Poverty Alleviation and Environmental Law

THE IUCN ACADEMY OF ENVIRONMENTAL LAW SERIES

Series Editors: Kurt Deketelaere, *University of Leuven, Leuven, Belgium* and Zen Makuch, *Imperial College, London, UK*

As environmental law increases in importance as an area of legal research, this new series will bring together some of the most current research carried out by the IUCN Academy of Environmental Law, a global network of environmental law scholars. The important issues addressed in the papers in this series were first presented at the Academy's annual colloquia. The series will present original research analysis and assessment, along with a much-needed synthesis of the state of environmental law. Directions as to the positive role that environmental law can play at a global level are also emphasized. This series will prove essential reading for scholars throughout the world with an interest in cutting edge environment-related issues, and will no doubt play an important role in shaping future debate.

Titles in this series include:

Compliance and Enforcement in Environmental Law
Toward More Effective Implementation
Edited by Lee Paddock, Du Qun, Louis Kotze, David L. Markell, Kenneth J. Markowitz and Durwood Zaelke

Environmental Law and Sustainability after Rio
Edited by Jamie Benidickson, Ben Boer, Antonio Herman Benjamin and Karen Morrow

Environmental Governance and Sustainability
Edited by Paul Martin, Li Zhiping, Qin Tianbao, Anel Du Plessis and Yves Le Bouthillier

Poverty Alleviation and Environmental Law
Edited by Yves Le Bouthillier, Miriam Alfie Cohen, Jose Juan Gonzalez Marquez, Albert Mumma and Susan Smith

Poverty Alleviation and Environmental Law

Edited by

Yves Le Bouthillier

Professor of Law, University of Ottawa, Canada

Miriam Alfie Cohen

Professor-Researcher, Universidad Autónoma Metropolitana, Cuajimalpa, Mexico

Jose Juan Gonzalez Marquez

Professor of Law, Universidad Autónoma Metropolitana, Azcapotzalco, Mexico

Albert Mumma

Professor of Law, University of Nairobi, Kenya

Susan Smith

Professor of Law, Willamette University, USA

THE IUCN ACADEMY OF ENVIRONMENTAL LAW SERIES

Edward Elgar

Cheltenham, UK • Northampton, MA, USA

Published by
Edward Elgar Publishing Limited
The Lypiatts
15 Lansdown Road
Cheltenham
Glos GL50 2JA
UK

Edward Elgar Publishing, Inc.
William Pratt House
9 Dewey Court
Northampton
Massachusetts 01060
USA

A catalogue record for this book
is available from the British Library

Library of Congress Control Number: 2012935321

FSC www.fsc.org MIX Paper from responsible sources FSC® C018575

ISBN 978 1 78100 328 2 (cased)

Printed and bound by MPG Books Group, UK

Contents

Contributors

Carla D. Aceves-Ávila is an attorney from the Universidad de Guadalajara, Mexico; LLM with American University, Washington College of Law, Washington D.C., USA; currently PhD candidate at the Universidad San Pablo CEU de Madrid, Spain. She received the Academic Merit Prize from the Universidad Nacional Autónoma de México in 2005 for her contribution in the development of Mexican environmental law through her first national publication *Bases Fundamentales de Derecho Ambiental Mexicano* (Fundamental Basis of Mexican Environmental Law). She is a full-time professor and researcher at the *Centro Universitario de Ciencias Económico Administrativas* of the *Universidad de Guadalajara* (economics and administration campus of the University of Guadalajara) concentrating on Mexican and international environmental law, particularly environmental public policy and access to environmental information, but continues with private consultation on environmental law in Mexico. She is currently the Head of the Social and Legal Sciences Department of the Center of Economic and Administrative Sciences of the Universidad de Guadalajara and the President of the Environmental Law Academy of the Masters Degree in Environmental Law and Sustainable Development of the University of Guadalajara.

Daniel Behn is a PhD Candidate in International Economic Law at the University of Dundee's Centre for Energy, Petroleum, and Mineral Law and Policy. He holds a Juris Doctorate degree from Tulane University's School of Law where he was Executive Editor of the Tulane Journal for International and Comparative Law. He is a licensed attorney in New York and Washington D.C. His research focuses on international economic law and natural resources law. His current research focuses on the role of subjective knowledge in the development of international legal norms. Through the use of Q methodology, his PhD thesis explores how values, such as fairness, influence and motivate the development of legal norms in investment treaty arbitration.

Karen Bubna-Litic is an Associate Professor in the School of Law at the University of South Australia (UNISA). She is a member of the IUCN Commission of Environmental Law and was co-chair of the IUCN Academy of Environmental Law's Teaching and Capacity Building Committee from 2007–2011. She researches in the areas of environmental law, corporate social responsibility and climate change law. She has written in the field of corporate environmental responsibility, with book chapters on eco-taxation and environmental reporting and articles on the linkages between sustainability and corporate practice. Her current research examines climate change and its associated economic incentives, particularly emissions trading, as a driver for better corporate environmental performance, and the social justice outcomes of carbon pricing policy, with particular reference to indigenous communities. She has been a visiting professor at the Boalt School of Law, UC (Berkeley), the School of Environmental Negotiation, University of Virginia and the Program for Research and Documentation for a Sustainable Society at the University of Oslo. In 2010 she was a visiting professor at the University of Ottawa, the University of Cape Town, North-West University and the University of Maastricht.

Miriam Alfie Cohen is Professor-Researcher in the Social Science Department in the Universidad Autónoma Metropolitana, Cuajimalpa, Mexico City. PhD in Social Science, Universidad Iberoamericana, Santa Fe, Mexico City; author of numerous essays and books about environmental movements, governance and democratic construction, including: *Sistema Mundial y Nuevas Geografías* (UAM-C, UAM-A, UIA, México, 2010); *Agencias Ambientales: América del Norte y Europa, perspectivas y alcances* (UAM-A, Pomares, Barcelona-México, 2006), and *Democracia y Desafío Medio Ambiental en México: retos, riesgos y opciones en la nueva era de la globalización* (UAM-A, Pomares, Barcelona-México, 2005).

Ed Couzens holds the degrees of PhD from the University of KwaZulu-Natal; LLM (Environmental Law) from the Universities of Natal and Nottingham; and BA Hons LLB from the University of the Witwatersrand. He is currently an Associate Professor in the Faculty of Law, Howard College Campus, University of KwaZulu-Natal, Durban. He is an admitted Attorney of the High Court, RSA; and a qualified Field Guide, RSA. His main research interest is national and international wildlife law and policy – his Doctoral thesis considered the positions in international law of elephants and whales, and the links between them. He has been since 2006 a co-editor of the University of Eastern Finland/United Nations Environmental Programme *Review of International Environmental Law-making and Diplomacy*; and is an Assistant Editor on the *Journal of South African Environmental Law and Policy*. He has been a member of the IUCN Academy of Environmental Law since its inception in 2003; and has attended several of its international Colloquiums, his first being in Nairobi in 2004.

Jose Juan Gonzalez Marquez is a Professor of Environmental Law at the Universidad Autonoma Metropolitana, Azcapotzalco, Mexico. He is a fellow of the Mexican National System of Researchers, and has published a number of treatises in the field of environmental law. From 1992 to 1996 he was the

Chief of the Legal Office of the General Attorney's Office for Environmental Protection. He has collaborated as external adviser for the Commission for Environmental Cooperation, the Inter-American Development Bank, the United Nations Environment Programme, the United Nations Development Programme and the World Meteorological Organization. He is a member of the IUCN Academy's Governing Board.

Stefan Gruber is a lecturer at Sydney Law School. He is also active as a legal practitioner and consultant. Stefan was educated at the Universities of Sydney, Frankfurt, Mainz, and at Harvard Law School, and holds degrees in law, philosophy, and political science. His PhD thesis focused on the conservation of cultural heritage in China and explored the need for more decisive legal and political action in that area. Other research interests include cultural heritage law and policy, international and comparative environmental law, sustainable development in Asia-Pacific, and international humanitarian law. He has been elected to the Executive Committee of the Association of Pacific Rim Universities Doctoral Students Network (APRU DSN) and is currently serving as the Director of Research and Development. Representative publications include a book on Just War Theory which was published in Germany in 2008 (Die Lehre vom gerechten Krieg: Eine Einführung am Beispiel der NATO-Intervention im Kosovo), 'Protecting China's Cultural Heritage Sites in Times of Rapid Change: Current Developments, Practice and Law' (2007) 10(3&4) *Asia Pacific Journal of Environmental Law* 253-301, and 'Heritage Discourses' in Kim Rubenstein and Brad Jessup (eds) *Environmental Discourses in International and Public Law* (Cambridge University Press 2012) (with Ben Boer).

Oscar Flores Jáuregui is Research Assistant at the Department of Social Sciences, Universidad Autónoma Metropolitana-Cuajimalpa in Mexico City. Masters Degree in Public Administration, Faculty of Law, Universidad Anahuac-México Norte. His main interest is in Local Government, Environmental Policy, Budget and Accountability.

Michael Kidd is Professor of Law at the University of KwaZulu-Natal, South Africa. He teaches and researches in the fields of environmental law and administrative law. He is author of *Environmental Law* (second edition appeared in 2011) and numerous articles on a wide range of topics within environmental law especially, particularly aspects relating to water. He is a member of the IUCN Academy's Governing Board.

Yves Le Bouthillier is a Professor at the Faculty of Law of the University of Ottawa, Canada, and Director of the IUCN Academy of Environmental Law.

The Secretariat of the Academy is located at the University of Ottawa. He teaches in international law, specifically in the areas of international human rights law, international environmental law, and in related areas such as immigration and refugee law. From June 2005 to December 2006 he was President of the Law Commission of Canada. He was Scholar in Residence at the Oceans, Environmental and Economic Law Division at the Department of Foreign Affairs and International Trade from August 2000 to June 2002.

Paul Martin is the Director of the Australian Centre for Agriculture and Law, and the Research Director for the Faculty of the Professions at the University of New England, Armidale NSW. He also serves on the editorial panels for the IUCN Academy of Environmental Law eJournal and the International Journal of Rural Law and Policy.

Albert Mumma is a law graduate of the Universities of Nairobi, Yale and Cambridge. He currently holds the position of Associate Professor at the University of Nairobi, and specialises in environmental and natural resources. He served for two terms as a member of the National Environment Tribunal in Kenya.

LeRoy C. (Lee) Paddock is Associate Dean for Environmental Law Studies at The George Washington University Law School. His work focuses on environmental compliance and enforcement, environmental governance with particular emphasis on integrating the regulatory system with economic and values-based drivers of environmental behavior, and on environmental management in the context of emerging nanotechnologies. He is a member of the Council of the ABA Section of Environment, Energy and Resources and chairs its Strategic Response. He also serves on The George Washington University Sustainability Implementation Team. Prior to coming to George Washington University, he was Director of Environmental Law Programs at Pace University School of Law. Before Pace, he served for 20 years in the Minnesota Attorney General's Office, including 13 years as Director of Environmental Policy for Minnesota Attorney General Hubert H. Humphrey III. He holds a BA from the University of Michigan and a JD with High Honors from the University of Iowa. Lee's recent publications include Paddock, Kotze, Markell, Markowitz, Qun and Zaelke (eds), *Compliance and Enforcement in Environmental Law: Toward More Effective Implementation* (Cheltenham, UK and Northampton, MA, USA: Edward Elgar, 2011).

Catherine G. (Kitty) Pring is an award-winning professional mediator and facilitator and founder of ReSolution Resources LLC, an alternative dispute resolution practice. Her work includes individual and group conflict resolution, program design, and systems evaluation in health and human services, environment, domestic violence, employment, family, real estate, medical, contracts, and neighborhood issues. With husband Rock, she is co-author of *Greening Justice: Creating and Improving Environmental Courts and Tribunals* and other ECT publications and co-directs the University of Denver's Environmental Courts and Tribunals (ECT) Study (www.law.du.edu/ect-study). She is also a Principal in Global Environmental Outcomes LLC (GEO), an international consulting service. She has served as the State of Colorado Ombudsman for Medicaid Managed Care, following her retirement after 15 years as the Director of the Adult Services Division for the City and County of Denver Department of Human Services, managing 10 major human services programs, and has worked for a non-profit foundation, directed the State of Colorado's Long Term Care system development, and as a consultant. She is a graduate of Vassar College (BA) and Michigan (MPA and Certificate in Gerontology).

George W. (Rock) Pring is Professor of Law at the University of Denver Sturm College of Law, Denver, Colorado, USA, where he teaches International, Constitutional, and Environmental Law courses. A graduate of Harvard (BA) and Michigan Law (JD), he has practiced in a national law firm, served as Chief of Environmental Litigation for the State of Ohio Attorney General's Office, directed an office of the Environmental Defence Fund, and is a Principal in Global Environmental Outcomes LLC (GEO), an international consulting service. With wife Kitty, he is co-author of *Greening Justice: Creating and Improving Environmental Courts and Tribunals* and other ECT publications and co-director of the University of Denver's global Environmental Courts and Tribunals (ECT) Study (www.law.du.edu/ect-study). Additional publications include *International Environmental Law & Policy for the 21st Century*, *Human Rights in Natural Resources Development* (Oxford: Oxford University Press). He also co-authored *SLAPPs: Getting Sued for Speaking Out* – which first named and drew international attention to 'Strategic Lawsuits against Public Participation' in government or 'SLAPPs' (lawsuits to chill citizens' communications to government).

Dinah Shelton holds the Manatt/Ahn Professorship in International Law at the George Washington University Law School, where she has taught since 2004. She previously taught international law and was director of the doctoral program in international human rights law at the University of Notre Dame Law School (1996–2004). She has also lectured at the University of California (Davis), Santa Clara University, Stanford University, University of California (Berkeley), the University of Paris, and the University of Strasbourg, France. Professor Shelton is the author of three prize-winning books, *Protecting*

Human Rights in the Americas (co-authored with Thomas Buergenthal), *Remedies in International Human Rights Law*, and the three-volume *Encyclopedia of Genocide and Crimes against Humanity*. She has also authored many other articles and books on international law, human rights law, and international environmental law. Professor Shelton is a member of the board of editors of the American Journal of International Law. She has served as a legal consultant to many international organizations and is on the board of numerous human rights and environmental organizations. In 2006, Professor Shelton was awarded the Elisabeth Haub Prize for Environmental Law. In June 2009, the General Assembly of the Organization of American States elected her to a four-year term as a member of the Inter-American Human Rights Commission. In 2010 she served as president of the Commission.

Sidra Sabzwari is a lawyer in Toronto, Ontario, Canada. Her interests are in administrative, environmental, indigenous and mental health law, as well as access to justice issues. She received a JD from Osgoode Hall Law School in 2009 and an Honours BSc from the University of Ottawa in 2006.

Dayna Nadine Scott is an Associate Professor at Osgoode Hall Law School, York University in Toronto. She teaches in the areas of administrative law, environmental law and international environmental governance. Since 2009, she has also been the Director of the National Network on Environments and Women's Health, a Center of Excellence funded by Health Canada and located at York University.

Susan Lea Smith is Professor of Law and Director of the Law and Government Certificate Program at Willamette University in Salem, Oregon, USA. Before joining the Willamette faculty, Professor Smith was Assistant Chief of the Environmental Defense Section, U.S. Department of Justice. At the beginning of her career, she specialized in natural resources and environmental litigation on behalf of the mining and oil and gas industries at Holland & Hart. Professor Smith teaches a host of environmental and natural resources courses as well as administrative law and the lawmaking process. She has taught intermittently as a visitor at the University of Sydney in New South Wales, Australia, Golden Gate University in San Francisco, California, USA, and other universities. She is co-author of the leading treatise on environmental crimes 'Crimes Against the Environment' as well as the Clean Air Act volume of Michael Gerrard's environmental law treatise. Her current scholarly interests revolve around governance, water and alleviating global poverty. Professor Smith has long advocated incorporating sustainability concepts into takings law, corporate law, and other bodies of legal doctrine in addition to focusing environmental and natural resources law on ecological sustainability.

1. Introduction

We can all agree that the international community, through legal and other means, needs to pursue both the alleviation of poverty and the protection of the environment. Ending poverty would be to truly respect Article 1 of the Universal Declaration of Human Rights that states that 'All human beings are born free and equal in dignity and rights'. Protecting the environment is the only way to ensure the survival of this and future generations and to also acknowledge, as stated in Article 1 of the Earth Charter, that 'all beings are interdependent and every form of life has value regardless of its worth to human beings.'

The relationship between the alleviation of poverty and the protection of the environment is a complex one. There is every reason to believe that poverty and environmental degradation go hand in hand: extreme poverty, with the need to survive until the next day or the next year, can lead to severe environmental depletion and irreversible damages. In turn, depletion of natural resources by both private and public actors, resources on which communities have relied for their economic, social and cultural well being, can cause a long slide into poverty. All around the world, poverty is found in contaminated lands, near waste sites, and close to polluting industries. This is no mere coincidence (Shelton, Sabzwari and Scott, Cohen and Jáuregui, Paddock). There are, however, situations where alleviation of poverty and the protection of the environment appear to be at odds with one another: when the need to increase the standard of living of poor communities can disrupt fragile ecosystems (Mumma) or when economic sustainability through the preservation of traditional practices can arguably constitute a threat to the conservation of species at risk (Couzens). In other cases, economic development threatens both the environment and the cultural heritage of poor ethnic minorities (Gruber). As will be seen throughout this volume, the role that law plays in the relationship between poverty and the environment will vary depending on the situation and will be more successful at pursuing environmental justice in some cases than in others.

This volume is the result of a conference organized in Mexico by the IUCN Academy of Environmental Law on the theme of Poverty and the Environment. The Academy is an international network of more than 150 law faculties and academic research institutions around the world. Its mission is to promote the teaching and research of environmental law at the international, regional and national level, with a particular emphasis on developing countries. Following the Mexico City conference, the editors selected 14 papers for publication. Together they provide an excellent sample of the many issues that were explored at the conference.

The book is divided into six Parts: (1) linkages between human rights, the environment and poverty; (2) environmental degradation and poverty: what is at stake for Aboriginal peoples? (3) the need for public participation in environmental issues to combat poverty; (4) states' approaches to environmental degradation and poverty; (5) the role of environmental courts and tribunal in the fight against poverty and environmental degradation; (6) global challenges: international mechanisms to address poverty and environmental degradation.

1.1 LINKAGES BETWEEN HUMAN RIGHTS, THE ENVIRONMENT AND POVERTY

In 'Using Law and Equity for the Poor and the Environment', Dinah Shelton (United States) explains how poverty alleviation and environmental protection are interdependent and how the pursuit of environmental justice is essential to achieve these two objectives. Looking at key principles of environmental justice, she explores how these have manifested themselves in the interplay between human rights law and environmental law and have contributed to the protection of the most vulnerable groups in society and the least developed states in the international community. She identifies four legal constructs that have, at the domestic and international level, incorporated these principles, with a particular emphasis on the rights-based approach. Her careful analysis of the latter approach allows the reader to appreciate its benefits and limits. This comprehensive chapter touches on many themes that are revisited in specific contexts in subsequent chapters and provides an excellent initial analysis to the theme of this volume.

By contrast to the broad approach of Shelton, Michael Kidd's chapter (South Africa), 'The Right of Access to Water in South Africa', focuses on a recent case dealing with the access to clean water by impoverished individuals living in the Phiri Township in South Africa. At the core of the decision is the question of the appropriate balance between the rights of individuals versus the public interest. The case made its way through three levels of courts. The decision of the last tribunal, the Constitutional Court, unfortunately illustrates the limits of the rights-based approach as Kidd concludes that: 'At the end of the day, there are people in Phiri who do not have access to even 25 litres per person per day, something which the Court did not realize or chose to ignore.'

1.2 ENVIRONMENTAL DEGRADATION AND POVERTY: WHAT IS AT STAKE FOR ABORIGINAL PEOPLES?

Modern society, with its emphasis on progress and development, has left very little space and resources for Aboriginal peoples and their traditional values. Aboriginal peoples are among the most impoverished groups in all corners of the world. Organizers of the conference at the genesis of this book were therefore not surprised to receive a number of submissions on this topic. The three chapters in this Part illustrate the diversity of challenges facing these Aboriginal groups around the world.

The cost of climate change will be disproportionally high for Aboriginal peoples. In Australia, for instance, a significant proportion of Aboriginal communities are located in remote or, in some cases, very remote areas. Because these remote communities also face a high level of poverty, they are particularly ill-equipped to adapt to climate change. Therefore, the government has to be alert and sensitive to the unique challenges facing aboriginal peoples. When designing policies and laws to reduce greenhouse gas emissions, such as carbon pricing, the government needs to be able to rely on solid data concerning the impact of these policies on Aboriginal peoples. Of course, it should also seek the active participation of Aboriginal peoples in the process to develop relevant laws and policies. In her chapter, 'Climate change impacts on the poor – a case-study of Australia's indigenous population and the impact of Australia's response on the population', Karen Bubna-Litic (Australia) questions the approach of the Australian government on both scores.

Three 'Rs' are what comes to mind when ones reads the chapter by Sidra Sabzwari and Dayna Nadine Scott (Canada): Resilience, Resistance and Respect. 'The Quest for Environmental Justice on a Canadian Aboriginal Reserve' is the story of the continued struggle of a small Aboriginal community, the Aamjiwnaang First Nation, to preserve its health and dignity as its traditional territory is surrounded by chemical factories. Having to deal with the health consequences of the long term cumulative effects from multiple pollution sources, the community has decided to deploy its own empowerment strategies. While in her chapter Karen Bubna-Litic deplores the gaps in the data collected by the Australian government regarding Aboriginal Australians, in this chapter the authors explain that the community has to produce its own data through biomonitoring and 'bucket brigades'. In doing so, the community has not only gathered crucial information that would not otherwise have been available but has also prompted action by the government. For Sabzwari and Scott, aboriginal communities around the world can draw positive lessons from this case study: 'For aboriginal communities to obtain environmental justice, they need to share strategies for community empowerment and for the generation of data and knowledge that can change the conventional dynamics of power, authority and credibility that prevail with respect to environmental law and policy.'

'A clash of rights and interest' is how Ed Couzens (South Africa) characterizes the negotiations in the International Whaling Commission on the issue of quotas for aboriginal subsistence whaling. His chapter, 'Whaling and Dealing: Aboriginal Subsistence Whaling, Politics and Poverty', provides an in-depth and fascinating account of the last 30 years of discussion on this issue within the Commission. While the core question is how to protect endangered species and at the same time preserve traditional fishing practices in communities that have depended on whale fishing since time immemorial, Couzens argues that political dealing has been marked by a great deal of hypocrisy at various times on the part of parties supporting one or the other position. He concludes that until this issue is resolved 'Poverty, culture and conservation will continue to be horses traded in a dodgy marketplace – and both indigenous peoples and whales might in the end be the poorer for it.' His analysis demonstrates how it can be difficult in the international arena to find the right balance between conservation, poverty and cultural issues when the interests of powerful States are involved and there are disagreements on key concepts such as 'traditional peoples' as well as on scientific evidence.

1.3 THE NEED FOR PUBLIC PARTICIPATION IN ENVIRONMENTAL ISSUES TO COMBAT POVERTY

Some of the authors in earlier Parts of this volume have noted the key role of public information and public participation in the pursuit of environmental justice for poorer communities (Bubna-Litic; Sabzwari and Scott). This important question is the central theme of the next two chapters.

LeRoy C. Paddock (United States), in his chapter titled 'The Role of Public Engagement in Achieving Environmental Justice', provides an overview of initiatives in the last 25 years by the federal government as well as some states in the United States to more effectively engage the public, and in particular low income communities and communities with large minority populations, in environmental issues that affect them. Like Sabzwari and Scott, his starting point is that environmental justice is very much about remedying the disproportionate adverse environmental burden placed on these communities. This can only be achieved by ensuring their meaningful involvement in the decision-making process. As Paddock convincingly explains, this means much more than simply setting up a public meeting. His study of various current practices in the United States provides an impressive list of innovative methods by which public participation can be made more inclusive and effective.

Carla D. Aceves-Avila (Mexico), in her chapter, 'The Right of Access to Information as a Tool for Environmental Protection and Poverty Eradication in Mexico', details the various databases in existence in Mexico, and the key actors responsible to provide environmental information. However, there are serious problems that need to be tackled such as the poor quality of some of the information, insufficient attention to the means by which this information is conveyed to marginalized groups, and a need to adopt an active approach to access to information. There is a public information infrastructure to build on but more resources as well as political will are needed to make it effective.

1.4 STATES' APPROACHES TO ADDRESS ENVIRONMENTAL DEGRADATION AND POVERTY

How can a state achieve conservation objectives effectively through environmental regulation while benefiting the poorer segments of society? This is the issue that Paul Martin (Australia) explores in 'Embedding Social Justice in the Design of Environmental Regulation'. State constraints or market instruments will likely result in inequalities unless regulatory regimes integrate social justice values alongside economic concerns. Therefore, Martin puts forward a number of proposals that could go a long way to ensure that the process of regulatory review in the environmental realm results in social equity.

Improved urban planning to address poverty and environmental degradation in megacities is the key topic of Miriam Alfie Cohen and Oscar Flores Jauregui's chapter (Mexico), 'Planning and Environment in Mexico City's Metropolitan Zone: Trying to Defeat Poverty'. Economic growth and urbanization has and will continue to produce environmental degradation and increase in inequalities until urban governance is driven by transversal and integral environmental-poverty plans. The need for a comprehensive and innovative approach to local governance is exemplified by a look at recent initiatives by municipal authorities and community groups in Mexico City.

1.5 THE ROLE OF ENVIRONMENTAL COURTS IN THE FIGHT AGAINST POVERTY AND ENVIRONMENTAL DEGRADATION

As thoroughly demonstrated by George (Rock) Pring and Catherine (Kitty) Pring (United States) in 'Specialized Environmental Courts & Tribunals: Improved Access to Justice for Those Living in Poverty', an increasing number of countries have opted to create environmental courts and tribunals.

The two authors have recently published the most comprehensive multidisciplinary study to date on the topic. In that study they identified 12 building blocks that are essential to consider in the development and implementation of these institutions. For the purpose of this volume, they have emphasized six of these blocks as particularly relevant to ensure greater access to environmental justice for the poor. These factors are (1) geographic coverage; (2) standing; (3) costs; (4) expert evidence; (5) alternative dispute resolution; and (6) operational tools.

Albert Mumma's chapter (Kenya), 'The Resolution of Urban Housing Development Disputes as a Mechanism for Poverty Alleviation: A Case Study of Kenya's National Environment Tribunal' dovetails nicely with the previous chapter. In the specific context of the role of the National Environmental Tribunal in housing projects in Kenya, Mumma identifies and discusses how some of an administrative tribunal's key attributes, can work to the advantage of poor communities. The three elements he focuses on (costs, timely process, rules on standing) are among those listed by Catherine and Rock Pring as important to the pursuit of environmental justice. Similarly to Michael Kidd's discussion in the water context, Mumma also explores the need for balancing between conflicting interests, in this case the need for housing projects for poor communities on one hand, and environmental protection on the other. His overall assessment of the Tribunal's contribution to find the right balance is positive. In the last part of the chapter, the author considers whether the Tribunal should have a larger competence in matters of environmental protection.

1.6 GLOBAL CHALLENGES: INTERNATIONAL MECHANISMS TO ADDRESS POVERTY AND ENVIRONMENTAL DEGRADATION

The dual challenge of reducing poverty and preventing environmental degradation calls for international mechanisms that effectively tackle both issues. As illustrated in the first two chapters in this Part, legal instruments developed by the international community to address specific problems, namely the development of the Clean Development Mechanism in the fight against climate change and the adoption of the World Heritage Convention for the preservation of unique cultural sites, could be improved upon to better meet these challenges. It is fitting that the third text of this Part, and the last one in the book, suggest a new legal mechanism as new ideas have to be considered to give hope for significant progress in combating poverty and environmental issues in the current century.

It is ironic that the emergence of some new powerful economies in the developing world coincided with the scientific realization that the increased emission of greenhouse gas from anthropomorphic origins to sustain economic development has endangered the planet. While the awareness of potential conflicts between the eradication of poverty and the protection of the environment preceded the rise of a global consciousness regarding the dangers of climate change, this issue has since taken on a new dimension. Many have pointed out that climate change will create greater hardship for the most vulnerable on this planet. Fortunately, the sense of self-preservation within the international community has encouraged the search for solutions to meet the rising need for energy to pursue the simultaneous development of the emerging countries as well as the ones still mired in poverty while reducing greenhouse gas emissions.

In the chapter titled 'Linking Climate Change Mitigation and Poverty Reduction: Continued Reform of the Clean Development Mechanism in the post-Kyoto Era to Promote Sustainable Energy Development on the African Continent', Daniel Behn (United Kingdom) looks at the promises and pitfalls of one the mechanisms designed to meet these two objectives, the Clean Development Mechanism (CDM). He agrees with many other experts that this mechanism, since its implementation, has fallen short of fulfilling its promises for the poorest countries. Taking the African continent as a case study, he points out that it has not, for instance, resulted in significant development of sustainable energy projects that could reduce extreme poverty on that continent. Nevertheless, noting that a number of steps have been taken to address these deficiencies, Behn argues for retaining the CDM in a post-Kyoto framework. The reader is introduced to the key structures and functions of the CDM, appraised of the operational deficiencies as well as institutional governance issues in Africa that have limited the benefits promised by this mechanism and, finally, is invited to consider various options in a new CDM framework designed to better answer the pressing need of the least developed countries.

In 'Poverty and the Loss of Cultural Heritage Sites', Stefan Gruber (Australia) examines another undesirable consequence of the struggle by states to decrease poverty: the loss of cultural heritage. Poorer states do not have the resources needed to protect significant cultural sites adequately. Other states endorsing aggressive economic development policies do so without erecting sufficient protection for these sites. In particular, as Gruber points out, economic inequalities within a state lead to the transformation, and ultimately the loss of authenticity, of cultural sites inhabited by poorer populations. Economic development is also threatening the existence of the cultural diversity that one finds in rural regions while increasing the ranks of poor people in urban areas. The author examines how the primary instrument for the protection of these sites, the World Heritage Convention, can assist states in meeting poverty related threats to their cultural heritage while also pointing out the limits of this instrument in these situations. All along the author formulates a number of proposals to better protect the cultural sites and poorer communities that inhabit and breathe life into these sites. In the end, Gruber reminds us that 'By fighting poverty, the task of conserving cultural heritage becomes much easier'.

While the reach of international law, including international environmental law, has greatly expanded in the last quarter of the twentieth century, both in terms of issues and actors, many would consider its influence on transnational corporations as negligible. Susan Smith (United States), in 'Chartering Sustainable Transnational Corporations', makes the case that new approaches to create 'sustainable transnational corporations' are needed as these entities do play a key role in issues of poverty and environmental degradation. She proposes to transform corporate charter law, taking as a point of departure for her analysis a recent legislative initiative in the state of Oregon in the United States. While she supports this initiative, she also explains what is lacking in it to make it truly transformative when applied to transnational corporations. Finally, she tackles some of the central questions that would need to be raised by the design of a new international model for sustainable transnational corporations.

In closing, we also want to take the opportunity to thank those who played a key role in making this book possible. As mentioned previously, this book is the end product of a colloquium organized in Mexico City under the leadership of one of the co-editors of this volume, Jose Juan Marquez Gonzalez. Thanks are due to him and his team at the Universidad Autonoma Metropolitana in Mexico for having organized a week-long conference with more than 150 speakers from all over the world. Thanks are also due to the United Nations Environment Programme for having made it possible, through a contribution, for scholars from developing nations to participate in this conference. Finally, we also want to thank our publisher, Edward Elgar, for the continued and essential support, assistance and expertise provided while we were working on this book.

Yves Le Bouthillier
Miriam Alfie Cohen
Jose Juan Gonzalez Marquez
Albert Mumma
Susan Lea Smith

PART I

Linkages between human rights, the environment and poverty

2. Using law and equity for the poor and the environment

Dinah Shelton

In October 1991, the periodic shift of wind direction that Californians experience, usually in the autumn, arrived around the San Francisco Bay. The normal off-shore coastal breeze disappeared and the so-called 'Santa Ana' winds blew in from the desert, coinciding with unusually hot and dry days. The winds were much stronger than normal and they picked up embers from a construction site high in the East Bay hills, creating a conflagration known as the 'Oakland Firestorm'. The fire destroyed nearly 4000 homes and killed 28 people in the space of a day. Some of the displaced persons were given refuge temporarily in the Claremont Resort Hotel, where each one was registered as a 'Distressed Person'. Most of the fire victims were insured and the insurance companies had agents available within 24 hours, providing funds to meet initial expenses. The insurance policies largely covered the costs of rebuilding and refurnishing a destroyed home; they also covered the cost of renting a comparable residence until the rebuilding project was completed. In the meantime, local, state and federal officials provided assistance to those burned out of their homes. Shops gave discounts for the purchase of replacement goods. Other communities reached out to help. The neighborhood rebuilt itself completely within a couple of years and became a highly-desirable area in which to live. Only the elderly did not return, because the stress of the fire took their lives within months.

In New Orleans, the Lower Ninth Ward is not elevated. It is in the flatlands and like most such areas, its residents are poor; over 98 per cent of them are African-American. When Hurricane Katrina threatened in 2005, most of those living in the wealthier parts of the city were able to leave before the storm made landfall. Those in the Ninth Ward could not. Of the nearly 2000 people killed during Katrina, 70 per cent of them were black and poor; most of them came from the Ninth Ward. Those who could escape their houses had no resort hotel to house them; instead, thousands of them were herded into a football arena, the Super Dome, where they were kept with little food or water, and where the sanitation facilities were overwhelmed after the first day. The aftermath further exacerbated the disproportionate impact of Katrina on the poor, as the latter were wholly underserved by the government and private relief agencies, creating a second disaster. The residents of the Ninth Ward had no insurance to cover immediate expenses or long-term rebuilding, because they could not afford it; they had no funds with which to obtain alternative shelter. The federal government eventually provided some temporary housing, in mobile homes later revealed to be contaminated with toxic chemicals, contamination known to the manufacturer and the government at the time they made available the mobile homes. Eventually some of the residents of the Ninth Ward were relocated as far away as Texas and Colorado, never to return to their former homes. Nearly five years later, the community has not been rebuilt; much of it looks the same as it did shortly after the hurricane. New Orleans as a whole is whiter, older and richer.

Desmond Tutu has accurately described the global version of this tale of two cities as 'adaptation apartheid' (UNDP, 2007, p. 13). It is not limited to the consequences and impacts of abrupt natural disasters, but can also be observed in measures being taken to adapt to more long-term anthropogenic climate change. In some wealthy countries, adaptation means ski resort operators are buying artificial snow machines; along coastlines, residents are constructing luxurious floating homes. In poor countries, the women and children in coastal areas are being taught to float and to swim, so they can survive storm surges and flooding.

This chapter examines legal concepts and strategies to overcome adaptation apartheid and to make environmental protection and poverty alleviation equally and mutually-reinforcing international priorities. The aim is to ensure that neither environmental protection nor poverty alleviation is viewed simply as instrumental to achieving the other goal. While conditions of poverty are among the factors contributing to environmental degradation, poverty must be addressed not for that reason alone, but because every human being has an equal right to a life of dignity, with an adequate standard of living, health and well-being. Alleviating poverty is not about charity, but it is about justice and rights, for which there must be an effective legal framework empowering those in need.

Similarly, while recognizing that a healthier environment can help improve the lives of the poor, environmental protection is its own goal, nature has intrinsic value and the global resource base and ecological services should be conserved for this reason alone. Putting the two goals together is not only possible, it is essential and leads directly to legal approaches based not only on environmental protection, but on environmental justice and human rights.

2.1 LINKS BETWEEN POVERTY AND ENVIRONMENTAL HARM

The World Bank recently raised its benchmark for extreme poverty from $1 a day to $1.25, but still had to announce on 27 August 2008 that more people are living in that condition than ever before.[1] Over 1.4 billion people – a quarter of the developing world – are living on less than this amount in the 20 poorest countries, where human development indicators declined significantly over the past decade.[2] Globally, one in five girls of primary school age is not in school; more than 55 million girls receive no formal schooling whatsoever; in the least developed countries, women are 30 per cent less likely to be literate than men (OHCHR, 2008, p. 25). Those living in such poverty suffer loss of life and health as a direct consequence of the environmental degradation that surrounds their communities. While wealthy families are able to choose where they live and thus largely isolate themselves from pollution and contamination, poor people, especially the oldest and youngest, are less able to escape exposure to pollutants, with disastrous effects on their well-being. NIMBY ('not in my back yard') is a principle that can be successfully invoked almost exclusively by the wealthy and powerful.

Overall, '[a] fifth of the disease burden in developing countries can be linked to environmental risk factors' (OHCHR, 2008, p. 37). The burden of such diseases falls especially hard on the poor who often lack the resources to seek medical treatment. Although some four million infants die in their first month of life and another nearly seven million before they reach the age of five, an estimated 60 per cent of these deaths is preventable (OHCHR, 2008, p. 27). In tropical developing countries, endemic diseases are spread through the poorest communities by ecological disruptions stemming from irrigation projects, dams, construction sites, standing water and poor drainage.[3] The same connection between ecological damage and other vector-borne diseases has been observed across a range of developing countries (Platt, 1996).

Even in rich countries, like the United States, mortality rates from respiratory illnesses due to pollution are higher among minorities, who make up the ranks of the poor, than they are among whites. Rates of lead poisoning are two to three times higher among poor African-American children than among wealthier white children (Ballard, 1993, pp. 320–325). Extreme local weather events, like the 1996 Chicago heatwave, also have a disproportionate impact on poor minority communities (Sze, 2005, p. 114, n. 4). The impacts are especially felt by the most vulnerable: children born during a drought are 50–79 per cent more likely to be malnourished (UNDP, 2007, p. 9).

It should not be surprising, therefore, to learn that anthropogenic climate change (IPCC, 2001) is predicted to have its most devastating impacts on poor and minority communities. The April 2007 IPCC report on climate change impacts, adaptation and vulnerability confirmed that 'the poorest of the poor in the world – and this includes poor people in prosperous societies – are going to be the worst hit'.[4] They already are. The Red Cross estimates that 1998 was the first year in which the number of refugees from environmental disasters exceeded those displaced as a result of war (ICRC, 1999). Between 2000 and 2004, some 262 million people were affected by climate disasters and 98 per cent of them were in the developing world. In OECD countries, 1 in 1500 persons was affected; in developing countries the figure was 79 times higher – one person out of every 19 (UNDP, 2007, p. 8).

Climate change is already having devastating impact on the lives and well-being of inland pastoral nomads of Kenya, whose lands and herds have been decimated by persistent drought. In the North the impacts being felt by the Inuits in the Arctic were documented by villagers in the *amicus curiae* legal brief they filed in the US Supreme Court case *Massachusetts v. EPA*.[5] They observed that their very existence is threatened by climate-related disruptions of soils, water, vegetation, and wildlife. Subsistence communities dependent on the ecosystem are hunting at their peril due to thinning ice. There is no practicable alternative food supply and even if alternative sources existed, the loss of traditional foods and the means of acquiring them bring with it a loss of culture and religion. Arctic storms are growing more fierce and frequent; one village lost 15 meters of land overnight in a storm. Afterwards, the residents voted to leave the community they and their ancestors had inhabited for the past 4000 years.

The links between poverty and environmental conditions become more obvious when one considers that poverty is not merely about income or wealth, but encompasses the capability of an individual or group to access the various elements that contribute to well-being.[6] These elements are very closely linked with ecosystem services such as sufficient clean water for drinking and bathing. Persons with money can buy clean water or the equipment to filter and purify water if it is contaminated. The poor have limited resources to pursue these options and usually have to depend on natural and/or public water supply systems. The result is that more than one billion persons lack access to safe drinking water.

The issue, however, is not only, or even primarily one of access to resources. The World Bank's *Voices of the Poor* found that the poor define poverty as disempowerment and exclusion.[7] For them, development is about human choice and freedom, the self-determination to decide on a future that is not constrained by sickness, hunger, illiteracy, or oppression. It is about allowing each person to lead the life that he or she values. The emphasis thus has to be on empowering the poor, seeing them as rights-bearing agents of change rather than victims requiring aid.

The eight Millennium Development Goals (MDGs)[8] which emerged from long discussions about poverty, development and the environment, take a different approach, setting discrete, time-bound and measurable poverty reduction goals. The MDGs view environmental protection as an instrument of poverty alleviation, rather than as a goal in and of itself. They fail to give sufficient attention to arresting and reversing the erosion of natural resources as an independent and valuable aim (World Bank, 2002). In addition to having narrow substantive focus, the MDGs lack mechanisms of accountability, public participation, access to information, and discussion of transboundary obligations in the field of economic, social and cultural rights. They are weak on empowerment, being state-centric and top-down in their approach.

In contrast, the constructs of environmental justice and human rights law provide support to development practices that help realize poverty alleviation through empowering the vulnerable and marginalized in society while ensuring an equitable allocation of resources. Poverty is a legitimate human rights issue, because the poor lack basic social goods, such as health, freedom from violence and intimidation, cultural and spiritual guarantees, and the ability to participate in the political process. Human rights law also has the advantage of offering accountability mechanisms to monitor compliance with the obligations that correspond to the rights bearers and their rights.

2.2 THE MEANING AND CONTRIBUTION OF ENVIRONMENTAL JUSTICE

The ethics and morality of any society can be measured partly on the basis of how it treats its most vulnerable members. By this measure, modern society is failing by placing its heaviest environmental burden on those who have been least responsible for creating environmental harm, including climate change, and on those who have the fewest resources to combat or adapt to environmental degradation. More specifically, the poorest 2.6 billion people on earth are being forced to confront climate change which they did not create and over which they have no control, in countries where they have little or no political voice. These facts raise issues of international and domestic environmental justice.

The term environmental justice can be used in many different senses. It may signify a fundamental moral source or rationale providing the underpinnings from which law emerges. Alternatively, it may refer not to a source of law, but to the ultimate goal or outcome to be achieved by legal norms. Environmental justice can also be considered to mean fairness or equity, or more narrowly it can refer to legal institutions and procedures for accountability and dispute settlement.

To some extent, the different meanings of environmental justice correspond to classic distinctions between procedural, reparative (or corrective) and distributive justice. Consolidating them all, environmental justice can be said to describe a system of norms, institutions and procedures aimed at maximizing the well-being of present and future life on the planet. The primary modalities for achieving this goal include allocation and management of scarce resources, restraints on the exercise of power, and enforcement of the rule of law, aiming to achieve inter-generational, intra-generational and inter-species equity.

Legal scholars for years have equated notions of justice with principles of natural law, the moral foundation of law (Philimore, 1871, p. 20 et seq.). National courts have referred to positive law as deriving from and conforming to 'larger considerations of the public good, of commercial liberality, and of international justice …'.[9] In the first decades of the twentieth century, writers expressed a conviction that all positive law emerges from and is inferior to international morality or natural law precepts of justice (Humphrey, 1945). Environmental justice fits into this construct because it reflects and expresses the fundamental values of contemporary society as it combines concern for the environment with concern for the rights and well-being of the poor and vulnerable.

The notion of justice as a set of moral values which precedes, is superior to, and fills in gaps in the law, finds expression in the well-known Martens Clause and its reference to 'the principles of the law of nations, as they result from the usages established among civilized peoples, from *the laws of humanity, and the dictates of the public conscience*'.[10] In the aftermath of World War II, the proclamation of *jus cogens* or peremptory norms also reflects the acceptance of a superstructure or international public order within which law and policy function (Silving, 1961).

Environmental justice may also be equated with equity, in the sense of fairness. Equity can allow for exceptions to an otherwise uniformly applied law, in order to provide individualized justice. In international environmental law, some developing countries have negotiated equitable exemptions from legal norms or for preferential treatment on the grounds that the application of the general legal rules without modification would leave them with a disproportionate environmental burden due to the export of pollution from wealthier countries, while they are unable to share in the benefits derived from the polluting activities, and have the least capacity to respond to the resulting environmental challenges.

Equity may also provide a basis for decision in the absence of law or when it is necessary to fill in gaps in existing norms, such as when new issues emerge that give rise to disputes. International tribunals have applied equity in this way, but usually on the basis that the equitable principle being invoked is a general principle of law.[11]

Positive law itself may designate equity as the basis for allocating rights and duties.[12] Equity is most often chosen as the rule of decision when the different circumstances or situations of subjects of the law necessitate differential treatment in order to achieve a just result (Akehurst, 1976). Equity has been utilized this way in international environmental law in an effort to fairly allocate and regulate scarce resources in order to ensure that the benefits of environmental resources, the costs associated with protecting them, and any degradation that occurs (that is, all the benefits and burdens) are fairly shared by all members of society.

Distributive justice represents an ethical imperative based on the notion of moral reciprocity, in which all human beings are treated as equals. Modern law and policy is based on recognition of 'the inherent dignity and of the equal and inalienable rights of all members of the human family [as] the foundation of freedom, justice and peace in the world'.[13] Since all human beings are born free and equal in dignity and rights, values and policies should be legitimized through individual consent, equal rights, and democratic procedures rather than through utilitarian philosophies based on abstract notions of welfare or economic efficiency. Nonetheless, given the social dimension of all human lives, justice 'cannot be related to any one value, be it equality or any other, but only to the complex value system of a man, a community, or mankind'.[14]

Distributive justice begins with equality but acknowledges that imposing equal obligations on subjects of law that are unequal in relevant ways is likely to exacerbate inequalities or impose unfair burdens on those least able to bear the burdens. Legal systems, including the international legal system, therefore often seek substantive equality in the distribution of societal goods and burdens by treating like alike and unlike differently. Distributive justice of this type is promoted through enactment of specific legal norms that address equitably the consequences of wrongful actions (state responsibility and liability); norms of humane treatment (human rights and humanitarian law); and norms allocating scarce resources.

Relations that have existed between rich and poor countries and rich and poor individuals can be viewed as unjust if they fail to promote equality and to narrow the gap between the haves and have-nots. Moral reciprocity demands redistribution as a matter of justice. Responses to pervasive inequalities in economic development or lack of capacity to tackle a given problem could include imposing differential obligations or providing preferential treatment. Such temporary unequal relationships seek to foster true equality, largely through favoring the least developed or most affected individuals or states. At the national level, this notion led US President William J. Clinton in 1994 to sign an Executive Order on Environmental Justice, which called on each federal agency to identify and address 'disproportionately high and adverse human health or environmental effects of its programs, policies, and activities on minority populations and low-income populations'.[15]

Distributive justice is inherent in the doctrine of equitable utilization of shared natural resources, taking into account the needs and capabilities of those involved.[16] The status of equitable utilization as a fundamental and just norm in the field of shared natural resources was affirmed by the ICJ in the *Case Concerning the Gabčíkovo-Nagymaros Project (Hungary/Slovakia).*[17] In the *Fisheries Jurisdiction Cases (UK v. Iceland; FRG v. Iceland*), the ICJ stressed the obligation of reasonable use and good faith negotiations aimed at an equitable result, taking into account the needs of conservation and the interests of all exploiters of the resource.[18]

Equitable utilization, as an application of the principle of distributive justice, attempts to reach a fair result based on what are deemed to be relevant factors, such as need, prior use or entitlement, and other interests. Societal values like environmental protection or human rights may affect the scope and application of equitable principles through insisting on the importance of one or more of the factors. The Watercourses Convention, for example, states that equitable and reasonable uses are to be 'consistent with adequate protection of the watercourse'.[19] The phrase implies that uses causing substantial harm to the watercourse might be considered inherently inequitable. It also now appears increasingly accepted that some resource uses have priority over others. In the utilization of freshwater, for example, priority is given to the satisfaction of basic human needs through the provision of safe drinking water and sanitation.[20] The UN Committee on Economic, Social and Cultural Rights, in its General Comment 12 on the Right to Water, insists that priority be given to safe drinking water and sanitation, with a guaranteed minimum amount to be provided to every person.[21] Thus, substantive human rights considerations take precedence over other factors in allocation.

Positive law supports other measures of distributive or corrective justice. At the international level, concern about the equitable distribution of the burdens of environmental protection has led to the creation of a series of financial mechanisms, exemptions, provisions for the transfer of technology, and flexibility in the time required for compliance with international obligations, all part of the concept of common but differentiated responsibilities (Drumbl, 2002). Capacity building through the provision of financial resources and the transfer of technology is widely included in global multilateral environmental agreements. Treaty provisions that explicitly recognize economic and social development and poverty eradication as the first and overriding priorities of developing country parties generally make the provision of financial resources and the transfer of technology from developed country parties a condition for the implementation of treaty obligations by developing country parties. Thus, Article 5(5) of the amended Montréal Protocol on Substances that Deplete the

Ozone Layer (Montréal Protocol) provides that developing countries' capacity to fulfil the obligations and implement the control measures specified in the Montréal Protocol will depend upon the effective implementation by developed nations of financial cooperation and transfer of technology as set out in the Protocol.[22] Similar statements are contained in Article 4(7) of the United Nations Framework Convention on Climate Change (FCCC)[23] and Article 20(4) of the Convention on Biological Diversity (CBD).[24]

The principle of corrective justice supports the demand that developed nations pay for any reductions or modifications the developing world has to make in the process of industrialization, because developed-world industrialization has unfairly circumscribed the ability of the developing world to pass off the negative externalities of development on the environment. The global community finds itself at the tipping point because of the conduct of the developed world. It is precisely because of this conduct that the marginal environmental costs of developing-nation industrialization today are high. It is thus unfair to allocate each state or each person an equal share of total permissible pollution in the present, given the past high levels of pollution emitted by some countries and persons.

Corrective justice thus substantiates the notion that developing nations and the poor today are entitled to the resources and technology from developed nations. Developed nations should have to internalize the environmental costs of ongoing and future developing-nation industrialization. While the corrective justice model brushes against theories of formal equality of states and individuals, achieving justice in the present requires taking into account elements from the past.

Environmental justice, in sum, means a rational sharing of the burdens and costs of environmental protection, discharged through the procedural and substantive adjustment of rights and duties. While certain stated principles of environmental law seem to aim for such international justice, there has been an evident strong resistance to aiding the 'have-nots' on the part of some of those who 'have', within and across states. To the extent progress has been made in fairly allocating benefits and burdens in international environmental law, it may be considered the result of ecological interdependence and issue-linkages. Developed countries increasingly recognize that they *must* have the cooperation of developing states if the global environment is to be restored and maintained; they cannot do it on their own. Benefit and burden-sharing then becomes the just price demanded by the developing world for its cooperation.

Justice and equity, with their emphasis on fairness, are more attractive concepts than economic efficiency or open conflict as a means of deciding how to allocate and sustain limited common resources. Without a cooperative and just solution to the issue of allocation, competitive utilization of the resource may continue until the resource is depleted. Equitable or differentiated obligations may induce participation in action among the competing states as well as among states that may not have any direct interest in a specific environmental issue.

Equity also may be justified on the basis of self-interest. An allocation of burdens that takes into account the more vulnerable position of developing states may benefit all through inducing the cooperation of such states to improve global environmental conditions.[25] Thus, environmental justice is not only a matter of morality and equity but may also foster more effective action on issues of common concern and more effective implementation of legal norms. Equity, as reflecting notions of fairness and legitimacy, may produce more or better compliance with environmental agreements. In practice, therefore, equitable differentiation is the price to be paid to ensure universal participation in measures to tackle global environmental problems. Yet, it should not be forgotten, as Thomas Franck has noted, that '[t]he law promotes distributive justice not merely to secure greater compliance, but primarily because most people think it is *right* to act justly' (Franck, 1995, p. 8).

2.3 LEGAL CONSTRUCTS TO GIVE EFFECT TO ENVIRONMENTAL JUSTICE

Principles of environmental justice (distributive, procedural and corrective) provide organizing principles in the efforts to combat poverty and environmental degradation. It remains to be seen how such principles can be integrated into domestic and international laws and policies. There are four legal constructs or approaches which have had some success and where further achievements are possible. These are not mutually exclusive approaches; indeed, all of them are necessary and must be pursued. In general, legal measures to combat disproportionate environmental impacts on the poor and address poverty can be grouped into the following broad categories: traditional private law, especially tort and property law; public regulation; market mechanisms; and constitutional or human rights law.

2.3.1 Private Law

Private law first incorporated principles of justice, especially corrective justice, in response to claims of environmental harm. Private law concepts can be seen internationally in the inter-state *Trail Smelter* arbitration.[26] The arbitral panel, which found no international treaties or precedents on point for transboundary air pollution, relied heavily on inter-state cases from within federal systems. Most of these judgments were, in turn, founded on private law concepts of nuisance. Nuisance is an equitable doctrine that imposes liability when, after examining and balancing the benefits and burdens accruing to litigating parties, one party's use of property or resources is found to be an unreasonable or unjust interference with the other party's property or other interests. Private tort actions were long the primary avenue for mitigating or halting pollution. A modern variant can be seen in the application of the polluter pays principle in liability regimes.

Significantly, the recent US Supreme Court judgment in *Massachusetts v. EPA*[27] relied on *Georgia v. Tennessee Copper Company and Ducktown Sulphur, Copper and Iron Company, Ltd.*,[28] the same key 1907 case utilized by the Trail Smelter tribunal. It did so in its analysis that found standing for states and local communities to sue the EPA for its failure to regulate greenhouse gases. The judgment and the multitude of briefs filed in the case suggest that the possibility remains open for a variety of actions to combat transfrontier pollution as a form of international nuisance, including from emission of greenhouse gases.

The challenge today is to use concepts like nuisance on behalf of the poor, indigenous, and minorities who are bearing a disproportionate environmental burden without obtaining corresponding benefits. Domestically it means challenging the siting of polluting activities in poor neighbourhoods. Internationally, it requires addressing the export of polluting industries and activities, as well as toxic waste, to poor countries and acknowledging and addressing the impacts of climate change. Applying past doctrines to contemporary problems requires research into the facts and potential causes of action, making use of legal clinics at law schools, *pro bono* representation, and participation in *amicus curiae* briefs.

In addition to allowing private actions based in tort, some countries have relied on the long-established property doctrine of public trust to protect those resources deemed to fall within the public domain. The doctrine of public trust, traced to Roman law, holds that navigable waters, the sea, and the land along the seashore are common property open to use by all (Justinian Institutes, translation 1876). Given its long-standing recognition as a legal doctrine, courts may recognize and enforce public trusts without legislation.[29]

The public trust doctrine emphasizes the equal right of access and use of the trust corpus by all in the present and the preservation of the trust for the future. It emphasizes the duties of the government as trustee, imposing on it an obligation to conserve the public trust asset and ensure common access to and use of it by present and future generations.[30] One limitation is that the public trust doctrine extends only to those natural resources which are viewed as part of the corpus of the trust and not to the environment as a whole.[31] However, the publication of Joe Sax's influential law review article in 1970,[32] has led some legislatures, litigants and courts to expand the doctrine and apply it to other resources, including wildlife and public lands.[33]

Efforts to invoke the public trust doctrine to protect the environment more broadly face three challenges. The first challenge is to examine comparatively the concept of the public trust to determine the extent to which it has already been applied to protect natural resources. The second challenge is to follow through on the implications of the public trust doctrine. Several subsidiary rules of trust law could be important in fleshing out the application of justice principles, such as those that require the trustee to monitor and report on the status of the trust corpus and those that ensure equal access for all, including the poor. These rules should impose legal obligations on public officials to monitor the state of the environment and provide information periodically to the public in an accessible form and through an accessible medium.

The third challenge is to examine the appropriateness of extending the public trust doctrine to the air, ecological processes, biodiversity and other components of the environment. Some laws already extend beyond the traditional coastline and fishing resources. Hawaii's constitution, for example, creates a public trust over all of the state's natural resources:

> For the benefit of present and future generations, the State and its political subdivisions shall conserve and protect Hawaii's natural beauty and all natural resources, including land, water, air, minerals and energy sources, and shall promote the development and utilization of these resources in a manner consistent with their conservation and in furtherance of the self-sufficiency of the State. All public natural resources are held in trust by the State for the benefit of the people.[34]

In international law, there are aspects of the doctrine already inherent in the concept of the common heritage of mankind, which recognizes that certain resources, such as those on or under the deep seabed, belong to the common heritage of mankind by virtue of their location in commons areas. Inclusion of the word 'heritage' connotes a temporal aspect in the communal safeguarding of areas or resources incapable of national appropriation. The nature of the common heritage is a form of trust, whose principal aims include restricting use to peaceful purposes, rational utilization in a spirit of conservation, good management or wise use, and transmission to future generations. Benefits derived from the common heritage may be shared through equitable allocation of revenues, or a sharing of scientific knowledge. It would be useful to consider how this might be expanded to the oceans as a whole, to ecosystems like coral reefs, to biodiversity, or the atmosphere.

2.3.2 Regulation

In the 1960s environmental law shifted from a reliance on property and tort law to one of public regulation. General environmental protection statutes were enacted along with specific laws to ensure clean water, clean air, and the survival of endangered species. Christopher Schroeder has pointed out that the shift from private to public law has three advantages in theory – 'one procedural, one remedial and one substantive' (Schroeder, 2002). On a procedural level, environmental regulation done right determines levels of environmental quality through a public process that involves collective choices, rather than through a series of private actions and reactions (negotiation or litigation). Of course, this process may be distorted by a lack of transparency or lobbying by powerful interests, but in theory it offers the benefits of a democratic and participatory process, especially if governance is based on theories of subsidiarity or decentralization in which those affected are directly involved in the decision-making.

Secondly, regulation emphasizes prevention rather than liability (although successful nuisance actions often lead to injunctive relief to prevent further harm). Prevention is a more efficient, cost-effective approach and also one that can help avoid irreparable harm. Finally, substantively, the regulatory system sets levels of environmental quality that the cost-benefit or balancing approach used in tort actions cannot normally achieve, because the latter tend to rely on corrective justice rather than deterrence and they may underestimate the collective losses caused by environmental harm (Schroeder, 2002).

There are several current challenges posed with the regulatory model: (1) determining at what level of governance – local, state, regional or international – regulations should be enacted; (2) coordinating the various regulations across governance units to ensure compatibility and synergies; (3) ensuring that the legal measures adopted are scientifically sound and aim at a high level of protection; (4) making sure that the measures are equitable, that the poor and vulnerable are not made worse off, at a minimum. Thought should be given to amending environmental impact assessment procedures to require that the social as well as the natural impacts of proposed activities and measures be assessed.

2.3.3 Market Mechanisms

The third construct became popular beginning in the 1980s, with deregulation and privatization. Market-based approaches to changing human behavior emerged in preference to command-and-control measures (Bosselmann and Richardson, 1999). In part, this move constituted a reaction to dense regulatory networks that were deemed inefficient and a drain on competitiveness and investment (Reitze, 1989). Economic instruments, however, largely remain within the regulatory framework because they require laws and institutions to oversee their operation. Purely market-based approaches such as voluntary agreements tend to be inequitable, ineffective, and unable to truly account for harm to public goods like air, water and other parts of the commons

(Rehbinder, 1999). They do not, and perhaps cannot, serve to protect long term interests such as future generations.

For those who believe in market mechanisms, the challenges are to study and learn from the efforts of human rights activists who sought to reduce and eventually end corporate complicity in apartheid by buying shares in companies with poor records and mounting shareholder actions at company meetings. Other techniques include naming and shaming, labelling to encourage consumer awareness and purchasing choices, and challenging deceptive advertising by companies that claim they are green when they are engaged in the worst industry practices.

2.3.4 Rights-based Approaches

The fourth paradigm is the rights-based approach to environmental protection and poverty alleviation. In addition to its focus on ensuring the enjoyment of all civil, political, economic, cultural and social rights, it emphasizes the right to a certain quality of environment because that quality is linked to, indeed a prerequisite for, the enjoyment of internationally and domestically guaranteed rights. Rights-based approaches were initially thought to have the defect of being non-justiciable, but courts are increasingly enforcing constitutional and international rights to environmental quality. Many courts have broadened standing to permit legal redress for violations of environmental rights, without requiring individualized injury to health or property, because one major motive for guaranteeing environmental rights is to prevent injury from occurring.[35]

Looking at the domestic level and using the US as an example, on the first Earth Day in 1970 the Pennsylvania legislature approved a proposed amendment to the state constitution, intending to 'give our natural environment the same kind of constitutional protection that [is] given our political rights'.[36] The proposed amendment was approved overwhelmingly by voters in the state on 18 May 1971[37] and added what is now Article I, section 27 of the state constitution. It specifies the right of the people 'to clean air, pure water, and to the preservation of the natural, scenic, historic and aesthetic values of the environment'.

Following this example, more than 30 of the 50 states in the United States,[38] and more than 130 states around the world, have added constitutional provisions that refer to environmental or natural resource protection as a constitutional right or governmental duty. The amendments generally were enacted for two stated purposes. First, they aim to elevate environmental protection as a fundamental value to a constitutional status above the states' legislative and regulatory norms. Second, they seek to expand the doctrine of standing to allow public interest litigation on behalf of the environment. The phrasing differs among the provisions, which in turn impacts their justiciability and scope. Where such provisions are being enforced nationally and internationally, a growing caseload is elaborating the content of environmental rights.

The rights-based approach to implementing principles of justice in law emphasizes each individual's right to a certain quality of environment, because environmental quality is linked to the enjoyment of internationally and domestically guaranteed rights that cannot be exercised in a degraded environment. Even when explicit guarantees of environmental rights are lacking, courts are finding it necessary to take into account environmental quality in order to ensure the effective enjoyment of other human rights. For these reasons, numerous national and international tribunals today address and provide redress for at least some environmental harm.

At the international level, most human rights treaties were drafted and adopted before the 1972 Stockholm Conference on the Human Environment and therefore they contain few references to the environment.[39] Later treaties[40] and declarations,[41] especially at the regional level,[42] do refer to the right to a safe and healthy or sound environment, while environmental agreements have incorporated procedural human rights deemed necessary or advantageous to achieving environmental protection.[43] The protections afforded increased in scope and number after the adoption of Principle 10 of the Rio Declaration on Environment and Development.[44]

At the global level, the former United Nations Human Rights Commission took several initiatives relating to human rights and the environment, most of which have been maintained by the new Council. The Special Rapporteur on the adverse effects of the illicit movement and dumping of toxic and dangerous products and wastes on the enjoyment of human rights,[45] has a mandate that includes investigating complaints about illicit waste trade as a violation of the rights to life, good health and a sound environment.[46] The mandate of the Special Rapporteur on the right to food includes the issue of access to water,[47] affirmed as the 'right to drinking water supply and sanitation for every woman, man and child'.[48] The Human Rights Council that replaced the former UN Commission has also taken up the human rights implications of climate change.[49]

One advantage to a rights-based approach is accountability. International human rights treaty bodies have received and decided cases from applicants who allege that environmental conditions affecting them have deteriorated to the point that their internationally-guaranteed human rights have been violated. The three fully operational regional human rights systems have examined the greatest number of the complaints that environmental deterioration has affected guaranteed human rights. The coming into force of the 2004 Revised Arab Charter on Human Rights[50] and the insertion of human rights clauses in the ASEAN Charter in 2007[51] expand regional human rights systems into new geographic areas and offer possibilities for lawyers to propose action that reflects and reinforces the jurisprudence of the other regions, just as the older systems have learned from each other.

On the merits of the cases, human rights tribunals are increasingly utilizing environmental standards to adjudicate human rights claims related to the environment and to judge whether or not states have complied with their legal obligations. This suggests an integration of environmental law with concern for individuals that reflects and reinforces the principles of environmental justice.

The European Convention for the Protection of Human Rights and Fundamental Freedoms (ECHR)[52] contains neither a right to health nor a right to environment, but cases have been brought for injury due to environmental harm, invoking the right to life (Article 2), the right to information (Article 10), and the right to privacy and family life (Article 8). In responding to these complaints, the European Court has determined that it must have regard to the changing conditions within its Contracting States generally and must respond to evolving convergence as to the standards to be achieved. The European Court maintains this dynamic and evolutive approach because it finds it is 'of critical importance that the Convention is interpreted and applied in a manner which renders its rights practical and effective, not theoretical and illusory'.[53] Such an approach benefits environmental rights, which might be excluded from consideration using an 'originalist' interpretation, because most human rights agreements were written before environmental law developed and thus environmental conditions were not contemplated by the treaty drafters.[54]

Applying its evolutive approach, the European Court has indicated that the scope of guaranteed rights is affected by the 'growing and legitimate concern both in Europe and internationally about offenses against the environment'.[55] It thus concluded that governments may adjust the amount of permissible bail that can be demanded and the length of pre-trial detention according to the particular circumstances of an environmental disaster.[56] In reaching this conclusion, the Court took into account the 1982 Convention on the Law of the Sea and its provisions on offenses against the marine environment, MARPOL,[57] and European law on environmental crimes and liability.[58]

In its first major decision[59] involving environmental harm as a breach of Article 8 ECHR, the European Court held that severe environmental pollution may affect individuals' 'well-being' to the extent that it constitutes a violation of Article 8. The pollution need not reach the point of affecting health, if the enjoyment of home, private and family life is reduced.[60] Moreover, the harm may be excused if it results from an authorized activity of economic benefit to the community in general, provided the principle of distributive justice is respected: that is, as long as there is no disproportionate burden borne by any particular individual or group (including the poor). The Court applies a three part test: the measure must have a legitimate aim, be lawfully enacted, and be proportional.[61] States enjoy a margin of appreciation or certain discretion in determining the legitimacy of the aim pursued, but the Court will hold the state to the level of environmental protection it has chosen and nearly always finds a violation if the state fails to enforce its own laws.

The Court further explained its standard in *Fadayeva v. Russia*,[62] noting that because 'no right to nature preservation is as such included among the rights and freedoms guaranteed by the Convention', the adverse effects of environmental pollution must attain a certain minimum level if they are to fall within the scope of Article 8. The requisite effects or interference need not reach the level of proven injury to health; it is enough if there are serious risks posed. In *Fadayeva*, the applicant succeeded on her claim because she was made more vulnerable to various diseases, even though quantifiable harm to her health was deemed not proved; in addition, the Court found that her quality of life at her home was adversely affected.

In these and other cases, the European Court has given effect to various human rights linked to environmental protection by reference to international environmental principles, standards and norms. In addition, it has emphasized the importance of enforcing national environmental rights provisions. In so doing the Court has given substantive content to environmental rights and corresponding state obligations.

In *Oneryildiz v. Turkey*,[63] the European Court of Human Rights made reference to several environmental texts, both binding and non-binding in holding the Turkish government responsible for the loss of life and property resulting from a methane explosion at a waste site. The binding texts deemed relevant were the Lugano Convention on Hazardous Activities[64] and the Strasbourg Convention on Protection of the Environment through Criminal Law.[65] The European Court used the Lugano Convention to define 'dangerous activity' and 'damage' incurring the liability of public authorities. It noted the duty under the Strasbourg Convention for authorities to establish criminal offenses for loss of life involving the disposal or treatment of hazardous wastes.

The Court also made reference to non-binding Council of Europe texts, including Parliamentary Assembly Resolution 587 (1975) on problems connected with the disposal of urban and industrial waste;[66] Resolution 1087 (1996) on the consequences of the Chernobyl disaster;[67] and Recommendation 1225 (1993) on the management, treatment, recycling and marketing of waste.[68]

In *Taşkın and Others v. Turkey*,[69] the Court utilized principles enshrined in the Aarhus Convention on Access to Information, Public Participation in Decision-making and Access to Justice in Environmental Matters,[70] despite the fact that Turkey had not signed the Aarhus Convention. The applicants were challenging under Article 8 the decision of Turkish authorities, taken after appropriate decision-making procedures, to allow development and operation of a gold mine which the applicants alleged would cause environmental damage to the detriment of people in the region. The applicants litigated the matter and won in domestic courts. The Turkish Supreme Administrative Court repeatedly concluded that the operating permit in issue did not serve the public interest and that the safety measures which the company had taken did not suffice to eliminate the risks involved in such an activity.

In reviewing the applicable legal framework, the Court referred to *Rio* Principle 10 and the Aarhus Convention, as they set forth procedural rights including access to justice. In addition, however, the Court also quoted from a Parliamentary Assembly resolution on environment and human rights[71] which recommended that member states ensure appropriate protection of life, health, family and private life, physical integrity and private property, taking particular account of the need for environmental protection, and that member states recognize a human right to a healthy, viable and decent environment including the objective obligation for states to protect the environment in national laws, preferably at the constitutional level. Given this recommendation and the domestic constitutional guarantees, the Court found a violation despite the absence of any accidents or incidents with the mine.

Enforcement of environmental rights involves courts in not only determining what environmental quality the law requires, but also in assessing whether or not the government has taken the requisite actions to achieve that quality. Human rights tribunals have made clear that the state may be responsible whether pollution or other environmental harm is directly caused by the state or whether the state's responsibility arises from its failure to regulate properly private-sector activities.[72] States must not only respect the observance of rights and freedoms but also guarantee their existence and the free exercise of all of them against private as well as state actors. Thus any act or omission by a public authority which impairs guaranteed rights may violate a state's obligations.[73] This is particularly important in respect to the environment, where most activities causing harm are undertaken by the private sector.

As noted above, the Court requires at a minimum that the state should have complied with its domestic environmental standards.[74] The issue of compliance with domestic law is particularly important when there is a domestic constitutional right to environmental protection. The European Court will review governmental actions in the light of the domestic law. In *Okyay and Others v. Turkey*[75] the applicants had successfully challenged in domestic courts the operations of thermal-power plants in South-west Turkey, which they claimed would damage the environment and pose risks for the life and health of the Aegean region's population. They explicitly argued that Article 56 of the Turkish Constitution guaranteed them the right to life in a healthy and balanced environment. They did not argue that they had suffered any economic or other loss. The European Court agreed that they had a right under Turkish law to protection against damage to the environment and that their rights under Article 6(1) ECHR had been violated due to the failure of Turkish authorities to comply in practice and within a reasonable time with the domestic court's judgments.

Domestic constitutional laws and provisions are particularly important in cases where the applicants have no independent claim under the ECHR for severe pollution, but instead are seeking nature protection or protection of the environment more generally. In *Kyrtatos v. Greece*,[76] as in the *Okyay* case, the applicants' claim involved a constitutional provision protecting the environment. In domestic courts, the applicants and the Greek Society for the Protection of the Environment and Cultural Heritage asserted that the local prefect's decisions to allow development projects and to issue building permits were illegal, because the area concerned was a swamp safeguarded by Article 24 of the Greek Constitution, which protects the environment. The domestic court held that the prefect had violated Article 24 of the Constitution, because the decision put in jeopardy an important natural habitat for various protected species, including birds, fishes and sea-turtles. It followed that the building permits were also unlawful and had to be quashed. The decision was not enforced by the local authorities, who instead issued further building permits. Given the constitutional provision, the European Court found a violation of Article 6(1), because the domestic law gave environmental rights to the applicants and the government had failed to enforce them.

The African Commission also has identified governmental human rights obligations by reference to environmental norms. In *SERAC v. Nigeria*, the African Commission held that Article 24 'imposes clear obligations upon a government to take reasonable and other measures to prevent pollution and ecological degradation, to promote conservation, and to secure an ecologically sustainable development and use of natural resources'.[77] Compliance with these obligations includes ordering or permitting independent scientific monitoring of threatened environments, requiring environmental and social impact studies, monitoring hazardous materials and activities, as well as providing information and an opportunity for the public to participate in decision-making.[78] While the Commission did not cite specific environmental agreements, the obligations it mentions are part of international environmental law.

Beyond ensuring that any domestic environmental rights are enforced, the European Court scrutinizes the adequacy of the domestic law, to see if the state has ensured a fair balance between the interests of the community and the rights of those affected. The Court accords each state a wide margin of appreciation in this respect, because national authorities 'are in principle better placed than an international court to assess the requirements' in a particular local context and to determine the most appropriate environmental policies and individual measures while taking into account the needs of the local community,[79] especially in a technical sphere like environmental protection.[80] The wide margin of appreciation afforded governments means that the Court will only find a violation if there is a 'manifest error of appreciation' by the national authorities in striking a fair balance between the competing interests of the different private actors.[81] The final evaluation as to whether the justification given by the state is relevant and sufficient remains subject to review by the Court[82] but 'only in exceptional circumstances' will the court look beyond the procedures followed to disallow the conclusions reached by domestic authorities on the environmental protection measures to be taken on the projects and activities allowed to proceed.[83] Even if it finds that the state decided wrongly, the Court will not determine exactly what should have been done to reduce the pollution in a more efficient way.[84]

Another European supervisory body has also found violations of substantive guarantees due to the failure of the government to legislate to protect the environment. The first and, to date, only European Social Charter complaint to concern environmental conditions, lodged on 4 April 2005, claimed violations of the Charter's right to health provisions[85] because the state had not adequately prevented negative environmental impacts nor had it developed an appropriate strategy to prevent and respond to the health hazards stemming from lignite mining. The complaint also alleged that there was no legal framework guaranteeing security and safety of persons working in lignite mines. The European Committee of Social Rights concluded that the government had violated the Charter[86] after examining the Greek National Action Plan for greenhouse gas emissions and finding it inadequate in the light of the state's obligations under the Kyoto Protocol and the principle requiring use of the 'best available techniques'.[87] While the Committee found that Greek regulations on information and public participation were satisfactory, the evidence showed inadequate enforcement of the relevant legislation.

The imposition of substantive environmental quality standards does not exclude, but rather reinforces procedural rights. Indeed, human rights tribunals have read the procedural rights and corresponding state obligations into substantive human rights guarantees such as the right to life and to privacy and home life. This approach has been important in instances where the guarantees of procedural rights in human rights instruments are not strong, as is the case in the European Convention. In *Guerra v. Italy*,[88] the applicants alleged that the Italian authorities violated Articles 2, 8 and 10 ECHR by failing to mitigate the risk of a major accident at a nearby chemical factory and by withholding information from local residents about the risks and emergency procedures. The 'right to information' claim was dismissed, because the European Convention does not require the collection and dissemination of information about the environment, but the European Court effectively incorporated this requirement into the applicant's Article 8 claim as the 'procedural dimension' of the obligation of states to secure effective respect for the applicants' right to family and home life.

On the merits of the *Oneryildiz* case, the Court explained that Article 2 ECHR, which guarantees the right to life, applies 'in the context of any activity, whether public or not, in which the right to life may be at stake, and a fortiori in the case of industrial activities, which by their very nature are dangerous, such as the operation of waste-collection sites'.[89] According to European environmental standards, waste disposal is a hazardous activity, therefore Article 2 applies. The resulting duty of care depends on several factors: the harmfulness of the phenomena inherent in the activity; the contingency of the risk to the applicant; the status of those involved in creating the risk, and whether or not the conduct was deliberate. The court merged procedural rights into the substantive evaluation, finding that 'particular emphasis' should be placed on the public's right to information concerning the risks to life and the duty to investigate when loss of life occurs.[90] Assessing the evidence, the Court found that the authorities must have known of the risk and of the need to take preventive measures 'particularly as there were specific regulations on the matter'.[91] As such they had an obligation as well under Article 2 ECHR, 'to take such preventive measures as were necessary and sufficient to protect those individuals ...'.[92]

Like *Oneryildiz*, the case of *Budayeva and Others v. Russia*,[93] concerned governmental knowledge of hazards and the failure to act upon that knowledge. The latter case, however, involved repeated natural disasters rather than hazards originating in human activities. The standard of care did not differ appreciably on many of the issues. Governmental authorities aware of mudslide hazards in a mining district failed to take reasonable precautions, with resulting deaths in a village and loss of property. The Court placed special emphasis on the adoption of regulations to mitigate the potential risk to human life from the activity involved.[94] Regulations must govern the licensing, setting up, operation, security, supervision, and monitoring of the activity and must make it compulsory for all those concerned to take practical measures to ensure the effective protection of citizens whose lives might be endangered by the inherent risks.[95] The choice of particular practical measures is in principle a matter within the state's margin of appreciation and the Court will seek to avoid placing an impossible or disproportionate burden on authorities,[96] but the unjustified failure to act regarding foreseeable mortal risks will constitute a violation of Article 2 if deaths result due to the inaction.

The margin of appreciation opens wider in the sphere of emergency relief during and after natural disasters, 'which are as such beyond human control', than in regulating dangerous activities of a man-made nature. This deferential standard determined the outcome of the applicants' claim for breaches of the right to peaceful enjoyment of their possessions. The Court held that the state must only do what is reasonable in the circumstances to protect property,[97] but it has a greater obligation to do everything within its power when the risk involves potential loss of life. The origin of the threat and the extent to which one or another risk is susceptible to mitigation are factors to be evaluated in determining the scope of the state's positive obligations.[98] In this case, the authorities had been warned about the risks of devastating mudslides and had failed to provide resources for strengthening the local dams, known to be in a state of disrepair. No alternative land-planning policies were implemented or monitoring stations set up. The government provided no explanation. The Court noted that the public's procedural right of information can only be enjoyed if the government obtains the relevant information, which in this case was indispensable for ensuring the residents' safety. The authorities' failure to ensure the functioning of an early warning system thus was also unjustified.

Assessing risk is an important issue in litigating substantive environmental rights. Some human rights procedures limit standing to 'victims' of violations and there must be a sufficient threat for the applicants or petitioners to qualify as a victim.[99] The precautionary principle has begun to play a role in bringing more risks within the ambit of human rights litigation. The case of *Taşkin v. Turkey*[100] was one based on risk, stemming from the use of cyanide in gold extraction. The Court referred to the various reports that had been done on site which highlighted the risks. Domestic judicial findings also demonstrated the threat to the environment and lives of the neighbouring population. The Court found Article 8 to be applicable 'where the dangerous effects of an activity to which the individuals *are likely to be exposed* have been determined as part of an environmental impact assessment procedure in such a way as to establish a sufficiently close link with private and family life for purposes of Article 8 of the Convention.'[101] The Court held that this broad reading was necessary to ensure the effectiveness of Article 8.

Lack of judicial expertise and problems of evidence, especially causality, are frequently invoked as hurdles to giving substantive content to environmental rights. At the international level, they have not proved to be high hurdles thus far, because in most of the cases domestic fact-finding had already revealed the risks entailed or the harm. This was the case in *Oneryildiz*,[102] *Taşkin*[103] and *Fadayeva*.[104] In the last-mentioned case, a government decree had recited statistics on the increases in respiratory and blood diseases linked to air pollution, as well as the increased number of deaths from cancer.[105] The government had also determined by legislation the safe levels of various polluting substances, many of which were exceeded in the security zone where the applicant lived. The mayor of the city said the steel plant was responsible for more than 95 per cent of industrial emissions into the town's air,[106] while a state Report on the Environment indicated that the plant in question was the largest contributor to air pollution of all metallurgical plants in Russia. The two statements substantially reduced questions about causality.[107] In the end both parties agreed that the applicant's place of residence was affected by industrial pollution caused by the steel plant, but they disagreed over the degree and effects of the pollution. The government claimed that the disturbance caused by the pollution was not so severe as to raise an issue under Article 8. The applicant and the European Court disagreed, the latter explaining:

> The assessment of that minimum is relative and depends on all the circumstances of the case, such as the intensity and duration of the nuisance, and its physical or mental effects. The general context of the environment should also be taken into account. There would be no arguable claim under Article 8 if the detriment complained of was negligible in comparison to the environmental hazards inherent to life in every modern city.[108]

Causality remained an issue on the applicant's health claims. Her medical records indicated problems, but did not attribute them to any specific causes. The doctors stated, however, that her problems would be exacerbated by working in conditions of vibration, toxic pollution and an unfavorable climate.[109] The applicant also submitted an expert report[110] which linked the plant specifically to increased adverse health conditions of persons residing nearby. The Court found that the medical evidence did not establish a causal link between the pollution at her residence and her illnesses, but accepted that the evidence, including submissions by the government, was clear about the unsafe excessive pollution around her home. The Court also made reference to the expert report and the findings of the domestic courts. The Court noted that Russian legislation defined the maximum permissible concentrations as 'safe concentrations of toxic elements'.[111] Therefore, exceeding these limits produced a presumption of unsafe conditions potentially harmful to the health and well-being of those exposed to it. This presumption, together with the evidence submitted, led the Court to conclude that the applicant's health deteriorated as a result of her prolonged exposure to the industrial emissions from the steel plant. Alternatively, even if that harm could not be quantified, the pollution 'inevitably made the applicant more vulnerable to various illnesses' and affected her quality of life at home.[112] Therefore Article 8 applied.

The Court's analysis raises the question of what evidence would be sufficient to raise the presumption the Court creates in the *Fadayeva* case. It should not be limited to legislative findings, because as *Zander v. Sweden*[113] indicates, safe levels may be changed to accommodate economic interests without necessarily being based on sound science. The World Health Organization (WHO) and other scientific bodies have determined through epidemiological studies what constitutes safe levels of concentration of toxic, carcinogenic, mutagenic and other hazardous substances.[114] Reliable evidence of such studies can and should be introduced to demonstrate presumed harm when such levels are exceeded, even if local legislation permits higher concentrations. A petition to the Inter-American Commission, recently declared admissible, relies on such WHO standards to assert that the average sulphur dioxide levels from a metallurgical complex are detrimental to the lives and health of the nearby community in Peru.[115]

The European Court's standard of proof is high[116] but flexible and takes into account the fact that governments often are the sole repository of relevant evidence. Indeed, in the case of *Fägerskiöld v. Sweden*[117] the Court cited the World Health Organization guidelines[118] on noise pollution, in rejecting the admissibility of an application concerning wind turbines constructed and operating near the applicants' property. The Court noted that the guidelines are set at the level of the lowest adverse health effect associated with noise exposure. The Court also referred to even lower maximum levels adopted by most European countries. Applying these standards to the noise level tests submitted in the case, the Court found that the levels of noise did not exceed the WHO guidelines and were minimally above the recommended maximum level in Sweden. Therefore the environmental nuisance could not be found to reach the level of constituting severe environmental pollution. The Court also rejected the applicants' claims that their property rights were violated because the wind turbines decreased the value of their property. Assuming that there was an interference with property rights, the Court found that it was justified on several grounds, one of them being that the operation of the wind turbines was in the general interest as it is an environmentally friendly source of energy which contributes to the sustainable development of natural resources. The Court considered whether these beneficial environmental consequences were sufficient to outweigh the negative impact on the applicants. The Court reiterated its findings that the negative consequences were not severe, while the availability of renewable energy is beneficial for both the environment and society. Moreover the government had taken measures to mitigate the negative impacts on the applicants. In sum, the alleged interference was proportionate to the aims pursued and no violation of property rights occurred.

In the Western Hemisphere, the Inter-American Commission has also devoted attention to environmental quality as it affects human rights. In many cases, litigants have sought protections for indigenous peoples' lands and resources threatened by environmental harm. In the case of *Yanomami v. Brazil*[119] the Inter-American Commission found that the government had violated the Yanomani rights to life, liberty and personal security guaranteed by Article I of the American Declaration on the Rights and Duties of Man,[120] as well as the right of residence and movement (Article VIII) and the right to the preservation of health and well-being (Article XI)[121] because the government failed to implement measures of 'prior and adequate protection for the safety and health of the Yanomami Indians'.[122]

The *Yanomami* case did not go into detail about the conduct required of a government or the standard of care the Commission would expect. Other cases and country studies[123] have helped to clarify some issues in this respect, specifying that governments must enact appropriate laws and regulations, and then fully enforce them. In a country report on Ecuador, the Commission referred generally to the obligation of the state to respect and ensure the rights of those within its territory and the responsibility of the government to implement the measures necessary to remedy existing pollution and to prevent future contamination which would threaten the lives and health of its people, including through addressing risks associated with hazardous development activities, such as mining.[124] Governments must regulate industrial and other activities that potentially could result in environmental conditions so detrimental that they create risks to health or life.[125] Furthermore, the government must enforce the laws that it enacts as well as any constitutional guarantee of a particular quality of environment.[126] The Commission was clear: 'Where the right to life, to health and to live in a healthy environment is already protected by law, the Convention requires that the law be effectively applied and enforced.'[127]

The state must also comply with and enforce the international agreements to which it is a signatory, whether these are human rights instruments or ones related to environmental protection. In the Ecuador report, the Commission noted that the state is party to or has supported a number of instruments 'which recognize the critical connection between the sustenance of human life and the environment',[128] including: the Additional Protocol to the American Convention in the Area of Economic, Social and Cultural Rights,[129] the International Covenant on Civil and Political Rights (ICCPR)[130] and the International Covenant on Economic, Social and Cultural Rights (ICESCR),[131] the Stockholm Declaration,[132] the Treaty for Amazonian Cooperation,[133] the Amazon Declaration,[134] the World Charter for Nature,[135] the Convention on Nature Protection and Wildlife Preservation in the Western Hemisphere,[136] the Rio Declaration on Environment and Development,[137] and the Convention on Biological Diversity.[138] Through the standard-setting and enforcement process, the state must 'take the measures necessary to ensure that the acts of its agents ... conform to its domestic and inter-American legal obligations'.[139]

States thus are not exempt from human rights and environmental obligations in their development projects: 'the absence of regulation, inappropriate regulation, or a lack of supervision in the application of extant norms may create serious problems with respect to the environment which translate into violations of human rights protected by the American Convention'.[140] In the case of the *Saramaka People v. Suriname*,[141] the Inter-American Court set forth three safeguards it deemed essential to ensure that development is consistent with human rights and environmental protection: (1) the state must ensure the effective participation of the members of the Saramaka people, in conformity with their customs and traditions, regarding any development, investment, exploration or extraction plan within Saramaka territory; (2) the state must guarantee that the Saramakas will receive a reasonable benefit from any such plan within their territory; and (3) the state must ensure that no concession will be issued within Saramaka territory unless and until independent and technically capable entities, with the state's supervision, perform a prior environmental and social impact assessment.[142] It is notable that these requirements parallel the Bonn Guidelines on Access and Equitable Benefit-Sharing,[143] adopted pursuant to the Convention on Biological Diversity, although the Court does not cite them, referring instead to views of the UN Human Rights Committee,[144] ILO Convention No. 169,[145] World Bank policies,[146] and the 2007 UN Declaration on the Rights of Indigenous Peoples.[147] The Court viewed benefit-sharing as inherent to the right of compensation recognized under Article 21(2) of the Inter-American Convention.[148]

2.4 CONCLUSION: PROSPECTS AND PROBLEMS

The advantages of rights-based approaches to environmental protection are several. First, because human rights are maximum claims on society, elevating a clean environment to a right raises it above a mere policy choice. Rights are inherent attributes that must be respected in any well-ordered society. The moral weight attached to a rights label exercises an important compliance pull on members of society.

Second, all legal systems establish a hierarchy of norms. Constitutional or human rights guarantees usually are at the apex and 'trump' conflicting norms of lower value. Thus, to include respect for the environment as a constitutional right, or international human right, should ensure that it will be given precedence over other legal norms that are not rights-based. The Montana Supreme Court indicated some of the implications in the case *Cape-France Enterprises v. The Estate of Peed,* describing the right to a clean and healthful environment as 'a fundamental right that may be infringed only by demonstrating a compelling state interest ...' one that is, 'at a minimum, some interest "of the highest order and ... not otherwise served," or "the gravest abuse endangering [a] paramount [government] interest [ ]"'[149] Thus, environmental protection is not an ordinary policy choice and the burden of proof will be on the government to demonstrate a compelling reason for permitting the environment to deteriorate. This is important given the short-term costs that may make it unpopular politically to adopt and implement measures of environmental protection. A right to environmental quality can act as the brake or limitation on domestic political processes that otherwise might take a short-term view and permit activities that are significantly harmful to the environment and the people in it.

Third, the emphasis on procedural rights of information, participation, and access to justice encourages an integration of democratic values and promotion of the rule of law in broad-based structures of governance. Thus, ensuring these rights is not only a means to produce decisions favorable to environmental protection, but can reinforce respect for human rights, the rule of law and democratic values more generally. Experience suggests that repressive regimes also tend to ignore environmental conditions, that is, 'governments that show a disregard for their citizens' basic rights often protect the environment poorly as well' (Osofsky, 2005, p. 88). Citizen efforts to counter environmental harm tend to promote democratic governance as well as enhance compliance with environmental norms, something seen in particular over the past decade in Central and Eastern Europe.

This link should not be surprising: the process by which rules emerge, how proposed rules become norms and norms become law, is highly important to the legitimacy of the law and legitimacy in turn affects compliance. To a large extent, legitimacy is a matter of participation: the governed must have and perceive that they have a voice in governance through representation, deliberation or some other form of action.

Fourth, as already mentioned a rights-based approach enhances accountability by allowing utilization of international petition procedures to bring international pressure to bear when governments lack the will to prevent or halt environmental harm that threatens human health and well-being. In many instances, petitioners have been afforded redress and governments have taken measures to remedy the violation. Sometimes the problem is the result of a combination of governmental lack of capacity and lack of political will. Pollution may be caused by powerful enterprises whose business and investment are important to the state or the state may have inadequate monitoring systems to ensure air or water quality. In these instances, petition procedures can help to identify problems and encourage their resolution, including by the provision of technical assistance. States may even welcome complaints if the results give them leverage in the domestic political arena to overcome opposition to needed measures. The availability of individual complaints procedures has given rise to extensive jurisprudence from which the specific obligations of states to protect and preserve the environment are detailed.

Turning to the problems, there are limits to what can be achieved through a rights-based approach. First, relying on existing human rights guarantees is anthropocentric, because environmental harm must affect human well-being before human rights guarantees can be invoked. Unless there is a specific right to a healthy or ecologically-balanced environment, international human rights procedures cannot be used on behalf of the environment or to prevent threats to other species or to ecological processes.

A second limitation to a rights-based approach to environmental protection is found in the limited mandates of human rights bodies in respect to remedies. The European Court can award monetary damages, but has little power to order injunctive relief or mandate specific action. Thus, rights may be vindicated with money for the applicants to move away from the environmental harm, but it is not clear that the environmental conditions themselves are improved in the short term. *Fadayeva v. Russia*[150] is a case in point; she was awarded compensation, but the industrial facility, the steel mill, remained in operation as before. Yet, the Committee of Ministers (COM) does not close a case until there is compliance with the judgment, including general measures to ensure that the violation is not repeated. Subsequently, the COM invited the Russian authorities to hold consultations with the Council of Europe (COE) and experts on the general measures to be adopted to ensure that there is no repetition of the violation. It also requested the Russian authorities to draft an environmental code to be reviewed by the COE for compliance with regional standards.

A further limitation is that the decisions of the Inter-American Commission, the African Commission, and the UN bodies are recommendations that lack the binding force of judgments of the regional courts. While good faith cooperation with international bodies given monitoring power and the authority to hear complaints suggests that states should comply, they may take the view that recommendations need not be strictly followed.

Third, and less commonly, some states envisage rights as restraints on governmental power, with duties of governmental abstention, and do not accept human rights obligations that require affirmative management of resources and regulations to ensure that private conduct – which is responsible for the large majority of environmental harm – is properly controlled. But constitutional and human rights law now widely accepts affirmative state obligations to protect individuals against private as well as public violations of rights. It is important because the major difference between constitutional provisions that are based on traditional doctrines of public trust and those that enshrine environmental rights seems to be the extent to which private-source environmental harm is addressed. Including the right to environment in the constitution places it on an equal footing with rights to property and allows for a balancing of community and individual interests, more than does public interest doctrine.

A fourth limitation is inherent in the traditional scope of human rights law:

a right to an environment of a certain quality is complicated by both temporal and geographic elements absent from other human rights protections. Environmental degradation harms not only those currently living, but also future generations of humanity as well. Can those not born be said to have rights and if so, who represents such future generations and how should courts protect their interests?

The most politically-charged aspect of a right to environment may be the potentially vast expansion of the territorial scope of state obligations. Presently, human rights instruments require each state to respect and ensure guaranteed rights to all individuals within its territory and subject to its jurisdiction. This geographic limitation reflects the reality that a state normally will have the power to protect or the possibility to violate human rights only of those within its territory and jurisdiction. Nature recognizes no political boundaries, however. A state polluting its coastal waters or the atmosphere may cause significant harm to individuals thousands of miles away. States that permit or encourage GHG emissions or depletion of the tropical rain forest can contribute to global warming that threatens the entire biosphere.

Ultimately, the definition of a right to environment will have to include substantive environmental standards to restrict harmful air pollution and other types of emissions. Although establishing quality standards requires extensive international regulation of environmental sectors based upon impact studies, such regulation is by no means impossible. Adoption of quality standards demands extensive research and debate involving public participation, but substantive minima are a necessary complement to the procedural rights leading to informed consent. Otherwise, a human rights approach to environmental protection would be ineffective in preventing serious environmental harm.

Establishing the content of a right through reference to independent and variable standards is often used in human rights, especially with regard to economic entitlements, and need not be a barrier to recognition of the right to a specific environmental quality. Rights to an adequate standard of living and to social security are sometimes defined in international accords such as the European Social Charter[151] or Conventions and Recommendations of the International Labor Organization. States implement these often flexible obligations according to changing economic indicators, needs, and resources. The human rights treaties provide a 'framework' containing the basic guarantees on which international, national and local laws and policies are elaborated.

A similar approach can be utilized to give meaning to a right to environment. Both the threats to humanity and the resulting necessary measures are subject to constant change based on advances in scientific knowledge and conditions of the environment. Thus, it is impossible for a human rights instrument to specify precisely what measures should be taken, that is, the products which should not be used or the chemical composition of air which must be maintained. These technical requirements can be negotiated and regulated through international environmental norms and standards, giving content to the right to environment by reference to independent environmental findings and regulations capable of rapid amendment. The variability of implementation demands imposed by the right to environment in response to different threats over time and place does not undermine the concept of the right, but merely takes into consideration its dynamic character.

So we have four approaches. There are challenges with each that require research and legal action from lawsuits to new instruments. The litigation will not always, or perhaps even often, result in immediate success, but is useful and perhaps even indispensable. The December 2005 Inuit petition to the Inter-American Commission on Human Rights[152] led to the first hearing on human rights and climate change and the possible future appointment of a special rapporteur on human rights and the environment. Beyond litigation, there is a need for consideration of new problems and potentially new legal instruments articulating new rights.

Can there be a state without a territory? Already, in Kiribati people ask whether they will still have their citizenship if they have no territory – will they still have an exclusive economic zone if there is no land? Will they have a right to access other territory? How does the Responsibility to Protect apply in the environmental context? We should begin to consider the need to elaborate a legal instrument on population movements and perhaps on ecological intervention in cases of natural disasters where the government lacks resources to aid its own people, but rejects outside help.

In conclusion, human rights and environmental protection both ultimately seek to achieve the highest quality of sustainable life for humanity within the global ecosystem. Potentially conflicting differences of emphasis still exist, because the essential concern of human rights law is to protect individuals and groups within a given society, while the purpose of environmental law is to sustain all life and ecological processes by balancing the needs and capacities of present generations with those of the future. Nonetheless, these two fundamental objectives of society are as interdependent as are the economies and communications networks of the world today. They must be integrated and addressed in a holistic manner that is sustainable and just, using all the legal techniques of the past and present as they may be modified to protect the future.

NOTES

1. 'World Bank Finds That Adjustment Places More in Steep Poverty', *New York Times*, 27 August 2008, p.A7.
2. Ibid.

3. It is estimated, for example, that the deforestation and consequent immigration of people into the Brazilian interior increased malaria prevalence in the region by 500%: Smith, A.T.P. (2002), *The Wealth of Nations* (MIT Press).
4. See the statement of the Chair of the IPCC at the time of the launch of the second part of the IPCC's Fourth Assessment Report in 2007 as reported in http://environment.about.com/od/globalwarming/a/ipcc_report_two.htm (accessed 12 February 2012).
5. Brief of Amici Curiae Alaska Inter-Tribal Council et al. in Support of Petitioners, *Mass. v. EPA*, 127 S.Ct. 1438 (No. 05-1120).
6. The *World Development Report 2000/2001* of the World Bank defined poverty as 'the pronounced deprivation of well being.', http://siteresources.worldbank.org/INTPOVERTY/Resources/WDR/English-Full-Text-Report/ch1.pdf (accessed 2 February 2012), p. 15.
7. Ibid., p. 17, box 1.1.
8. The eight goals are: eradicate extreme poverty and hunger; achieve universal primary education; promote gender equality and empower women; reduce child mortality; improve maternal health; combat HIV/AIDS, malaria and other diseases; ensure environmental sustainability; develop a global partnership for development. See http://www.un.org/millenniumgoals/ (accessed 2 February 2012).
9. *The Henry Eubank,* 11 F. Cas. 1166, 1170 (D. Mass. 1833 (No. 6376); see also *The Blackwall*, 77 U.S. (10 Wall.) 1, 14, 2002 AMC 1808, 1815 (1869).
10. Convention (No. IV) Respecting the Laws and Customs of War on Land, with annex of Regulations (The Hague, Oct. 18, 1907), 36 Stat. 2277, T.S. No. 539, Preamble (emphasis added).
11. Thus, for example, in the case of *Diversion of the Waters of the Meuse*, the PCIJ held that it was inequitable for the applicant state to complain of a wrongful act which the applicant itself had committed in the past. (1937) PCIJ: Ser. A/B 70, p. 25.
12. For other meanings see Schachter, O. (1991) *International Law in Theory and Practice* (Nijhoff Publishers), pp.55–56.
13. Universal Declaration of Human Rights, http://www.un.org/en/documents/udhr/index.shtml (accessed 2 February 2012), Preamble.
14. See Petersmann, E-U. *Theories of Justice, Human Rights, and the Constitution of International Markets*, (2003) *Loy. L.A. L. Rev.* 37, 407 at p. 412: '[C]ontrary to the suggestion by John Rawls to base international justice on equal freedoms of peoples, human rights offer a more appropriate constitutional basis for national as well as international justice.'
15. Federal Actions to Address Environmental Justice in Minority Populations and Low-Income Populations, Exec. Order No. 12898, 3 C.F.R. sec. 859 (1994), reprinted in 31 U.S.C.A. sec. 4321 at 7629-32 (1994).
16. See for instance Article 2, 1997 UN Convention on the Law of Non-Navigational Uses of International Watercourses, http://untreaty.un.org/ilc/texts/instruments/english/conventions/8_3_1997.pdf (accessed 2 February 2012).
17. *Case Concerning the Gabčíkovo-Nagymaros Project (Hungary/Slovakia)*, Judgment of 25 September 1997, [1997] I.C.J. 7. See http://www.icj-cij.org/docket/files/92/7375.pdf (accessed 2 February, 2011).
18. *Fisheries Jurisdiction Cases (United Kingdom v. Iceland; Federal Republic of Germany v. Iceland),* Judgments of 25 July 1974, [1974] I.C.J. 3 and [1974] I.C.J. 175. See http://www.icj-cij.org/docket/index.php?p1=3&p2=3&k=f9&case= 56&code=bi&p3=4&PHPSESSID=757ee871185687f4805ea9f22cef75f6 (accessed 2 February 2012)
19. Above, note 16, Art. 5.
20. Ibid., Art. 10.
21. http://www.unhchr.ch/tbs/doc.nsf/0/3d02758c707031d58025677f003b73b9 (accessed 2 February 2012).
22. http://ozone.unep.org/new_site/en/Treaties/treaty_text.php?treatyID=2 (accessed 12 February 2012).
23. http://unfccc.int/essential_background/convention/background/items/2853.php (accessed 2 February 2012).
24. http://www.cbd.int/convention/text/ (accessed 2 February 2012).

25. Moreover, Scott Barrett's work has indicated that agreements perceived to be fair are not only likely to induce greater participation but are more likely to be self-enforcing and thus successful over the long term. Barret, S. (2003), *Environment and Statecraft: The Strategy of Environmental Treaty-Making* (Oxford University Press).
26. *Trail Smelter (U.S. v. Can.)* (1941) RIAA iii.1905 at 1965; Ann. Digest (1938-40) no. 104.
27. Above, note 5.
28. *Georgia v. Tennessee Copper Company and Ducktown Sulphur, Copper and Iron Company, Ltd.*, 206 U.S. 230 (1907). This case defined the nature of the suit as one brought by the state in its capacity as quasi-sovereign, a capacity that gives it an interest 'independent of and behind the titles of its citizens, in all the earth and air within its domain'. The Supreme Court found that 'it is a fair and reasonable demand on the part of a sovereign that the air over its territory should not be polluted on a great scale by sulphurous acid gas, that the forests on its mountains, be they better or worse, and whatever domestic destruction they may have suffered, should not be further destroyed or threatened by the act of persons beyond its control, that the crops and orchards on its hills should not be endangered from the same source'.
29. See, for example, *Illinois Central Railroad Co. v. Illinois*, 146 U.S. 387 (1892); *City of Milwaukee v. State*, 214 N.W. 820 (Wis. 1927). Fishing rights, free access to the shore, and navigation are traditional rights that are reaffirmed in several state constitutions as well as in jurisprudence. See, for example, Cal. Const. art. I sec. 25; R.I. Const. art. I sec. 17; Ala. Const. art. 1 sec 24.
30. Alaska's constitution, for example, guarantees the latter: 'Wherever occurring in their natural state, fish, wildlife, and waters are reserved to the people for common use.' Ala. Const. art. VIII, § 3. Rhode Island's Constitutional amendment, added in 1986, also focuses on public rights of access and use, coupled with a legislative mandate:

> The people shall continue to enjoy and freely exercise all the rights of fishery, and the privileges of the shore, to which they have been heretofore entitled under the charter and usages of this state; and they shall be secure in their rights to the use and enjoyment of the natural resources of the state with due regard for the preservation of their values, and it shall be the duty of the general assembly to provide for the conservation of the air, land, water, plant, animal, mineral and other natural resources of the state, and to adopt all means necessary and proper by law to protect the natural environment of the people of the state by providing adequate resource planning for the control and regulation of the use of natural resources of the state and for the preservation, regeneration and restoration of the natural environment of the state.

31. For various approaches to the reach of the public trust, see: Reed, S.W. (1986), 'The Public Trust Doctrine: Is it Amphibious?' *J. Envtl L. & Litig.* 1, 107, at pp. 107–08, 118; Wilkinson, C.F. (1980), 'The Public Trust Doctrine in Public Land Law', *U.C. Davis L. Rev.* 14, 269, at p. 316; Rieser, A. (1991), 'Ecological Preservation as a Public Property Right: An Emerging Doctrine in Search of a Theory', Harv. Envtl. L. Rev. 15, 393, at pp. 398–99.
32. Sax, J. (1970), 'The Public Trust Doctrine in Natural Resource Law: Effective Judicial Intervention', *Mich. L. Rev.* 68, 471. See also Cohen , B. (1970), 'The Constitution, the Public Trust Doctrine, and the Environment', *Utah L. Rev.* 388.
33. See, for example, *Wade v. Kramer*, 459 N.E.2d 1025, 1027 (Ill. App. Ct. 1984).
34. Haw. Const. art. XI, § 1.
35. See, for example, *Montana Environmental Information Center v. Department of Environmental Quality*, 296 Mont. 207, 988 P. 2d 1236 (1999).
36. Kury, F.L., 'The Pennsylvania Environmental Protection Amendment', *Pa. B. Ass'n Q.*, Apr. 1987, at 85, 87, quoted in Kirsch, M.T. (1997), 'Upholding the Public Trust in State Constitutions', 46 *Duke L.J.* 1169–1210, at 1170.
37. The vote was more than 3–1 in favor of the amendment, with close to 2 million voters. See Kury, F.L. (1980), 'The Environmental Amendment to the Pennsylvania Constitution:

Twenty Years Later and Largely Untested', *Vill. Envtl. L.J.* 1, 123, 123–24 (1990) in Kirsch, op cit, at note 3.

38. Kirsch, in fact, argues that all of the successfully invoked provisions rely upon public trust doctrine, asserting that '[e]ach of the successful provisions invokes some combination of the concepts undergirding the public trust doctrine: conservation, public access, and trusteeship'. Kirsch, op cit, at 1173. Provisions that refer to 'trust,' include Haw. Const. art. XI; Pa. Const. art. I, § 27; Va. Const. art. XI, § 3. For provisions outlining public trust principles, see Ala. Const. art. VIII; Cal. Const. art. X, § 2; Fla. Const. art. II, § 7; La. Const. art. IX; Mass. Const. § 179; Mich. Const. art. IV, § 52; Mont. Const. art. IX, § 1; N.M. Const. art. XX, § 21; N.Y. Const. art. XIV; N.C. Const. art. XIV, § 5; R.I. Const. art. 1, § 17; Tex. Const. art. XVI, § 59.
39. The International Covenant on Economic, Social and Cultural Rights (IESCR) (16 December 1966), http://www2.ohchr.org/english/law/cescr.htm (accessed 2 February 2012) speaks primarily to the working environment, guaranteeing the right to safe and healthy working conditions (art. 7 b) and the right of children and young persons to be free from work harmful to their health (art. 10 para. 3). The right to health (IESCR, art.12), however, goes further and expressly calls on states parties to take steps for 'the improvement of all aspects of environmental and industrial hygiene' and 'the prevention, treatment and control of epidemic, endemic, occupational, and other diseases'.
40. The Convention on the Rights of the Child (New York, 20 November 1989), http://www2.ohchr.org/english/law/crc.htm (accessed 2 February 2012) refers to aspects of environmental protection in respect to the child's right to health. Article 24 provides that states parties shall take appropriate measures to combat disease and malnutrition 'through the provision of adequate nutritious foods and clean drinking water, taking into consideration the dangers and risks of environmental pollution'. (Art. 24(2)(c)). States parties also are to provide information and education on hygiene and environmental sanitation to all segments of society. (Art. 24(2)(e)). ILO Convention No. 169 concerning Indigenous and Tribal Peoples in Independent Countries (Geneva, June 27 1989) see http://www.ilo.org/ilolex/cgi-lex/convde.pl?C169 (accessed 2 February 2012) contains numerous references to the lands, resources, and environment of indigenous peoples (for example, Arts. 2, 6, 7, 15). The Convention requires states parties to take special measures to safeguard the environment of indigenous peoples (Art. 4). In particular, governments must provide for environmental impact studies of planned development activities and take measures, in cooperation with the peoples concerned, to protect and preserve the environment of the territories they inhabit.
41. The most recent UN human rights text, the United Nations Declaration on the Rights of Indigenous Peoples, adopted by the General Assembly on 12 September 2007 see http://www.un.org/esa/socdev/unpfii/en/drip.html (accessed 2 February 2012) with only four dissenting votes (U.S., Canada, Australia and New Zealand) contains several provisions related to environmental rights. In addition to protection of indigenous lands (Arts. 10, 25–27) and resources (Arts. 23, 26) the declaration contains procedural rights of participation (Art. 18) and prior informed consent (Art. 19) as well as a specific article on the environment. Article 29 provides:

    1. Indigenous peoples have the right to the conservation and protection of the environment and the productive capacity of their lands or territories and resources. States shall establish and implement assistance programmes for indigenous peoples for such conservation and protection, without discrimination.
    2. States shall take effective measures to ensure that no storage or disposal of hazardous materials shall take place in the lands or territories of indigenous peoples without their free, prior and informed consent.
    3. States shall also take effective measures to ensure, as needed, that programmes for monitoring, maintaining and restoring the health of indigenous peoples, as developed and implemented by the peoples affected by such materials, are duly implemented.

42. The African Charter on Human and Peoples' Rights, (Banjul, 26 June 1981), see http://www1.umn.edu/humanrts/instree/z1afchar.htm (accessed 2 February 2012). Article 24 provides that 'All peoples shall have the right to a general satisfactory environment favorable to their development.' The Additional Protocol to the American Convention on Human Rights in the area of Economic, Social and Cultural Rights, http://www.oas.org/juridico/english/treaties/a-52.html (accessed 2 February 2012), also contains a right to environment, but did not add it to those rights subject to the individual complaint procedure. Article 11, entitled: 'Right to a healthy environment' proclaims:

    1. Everyone shall have the right to live in a healthy environment and to have access to basic public services.
    2. The States Parties shall promote the protection, preservation and improvement of the environment.

    The 2004 Revised Arab Charter on Human Rights, see http://www1.umn.edu/humanrts/instree/loas2005.html (accessed 2 February 2012) also guarantees a right to a safe and healthy environment. Its Article 38 specifies:

    > Every person has the right to an adequate standard of living for himself and his family, that ensures their well-being and a decent life, including food, clothing, housing, services and the right to a healthy environment. The States parties shall take the necessary measures commensurate with their resources to guarantee these rights.

43. See, for example, the Convention on Access to Information, Public Participation and Access to Justice in Environmental Matters (Aarhus, June 25, 1998), http://www.unece.org/env/pp/documents/cep43e.pdf (accessed 2 February 2012); Protocol to the 1979 Convention on Long-Range Transboundary Air Pollution Concerning the Control of Emissions of Volatile Organic Compounds or Their Transboundary Fluxes (Geneva, 18 November 1991), Art. 2(3)(a)(4), http://www.unece.org/env/lrtap/vola_h1.htm (accessed 2 February 2012) ; Convention on the Protection and Utilization of International Watercourses and International Lakes (Helsinki, 17 March 1992), Art. 16, see http://www.unece.org/env/water/ (accessed 2 February 2012; the regional seas agreements; Convention on Civil Responsibility for Damage Resulting from Activities Dangerous to the Environment (Lugano, 21 June 1993, Arts. 13–16, http://conventions.coe.int/treaty/en/treaties/html/150.htm (accessed 2 February 2012) ; and United Nations Framework Convention on Climate Change (Rio de Janeiro, 9 May 1992) , above, note 23, Art. 6. Non-binding texts include the European Charter on the Environment and Health, adopted 8 December 1989, http://whqlibdoc.who.int/euro/-1993/ICP-RUD_113.pdf (accessed 2 February 2012); Ministerial Declaration on Environmentally Sound and Sustainable Development in Asia and the Pacific (Bangkok, 16 October 1990), A/CONF.151/PC/38 (Para. 27 affirms 'the right of individuals and nongovernmental organizations to be informed of environmental problems relevant to them, to have necessary access to information, and to participate in the formulation and implementation of decisions likely to affect their environment'.); Arab Declaration on Environment and Development and Future Perspectives (Cairo, September 1991), A/46/632, cited in U.N. Doc. E/CN.4/Sub.2/1992/7, 20 (affirming the right to information about environmental issues).
44. http://www.unep.org/Documents.Multilingual/Default.asp?documentid=78&articleid=1163 (accessed 2 February 2012). For relevant instruments adopted after the Rio Declaration see for example, Protocol on Water and Health to the 1992 Convention on the Protection and Use of Transboundary Watercourses and International Lakes (London, 17 June 1999), http://www.unece.org/env/documents/2000/wat/mp.wat.2000.1.e.pdf (accessed 2 February 2012); the United Nations Convention to Combat Desertification in Those Countries Experiences Serious Drought and/or Desertification (14 October 1994), http://www.unccd.int/convention/text/convention.php?annexNo=0 (accessed 2 February

2012) which places human beings at the center of concern to combat desertification (Pmbl) and requires states parties to ensure that all decisions to combat desertification or to mitigate the effects of drought are taken with the participation of populations and local communities. (Art. 3). The Convention places an emphasis throughout on information and participation of local communities. The Rotterdam Convention on the Prior Informed Consent Procedure for Certain Hazardous Chemicals and Pesticides in International Trade (10 September 1998), EMuT, 998:26, http://www.pic.int/home.php?type=s&id=77 (accessed 2 February 2012), Art 15(2), requires each state party to ensure, to the extent practicable that the public has appropriate access to information on chemical handling and accident management and on alternatives that are safer for human health or the environment than the chemicals listed in Annex III to the Convention. The Cartagena Protocol on Biosafety to the Convention on Biological Diversity (Montreal, 29 January 2000), 39 I.L.M.1027, http://bch.cbd.int/protocol/text/ (accessed 2 February 2012), Art. 23 concerns public awareness and participation, requiring the Parties to facilitate awareness, education and participation concerning the safe transfer, handling and use of living modified organisms in relation to the conservation and sustainable use of biological diversity, taking into account risks to human health. Access to information on imported LMOs should be ensured and the public consulted in the decision-making process regarding such organisms, with the results of such decisions made available to the public. Further, each Party shall endeavour to inform its public about the means of public access to the Biosafety Clearing-House created by the Convention.

45. Resolution 2001/35, Adverse effects of the illicit movement and dumping of toxic and dangerous products and wastes on the enjoyment of human rights, E/CN.4/RES/2001/35.
46. All of the reported cases involved harm to persons as a result of the transboundary movement of hazardous materials, nearly always in violation of national and international environmental law. See the Report of the Special Rapporteur on the Adverse Effects of the Illicit Movement and Dumping of Toxic and Dangerous Products and Wastes on the Enjoyment of Human Rights, Addendum, Commission on Human Rights, E/CN.4/2001/55/Add.1 (21 Dec. 2000), documenting *inter alia* damage to tissues from arsenic poisoning, risks to health from the dumping of heavy metals, illnesses from pesticide use at banana plantations, deaths from petrochemical dumping, and kidney failure in children due to contaminated pharmaceuticals. In its resolutions on this matter, the Commission consistently recognized that such trade ‘constitute[s] a serious threat to the human rights to life, good health and a sound environment for everyone’. See Commission on Human Rights, Resolutions 199/23 and 2000/72.
47. Resolution 2001/25, *The right to food*, E/CN.4/RES/2001/25 of 20 April 2001. The Commission’s Sub-Commission on Promotion and Protection of Human Rights also pressed the issue of the right to drinking water and sanitation, conducting a detailed study on the relationship between the enjoyment of economic, social and cultural rights and the promotion of the realization of the right to drinking water supply and sanitation. Resolution 2001/2, *Promotion of the realization of the right to drinking water and sanitation*, E/CN.4/Sub.2/RES/2001/2 of 10 August 2001.
48. The Commission also adopted several resolutions linking human rights, health and the environment, such as Res. 2005/60 (20 April 2005), entitled *Human rights and the environment as part of sustainable development*. The resolution cited relevant UN conferences from Stockholm to Johannesburg and the goals and targets of the United Nations Millennium Declaration.
49. See Resolution 2/23 (28 March 2008) at http://www2.ohchr.org/english/issues/climate change/docs/Resolution_7_23.pdf (accessed 2 February 2012).
50. Above, note 42.
51. See Art. 1(7), Art. 2(2)(i), and Art. 14 for human rights provisions as well as Art. 1(9) with regard to the environment in the Charter of the Association of Southest Asian Nations, adopted 20 November 2007, www.asean.org (accessed 2 February 2012).
52. http://conventions.coe.int/treaty/Commun/QueVoulezVous.asp?NT=005&CL=ENG (accessed 2 February 2012).
53. *Christine Goodwin v. The United Kingdom* [GC], App. No. 28957/95, judgment of 11 July 2002, 35 EHRR 18 (2002), para. 74.

54. Recall that the Vienna Convention on the Law of Treaties, http://untreaty.un.org/ilc/texts/instruments/english/conventions/1_1_1969.pdf (accessed 2 February 2012), allows recourse to the drafting history (*travaux préparatoires)* as a subsidiary means of interpretation (Art. 32) only if the application of Art. 31 leaves the meaning absurd or ambiguous.
55. See *Mangouras v. Spain*, no. 12050/04, Decision of the Grand Chamber, 28 Sept. 2010, 8 Jan. 2009, para. 86. See http://cmiskp.echr.coe.int/tkp197/view.asp?item=1&portal=hbkm&action=html&highlight=mangouras%20|%20spain&sessionid=85911271&skin=hudoc-en (accessed 2 February 2021). Increased concern with the environment has also proved important in cases where states have taken measures to protect the environment and the actions are resisted on the grounds that they interfere with the right to property. In *Fredin v. Sweden* the applicant argued that nature protection was an inadequate reason to revoke a license to extract gravel on his property and therefore was a violation of Article I, Protocol 1. The Court found no violation, noting that the protection of the environment is an increasingly important consideration. *Fredin v. Sweden*, No. 12033/86, 13 EHRR. 784 (1991). The Court similarly found no violation of the same provision in *Pine Valley Developments Ltd v. Ireland*, where permission to carry out construction in a green belt area was revoked on grounds of environmental protection. *Pine Valley Devs. Ltd. v Ireland,* App. No. 12742/87, 14 EHRR. 319 (1992). The most difficult and contentious cases in this respect have concerned travellers or gypsies, whose lifestyle may bring them into contact with modern land use planning. The European Court has repeatedly refused to override local zoning restrictions, especially the creation of green belts, in order to ensure a permanent home for this minority group. See *Buckley v. United Kingdom*, 1996-IV Eur. Ct. H.R. 1271 (1996) and the four recent cases: *Smith v. United Kingdom*, App. No. 25154/94, 33 EHRR 712 (2001); *Lee v. United Kingdom*, App. No. 25289/94, 33 EHRR 677 (2001); *Chapman v. United Kingdom*, App. No. 27238/94, 33 EHRR 399 (2001); *Beard v. United Kingdom*, App. No. 24882/94, 33 EHRR (2001).
56. *Mangouros v. Spain,* op cit.
57. International Convention for the Prevention of Pollution from Ships, 2 November 1973 (MARPOL 73/78) and the Protocol thereto adopted 17 February 1978. See http://www.imo.org/about/conventions/listofconventions/pages/international-convention-for-the-prevention-of-pollution-from-ships-(marpol).aspx (accessed 2 February, 2012).
58. The Court cited two European Community directives, Directive 2004/35/CE of 21 April 2004 on environmental liability with regard to the prevention and remedying of environmental damage; and Directive 2005/35/EC of 7 September 2005 on ship-source pollution and on the introduction of penalties for infringements.
59. *Lopez Ostra v. Spain*, Eur. Ct. Hum. Rts [1994] Ser. A, No. 303C.
60. In *Powell & Raynor v. United Kingdom*, Eur. Ct. Hum. Rts [1990] Ser. A No. 172, the European Court found that aircraft noise from Heathrow Airport constituted a violation of Article 8, but was justified as 'necessary in a democratic society' for the economic well-being of the country and was acceptable under the principle of proportionality because it did not 'create an unreasonable burden for the person concerned'. The latter text could be met by the state if the individual had 'the possibility of moving elsewhere without substantial difficulties and losses'.
61. Many of the European environmental cases invoking the protection of privacy and home life involve noise pollution. See *Arrondelle v. United Kingdom*, (1980)19 DR 186; (1982) 26 DR 5; *Powell & Raynor v. United Kingdom*, 172 Eur.Ct. H.R. (1990); and *Hatton and Others v. The United Kingdom* (GC) 2003, 37 EHRR 28, applying a 'fair balance' test and finding no violation due to aircraft noise from Heathrow Airport.
62. *Fadayeva v. Russia*, no. 55723/00, judgment of 9 June 2005, 2005/IV Eur. Ct.H.R. 255 (2005).
63. *Oneryildiz v. Turkey*, no. 48938/99, (GC), Reports 2004-VI (30 Nov.).
64. Convention on Civil Liability for Damage resulting from Activities Dangerous to the Environment, above n. 43.
65. Convention on Protection of the Environment through Criminal Law, Strasbourg, 4 Nov. 1998, E.T.S. No. 172. See http://conventions.coe.int/treaty/en/Treaties/Html/172.htm (accessed 2 February 2012). The Court noted that the Strasbourg Convention was not in

force, but found it 'very much in keeping with the current trend towards harsher penalties for damage to the environment.'

66. http://assembly.coe.int/Main.asp?link=/Documents/AdoptedText/ta75/ERES587.htm (visited 2 February 2012)
67. http://assembly.coe.int/Main.asp?link=/Documents/AdoptedText/ta96/ERES1087.htm (visited 2 February 2012).
68. http://assembly.coe.int/Documents/AdoptedText/ta93/EREC1225.HTM (visited 2 February 2012).
69. *Taskın and Others v. Turkey*, no. 49517/99, §§ 99 and 119, 2004-X Eur. Ct. H.R. 145 (2005).
70. Aarhus Convention, above, note 43.
71. Parliamentary Assembly Recommendation 1614 (2003) of 27 June 2003. See http://assembly.coe.int/Main.asp?link=/Documents/AdoptedText/ta03/EREC1614.htm (visited 2 February 2012). See also *Okyay and Others v. Turkey*, *Okyay et autres c. Turquie/and Others v. Turkey*, no. 36220/97 (Sect. 2) (bil.),CEDH/ECHR 2005-VII.
72. *See: Mareno Gomez v. Spain*, no. 4143/02, 16 Nov. 2004, para. 55; *Giacomelli v. Italy*, no. 59909/60, 12 Oct. 2006, paras. 78–79; *Surugiu v. Romania*, no. 48995/99, 20 April 2004.
73. *Velasquez Rodriguez Case*, 4 Inter-Am. Ct. H.R. (ser. C) at 155 (Judgment of July 29, 1988) (concerning disappearance of civilians perpetrated by the Honduran army); *Godinez Cruz Case*, 5 Inter-Am. Ct. H.R. (ser. C) at 152-53 (Judgment of 20 January 1989).
74. See, for example. *Ashworth and Others v. the United Kingdom*, App. No. 39561/98, 20 Jan. 2004; , *Moreno Gomes v. Spain*, 2004-X Eur. Ct. H.R. 327 (2005).
75. *Okyay and Others v. Turkey*, above, note 71 at 57.
76. *Kyrtatos v. Greece*, no. 41666/98, 22 May 2003, 2003-VI.
77. *Social and Economic Rights Action Center/Center for Economic and Social Rights v. Nigeria*, Comm. 155/96, Case No. ACHPR/COMM/A044/1, 27 May 2002.
78. Ibid., para. 53.
79. *Giacomelli*, above, note 72, para. 80.
80. *Fadayeva v. Russia*, above note 62 at para. 104, citing *Hatton*, above, note 61, para. 122.
81. Ibid.
82. Ibid., paras. 102–103.
83. Ibid., para. 105, citing *Taskin and others v. Turkey* , above, note 69.
84. In particular, the Court says it would be going too far to assert that the state or the polluting undertaking were under an obligation to provide the applicant with free housing. Ibid.,para. 133. It is enough to say that the situation called for a special treatment of those living near the plant.
85. Complaint No. 30/2005 *Marangopoulos Foundation for Human Rights (MFHR) v. Greece,* http://www.coe.int/t/dghl/monitoring/socialcharter/complaints/CC30CaseDoc1_en.pdf (accessed 2 February 2012).
86. The Committee transmitted its decision on the merits to the Committee of Ministers and to the Parties on 6 December 2006. The Committee of Ministers adopted its resolution on the matter on 15 January 2008. See https://wcd.coe.int/wcd/ViewDoc.jsp?Ref=CM/Notes/994/4.2d&Language=lanEnglish&Ver=original&Site=CM&BackColorInternet=DBDCF2&BackColorIntranet=FDC864&BackColorLogged=FDC864 (accessed 2 February 2012).
87. According to the Committee, ibid, '[t]he Greek National Action Plan for 2005-2007 (NAP1) provides for greenhouse gas emissions for the whole country and all sectors combined to rise by no more than 39.2% until 2010, whereas Greece was committed, in the framework of the Kyoto Protocol, to an increase in these gases of no more than 25% in 2010. When air quality measurements reveal that emission limit values have been exceeded, the penalties imposed are limited and have little dissuasive effect. Moreover, the initiatives taken by DEH (the public power corporation operating the Greek lignite mines) to adapt plant and mining equipment to the "best available techniques" have been slow.'
88. *Guerra v. Italy*, App. No: 14967/89, Reports 1998-I, no. 64.
89. Above, note 63, para. 71.
90. Ibid. para. 90.
91. Ibid. para. 101.

92. Ibid.
93. *Budayeva and Others v. Russia*, App. No. (2008) ECHR 15339/02 & Ors (20 March 2008).
94. Ibid, para. 132.
95. Ibid.
96. Ibid, para. 135.
97. Ibid, at para. 174. While the Court found that the measures taken by the state were negligent, it found the causal link was not well-established. The mudslide of 2000 being exceptionally strong, the Court said it was unclear whether a functioning warning system or proper maintenance of the defence infrastructure would have mitigated the damage.
98. Ibid, at para. 137.
99. See *Bordes and Temeharo v. France*, Comm. No. 645/1995, CCPR/C/57/D/645/1995, 30 July 1996. The risk of harm from nuclear radiation due to nuclear testing by France in the South Pacific deemed too remote for the victims to qualify as victims.
100. *Taşkin,* above, note 69.
101. Ibid., para. 113 [emphasis added].
102. *Oneryildiz*, above, note 63.
103. *Taşkin*, above, note 83.
104. *Fadayeva v. Russia*, above note 62. See also *Ledyayeva, Dobrokhotova, Zolotareva and Romashina v. Russia*, nos. 53157/99, 53247/99, 53695/00 and 56850/00, judgment of 26 October 2006, also involving the same steel plant built during the Soviet era.
105. Russia's Constitution, art. 42 guarantees as follows: 'Everyone has the right to a favorable environment, to reliable information about its state, and to compensation for damage caused to his health or property by ecological disease.' The provision was not invoked in the case.
106. The Court noted that this made the case different from and more easily definable than other air pollution cases where multiple minor sources cumulate to produce the problem. Fadayeva, above, note 63, para. 91.
107. The Court noted that the parties produced official documents containing generalized information on industrial pollution, because basic data on air pollution are not publicly available. Ibid., para. 30.
108. Ibid., para. 69.
109. Ibid., para. 45.
110. The court made it a point to recite the qualifications of the expert when discussing the report. See ibid., para. 46, n. 1.
111. Ibid., para. 87.
112. Ibid., para. 88.
113. In *Zander v. Sweden*, App. No. 14282/88, Eur. Ct. Hum. Rts [1993] Ser. A, No. 279B, where the applicants complained about contamination of their well water by cyanide from a neighboring dump site. The municipality initially furnished temporary water supplies, but later, adhering to the normal regulatory procedures, the town raised the permissible level of cyanide in the city water supply. The permit for the dump was later renewed and expanded, while the applicant's request for safe drinking water was denied.
114. The WHO has developed guidelines for safe and acceptable water quality and quantity. World Health Organization, 'Guidelines for Drinking Water Quality' (3d edn. 2004). See http://www.who.int/water_sanitation_health/dwq/GDWQ2004web.pdf (visited 2 February 2012) Independent surveillance of water quality, quantity, accessibility, affordability and long term availability are part of the WHO framework.
115. Inter-American Commission on Human Rights, Report No. 76/09, Case 12.718, *Community of La Oroya, Peru,* admissibility decision of 5 August 2009, OAS/Ser/L/V/II.135, doc. 23.
116. It has long demanded 'proof beyond reasonable doubt.' Fadayeva, above, note 62, para. 79 which can follow from the coexistence of sufficiently strong, clear and concordant inferences or of similar unrebutted presumptions of fact.
117. *Fägerskiöld v. Sweden*, no. 37664/04, (admissibility), 26 February 2008.
118. World Health Organization, 'Guidelines for Community Noise' (Geneva 1999), http://www.who.int/docstore/peh/noise/guidelines2.html (accessed 2 February 2012).

119. *Yanomami Case*, Res. No. 12/85, Case 7615 (Brazil), in *Annual Report of the IACHR 1984–1985,* OEA/Ser.L/V/II.66, doc. 10, rev. 1 (1985), 24.
120. http://www.cidh.oas.org/Basicos/English/Basic2.American%20Declaration.htm (accessed 2 February 2011).
121. Above, note 119, at 33.
122. Ibid., at 32.
123. Inter-Am.C.H.R., *Report on the Situation of Human Rights in Ecuador*, OEA/Ser.L/V/II.96, doc. 10 rev. 1 (1997), also at http://www.cidh.oas.org/countryrep/ecuador-eng/Index%20-%20Ecuador.htm (accessed 2 February 2012) (hereinafter *Report on Ecuador*); Inter-Am.C.H.R., *Report on the Situation of Human Rights in Brazil*, OEA/Ser.L/V/II.97, doc. 29, rev. 1 (1997); Inter-Am. C.H.R., Third Report on the Situation in Paraguay, OEA/Ser.L/V/II.110, Doc. 52, 9 March 2001.
124. *Report on Ecuador,* op cit, at 94.
125. Ibid., p. v.
126. In the Ecuador report, the Commission heard allegations that the Government had failed to ensure that oil exploitation activities were conducted in compliance with existing legal and policy requirements. The Commission's onsite delegation also heard that the Government of Ecuador had failed to enforce the inhabitants' constitutionally protected rights to life and to live in an environment free from contamination. The domestic law of Ecuador recognizes the relationship between the rights to life, physical security and integrity and the physical environment in which the individual lives. The first protection accorded under Article 19 of the Constitution of Ecuador, the section which establishes the rights of persons, is of the right to life and personal integrity. The second protection establishes 'the right to live in an environment free from contamination'. Accordingly, the Constitution invests the state with responsibility for ensuring the enjoyment of this right, and for establishing by law such restrictions on other rights and freedoms as are necessary to protect the environment. Thus, the Constitution establishes a hierarchy according to which protections which safeguard the right to a safe environment may have priority over other entitlements. Ibid., pp. 78–86.
127. Ibid.
128. See Chapter 8 of the Report at http://www.cidh.oas.org/countryrep/ecuador-eng/Chaper-8.htm (accessed 2 February 2012).
129. Above, note 42.
130. http://www2.ohchr.org/english/law/ccpr.htm (accessed 2 February 2012).
131. Above, note 39.
132. http://www.unep.org/Documents.Multilingual/Default.asp? DocumentID=97&ArticleID=1503&l=en (accessed 2 February 2012).
133. Treaty for Amazonian Cooperation, 17 I.L.M. 1045 (1978).
134. Amazon Declaration, 28 I.L.M. 1303 (1989).
135. World Charter for Nature, G.A. Res. 37/7, U.N. Doc. A/37/51 (1982).
136. Convention on Nature Protection and Wildlife Preservation in the Western Hemisphere, 161 U.N.T.S. 229 (1940).
137. Above, note 44.
138. Above, note 24.
139. *Report on Ecuador*, above, note 123, 89 at 92.
140. Ibid., at 89.
141. *Case of the Saramaka People v. Suriname*, Inter-Am. Ct. Hum. Rts, Ser. C No. 172 (28 Nov. 2007).
142. Ibid., at para.129.
143. http://www.cbd.int/doc/publications/cbd-bonn-gdls-en.pdf (accessed 2 February 2012).
144. See ICCPR, General Comment No. 23, *The Rights of Minorities* (Art. 27), U.N. Doc. CCPR/C/21 Rev 1/Add.5, 4 August 1994 and *Apirana Mahuika et al. v. New Zealand*, U.N. doc CCPR/C/70/D/47/1993, 15 November, 2000.
145. Above, note 40.
146. See World Bank, Revised Operational Policy and Bank Procedure on Indigenous Peoples, OP/BP 4.10.

147. Supra, note 41.
148. http://www.cidh.oas.org/basicos/english/basic3.american%20convention.htm (accessed 2 February 2012). Article 21(2) provides that [n]o one shall be deprived of his property except upon payment of just compensation, for reasons of public utility or social interest, and in the cases and according to the forms established by law.
149. *Cape-France Enterprises v. The Estate of Peed*, 305 Mont. 513, 29 P.3d 1011 (2001), citing *Armstrong v. State*, 1999 Mt. 261, 296 Mont. 361, 989 P. 2d 364, at fn. 6.
150. Above, note 62.
151. http://www.coe.int/T/DGHL/Monitoring/SocialCharter/ (accessed 2 February 2012).
152. Above, note 5.

REFERENCES

Akehurst, M., (1976) 'Equity and General Principles of Law', *Int'l & Comp. L.Q.* 25, 801.

Ballard, R. (1993) 'Race and Environmental Justice in the United States', *Yale J. Int'l L.* 18, 319.

Bosselman, K. and B. Richardson (eds), (1999), *Environmental Justice and Market Mechanisms: Key Challenges for Environmental Law and Policy* (Kluwer International).

Drumbl, M.A. (2002), 'Poverty, Wealth, and Obligation in International Environmental Law', *Tulane L. Rev.*, 76, 843.

Franck, T. (1995), *Fairness in International Law and Institutions* (Clarendon Press).

Humphrey, J.P. (1945), 'On the Foundations of International Law', AJIL 39, 231.

Intergovernmental Panel on Climate Change (IPCC) (2001), *Climate Change 2001: Impacts, Adaptation, and Vulnerability* (A Report of Working Group II of the IPCC).

International Committee of the Red Cross (ICRC) (1999), *Annual Report.*

Justinian Institutes, 2.1.1 (T. Sanders Trans. 1st Am. ed. 1876).

Office of the High Commissioner for Human Rights (OHCHR), *Claiming the Millennium Development Goals: A Human Rights Approach* (2008). Geneva, HR/PUB/08/3, sales no. E.08.XIV.6.

Osofsky, H.M. (2005), 'Learning from Environmental Justice: A New Model for International Environmental Rights', *Stan. Envtl L.J.*, 24, 71.

Philimore, R. (1871), *Commentaries upon International Law*: Vol. 1 (2nd edn), (Butterworths).

Platt, A.E. (1996), *Infecting Ourselves: How Environmental and Social Disruptions Trigger Disease*, Worldwatch Paper 129 (World Watch Institute).

Rehbinder, E. (1999), 'States between Economic Deregulation and Environmental Responsibility' in K. Bosselmann and B. Richardson (eds), *Environmental Justice and Market Mechanisms: Key Challenges for Environmental Law and Policy* (Kluwer International).

Reitze, A.W. Jr. (1989), Environmental Policy – It is Time for a New Beginning,' 4 *Columbia J. Envtl L.* 4, 111.

Schroeder, C.H. (2002), Lost in Translation: What Environmental Regulation Does that Tort Cannot Duplicate, *Washburn L.J.* 41, 583.

Silving, H. (1961), 'In re Eichmann: A Dilemma of Law and Morality,' *AJIL* 55, 307.

Sze, J. (2005) 'Race and Power: An Introduction to Environmental Justice Energy

Activism', in N. Pellow and R.J. Brulle (eds), *Power, Justice, and the Environment: A Critical Appraisal of the Environmental Justice Movement* (MIT Press).
United Nations Development Programme (UNDP) (2007), *Human Development Report*.
World Bank (2002), *Linking Poverty Reduction and Environmental Management: Policy Challenges and Opportunities* (The World Bank).

3. The right of access to water in South Africa

Michael Kidd

> We live in a society in which there are great disparities in wealth. Millions of people are living in deplorable conditions and in great poverty. There is a high level of unemployment, inadequate social security, and many do not have access to clean water or to adequate health services. These conditions already existed when the Constitution was adopted and a commitment to address them, and to transform our society into one in which there will be human dignity, freedom and equality, lies at the heart of our new constitutional order. For as long as these conditions continue to exist that aspiration will have a hollow ring.[1]

3.1 INTRODUCTION

In 2008, only 70.9 per cent of South African households had access to water on site, and 7.7 per cent had no toilet facilities (Statistics South Africa, 2008). Most households lacking water and sanitation are black, mainly living in peri-urban and rural areas. Women and children, who spend time and effort in fetching water, are vulnerable to avoidable diseases resulting from inadequate sanitation and lack of clean water (DWAF, 1997). Clearly, one of the manifestations of poverty is inadequate access to water and the resolution of this problem is one step towards alleviation of poverty. Not only is inadequate access a symptom of poverty, but it also further entrenches existing poverty and disempowerment (Barrett and Jaichand, 2007, p. 544).

The right to water is acknowledged in some international instruments and is recognized in the South African Bill of Rights (s. 27 of the Constitution of the Republic of South Africa, 1996). In this chapter, I describe the right in its international context and reflect on how South African Courts are able to give effect to it, and other socio-economic rights in our Constitution. In particular, I analyse aspects of the recent case of *Mazibuko v. The City of Johannesburg*, for which there are now three judgments: in the Witwatersrand Division of the High Court, the Supreme Court of Appeal and the Constitutional Court. Whilst the paper considers the issue in the context of the South African Constitution and water legislation, the dynamics involved in issues of access to water and how the law can provide for this, are universal. These issues are particularly relevant to developing countries and the *Mazibuko* case and its ramifications should be of interest to other countries faced with similar situations.

3.2 THE RIGHT TO WATER ON PAPER

3.2.1 International Law

Although express provision to the right to water appears in some international documents, it is often invoked by necessary implication. As Gleick states, 'several of the explicit rights protected by international rights conventions and agreements, specifically those guaranteeing the rights to food, human health, and development, cannot be attained without also guaranteeing access to basic clean water' (Gleick, 1999, p. 489). This is not the place to set out an exhaustive list of international instruments recognizing the right to water – that has already been done elsewhere (see, for example, Kok and Langford, 2005). A good example, though, is found in the International Covenant on Economic, Social and Cultural Rights (ICESCR), Article 11(1) of which provides: 'The States Parties to the present Covenant recognize the right of everyone to an adequate standard of living for himself and his family, including adequate food, clothing and housing …'.[2] This provision makes no express reference to water. The body responsible for the oversight of the Covenant, the United Nations Committee on Economic, Social and Cultural Rights (UNCESCR), interpreted Article 11 as incorporating the right to water for personal and domestic uses (Kok and Langford, 2005, p. 193) stating: 'The right to water clearly falls within the category of guarantees essential for securing an adequate standard of living, particularly since it is one of the most fundamental conditions for survival' (UNCESCR, 2002, para. 3). This line of thinking cannot be faulted.

3.2.2 South African Constitution

Section 27 of the Constitution of the Republic of South Africa, 1996, reads:

> (1) Everyone has the right to have access to–
> (a) health care services, including reproductive health care;
> (b) sufficient food and *water*; and
> (c) social security, including, if they are unable to support themselves and their dependents, appropriate social assistance.
>
> (2) The state must take reasonable legislative and other measures, within its available resources, to achieve the progressive realisation of each of these rights. (emphasis added).

This section contains reference to several socio-economic rights, and there are others elsewhere (for example, the right to housing in s. 26). In cases where the state is required to provide the right in question (that is, the right has not yet been realized), the internal modifier in s. 27(2) comes into play – it must take reasonable legislative and other measures, within its available resources, to achieve the progressive realization of the rights. Prior to consideration of the right to water in *Mazibuko*, the Constitutional Court was faced with this issue primarily in the cases of *Government of the Republic of South Africa v. Grootboom*[3] and *Minister of Health v Treatment Action Campaign*.[4] In short, the approach of the Court can be characterized by the following:

- The 'reasonable legislative and other measures' aspect requires both legislation and implementation of that legislation. The courts may require the state to explain the measures they have chosen, and account for the progress of implementation of such measures (Currie and De Waal, 2005, p. 578). The Court uses the standard of reasonableness to evaluate this, with the standard being 'determined on the facts of each case'.[5]
- The state is required to achieve the 'progressive realization' of the rights, which clearly means that the state may realize these rights progressively over a period of time. This, however, does not relieve the state of the obligation to take those steps that are within its power immediately, followed by others as soon as possible (Currie and De Waal, 2005, p. 582).
- The state's obligation is to realize the rights 'within its available resources', which means that the absence of resources with which to achieve the rights would excuse the state from not realizing the right for the time being. The absence of resources, however, does not relieve the state of its duty to fulfil its 'core minimum obligations' (UNCESCR, 1990, para. 10). Fulfilment of the core minimum obligations may be excused only if the state is able to show that its resources are 'demonstrably inadequate'. Nevertheless, the state is still required to 'strive to ensure the widest possible enjoyment of the relevant rights under the prevailing circumstances' (Currie and De Waal, 2005, p. 584).
- In both *Grootboom* and *Treatment Action Campaign*, the Constitutional Court did not set a minimum core standard for the right to housing and health services respectively. In both cases, the Court preferred to evaluate the conduct of the state on the basis of whether the measures it had adopted were reasonable.

The right of access to water does not only operate in cases where the right has not yet been realized. It also has a 'negative' dimension, which refers to the protection afforded a right that has already been realized. Socio-economic rights such as housing and water may not be subjected to so-called 'deliberately retrogressive measures' (UNCESCR, 1990, para. 9). Such a measure is one 'that has the effect of denying individuals their existing access to water, food or housing, or preventing them from using whatever resources they have at their disposal to satisfy their water, food and housing needs' (Currie and De Waal, 2005, p. 572). Disconnection of an existing water supply has been held to be a limitation to the right of access to water (*Residents of Bon Vista Mansions v. Southern Metropolitan Local Council*;[6] see also Kidd, 2004; Pieterse, 2003). The issues outlined above in respect of the realization and protection of socio-economic rights are all directly relevant to the *Mazibuko* case, discussed below.

3.2.3 The Water Services Act 107 of 1998

Among the objects of the Water Services Act are to provide for the right of access to basic water supply and the right to basic sanitation necessary to secure sufficient water and an environment not harmful to human health or well-being (which echoes s. 24 of the Constitution, which provides that everyone has the right to an environment that is not harmful to their health or well-being) and the setting of national standards and norms and standards for tariffs in respect of water services (s. 2). To this end, the Act provides in s. 3 for everyone to have the right of access to basic water supply and basic sanitation. This is aimed at giving effect to the Constitutional right. Every water services institution is required to take reasonable measures to realize these rights (s. 3(2)), which are subject to the limitations contained in the Act (s. 3(4)). More specific responsibilities are set out in s. 4, which provides for conditions for water services, requiring the water services provider to provide such services in terms of conditions set by the provider.

Section 9 empowers the Minister to prescribe compulsory national standards relating to the provision of water services, amongst other related matters. Every water services institution (defined in s. 1 of the Act as 'a water services authority, a water services provider, a water board and a water services committee') is required to comply with such standards. The Minister has prescribed standards in a notice entitled 'Regulations relating to compulsory national standards and measures to conserve water' (RSA, 2001) Regulation 3 provides that the minimum standard for basic water supply is:

(a) the provision of appropriate education in respect of effective water use; and
(b) a minimum quantity of potable water of 25 litres per person per day or 6 kilolitres per household per month –

(i) at a minimum flow rate of not less than 10 litres per minute;
(ii) within 200 metres of a household; and
(iii) with an effectiveness such that no consumer is without a supply for more than seven full days in any year.

If the water supply is interrupted, reg. 4 provides that the water services institution must take steps to ensure that where water services are interrupted for a period of more than 24 hours for reasons other than those contemplated in s. 4 of the Act, a consumer has access to alternative water services comprising at least 10 litres of potable water per person per day; and sanitation services sufficient to protect health.

It is important to note at this juncture that water provision is not governed only by the Water Services Act, but also by municipal (that is, local government) by-laws.

3.3 THE *MAZIBUKO* CASE

3.3.1 The High Court Decision

The applicants in *Mazibuko and others v. City of Johannesburg and others*, Lindiwe Mazibuko and four others, were residents of Phiri township, part of Soweto. Residents of Phiri are described in the High Court judgment[7] as:

> mainly poor, uneducated, unemployed and are ravaged by HIV/AIDS. Each [water] account holder in the township has more than one household in his/her stand. Those who are employed earn about R1 100,00 per month. The majority of residents depend on either the government old age pension, or child grant.

In 2001, the City of Johannesburg and the water services provider, Johannesburg Water (Pty) Ltd decided to provide every household in the city with 6 kilolitres (kl) free water per household per month. Faced with huge water losses in the Phiri township, where residents had been entitled to unlimited water supply at a flat rate (which was often not paid), the City launched *Operation Gcinamanzi*, aimed at water conservation and improved water service delivery. Amongst other things, the project was aimed at reducing water losses and addressing a culture of non-payment for services such as water. To this end, the City decided to implement a system of pre-payment meters in Phiri. These meters would dispense the 6 kl of water provided free by the City, following which the consumer would have to purchase water credits for further water prior to the free water for the following month becoming available. This was seen as problematic due to many persons being unable to pay for water once the original allocation was exhausted, and hence having no access to water for a significant part of each month.

The case was essentially a challenge to the installation of the prepayment meters, on several grounds (not all of which are relevant to the present discussion). Not only did the applicants challenge the installation of the prepayment meters, but they also challenged the amount of free water of 25 litres per person per month (or 6 kl per household), seeking a declaratory order that each resident of Phiri is entitled to 50 litres per person per day (50 lpcd). The appropriateness and legality of the use of prepayment water meters and the setting of a minimum amount of water to be provided as a right is the central topic of discussion of the case.

In the Witwatersrand division (the first hearing), the Court decided that the installation of prepayment meters was not only *ultra vires* (in the sense that it was not authorized by the relevant by-laws) but that the implementation had been carried out in a way that was procedurally unfair – the residents had not been adequately notified, nor had they been given adequate opportunity to be heard in respect of the decision (which seems to have been established on the facts in the High Court, although the factual position presented in the Constitutional Court was different).

As for the appropriate amount of water, the Court found, first, that reg. 3(b) of the Water Services Act, which provides for a minimum quantity of potable water of 25 litres per person per day or 6 kl per household per month, was lawful. In the context of South Africa's water scarcity and the responsibility on the government to provide several basic socio-economic rights, the Court held that setting of the basic water supply at 25 litres per day is a realistic target in order to enable water services bodies to assure the basic provision of water. In other words, if the regulation had set the amount significantly higher, this would have been a difficult duty to fulfil. The Court consequently agreed with the submission of the Minister of Water Affairs and Forestry (the third respondent and the official responsible for enacting the regulation) that the standard set must be viewed as a floor and not a ceiling.[8]

In the light of this finding, the Court also decided that the city and the water services provider (the respondents) are, 'in terms of s. 27(2) [of the Constitution], obliged to provide more than the minimum [that is, 25 lpcd] if its residents' needs so demand and they are able, within their available resources, to do so'.[9]

The final aspect of the judgment that is discussed here is the applicants' request for a declaratory order that 'each of them' is entitled to 50 litres per person per day.[10] The respondents' basic water supply policy involved the provision of 6 kl of water per household per month. This entails a household of eight persons receiving 25 litres each per day. The judge indicated that it is 'common cause' that the number of residents per 'yard' in Phiri (on which the water supply is based – there is one account holder per yard) 'far outnumber members of a household' (para. 168). In short, the assumption that the basic water supply is based on eight persons per water account holder is invalid for Phiri township, where the average household consists of 'minimum persons (*sic*) of 16' (para. 169). In this context, and the fact that residents of Phiri are 'mainly poor, uneducated, elderly, sick and ravaged by HIV/AIDS', (the Court states that this is 'common cause') the Court relied on the evidence of experts (both experts in water access generally as well as medical experts) to conclude that '25 kilolitres (*sic*) per person per day is woefully insufficient' (para. 179: From the context, it is clear that the Court means 25 litres). The Court went on to decide that the city had the resources to provide 50 litres per person per day (para. 181), and, consequently, the Court ordered the respondents to provide each applicant and other similarly placed residents of Phiri Township with a free basic water supply of 50 litres per person per day and the option of a metered water supply at the cost of the City of Johannesburg (para. 183.5).

3.3.2 The Supreme Court of Appeal Decision

The respondents in the Court *a quo* appealed to the Supreme Court of Appeal, which delivered judgment in March 2009 (*City of Johannesburg and Others v. Mazibuko and Others,* 2009).[11] The Court held that the 25 lpcd amount was a minimum but that this amount would not in all circumstances constitute sufficient water (para. 14). In this light, the Court asked: (i) what would constitute sufficient water in terms of s. 27(1) of the Constitution; (ii) does the City have to provide residents of Phiri with access to that quantity of water; and (iii) does the City have to provide such access or access to a lesser quantity of water free? (para. 15). Highlighting the view that the right of access to water should be regarded as sufficient water to allow for a dignified existence, and taking into account a wider source of expert evidence than the court *a quo*, the Court held that 42 lpcd would constitute sufficient water for the purposes of s. 27(1) (para. 24). The Court also observed that the City did not take the position that it was unable to provide 42 lpcd, but that it disputed whether it had to provide that amount free. The second question was, consequently, not relevant in the current dispute (although clearly this may be a relevant question in situations where the water provider in question is unable to provide such amount of water). The Court decided, in answer to the third question, that the existing free water policy of the City was invalid as it was based on a mistaken interpretation of the empowering legislation (including s. 27(1) of the Constitution). Recognising, however, that the Court's functions are limited as to how to take into account all the factors relevant to determination of an appropriate free water policy, the Court decided that 'the matter should be referred back to the City to formulate a revised water policy in the light of the finding that it is constitutionally obliged to grant each Phiri resident who cannot afford to pay for water access to 42 litres of water per day free in so far as it can reasonably be done having regard to its available resources and other relevant considerations' (para. 43). It augmented this finding with an order that the City, pending determination of an appropriate policy, provide 42 lpcd to those households on the City's indigent list.

3.3.3 The Constitutional Court Decision

The Phiri residents then appealed to the Constitutional Court (and the authorities cross-appealed). Judgment was handed down on 8 October 2009 in *Mazibuko and Others v. City of Johannesburg and Others* (2010).[12] This decision was received with great disappointment, and was regarded by several critics as being 'anti-poor'. In my opinion, this was not a good judgment, for reasons that will be outlined below.

The Court identified two main questions for its consideration (both involving several sub-issues):

> the first is whether the City's policy in relation to the supply of free basic water, and particularly, its decision to supply 6 kilolitres of free water per month to every account holder in the city ... is in conflict with section 27 of the Constitution or section 11 of the Water Services Act. The second major issue is whether the installation of pre-paid water meters by the first and second respondents in Phiri was lawful (para. 6).

Discussion of all of the grounds of challenge raised in the Court is beyond the scope of this chapter, but, in essence, the Court held, first, that the City's Free Basic Water Policy was reasonable (and consequently not in conflict with s. 27), and that the installation of pre-paid water meters was not unlawful. In considering the Free Basic Water Policy, the Court decided that it was not appropriate for a court to decide on what a 'sufficient' amount of water should be, since courts 'are ill-placed to make these assessments for both institutional and democratic reasons' (para. 62), and that the approach of both the High Court and the Supreme Court of Appeal were flawed because they failed to consider the content of the obligation imposed on the state by s. 27 of the Constitution. In short, it was not appropriate for the courts *a quo* to have quantified the content of the right of access to water. Moreover, the numerous grounds raised by the applicant indicating (in its view) why the City's policy was unreasonable, were all rejected by the Constitutional Court. The main theme running through the Court's reasoning was the burden that would be imposed on the water provider if the (essentially) one-size-fits-all water policy were to be tailored to cater for poor consumers' individual circumstances.

As for the legality of the installation of the pre-paid meters, the Court held that: the installation was contemplated by (or, at least, not *ultra vires*) the relevant municipal by-laws (in other words, the City had legal authority to install them); the use of pre-paid meters did not result in the unauthorised discontinuation of water supply (because the Court interpreted 'discontinuation' as meaning permanent discontinuation); the installation of the meters had not been induced by an unlawful threat, nor as a result of a procedurally unfair process; it did not violate the duty to respect the right to water in terms of s. 27 (in respect of those members of the community who already had access to water); it was not unreasonable in the light of s. 27 of the Constitution and the Water Services Act; it was not irrational and in conflict with s. 9 of the Constitution (the right to equality) and the installation did not constitute unfair discrimination.

Consequently, the Constitutional Court dismissed the appeal of the Phiri residents and upheld the City's cross-appeal, setting aside the decisions of both the High Court and the Supreme Court of Appeal.

3.4 ANALYSIS OF THE CASES

3.4.1 Free Basic Water

There is much that could be said about the numerous strands of reasoning adopted by the Court in reaching the decision that the City's Free Basic Water Policy is reasonable, but space does not permit that analysis here – that will have to be left for another occasion. If, however, we take the view that the Constitutional Court seems to adopt – that the determination of the reasonableness of government attempts to realise the Constitutional right in s. 27 is determined by the context in which the decision is made – then the Court may well have missed a trick. There was an opportunity to make a meaningful contribution to the jurisprudence on access to water, but the Court failed to grasp it.

The core question that is relevant in the assessment of the free basic water policy of the City is whether the amount provided is reasonable. This must take into account what is necessary for sustaining life and health. Moreover, given that the Constitution provides that everyone has inherent dignity and the right to have their dignity respected and protected (s. 10) and that dignity is one of the Constitution's founding values (s. 1), 'sufficient' water must also encompass the amount of water required for a dignified existence. Would, for example, a person's dignity be respected if she were able to flush a toilet only once per day? In *Mazibuko*, one of the applicants had 20 people living on her stand. They would, consequently, on the basis of the City's policy (6 kl per month plus 4 kl extra) receive 16.7 litres per person per day. There would be other stands (according to the High Court, the average number of persons per stand in Phiri was 16) where persons would be receiving less than 25 lpcd per day. Is this reasonable?

I would submit that this is not reasonable. Admittedly, most stands would receive enough water proportionally to the number of persons on the stand, but does that mean that the rights of the exceptional people should be infringed? The Court accepted the City's argument that the establishment of a per-person allocation (which would cater for unusually large numbers of people on a stand) would be administratively unfeasible, but why would it be administratively possible for the City to establish and administer a database of indigent households and not similarly be able to establish a database of stands where there are more than a certain number of people?

In the *Treatment Action Campaign* case, the Court held that the government's actions in realising the right were unreasonable. The same position should have been taken in *Mazibuko*. If the Court had found this, it would have been possible for the Court to set an amount of water per day as a sufficient amount per person per day *in the circumstances*. Setting a 'minimum core' (or whatever one wants to call it) in a specific set of circumstances (in this case, in respect of persons in Phiri township who did receive water previously) would, in my view, not undermine the City's efforts to provide water to those who do not yet have water and nor would it run counter to the Court's approach in the *Grootboom* and *Treatment Action* cases.

3.4.2 Installation of Pre-paid Meters

The main issues relating to the lawfulness of installing pre-paid meters revolved around interpretation. The interpretation of the municipal by-laws determined whether there was lawful authority for their installation and the interpretation of s. 4 of the Water Services Act determined whether pre-paid meters allowed for discontinuation of water supply. In my opinion, both interpretations of the Constitutional Court were strained to ensure that the installation of pre-paid meters was lawful. The interpretations in both the High Court and Supreme Court of Appeal were not wrong. Why, then, did the Constitutional Court choose the interpretations it did? The City had embarked on the programme it called *Operation Gcinamanzi* in order to reduce rampant water wastage and to ensure that water that had been provided free (in effect) would now be paid for. Part of the plan required the installation of pre-paid water meters at a reported cost of approximately R336 million (approx US$44 million) (Bond and Dugard, 2008). A decision that the installation of these meters was unlawful would have crippling financial implications. Because, for the most part, consumers were not adversely affected by this, the Court clearly felt that it could not decide against the City, and hence interpreted the legislation in favour of allowing pre-paid meters. The rights of access to water of some Phiri residents would unfortunately, it would seem, simply have to be sacrificed to the greater good. Whilst this is understandable, the Constitutional Court's task is to ensure that the rights of individuals in the Constitution are protected, which they are not in this case.

Interestingly, the Supreme Court of Appeal must have been influenced by the same considerations, which would explain its somewhat unusual order that the installation of the meters is unlawful, but that the declaration of unlawfulness be suspended for a period of two years, within which time the City was required to amend its legislation in order to ensure that the installation became lawful. But even if this were done, I would have grave doubts as to the constitutionality of pre-paid meters, on the basis that they *do* constitute a limitation to the right of access to water, which I would view as unreasonable. Once the pre-paid limit has run out (in the case of many Phiri residents, this would be the amount of water provided free) then the persons in question do not have access to water. Until the following month, they have no water.

Because of this, people whose water credit has run out, and whose water supply has thus been discontinued (whatever the Constitutional Court may say about the meaning of 'discontinue'), are susceptible to disease from using contaminated water. The notorious cholera outbreak in the Uthungulu district between 2000 and 2002 was largely due to the conversion of free communal taps to pre-paid meters (Barrett and Jaichund, 2007, p. 551). The link between pre-paid meters and disease (in this case dysentery) has also been observed in the United Kingdom, where disconnection for non-payment and any sort of device which limits water have been made illegal by s. 1 of the Water Industry Act 1999 (Barrett and Jaichund, 2007, p. 551). According to Barrett and Jaichund (2007, p. 551 – emphasis in original), the government stated that '*where the water supply is disconnected the maintenance of good health and hygiene can only be put at risk*. In light of this and having considered the available evidence, the Government believes that disconnection *does not have to be an integral part of the process of collecting arrears of charges for water supplied to domestic premises*.' (House of Commons, 1998).

If one accepts the view that the exhaustion of pre-paid credit amounts to disconnection, this view ought to prevail in South Africa as well.

5 CONCLUSION

The provision of water, whether maintaining existing provision or rolling out new water services to those who have not been connected before, is a complex exercise. Not only must the impact on other human users be considered, but also the possible impact on the environment, particularly if the environment is recognised as a water user. Water providers must also take into account issues relating to the type of service that each user has, and what water supply is appropriate for that service. It is important, however, in the light of (South African) Constitutional obligations to provide for the right of access to water, not to lose sight of the individual whilst pursuing the public interest. This balancing act is very important and, arguably, this is what the Constitutional Court failed to do in *Mazibuko*. At the end of the day, there are people in Phiri who do not have access to even 25 litres per person per day, something which the Court did not realise or chose to ignore.

One of the central features of the case was the refusal of the Court to decide on an amount of water that would constitute sufficient water for purposes not only of s. 27 of the Constitution, but also to ensure dignity. Given that decisions on socio-economic rights must be made in the context within which the litigation is brought, which is something that the Court stressed in *Mazibuko*, it would surely be possible for a Court to insist on a certain amount of water as 'sufficient' in a particular situation. This would not be applicable beyond the ambit of the case itself, and could be provided for in a flexible manner to cater for exceptional circumstance such as severe drought. As long as the Court asks how the prospective decision in respect of the applicants will impact on other users, in particular those who do not yet have access, then a decision can be made that will not hamper efforts to provide new water services. It is also perfectly clear that such a decision does not mean that everyone will automatically be entitled to whatever amount the Court decides upon, because of the recognition of progressive realisation. Important, too, is the recognition that a Court does not have to spell out the manner of the provision of water, because this is something that is within the executive's jurisdiction. In the light of this, the order of the Supreme Court of Appeal is the kind of order that would be appropriate – insisting on a particular amount of water and requiring the water provider to establish a policy that provides for it.

Finally, the finding by the Court that pre-paid meters are legally acceptable is very disappointing, particularly in the light of the impact that they have on health. Unfortunately, the Court seemed to adopt the position that there was only one feasible manner of ensuring that the costs of water would be met – the pre-paid meter – without considering (or asking the City to consider) other methods.

Overall, this was an opportunity lost for the Constitutional Court and South Africa. While the City of Johannesburg has solved a problem, there are still many poor people who will be left without access to water for parts of every month. This cannot be what s. 27 of the Constitution contemplates.

NOTES

1. Chaskalson P. in *Soobramoney v. Minister of Health, KwaZulu-Natal* 1998 (1) SA 765 (CC), para. 8.
2. http://www2.ohchr.org/english/law/cescr.htm (accessed 2 February 2011).
3. 2001 (1) SA 46 (CC).
4. 2002 (5) SA 703 (CC).
5. *Grootboom*, above, n. 3, para. 92.
6. (2002) (6) BCLR 625 (W).
7. Case No. 06/13865 (W), http://www.iatp.org/files/451_2_102539.pdf (accessed 13 March 2012)
8. Ibid., para. 53.
9. Ibid., para. 126.
10. Ibid., para. 167.
11. (489/08) [2009] ZASCA 20; see http://www.saflii.org/za/cases/ZASCA/2009/20.html (accessed 13 March 2012)
12. (CCT 39/09) [2009] ZACC 28; see http://www.saflii.org/za/cases/ZACC/2009/28.html (accessed 13 March 2012)

REFERENCES

Barrett, D. and V. Jaichand (2007), 'The Right to Water, Privatised Water and Access to Justice: Tackling United Kingdom Water Companies', Practices in Developing Countries' *SAJHR*, 23, 543.

Bond, P. and J. Dugard (2008), 'The case of Johannesburg water: What really happened at the pre-paid "Parish pump"', *Law, Democracy and Development* 12, 1.

Currie, I. and J. De Waal (2005), *The Bill of Rights Handbook*, 5th edn, (Juta).

Department of Water Affairs and Forestry (DWAF) (1997), *White Paper on a National Water Policy for South Africa* (Pretoria: Government Printer).

Gleick, P.H. (1999), 'The human right to water', *Water Policy*, 5, 487.

House of Commons Research Paper 98/117 (1998), Water Industry Bill.

Kidd, M. (2004), 'Not a Drop to Drink: Disconnection of Water Services for Non-Payment and the Right of Access to Water' *SAJHR*, 20, 119.

Kok, A. and M. Langford (2005), 'The right to water' in D. Brand and C. Heyns (eds), *Socio-Economic Rights in South Africa* (Pretoria University Law Press).

Pieterse, M. (2003), 'Towards a useful role for section 36 of the Constitution in social rights cases? *Residents of Bon Vista Mansions v. Southern Metropolitan Local Council*' *SALJ*, 120, 41.

Republic of South Africa (RSA), GN R509 *GG* 22355 of 8 June 2001.

Statistics South Africa (2008), *General Household Survey* (Statistics South Africa)

UN Committee on Economic, Social and Cultural Rights (UNESCR) (2002), General Comment No 15 *The right to water (arts 11 & 12 of the Covenant)* (29th Session, 2002) (UN Doc E/C 12/2002/11).

UN Committee on Economic, Social and Cultural Rights General Comment 3 (1990), *The Nature of States Parties Obligations*, UN Doc HR1/Gen 1/Rev 1 at para. 10.

PART II

Environmental degradation and poverty: what is at stake for aboriginal peoples?

4. Climate change impacts on the poor – a case-study of Australia's indigenous population and the impact of Australia's response on this population

Karen Bubna-Litic

4.1 INTRODUCTION

Climate change is likely to affect indigenous communities significantly, as they often lack the economic and technical resources available to non-indigenous communities to respond to the social and environmental challenges of climate change. These challenges include the increased costs resulting from climate change policy, decreased availability of water and food, decreased security and availability of housing, and adverse health effects. These challenges will be more difficult for indigenous communities to meet because they generally already experience a lower economic standard of living and have less education and training.[1] Furthermore, climate change policies, unless carefully designed with attention to their impact on indigenous communities, are likely to disproportionately affect indigenous communities because those communities are generally located in physically isolated, fragile and harsh environments.

This chapter presents a case study of the impact of climate change and climate change policy on indigenous Australians. It attempts to answer two questions. The first question is whether climate change will disproportionately impact indigenous Australians? The second question is whether Australia's response to climate change, by putting a price on carbon, will disproportionately burden indigenous Australians?

The chapter concludes that the answer to both questions is 'yes'. Given that fact, the Australian government needs to pay particular attention to indigenous Australians, who may be disproportionately burdened because they are indigenous. To date, in the climate change debate in Australia, there has been little attention paid to the particular position of indigenous Australians, with the government treating them as just another group of disadvantaged members of the community.[2] This chapter demonstrates that there is something unique about indigenous people, which differentiates them from other disadvantaged groups.

Section 4.2 of this chapter briefly summarizes why it is important to recognize the impacts that climate change has on the poor. Section 4.3 identifies two factors that play a crucial role in determining why indigenous communities are inherently disadvantaged when Australia tries to produce effective climate change policy. These are the lack of a voice for indigenous people at the policy making table and the absence of statistical data on indigenous Australians. Section 4.4 details the impact of climate change on indigenous Australians and argues that they will be disproportionately affected by climate change. Section 4.5 sets out Australia's response to climate change and section 4.6 details the impacts that carbon pricing will have on Australia's indigenous communities. Section 4.7 draws some conclusions as to the disproportionate burden that will result from this carbon price and section 4.8 touches on some opportunities that exist due to use of an emissions trading system (ETS).

This chapter was first prepared at a time when Australia was about to price carbon, through an emissions trading scheme. The Carbon Pollution Reduction Scheme (CPRS) was designed following a report by Professor Ross Garnaut (the Garnaut Review). This initial proposal was not successful. However, in 2011 the government passed its clean energy legislation package which introduces a carbon tax from 1 July 2012, transitioning into an emission trading scheme in 2015. Due to the proposed similarities between the scheme to be introduced in 2015 and the CPRS, I have updated this chapter and have made my argument based on the impacts on indigenous communities, as if the CPRS had been implemented, as it is likely that the details of the new policy will be similar.

4.2 CLIMATE CHANGE, DEVELOPING COUNTRIES, AND POOR COMMUNITIES WITHIN DEVELOPED COUNTRIES

For many years, we have allowed the emission of greenhouse gases into the atmosphere without a view to the consequences of this activity. The damage caused by these emissions has been recognized[3] and countries around the world are looking at ways to reduce their output, mitigate their impact and adapt to the effects of climate change.

Originally, developing countries thought that global warming was a malaise of developed countries and as it was their problem, they should be the ones to solve it. But we now know that those in the poorest developing countries are likely to be the most vulnerable to the impacts of climate change and the least able to adapt to the effects of climate change.[4] The first impacts of global warming have been on the very things that the poorest depend on most, such as dry-land agriculture, tropical forests and subsistence fishing.[5] The Intergovernmental Panel on Climate Change (IPCC) has identified the most vulnerable as those living in low lying developing states and in coastal settlements in developing countries such as the mega-deltas of Asia and Africa.[6] Their economic reliance on climate-sensitive resources and constraints on their adaptive capacity add to this vulnerability. This includes their inability to develop public health programs to deal with the spread of pests and water-borne diseases.[7]

In addition to constraints on adaptation, many developing countries, and certainly the least developed ones, have a much smaller carbon footprint than developed countries. For this reason, climate change has been called the world's biggest regressive tax, with the poorest paying for the behaviour of the richest.[8]

Climate change and climate change policies can also disproportionately burden poor communities within developed countries. Climate change itself disproportionately impacts indigenous Australians. Indigenous communities in Australia are often more vulnerable than non-indigenous Australians to the impacts of climate change due to poverty and remoteness. They often have less access to the education and skills required to understand the impacts and take advantage of the opportunities offered by a carbon constrained world.

Poorly designed climate change policies can also exacerbate the disproportionate burden already borne by indigenous Australians. Consider the impact of extreme weather events and carbon pricing policy as an example. Scientists have observed a world-wide increase in extreme weather events as a result of climate change,[9] such as drought, higher winds, storm events, flooding, coastal inundation, and rising sea levels. Australia is already experiencing difficulty adjusting to drought, high winds, flooding, and other extreme weather events. Indigenous Australians, as some of the poorest Australians, are least capable of adapting to these events and their capacity to adapt may be further impaired by suggested climate change policies such as carbon pricing. Putting a price on carbon may be an attractive way to mitigate greenhouse gas emissions; however, it exacerbates the impacts of these extreme weather events on indigenous communities living in remote areas of Australia. Increased construction costs as a result of carbon pricing have a greater impact on remote communities that suffer infrastructure damage and damage to poorly built houses through flooding and storm – repairing that damage may be virtually impossible given the high transport costs and limited transport options available in remote communities.

4.3 THE ISSUE OF DISADVANTAGE OF INDIGENOUS AUSTRALIANS

Effective climate change policy making with respect to indigenous Australians has two elements: full participation in the policy-making process and adequate data on which to base decisions. Currently, in Australia, both of these are lacking.

Full participation in the policy-making process occurs when these communities have a significant role in the design, implementation and governance of programs and policies.[10] Currently in Australia, aboriginal people have been marginalized in the policy process.[11] The Aboriginal and Torres Strait Islander Commission (ATSIC) was abolished by the Howard government in 2005.[12] Since then there has not been a representative mechanism allowing a variety of indigenous voices to be heard. There is no treaty or move towards self-determination for indigenous communities and this places a severe limitation on the ability of these communities to effectively participate in the policy process. This can be contrasted with the experience in New Zealand where Maori actively participate in policy making, pursuant to obligations under the Treaty of Waitangi.[13]

Effective policy making also relies on having sufficient socio-economic data on indigenous Australians and their communities as well as adequate data about the probable impact of climate change on those communities. Australia has experienced problems obtaining meaningful general socio-economic data on indigenous Australians and their communities.

First, 25 per cent of indigenous Australians live in remote or very remote areas that are difficult to access and may not be properly sampled during data collection.[14] Second, a great deal of socio-economic data has been collected without appropriate indigenous indicators. In Australia, the main source of statistical data is the national census known as the ABS General Social Survey (GSS) conducted by the Australian Bureau of Statistics (ABS), every 4 years, from 2002. Until recently, the GSS did not have any indigenous indicators. This meant that specific data on Aboriginal and Torres Strait islander populations had to be separately collected in order to develop policies to alleviate the disadvantage suffered by these populations. Surveys collecting that data included a 1994 National Aboriginal and Torres Strait Islander Survey (NATSIS), a 2002–2003 National Aboriginal and Torres Strait Islander Social Survey (NATSISS, survey of 9400 aged 15+), and a 2007 Productivity Commission Report (Productivity Commission). Another NATSISS was conducted during 2008–09.[15]

The lack of an indigenous indicator in most ABS surveys has inhibited the gathering of indigenous data. Recently, ABS has improved collection of indigenous data by running a rolling survey program with an indigenous specific survey every three years. However, there are additional difficulties in the data that have been collected. NATSISS questions have changed between 1994 and 2002, which prevents comparisons over time. 'Cultural activity' and traditional hunting and fishing are not regarded as contributing to the 'real' economy and so economic data concerning these activities has not been collected. Problems with data collection from the 2002 NATSISS have been recognized[16] and there has been some improvement in the 2008 NATSISS. The main critique of the methodology of the NATSISS was that it was too general. The survey made no distinction between remote and non-remote communities. The public could not simultaneously examine detailed statistical information by remote and state indicators. More detailed data is necessary to conduct a meaningful analysis of carbon pricing impacts.

The 2002 NATSISS which attempted to collect data on the 'hybrid economy',[17] raised more problems. Fishing or hunting in a group was one indicator, but the 2002 and 1994 questions were not comparable. The 2002 survey only asked about group culture activity for the prior three months, which did not take account of seasonal variations and rendered survey data suspect because answers would have differed depending on the season in which the respondent was surveyed. The 2002 survey lacked any question about gathering, which had been asked in 1994.[18] These problems were overcome in the 2008 NATSISS but according to one commentator, the 2008 NATSISS data underestimates the value of the hybrid economy.[19]

The discussion so far has pointed out the difficulties involved in gathering even general indigenous data. Determining whether a policy will place a disproportionate burden on indigenous communities requires data that enables a comparison between indigenous and non-indigenous populations. The data that would be useful for such a comparison includes information on those living in remote areas, access to public transport or reliance on private transport, numbers living in rental or owner occupied accommodation, and the industries employing a higher percentage of indigenous employees. Changes in the GSS were supposed to facilitate comparisons to the non-indigenous population. However, when looking at the GSS, there is no indigenous identifier at more detailed data levels, which makes it impossible to compare indigenous populations with the non-indigenous population at a sufficiently detailed level. One can compare indigenous populations to the whole population but not to the non-indigenous population.

The unwillingness to include an indigenous identifier for the most detailed data level arises from a confidentiality concern: an indigenous identifier may compromise participants' privacy.[20] This problem needs to be rectified in order to assist in the question of a carbon price impact. The GSS, unlike the NATSISS, did not go to non-remote areas, which also impairs assessment of the impacts of the emissions trading scheme on aboriginal communities.

4.4 THE IMPACTS OF CLIMATE CHANGE ON AUSTRALIA'S INDIGENOUS POPULATION

The 2006 census found that 31 per cent of Australia's indigenous population lived in major cities[21] with 22 per cent living in inner regional areas,[22] 22 per cent in outer regional areas,[23] and 24 per cent living in remote or very remote, Australia.[24] Very remote Australia makes up 75 per cent of the Australian land mass.[25] Forty-five per cent of the population of very remote Australia is indigenous and, if one takes away mining and service towns, indigenous people by far comprise the majority (population) across very remote Australia. Overall, 25 per cent of the indigenous population lives in remote and very remote areas, while only 2 per cent of the non-indigenous population lives in those areas.[26] So, it is fair so say that a disproportionately high number of aboriginal Australians live in remote areas. The proportion of indigenous people living in remote areas, of course, varies between states and territories. For example, 70 per cent of the non-urban population of the Northern Territory is indigenous.

The disproportionate number of indigenous people living in remote areas alone makes the impact of climate change on indigenous communities disproportionate. First, emergency responses to extreme weather events are naturally slow in reaching remote indigenous communities. Second, the threats from extreme climatic events such as storms can be limited through active land management; however, in remote areas, these threats are difficult to address because there are simply too few people. For example, the more than 1000 remote communities in Australia with less than 100 people will likely have problems addressing floods.[27] These isolated communities have limited infrastructure to control flooding and little access to technology such as early warning devices.

Third, tourism in remote parts of Australia will be substantially affected by climate change. Indigenous communities who manage sites such as the Great Barrier Reef and Kakadu National Park will be far more severely affected by sea level rise. For example, climate change-induced rise in sea levels threatens about 90 per cent of Kakadu's coastal freshwater wetlands with saltwater intrusion.[28] This may diminish its attractiveness to visitors who come to see the birdlife in the wetlands, threatening the livelihood of traditional owners who play a prominent role in its tourism industry.

As 4.2 above indicated, coastal populations are more vulnerable to the impacts of climate change. Eighty-five per cent of the coastline of the Northern Territory is aboriginal-owned. Some of the Torres Strait islands have coastlines of less than one metre above sea-level and others have interiors below sea level. These islands are home to approximately 8000, mostly indigenous residents.[29] Clearly, due to their location of residence, climate change will have a significant impact on Australian indigenous communities though to date there has been very little analysis of this impact.[30] Indigenous communities on Australia's northern coasts are expected to face increased storm disturbance and coastal inundation.[31] Flow rates of river systems are predicted to be significantly reduced[32] and decisions may have to be made as to which wetland systems will be protected and which will be sacrificed. This will impact on those indigenous communities who rely on these wetlands for their livelihood.

The 2002 survey of aboriginal peoples shows that 80 per cent of adults living in discrete indigenous communities fish or hunt for their livelihood.[33] As mentioned previously, these activities are often referred to as part of the 'hybrid economy'. Loss of access to these resources, through changes in the distribution of species and species abundance as a result of climate change, will further impoverish indigenous people. The resulting loss of their traditional diet may result in a more processed diet, making people in these communities more susceptible to obesity, diabetes and other health related problems. This loss will also have an impact in the commercial farming of native foods and the use of native plants for art and craft industries.

Low-income earners are more vulnerable to climate change impacts because they tend to live in more marginal areas and in poor quality houses. Those living in poor quality housing with a lack of connection to essential services may be more heavily impacted by storm damage. In 2001, there were nearly 2000 temporary or improvised dwellings in discrete indigenous communities, while for permanent dwellings in these communities, 31 per cent required major repair or replacement and 153 had no organized sewerage supply.[34] The high proportion of indigenous Australians living in rental accommodation do not have the opportunities to invest in housing infrastructure to minimize climate change impacts. Indigenous Australians also tend to live in overcrowded housing, which can put additional stress on households when water, sanitation, and other services are limited by storm events.

The health impacts associated with rising temperature are also likely to affect indigenous Australians disproportionately. Heat stress and spread of infectious diseases will be far more deadly given their limited access to health services. Remote aboriginal communities are particularly vulnerable to water-borne diseases, which will increase due to the increased frequency of storms and droughts leading to increased flooding, contamination of drinking water and potentially unsafe releases of wastewater into the environment.[35]

4.5 AUSTRALIA'S POLICY RESPONSE TO CLIMATE CHANGE

The conservative government, which had been in power Australia since March 1996, lost power in November 2007. The new Rudd Labour government commissioned Ross Garnaut, a leading Australian economist, to report on the effect on Australia's economy and environment of human induced climate change; the costs and benefits of ameliorating these impacts; the role that Australia can play in international policy; and the medium and long-term policy options. The final Garnaut report was released in September 2008.[36] Previously, the government had released a discussion paper on the proposed Carbon Pollution Reduction Scheme (CPRS) in July 2008,[37] and the final white paper was released on 15 December 2008.[38] The government's chosen response to climate change was to introduce an emissions trading scheme scheduled to begin in July 2010, which was later delayed to July 2011. The draft legislation was introduced into Parliament on 10 March 2009[39] (Exposure draft) and was open for public comment until 14 April 2009. The emission trading legislation was rejected three times by the opposition, and in April 2010, the CPRS was shelved. This decision made Kevin Rudd's leadership untenable and in July 2010, he was replaced as leader by Julia Gillard who went on to win an election in November 2010. The Gillard government's policy on climate change is to put a price on carbon. On 8 July 2011 the Australian Parliament passed its clean energy legislation package which introduces a carbon tax from 1 July 2012, transitional into an emission trading scheme from 2015. Some details of this second phase have been released and are similar to the CPRS. For this reason, this chapter considers what would have been the impact if the CPRS had been adopted, as many of the details are likely to be the same.

Governments have recognized that (1) pricing carbon will increase costs of production, which will be passed onto consumers, and (2) low income households will be disproportionately affected by this policy because they spend a higher proportion of their income on emission intensive products. Higher production costs will increase the price of electricity, gas, petrol, diesel, chemicals, and fertilizers, which, in turn, will be passed on, increasing the price of products ranging from cement to plastic and the cost of transporting goods. Consumer prices for petrol and food will also increase. Overall, these price increases will be regressive, but the Australian government continues to argue that it will compensate low income earners.[40]

Most of Australia's emissions come from electricity generation, transport and agriculture. The CPRS was to cover stationary sources of emissions, transport, fugitive emissions, industrial processes, and waste emissions and all six greenhouse gases. The CPRS was to cover the largest emitters in Australia, those which emit 25 000 tonnes or more of CO_2e. Emissions from deforestation were not included at all and agriculture was not included from the beginning because of the difficulty in estimating agricultural emissions and imposing reporting requirements.

The government tried to lessen the impact of the CPRS on various sectors and avoid having these sectors automatically pass on the increases resulting from carbon pricing to consumers through increased prices. For example, the government dealt with the increased costs of the transport sector by compensating reductions in other tax burdens. The transport sector contributes 14 per cent of Australia's emissions and this has increased hugely since 1990.[41] It has been shown that transport choices can be influenced by price changes.[42] To compensate for the costs imposed as a result of transport emissions, the government planned to cut fuel taxes on a cent for cent basis for the first three years of the Scheme. A reduced fuel tax was to begin on 1 July 2010 with additional reductions every six months if needed for three years.[43] Reductions in fuel tax made within the three-year period would become permanent after that period expired. There would be a fuel credit system for some industries, including agriculture and fisheries.[44] Fuel taxes would also be cut for heavy vehicle road users who transported goods and this would be reviewed after one year.[45]

For those trade-exposed businesses that could not pass on these increased costs because they may lose competitiveness, the government would provide free permits to the most emissions intensive trade exposed (EITE) activities in various industries. It was suggested that 30 per cent of permits would be allocated to EITE activities, with those producing between 1000–1999 tonnes of CO_2e emissions per million dollar revenue, or between 3000–5999 tonnes of CO_2e emissions per million dollar revenue added during the specified assessment period to receive permits for 60 per cent of their baseline emissions and those who produce over 2000, or produce 6000 tonnes of CO_2e per million dollar revenue added during the assessment period to receive permits for 90 per cent of their baseline emissions.[46] This rate of assistance would be reduced at a rate of 1.3 per cent per year (which is the carbon productivity contribution) to encourage EITE industries to contribute to national carbon reduction.[47] When similar obligations are placed on competitors, either through domestic action or an international agreement, this assistance should cease.

Coal fired power generators were to get special assistance on the basis that they are highly emissions intensive, unable to fully pass on their carbon costs, owners of significant long-lived assets with limited alternative uses and able to access few, if any, economically viable abatement options.

The government was to rebate the effect of the carbon pollution permits on businesses in the agricultural and fishing industries for three years. This was seen to be necessary as the excise system effectively does not apply to this sector.

4.6 IMPACTS OF PRICING CARBON ON INDIGENOUS COMMUNITIES

The impact of pricing carbon depends on the consumption and production activities of indigenous communities and other disadvantaged groups. On the consumption side, the overall price impact of the scheme on an individual household's welfare depends on many factors. These include the carbon price, the extent to which the carbon costs are reflected in the prices of the goods, individual consumption patterns, the individual households' levels of disposable income, the assistance provided to households by the government to offset impacts of the scheme, and the ability of households to adjust consumption patterns in response to higher carbon prices.

The CPRS would increase energy and fuel prices. When examining the impact on households of a carbon price of around \$20/tonne, it is assumed that households will consume less of products whose prices have increased and more of those products whose prices have decreased. But with energy and fuel prices, this may not be possible, especially for low income households who cannot take advantage of more efficient energy options. At \$20/tonne, the electricity prices are predicted to rise by 16 per cent with the average price of all goods increasing by 0.9 per cent.[48] This will have the most severe effect on all low income households.

The proposed emissions trading scheme would also have an impact through the inability of many indigenous people to avail themselves of the assistance that the government would provide to offset the impacts of the scheme. For example, indigenous Australians would find it financially difficult to switch to less emission-intensive lifestyles even with government incentives. These incentives may include household retrofits, insulation and renewable energy options, which would be available only to home owners as well as for the purchase of energy efficient appliances and cars. On the issue of home ownership, in 2006 a majority of indigenous people (63 per cent), aged 18 years or over, were living in rented dwellings.[49] The proportion renting was lower in major cities and regional areas (around 58 per cent) than in remote areas (82 per cent).[50] Overall, in 2006, only 35 per cent cent of indigenous people aged 18 years and over lived in home owner/purchaser households.[51] Renters have less ability and no financial incentive to invest in capital energy efficiency improvements, such as insulation. Recently, the Australian government announced a monetary package to encourage insulation in houses.[52] Regulations that require landlords to insulate rental properties would improve energy efficiency but the costs of insulation may be passed on to renters through increased rents. The impact on renters is uncertain. Would they move to cheaper accommodation or simply be under increased financial stress?

Finally, there may be fewer employment options and income losses for workers in industry-affected communities. This is explored in more detail below.

4.7 DOES CARBON PRICING RESULT IN A DISPROPORTIONATE BURDEN ON INDIGENOUS COMMUNITIES?

Are there distinctive challenges for indigenous communities arising out of carbon pricing? That is, are indigenous communities more vulnerable than the non-indigenous population?

4.7.1 Poverty

In the absence of data on wealth, income data is the best available indicator of poverty or material disadvantage. From the 2006 census, the mean gross weekly equivalised household income for indigenous people was $460. This compares to $740 for non-indigenous households.[53] Indigenous Australians are disproportionately represented amongst Australia's low income households.[54] They are more than twice as likely as other Australians to be in the lowest income quintile, and almost four times less likely to be in the highest quintile.[55]

The measure of financial stress, or the poverty indicator, is a household's ability to raise $2,000 within a week in an emergency.[56] Comparing the 2008 NATSISS and the 2006 General Social Survey, 47 per cent of the indigenous population was under financial stress. This compares to 13 per cent for the non-indigenous population.

This means that cost increases will disproportionately impact indigenous communities in non-remote, urban areas because they make up a disproportionate percentage of the lowest income quintile.

4.7.2 Remoteness

In remote areas, the financial stress of indigenous Australians is even higher, being around 73 per cent.[57] So even though the percentage of indigenous people in the lowest quintile of equivalised income does not vary much between remote and non-remote communities, the poverty indicator increases hugely in remote communities. This means that cost increases will disproportionately impact indigenous communities, especially in remote Australia.

Under an Australian carbon pricing policy, goods and services that are carbon intensive will cost more over time than goods that are not. It has been recognised by the government that the price of consumer goods will increase.[58] The overall impact of the scheme on an individual household's welfare will depend, as mentioned previously, on factors including household consumption patterns and the ability of households to adjust consumption patterns in response to higher carbon prices. The disproportionate impact on indigenous communities, particularly those in remote Australia, through the poverty indicator, will be exacerbated because of their lack of ability to adjust their consumption patterns because of limited access to alternatives. Extra burdens may also be placed on indigenous communities because of their heavy reliance on customary ways of living, such as fishing and hunting. The increases in the cost of food due to a carbon price may put more pressure on the 'hybrid' economy of hunting and fishing and this, combined with the possible impacts on these natural resources in terms of changes in species abundance through climate change, may impact disproportionately on remote indigenous communities.

Fuel prices will increase as a result of a carbon price. The ability to minimize these costs will depend on the proximity of public transport services. Remote area indigenous communities are dependent on private transport options as they travel large distances to access services, such as shopping, schooling and medical care, and public transport options are not available. They are particularly vulnerable and disproportionately disadvantaged by rising fuel prices, which would result from an ETS since, as we have seen, a higher percentage of the indigenous population than the non-indigenous population lives in remote areas. Reducing reliance on private transport is a way of keeping costs down but there is the danger that reducing mobility can lead to isolation and social exclusion.

Tourism in remote areas will also be impacted through increased costs, less consumer demand and longer term environmental degradation, especially those that rely on currently vulnerable ecosystems, such as the Great Barrier Reef. Domestic aviation and shipping costs was not going to be offset under the CPRS while international costs were excluded from the scheme.[59] This could make domestic tourism less competitive compared to international tourism and hurt the indigenous tourism market.

4.7.3 Household Type

We have seen that a carbon price of \$20 per tonne will increase the average price of all goods by around 0.9 per cent. Australian studies have showed the predicted price effects by household type as a result of this \$20 carbon price.[60] These price impacts across different types of households seem to be slightly regressive with the highest impact of a 1.2 per cent increase being felt in the lowest quintile and in single parent households.[61] The Productivity Commission Report of 2007[62] shows that indigenous Australians are twice as likely as non-indigenous Australians to have their household income in the lowest quintile and substantially more likely to live in single parent households and thus will carry a disproportionate burden of these price increases.

4.7.4 Home Ownership and Overcrowding

Many of the incentives offered by the government relate to options that only home owners can take advantage of. These include insulation rebates, solar panel rebates, incentives for solar hot water systems and rating systems for appliances. However, a much lower proportion of indigenous adults (27.4 per cent) than non-indigenous adults (73.7 per cent) live in homes owned or being purchased by a member of the household.[63] Close analysis of this data shows that non-indigenous households were between 1.9 and 2.5 times more likely than households with indigenous people to own their own homes in major cities, inner and outer regional areas and remote areas. Non-indigenous households were 6.0 times more likely than households with indigenous people to own their own homes in very remote areas.[64] This indicates that the impacts of an ETS on those households who rent[65] will disproportionately impact on indigenous populations, with a higher burden in remote Australia.

Overcrowding is another problem with indigenous rather than non-indigenous communities, especially in remote and very remote areas.[66] Overcrowding often results from an inadequate, inappropriate or poorly maintained housing stock. This can have very serious health risks: if a house has sufficient working taps, tubs, showers, toilets, insect screens and protection from the weather, the household will be much better able to prevent disease transmission than the household with inadequate housing typical of crowded households. In remote and very remote areas in particular, it is more expensive and logistically more difficult to construct and maintain infrastructure. Pricing carbon will only increase construction costs and this will disproportionately impact on these remote indigenous communities that need to improve their housing infrastructure.

4.7.5 Employment in ETS Impacted Industries

According to the Garnaut review, industries that would be most affected by a carbon price are those with a high emissions intensity, with access to few substitutes, with limited capacity to pass on the emissions price (those with overseas competitors).[67] These impacted industries, of course, will often pass on these impacts to the communities in which they operate. Their viability may depend on whether they can use low-emission technology. Former employees may have to leave the region to get other work and this may result in the loss of viability of the area. The two areas likely to be most affected are coal-fired electricity production and agriculture. If this is the case, to determine if there is an unfair burden placed on indigenous communities, we need statistics to look at the percentage of the indigenous workforce in these two industries. There are statistics from the ABS and NATSISS in 2002 and 2004. The 2001 statistics give a more specific breakdown of industries. The 2004–05 statistics are too general to be helpful in determining whether a distributional burden exists. The 2001 statistics show that a higher percentage of total employment of indigenous workers than non-indigenous workers worked in the agriculture, forestry and fishing industries, the mining industry, government industry and defence, education and health and community services.[68]

It seems that an unfair burden may fall on indigenous workers due to their employment in the mining sector and agricultural sector, though this is based on 2001 data. Statistics from 2006[69] show that there was a higher percentage of total employment, of indigenous workers than non-indigenous workers in the mining industry, administration, safety and support services, education and training, and health care and social assistance. It therefore seems that an unfair burden may fall on indigenous workers due to their employment in these impacted sectors.

4.8 OPPORTUNITIES

Having set out the reasons why indigenous Australians will be disproportionately impacted by both climate change and Australia's response to climate change, there are a number of opportunities that could flow to Australia's indigenous communities as a result of carbon pricing. These lie in the areas of reforestation and carbon pricing. Opportunities for the use of the indigenous estate in Australia could include reforestation and land use for renewable energy and carbon capture and storage (CCS) technologies. The former may be regarded as high risk because of unknown future extreme weather events. The latter requires high capital costs and CCS is still in the developmental stage.

An opportunity that is starting to be realized in Australia is that of fire management. The West Arnhem Land Fire Abatement Project[70] is a partnership between traditional owners, the Northern Land Council, fire ecologists, five aboriginal-based ranger groups, the Northern Territory government and the energy company Darwin Liquified Natural Gas Ltd. Bushfires contribute about half of the Northern Territory's greenhouse gas emissions and this 17-

year agreement is intended to offset some of the greenhouse gas emissions from the Liquefied Natural Gas plant at Wickham Point in the city of Darwin and reduce the emissions through bushfire management. Their abatement target is 100 000 tonnes/yr and the first two years have abated 256 000 tonnes of carbon.

4.9 CONCLUSION

Indigenous communities in Australia are likely to bear a disproportionate burden compared to non-indigenous Australian communities, as a result of climate change and Australia's response to it. This burden arises because of the disproportionate number of indigenous Australians in remote and very remote areas; their increased likelihood to be in the lowest quintile of income earners and their high proportion of single parent households. They are also much less likely to own their own home in both urban and rural settings and they are disproportionately represented amongst those who live in poor quality housing.

Indigenous Australians suffer from a lack of education and access to information and this, together with their disproportionate representation amongst remote and poverty stricken populations, will result in limited access to emission intensive product substitutes, and alternative transport options. Extra stress may be put on the hybrid economy, and the industries most impacted by carbon pricing through an ETS are likely to have a disproportionate percentage of indigenous employees. This means an unfair burden will be carried by indigenous Australians as a result of the Australian government response to climate change.

Australia needs better statistical data for indigenous Australians, particularly in the areas of employment, household expenditure and rental statistics, collected in a manner that facilitates statistical comparisons with the non-indigenous population. This could be achieved by the simple change of including an indigenous indicator in the GSS. There was some improvement in the 2008 NATSISS, but there is room for more.

It is crucial to involve the indigenous population in setting carbon pricing policy. Indigenous Australians have been put into the general basket of disadvantaged communities (for which the Australian government promises tax relief to offset the adverse impacts of the ETA on disadvantaged communities). Blanket tax relief will not work. Tax relief must be fine-tuned to avoid placing a disproportionate burden on indigenous communities by carbon pricing mechanisms.

NOTES

1. Indigenous Business Australia (IBA) – submission to the Carbon Pollution Reduction Scheme Green Paper 10 September 2008 (on file with author),
2. Garnaut Climate Change Review ,http://www.garnautreview.org.au/index.htm (accessed 3 February 2012).
3. Intergovernmental Panel on Climate Change (IPCC) (2007) 'Fourth Assessment Report: Working Group II Report 'Impacts, Adaptation and Vulnerability' http://www.ipcc.ch/publications_and_data/publications_and_data_reports.shtml (accessed 3 February 2012).
4. Ibid.
5. '*Adapt or Die*' The Economist, 11 September 2008, http://www.economist.com/world/international/displaystory.cfm?story_id=12208005 (accessed 3 February 2012).
6. IPCC Summary for Policymakers, http://www.ipcc.ch/pdf/assessment-report/ar4/wg2/ar4-wg2-spm.pdf (accessed 3 February 2012).
7. Ibid.
8. Smith, K., 'The IPCC: Impressions from a Foot Soldier', Speech delivered at the United Nations Association, International House, UC Berkeley, 24 October 2007 (on file with author).
9. Above, n. 3.
10. Oxfam Australia 'Rights of Indigenous Peoples in Australia', http://www.oxfam.org.au/resources/filestore/originals/OAus-PositionPolicies-0710.pdf (accessed 3 February 2012).
11. Ibid.
12. ATSIC website, http://www.smh.com.au/news/National/ATSIC-abolished-after-bill-passes-Parliament/2005/03/16/1110913660843.html (accessed 3 February 2012).
13. For a full discussion of this in relation to New Zealand's climate change policy, please see Bubna-Litic, K, (2009), 'The Impacts of Carbon Pricing on Indigenous Communities: A Comparison of New Zealand and Australia' in Lye, L.H.; J. Milne, H. Ashiabor, L. Kreiser, K. Deketelaere, (eds), *Critical Issues in Environmental Taxation*, New York: Oxford University Press, pp. 349–373.
14. Taylor, J. (2006) 'Population and diversity: Policy implications of emerging Indigenous demographic trends', CAEPR DP 283 cited in Altman J. and K. Jordan, (2008), 'Impact of Climate Change on Indigenous Australians: Submission to the Garnaut Climate Change Review.' Centre for Aboriginal Economic Policy Research ANU, http://anu.edu/caepr/Publications/topical/Altman_Jordan_Garnaut%20Review.pdf (accessed 3 February 2012).
15. Australian Bureau of Statistics, *4714.0 – National Aboriginal and Torres Strait Islander Social Survey, 2008* (2008), online: ABS http://www.abs.gov.au/ausstats/abs@.nsf/Latestproducts/4714.0Main%20Features22008?opendocument&tabname=Summary&prodno=4714.0&issue=2008&num=&view= (accessed 3 February 2012).
16. CAEPR website, http://www.fabian.org.au/1043.asp (accessed 3 February 2012).
17. 'The hybrid economy, as already noted, is about a three sector economy that includes the customary rather than the more conventional two sector private and public model.' From 'The Indigenous Hybrid Economy', Address to the Australian Fabian Society, 26 October 2005 by J. Altman, http://www.fabian.org.au/1043.asp (accessed 3 February 2012).
18. Biddle, N. and B. Hunter, 'NATSISS 2002 General Methodological Issues' ch. 4 in *Assessing the evidence on Indigenous socioeconomic outcomes*, CAEPR Research Monologue, No.26 http://epress.anu.edu.au/wp-content/uploads/2011/08/ch0412.pdf (accessed 16 February 2012).
19. Altman, J., 'Important questions for indigenous policy makers', May 2011, http://www.abc.net.au/unleashed/2692730.html (accessed 3 February 2012).
20. Webster. A, A. Rogers and D. Black, 'The 2002 NATSISS – the ABS survey methodology and concepts', ch. 3 in 'Assessing the evidence on Indigenous socioeconomic outcomes' CAEPR Research Monologue, No.26 http://epress.anu.edu.au/wp-content/uploads/2011/08/ch0312.pdf (accessed 16 February 2012).
21. Australian Bureau of Statistics (ABS) *4705.0 – Population Distribution, Aboriginal and Torres Strait Islander Australians*, (2006), http://www.abs.gov.au/AUSSTATS/abs@.nsf/Lookup/4705.0Main+Features12006?OpenDocument (accessed 3 February 2012).

22. Hobart is classified as inner regional, ibid.
23. Darwin is classified as outer regional, ibid.
24. Ibid.
25. Altman J., et al (2007) 'The Environmental Significance of the Indigenous Estate: Natural Resource Management as Economic Development in Remote Australia', CAEPR Discussion Paper No. 286/2007, http://caepr.anu.edu.au/sites/default/files/Publications/DP/2007_DP286.pdf (accessed 16 February 2012)
26. ABS *4704.0—The Health and Welfare of Australia's Aboriginal and Torres Strait Islander Peoples*, 2008 http://www.abs.gov.au/ausstats/abs@.nsf/mf/4704.0/ (accessed 3 February 2012).
27. ABS *4714.0—National Aboriginal and Torres Strait Islander Social Survey*, 2002 http://www.abs.gov.au/AUSSTATS/abs@.nsf/mf/4714.0/ (accessed 3 February 2012).
28. CANA, *The Social Impacts of Climate Change* http://www.cana.net.au/socialimpacts/australia/indigenous.html (accessed 3 February 2012).
29. McLucas J., (2006) 'The impacts of climate change on Torres Strait Islanders, Commonwealth', *Parliamentary Debates*, Senate, 10 October 2006, 142.
30. Above, n. 3.
31. CAEPR submission to the Garnaut Review, http://www.anu.edu.au/caepr/Publications/topical/Altman_Jordan_Garnaut%20Review.pdf (accessed 3 February 2012).
32. Ibid.
33. National Aboriginal and Torres Strait Islander Social Survey 2002 http://www.ausstats.abs.gov.au/ausstats/subscriber.nsf/0/AE3942DB21AD4A27CA256EBB0079843D/$File/47140_2002.pdf (accessed 3 February 2012).
34. ABS *4710.0 – Housing and Infrastructure in Aboriginal and Torres Strait Islander Communities, Australia*, 2001 http://www.abs.gov.au/AUSSTATS/abs@.nsf/Lookup/4710.0Main+Features12001?OpenDocument (accessed 3 February 2012).
35. Above, n. 3.
36. Above, n. 2.
37. Carbon Pollution Reduction Scheme Green Paper July 2008 http://www.plantations2020.com.au/assets/acrobat/Greenpaper.pdf (accessed 3 February 2012) .
38. Carbon Pollution Reduction Scheme White Paper http://www.climatechange.gov.au/publications/cprs/white-paper/~/media/publications/white-paper/V100eExecutive Summary-pdf.ashx (accessed 16 February 2012) .
39. Exposure draft of the Carbon Pollution Reduction Scheme legislation http://www.aph.gov.au/senate/committee/economics_ctte/cprs_09/ (accessed 3 February 2012).
40. Labour to offer carbon tax break for low earners. http://www.smh.com.au/environment/climate-change/labour-to-offer-carbon-tax-break-for-low-earners-20110319-1c1mo.html (accessed 3 February 2012)
41. Emissions from transport were predicted to increase by 57% since 1990 in 2010, increasing by 78% by 2020 Greenhouse Gas Emissions From Australian Transport: Base Case Projections to 2020 http://www.bitre.gov.au/publications/34/Files/BTRE_AGO_05.pdf (accessed 3 February 2012).
42. A 10% per cent increase in price leads to a fall in fuel use in the longer term of up to 7% (Australia's green paper). See above, n. 38.
43. Above, n. 40.
44. Ibid.
45. Ibid.
46. Above, n. 41.
47. Ibid.
48. Above, n. 2.
49. Australian Bureau of Statistics, *47130 – Population Characteristics, Aboriginal and Torres Strait Islander Australians, 2006* (2006), online: Australia http://www.ausstats.abs. gov.au/Ausstats/subscriber.nsf/0/BD4AECC58BB2B97 4CA257718001E0CBC/$File/national%20tables47130do001_2006.xls#Table_33!A1 [accessed 3 February 2012) at Table 33 'Household Income Distribution by Tenure, Persons in occupied dwellings by Remoteness Areas'.

50. Ibid.
51. Ibid.
52. This was to minimize energy costs as they became less affordable as a result of the economic downturn, but renters would not be able to take advantage of this and would only benefit if their landlords decided to take up this offer.
53. Australian Bureau of Statistics, *47130DO001 Population Characteristics, Aboriginal and Torres Strait Islander Australians 2006* (4 May 2010), online: ABS http://www.ausstats.abs.gov.au/Ausstats/subscriber.nsf/0/BD4AECC58BB2B974CA257718001E0CBC/$File/national%20tables47130do001_2006.xls (accessed 3 February 2012).
54. Ibid.
55. Ibid.
56. This measure is an ABS indicator, introduced in the 2001 Census and expanded in the 2008 NATSISS. Australian Bureau of Statistics, *4714.0 – National Aboriginal and Torres Strait Islander Social Survey, 2008* (2008), online: ABS http://www.abs.gov.au/ausstats/abs@.nsf/Latestproducts/4714.0Main%20Features112008?opendocument&tabname=Summary&prodno=4714.0&issue=2008&num=&view= (accessed 3 February 2012).
57. This is based on the poverty indicator. Ibid.
58. Above, n. 41.
59. Above, n. 40.
60. Overcoming Indigenous Advantage http://www.pc.gov.au/gsp/reports/indigenous/keyindicators2007 (accessed 3 February 2012).
61. Ibid.
62. Ibid.
63. Ibid.
64. Ibid.
65. The nature of this disadvantage is that they find it hard to take advantage of emission reduction initiatives. Renters have less incentive to outlay the capital costs of emission reduction activities such as insulation, renewable energy options, hot water systems and cooking appliances.
66. In 2008, in remote areas, 48% of indigenous people lived in overcrowded housing http://www.abs.gov.au/AUSSTATS/abs@.nsf/lookup/4704.0Chapter865Oct+2010 (accessed 3 February 2012).
67. Above, n. 2.
68. ABS 2001 Census; table 11A.1.3.
69. Australian Bureau of Statistics, *47130DO001 Population Characteristics, Aboriginal and Torres Strait Islander Australians, 2006* (4 May 2010), Table 20 online: ABS http://www.ausstats.abs.gov.au/Ausstats/subscriber.nsf/0/BD4AECC58BB2B974CA257718001E0CBC/$File/national%20tables47130do001_2006.xls#Table_23!A_'Table of Contents' (accessed 3 February 2012).
70. Savanna website: http://savanna.cdu.edu.au/information/arnhem_fire_project.html (accessed 3 February 2012).

5. The quest for environmental justice on a Canadian aboriginal reserve

Sidra Sabzwari and Dayna Nadine Scott

5.1 INTRODUCTION

Indigenous peoples worldwide suffer from environmental injustice. Although Canada prides itself on its environmental record, health care and social programs, there are indigenous groups, or First Nations, Metis and Inuit Aboriginal peoples, within Canada who do not have basic access to safe and healthy environments. Many First Nations in Canada have a unique temporal and spatial connection to the land, whereby they have inhabited or hunted through traditional land areas for several generations spanning hundreds of years. Since cultural identity is associated with specific land areas and practices, migration is minimal between lands and over time. As a result, although every Canadian is affected by chemical pollutants in our environment, First Nations in Canada experience a disproportionate burden of the harm from localized and cumulative environmental toxins. The prevailing regulatory schemes for air pollution in place across the country fail to address these particular impacts that chronic pollution has upon aboriginal communities (see for example Scott, 2008). In this chapter, we take the Aamjiwnaang First Nation as a case study in how a community experiencing chronic contamination and environmental injustice can take direct action to mobilize and catalyze changes in government environmental policy.

Section 5.2 of this chapter gives the background of the environmental justice movement, chronic pollution, and the rise of popular epidemiology. Section 5.3 provides some historical context for the Aamjiwnnang First Nation's chronic contamination and the acts of resistance they have employed. Section 5.4 examines exciting new methods of community action influenced by the environmental justice movement, such as body burden testing and community environmental monitoring. We conclude with comments on how other indigenous groups worldwide can apply lessons from the experience of the Aamjiwnaang community in their pursuit of environmental equity and justice, by transitioning from victims of pollution to agents of change.

5.2 THE ENVIRONMENTAL JUSTICE MOVEMENT, CHRONIC POLLUTION AND EPIDEMIOLOGY

Environmental justice can be defined as 'the fair treatment and meaningful involvement of all people regardless of race, color, national origin, or income with respect to the development, implementation, and enforcement of environmental laws, regulations, and policies'.[1] A broader view of environmental justice incorporates aspects of social justice, such as livable wages, safe communities, quality education, health care, and democratic decision making (Zilney *et al.*, 2006; Bradley, 2008). The environmental justice movement is a rising broad-based social movement focusing mainly on the concept of 'disproportionate burdens' (Bullard, 2005; Cole and Foster, 2001). It has emerged in response to concerns about how the state of the everyday 'environment' affects human health. It has a more urban focus than conventional environmentalism and key campaigns have unfolded mainly around air pollution, water contamination, chemicals and pesticides (Brown, 2007). The central claim of the movement is that environmental health burdens are heaviest for the poor, the racialized and the most marginalized in our society (Luke, 2000).

Much of this disproportionate environmental health burden comes in the form of chronic pollution, which is the continuous or continuously recurring exposure to low doses of pollutants that is part of everyday life in most parts of the urban industrialized world. Usually in the case of chronic pollution, it is difficult to trace and link environmental health harms to any one cause, chemical or polluter (Colborn *et al.*, 1996, p. 220). This is aggravated because the actual injury occurs at the molecular level (Collins, 2001, p. 107); multiple chemicals are dispersed into the environment by multiple polluters; and there are long latency periods between the time of exposure to the time the injury effectually presents itself. Exposures to toxic chemicals in one generation may produce effects in the next. Chronic polluters can often point to several possible intervening causal events, thereby escaping tort liability. In response to this challenge, environmental justice activists are experimenting with new ways to gather the required evidence to demonstrate that chronic exposures to pollution are *causing* environmental health harms, even at the supposed 'safe doses' currently permitted by existing laws.

Often, these communities employ the science of epidemiology. Epidemiology is the study of disease in the population as a whole, as distinguished from the study of disease in individuals.[2] It is concerned with the distribution of a disease or physiological condition in human populations, and of the factors that influence that distribution (Cranor, 2006, p. 9). Most toxic substances in the environment, however, have not been subjected to systematic epidemiological study (Brown, 2007, p. 265; Wolff, 2006, p. 234). Even when there are studies to draw on, the evidence is generally treated as useful for demonstrating associations or correlations between particular illnesses and potential toxins, but not for providing conclusive or definitive causal links (Scott, 2008).

The downside of employing epidemiological evidence from a community's perspective is that '[s]ubjective claims about the body are subordinated to statistical correlations between exposure and [populations]' (Jasanoff, 2002, p. 37). The focus moves from personal stories of individual suffering, or community-wide illness, to aggregated and probabilistic harm across disembodied 'populations'. It tends to blur the details of individual lives and community struggle in the hopes of creating a pattern or revealing a cluster. Thus, the critique of epidemiology's 'statistical vision' is that it tends to turn individuals suffering from the effects of chronic contamination into mere 'victims of chance', denying the social origins of pollution and the blameworthiness of those who perpetuate it. But individuals who confront risks are not generic human beings. Their narratives are important to increase our understanding of chronic pollution. On the Aamjiwnaang reserve for example:

> they are young Aboriginal mothers, parents who routinely receive 'emergency alerts' over the radio indicating that they should 'Shelter in Place' as a result of an incident or a 'fugitive release' from neighbouring industry, daycare workers responding to the sirens by shuffling toddlers inside and closing the vents, health clinic staff staring down bewildering statistics, teenagers struggling with asthma, as well as developmental and attention-deficit disorders, and young children prevented from swimming in the contaminated creek that passes through their traditional powwow grounds (Scott, 2008, p. 311).[3]

Since environmental risks are virtually undetectable without scientific investigation, the result is a growing tension between those who have 'knowledge' and those who do not, leading to a social dependency on expert institutions (Hajer, 1995; Harvey, 1999, p. 153; Wynne, 1996, p. 45). Overcoming a community's dependence on those who have the 'knowledge' is a key goal of the environmental justice movement and the driving force behind the rise of 'popular epidemiology' (Fischer, 2000, p. 121). Popular epidemiology is a form of political struggle through which community members take initiative and engage in the collection of data, knowledge and evidence needed to explain their experience of contamination (Brown and Mikkelson, 1990). This type of evidence may be useful for telling a community's story, for proving claims in court, or for quantifying environmental damages. To varying extents, residents involved in this type of struggle will also enlist the knowledge and resources of experts. However, when they engage in popular epidemiology, community members tend to include social and structural factors as part of the causal disease chain more often than experts do (Brown, 1992).

Traditional pollution control regimes, because they often fail to account for the cumulative effects from all pollution sources, are completely ineffective against chronic low-dose exposures to toxic chemicals, such as endocrine disruptors (Scott, 2008). The legal regimes thus enable the continued release of contaminants at levels that are scientifically sanctioned as tolerable. However, new evidence indicates that certain classes of chemicals in widespread use, such as endocrine disruptors, 'are capable of exerting population-wide effects at current levels of exposure' (National Wildlife Federation & Canadian Institute for Environmental Law and Policy, 1991). Although these low-dose, chronic exposures were once thought to be 'safe' or 'tolerable' by the human body, epidemiological studies are now forwarding multiple claims of irreversible developmental effects at low levels of exposure to certain chemicals (van Larebeke *et al.*, 2008, p. 140; Brouwer *et al.*, 1999; Kuriyama *et al.*, 2005; Parmigiani *et al.*, 2003; Vom Saal and Hughes, 2005; Welshons *et al.*, 2006).[4] A possible solution to the contemporary problem of chronic pollution is for regulators to take an ecosystem approach. This would focus on cumulative effects of chemicals rather than on individual facility emissions. We are exposed to complex mixtures, and not mere individual chemicals in unique instances of space and time. 'Scientific studies make it clear that chemicals can interact or act together to produce an effect that none could produce individually' (Colborn *et al.*, 1996, p. 220), yet most legal regimes currently in place ignore the possible additive and synergistic effects.

Public participation and community empowerment are fundamental to achieving environmental justice (Pirk, 2002, p. 212). '[T]rue public participation and environmental justice cannot be realized until the communities that are impacted by environmental regulations have a voice in the process equal to that of regulated industry' (Kuhn, 1999, p. 648). However, as is the case with many indigenous groups worldwide, the Aamjiwnaang community has not been given any voice at all in regards to industrial activity that affects their traditional ancestral lands (Bradley, 2008). The Aamjiwnaang situation provides a particularly distressing example of the failure of our regulatory system to uphold environmental justice.

5.3 THE AAMJIWNAANG FIRST NATION: A CHRONICALLY CONTAMINATED COMMUNITY

The Aamjiwnaang First Nation is a community of approximately 900 Aanishnaabek people living on a reserve near Sarnia, Ontario, Canada. In 1827, the Band surrendered title to over two million acres of traditional lands in exchange for reserve land from the British Crown, now represented by the Government of Canada.[5] After a century of petrochemical production, the reserve has become surrounded by industry. Sixty-two large industrial facilities now operate within 25 km of the Aamjiwnaang reserve, including several large petrochemical, polymer, and chemical industrial plants.[6] In 2005, Sarnia's 'Chemical Valley' was responsible for releasing 5.7 million kilograms of toxic air pollutants. The airshed is further saturated by non-point source pollution, as Sarnia is a popular border-crossing point for trucks passing between the United States and Canada (Parker and Diamond, 2005).

The attention to pathways for chemical migration is critical, because the notion of disproportionate burdens deployed by the environmental justice movement has a fundamentally spatial character (Scott, 2008). As Steingraber has noted, '[t]he distribution of illness in space reveals clues about its causes' (1997, p. 100). Indigenous populations may in fact experience a disproportionate burden of the harms from chronic pollution precisely due to the unique combination of the spatial arrangements of their reserves in relation to industrial sources of pollutants and their lasting connections with the land. This is especially evident in Sarnia, where the Aamjiwnaang reserve is located immediately downwind of the 62 factories of Chemical Valley. For years, Aamjiwnaang residents have been complaining about the prevailing winds and the way they disperse and distribute the pollution. The mantra of the environmental justice movement, 'some live more downstream than others', is thus an obvious reality in this community (Tarter, 2002, p. 213; Scott, 2008). South Sarnia is a working-class area of town which might receive similar exposures to air pollutants as indigenous reserve residents, and recently saw the elimination of their only representative position at Sarnia's city council (Plain, 12 June 2008). North Sarnia is where the city's wealthier residents live, upwind and out of harm's way from the concentrated air emissions.

The attention to temporal effects of chronic pollution on Aboriginal peoples is also critical. Non-Aboriginal populations who are more transient may act as a control group when demonstrating the spatial and temporal effects of chronic pollution. For example, although South Sarnia is also downwind of 'Chemical Valley', it is a non-Aboriginal population where people come and go, moving between residences and neighbourhoods, shifting their spatial location over a lifetime and between generations (Pellow, 2000, p. 590). Most people in Sarnia have not lived there all of their lives, and they may have been born anywhere in Canada, if not the world. Thus, the effects of the chronic contamination on their bodies are muted. In contrast, aboriginal peoples in general are not a transient population and will usually not abandon their homeland even to find cleaner air or water (Tarbell and Arquette, 2000, p. 99). Their connection to the land is tied to identity. Native people, 'like resident ... plants and animals, will live adjacent to these [contaminated] sites forever and experience the effects of persistent contaminants for generations to come' (Tarbell and Arquette, 2000). The Aamjiwnaang people have occupied their traditional lands for hundreds of years. The geography is sacred and helps the Aamjiwnaang practice their spirituality within their worldview (Jackson, 2010, p. 256). Story-telling by Elders is used to teach the younger generations, and is facilitated by making reference to shared locations known and frequented by the entire community (Jackson, 2010, p. 256). On the Aamjiwnaang burial grounds, you will find the remains of four generations of ancestors, literally on the fenceline of a large refinery (Scott, 2008).[7] Most non-aboriginal residents of Sarnia cannot describe the same historical permanence of their family on the landscape. This may explain why we might see a disproportionate effect of chronic pollution in this indigenous community, as it is grounded both spatially and historically. It also demonstrates clearly how toxic chemical pollution exists in social contexts that can intensify its effects (Luke, 2000, p. 248), as those downwind of 'Chemical Valley' are not wealthy, and have little to no political power or influence on environmental, city planning, or regulatory decisions.

Several years ago community activists from the Aamjiwnaang First Nation commenced a participatory research project with the assistance of researchers affiliated with the University of Ottawa and the Occupational Health Clinic for Ontario Workers. The study confirmed that the community's sex ratio (the number of boys born relative to the number of girls) is declining at an alarming rate (Mackenzie *et al.*, 2005). Using data reported to the Government of Canada's Department of Indian and Northern Affairs, the researchers assessed trends in the ratio of male to female births for the years from 1984 to 2003 and noticed that the proportion of male births has declined sharply. Globally, the percentage of male births typically hovers at just about 50 per cent and in Canada it is 51.2 per cent. However, from 1994–2003, Aamjiwnaang males accounted for only 41.2 per cent of births, and from 1999 to 2003, only 34.8 per cent. The biologists determined that the decline is statistically significant and growing steadily (Mackenzie *et al.*, 2005, p. 1295; Scott, 2008). At this point, there is only one boy born in Aamjiwnaang for every two girls, and the Aamjiwnaang First Nation now has the unwelcome distinction of the world's lowest documented birth ratio.[8]

The biologists who studied this effect found many contaminants in the soil and sediment that exceeded the provincial guidelines, including arsenic, PCBs, mirex, lead, and mercury.[9] The study recommended further research to determine whether the noted decline in sex ratio was correlated with the community members' exposure to industrial pollutants. It is now speculated that chronic environmental exposures to a group of endocrine disrupting chemicals, the 'gender-benders', are responsible. Endocrine disrupting chemicals include a diverse set of compounds that includes persistent organic pollutants (like dioxins and polychlorinated biphenols), several insecticides and fungicides, and a number of widespread industrial chemicals (such as brominated fire retardants) (Mantovani, 2006, p. 240). Endocrine disruptors are said to have a 'hormone-mimicking' effect (Colborn *et al.*, 1996). They may induce long-term effects upon low-dose exposures in susceptible developmental phases. It is hypothesized that these environmental contaminants disrupt the human endocrine system, possibly influencing the sex ratio by changing parents' hormonal milieu or by inducing sex-specific mortality in early miscarriage.[10] Other studies conducted in this region have found changes in the sex ratios and reproductive abilities of fish, bird, and turtle populations, which are also thought to be due to exposures to endocrine-disrupting chemicals.[11]

The publication of the sex ratio problem has drawn international attention to the community, and members are now using this to focus the media on other more tangible health problems caused by the pollution. In 2006, the Aamjiwnaang Health and Environment Committee interviewed community members and conducted a 'body mapping' exercise. Body mapping is a way of pooling the collective health complaints of people so that patterns can be identified. Residents were asked to place colour-coded sticky dots on maps of a human body to represent their symptoms. The result, when all of the maps were laid on top of each other, was a visual representation showing that 17 per cent of adults and 22 per cent of children surveyed had asthma; about 25 per cent of adults experienced high blood pressure and/or chronic headaches; about 25 per cent of children suffered from learning and behavioural problems; and about 40 per cent of women had experienced miscarriage or stillbirth.[12]

Contamination of their bodies and their traditional territory has also had an enormous emotional effect on community members.[13] Residents of the Aamjiwnaang First Nation have expressed a building anger and lingering sadness upon learning the extent of their health problems and the mounting evidence linking those problems to the polluting actions of their industrial neighbours.[14] The unknowns can have an equally corrosive effect. It is widely accepted that exposures to toxic chemicals in one generation may produce effects in the next, but no one can tell the Aamjiwnaang community whether they face a present danger or are experiencing the latent manifestation of previous exposures (Plain, 2008; Scott, 2008).[15] Early exposure for children, even in the womb, can be linked to diseases that show up later in life, and failure to conceive is part of this continuum.[16]

Most residents of the Aamjiwnaang First Nation accept that there is a causal relationship between chronic exposures to chemicals and injuries to human health. But they acknowledge that the evidence is only now starting to come in, and that there is still much to be learned. Activists from the community have teamed up with progressive environmental epidemiologists who are working on compiling the growing evidence around these chronic exposures

(Grandjean and Landrigan, 2006, p. 2167). The people of Aamjiwnaang are actively resisting this pollution, and their strategies have the potential to expose the failure of the prevailing regulatory approach as an answer to contemporary pollution problems.

5.4 COMMUNITY ACTION INFLUENCED BY THE ENVIRONMENTAL JUSTICE MOVEMENT

The linkage between public participation, community empowerment and environmental justice requires that the community itself determine which strategies to undertake, both inside and outside the legal system. In the course of their ongoing struggles against chronic pollution, the Aanishnaabek of Aamjiwnaang have employed several strategies for community empowerment which demonstrate the growing influence of the environmental justice movement.

Two of the most exciting new strategies employed by activists and communities inspired by the movement are biomonitoring (or 'body burden' testing) and community environmental monitoring, such as the deployment of so-called 'bucket brigades'.

5.4.1 Biomonitoring, or 'Body burden' Testing

Biomonitoring is emerging as a very powerful method for marshalling the kind of evidence that is useful for communities facing contamination.[17] It 'derives from critical epidemiology and citizen-science alliance' and its goal is to generate a measure of a person's 'body burden', which is thought to give direct information about total exposures to pollutants across time and from all sources (Brown, 2007, p. 265). A 'body burden' is a measure of a person's chemical load; it is the sum total of exposures from all routes of entry (inhalation, ingestion, and skin absorption) and from all sources (food, air, and water) from all the places we inhabit. For a complete measure of the total burden, one would need samples from every fluid and compartment of tissue in the exposed body. More commonly though, a sample of blood, urine, semen, umbilical cord fluid, or fingernails is extracted and subjected to expensive analysis.

For fat soluble, persistent chemicals, the body burden shows a measure of cumulative exposures that have slowly built up over time. For chemicals which are quickly metabolized and excreted, the body burden is an indicator of 'immediate and ongoing exposures to particular contaminants at single points in time' (Steingraber, 1997). If these are found regularly, it means the person is exposed to this contaminant every day, on a continual and chronic basis. When receiving the results of these tests, participants will differ in their 'exposure experience', or how they interpret their results, depending upon their own past life experiences (Altman *et al.*, 2008, p. 428). Participants may gain new information about the chemicals that surround them during their daily routine; they may request a scientist's evaluation on the significance and health implications of said results; and they may ask follow-up questions seeking knowledge of other potential health risks (Altman *et al.*, 2008, p. 423).

The testing is expensive, and the more mediums tested for, the pricier it is. Less affluent communities will have to attract foundation money or partner with a non-governmental organization to help fund the tests. The community can set up a steering committee to have some control over the study design. This avoids the situation of getting funded by the regulator, and being dependent on obtaining information from them. The testing is also risky, as there is always a chance the test results will be found within the range of 'normal'. Nevertheless, communities are moving forward with this strategy, confident that they will generate evidence that cannot be ignored.

Biomonitoring campaigns are useful because they demonstrate that our current laws and regulations are failing to prevent a toxic build-up of chemical residues in our own bodies. They also serve to promote awareness that pollution causes health effects at levels below the 'safe doses' currently set by regulatory agencies, and to demonstrate the omnipresence of certain substances in the environment. Further, while we are all subject to some degree of chronic pollution, it is clear that racialized and marginalized communities are more vulnerable than others. With respect to low-dose chronic exposures, while it may be true that 'no one can fully escape', some of us can and do avoid exposures to the most toxic local contaminants that others are unable to dodge. Radioactive waste disposal sites, incinerators, refineries, coal-fired utilities, and cement kilns are not located in wealthy neighbourhoods (Scott, 2008).

5.4.2 Community Environmental Monitoring

Launching their own 'bucket brigades' is a second new strategy which allows residents of contaminated communities to actively participate in environmental monitoring and regulation.[18] The bucket brigades are trained and motivated teams of local community residents who are recruited to monitor air quality near the refineries, chemical factories, or power plants that surround the community, using low-cost 'grab samplers'.[19] These teams are 'deployed on the frontlines of efforts to improve environmental monitoring and reinvigorate environmental enforcement' (O'Rourke and Macey, 2003, p. 385). The driving motivation behind the bucket brigades is the goal of generating evidence that can be used to force regulators into action.

In essence, the team of residents is equipped to sample the ambient air in their communities at times and locations of their own choosing. The team consists of 'sniffers' and 'samplers' in a coordinated network using tools that are 'explicitly designed to be inexpensive, easy to use, and made of materials that can be found at a local hardware store' (O'Rourke and Macey, 2003, p. 389). At the same time, these buckets are capable of storing a sample of ambient air that can be subject to sophisticated analysis with proven credibility. The strategy is motivated by the firm belief that the current monitoring systems in place are wholly inadequate and that they in fact 'perpetuate an environment in which firms pollute beyond safe levels, and with little threat of punishment' (O'Rourke and Macey, 2003, p. 384). It is also motivated by the realization of communities that the 'location, range, and focus of ambient monitors are determined through an inherently political process' (O'Rourke and Macey, 2003).

For example, until recently, there were no ambient air quality monitors located downwind of Chemical Valley in Sarnia. But, when faced with the recent publication of some test results from an air sample captured by the Aamjiwnaang bucket brigade, the government regulator acted quickly to install an air quality monitoring station on the reserve. Without the monitors or the capacity to do its own monitoring, the Aamjiwnaang First Nation would face this very typical scenario: '[i]ndustry has an accident that results in a chemical release; government officials arrive too late to inspect or evaluate the release; and industry announces that there is no risk to the community' (O'Rourke and Macey, 2003, p. 391; Scott, 2008, p. 337). The common complaint of community residents is that they simply cannot get someone to come out to the community to test the air in time to get an accurate sample.[20] In this key respect, the bucket brigades are intended to alter the essential power relations by providing the community with the indispensable tool of information that it can control.

A central concern for those worried about the cumulative effects of exposures is that government agencies 'are not monitoring the full range of chemicals that [residents] are exposed to' (O'Rourke and Macey, 2003, p. 395). For example, past Aamjiwnaang bucket brigade results have revealed unusually high levels of benzene. Benzene is a volatile organic compound which can be hazardous to human health when inhaled. Because benzene has been noted as toxic and is a probable human carcinogen, the official provincial position is that its emissions should be prevented or limited to the greatest extent possible (*Environmental Protection Act*; *Bogan* [2007]).[21] The regulator in Ontario does not have an ambient air quality standard for this chemical.[22] Due directly to the Aamjiwnaang bucket brigade results, the regulator is now looking into establishing a standard for benzene. Thus, for communities under seige from toxic emissions, the mobilization of a bucket brigade can signal the 'transition from victims to agents of change' (O'Rourke and Macey, 2003, p. 398).

5.5 CONCLUSION

Current regulatory regimes are incapable of addressing all health impacts from low-dose long-term exposure to toxins in the environment, as they typically do not address synergistic effects or cumulative impacts of pollution. Further, the concept of 'safe doses' is unraveling. The unjust nature of political power relations between a government and historically disadvantaged groups such as aboriginal tribes has often resulted in these groups being made to suffer for the benefit of industrial and economic development for the good of society, as the Aamjiwnaang case clearly demonstrates.

Less politically powerful communities are using the values embodied by the environmental justice movement and creatively fashioning their own methods of encouraging or forcing environmental policy change. When communities design culturally and locally relevant research methods, the knowledge acquired serves to empower the community and gives them a stronger bargaining chip when lobbying or negotiating with more powerful government institutions. With this knowledge comes power and confidence. Methods of direct community action such as biomonitoring, body mapping, and the bucket brigades are easily designed and could be used in parallel situations with other indigenous groups globally who suspect they are experiencing the health effects of chronic pollution. Even if the knowledge acquired does not impact policy decisions, at the very least it eliminates some of the uncertainty involved with chronic pollution and could serve to answer health questions in the minds of the community members. While there is some indication that the government may be planning to bring in new legislation to 'modernize' the air pollution permit regime in Ontario, a recent discussion paper on the topic issued by the Ministry of Environment does not address the problem of cumulative impacts, and activists from the Aamiwnaang community have expressed frustration with the slow progress.[23]

That frustration may have now reached a boiling point: in November 2010, Band members Ron Plain and Ada Lockridge of the Aamjiwnaang First Nation launched litigation claiming that the chronic exposures to pollution, and the Ministry's failure to assess the cumulative effects on their health, constitute a violation of their constitutional rights to life, liberty and security of the person and equality.[24] In the context of the high rates of cancer, respiratory illness, cardiovascular disease, neurological and developmental disabilities, and the declining birth ratio that have been brought to light through the work of local community activists, it is undeniable that the location of this reserve matters. For aboriginal communities to obtain environmental justice, they need to share strategies for community empowerment and for the generation of data and knowledge that can change the conventional dynamics of power, authority and credibility that prevail with respect to environmental law and policy.

NOTES

1. U.S. Environmental Protection Agency (2009), 'Environmental Justice', http://www.epa.gov/ compliance/environmentaljustice/ (accessed 3 February 2012).
2. *Rothwell v. Raes* (1988), 66 O.R. (2d) 449, (Ontario High Court of Justice).
3. Poirier, J. (2008), 'Sarnia issues warning after benzene vapour leak at plant', The Times Herald, 15 March.
4. Gee, D., D. Stanners, D. Jiménez-Beltrán, P. Bourdeau, B. Jansson, D. Ogden and J. Willis (1998), 'Chemicals in the European Environment: Low Doses, High Stakes?', Copenhagen: European Environment Agency, http://www.eea.europa.eu/publications/NYM2 (accessed 3 February 2012); Hogg, M. (2007), 'Chemicals Harmful to Health in Low As Well As High Doses' The Environmental Illness Resource, http://www.ei-resource.org/news/general-environmental-health-news, 23 January (accessed 3 February 2012).
5. *Chippewas of Sarnia Band v. Canada (Attorney General)* (2000), 195 D.L.R. (4th) 135, 51 O.R. (3d) 641 (Ontario Court of Appeal).
6. MacDonald, E. and S. Rang (2007), 'Exposing Canada's Chemical Valley: An Investigation of Cumulative Air Pollution Emissions in the Sarnia, Ontario Area', Ecojustice, http://www.ecojustice.ca/publications/reports/report-exposing-canadas-chemical-valley/attachment, p.8. (accessed 3 February 2012).
7. Jonston, S. and R. Plain (2000), 'Environmental Health Status of First Nations: Aamjiwnaang First Nation Health Studies', presented to the Aamjiwnaang Environmental Health Symposium, unpublished; notes on file with author.
8. Colihan, M.A. (2008), 'Chemical Valley: Aamjiwnaang First Nation in Sarnia Sounds Alarm Over Toxins' CBC News In Depth, http://www.cbc.ca/news/background/aboriginals/health.html, April 1 (accessed 3 February 2012).
9. See Mackenzie et al. (2005) p. 1297.
10. Foster, W. (2008), 'Panel Discussion on Sex Ratio Changes', Panel discussion held at the Aamjiwnaang Environmental Health Symposium, Sarnia: [unpublished], 26 March.
11. Environment Canada Canadian Wildlife Service (2003), 'Fish and Wildlife Health Effects in the Canadian Great Lakes Areas of Concern', Ottawa, Ontario, Canada: Minister of Public Works and Government Services Canada, http://www.ec.gc.ca/Publications/A793CA48-2A8C-4F38-8B1C-B3AEBEAE2342%5CFishAndWildlifeHealthEffectsInTheCanadianGreatLakesAreasOfConcern.pdf (accessed 15 February 2012).
12. Above, n. 7.
13. Jacobs, D. (2008), 'Environmental Health Status of First Nations', Lecture presented at the Aamjiwnaang Environmental Health Symposium, Sarnia: unpublished, notes on file with author, March 26.
14. Aamjiwnaang Environmental Health Symposium (2008), 'Letter of Invitation', Sarnia, 26 March. See also Luginaah, I., K. Smith and A. Lockridge (2010), 'Surrounded by Chemical Valley and "living in a bubble": the case of the Aamjiwnaang First Nation, Ontario', *Journal of Environmental Planning and Management*, 53(3), 353.
15. Plain, R. (2008), 'The Costs of Chronic Pollution: Stories from the Aamjiwnaang First Nation, Lecture delivered at the "Exposing Canada's Toxic Shame" event, Faculty of Environmental Studies, York University, notes on file with author,
16. Above, n. 8. The link between chronic pollution and reproductive health is contested and fraught. For example, critics content that women bear a disproportionate burden of the anxiety and guilt around reproduction and reproductive outcomes when women become viewed as 'mediums' of pollution or contamination. See for example, Scott, D.N. (2009), 'Gender-Benders: Sex and Law in the Constitution of Polluted Bodies', *Feminist Legal Studies*, 17, 241.
17. Environmental Defence (2007), 'Toxic Nation', http://www.toxicnation.ca/ (accessed 3 February 2012).
18. McLean, J (2007), 'A toxic drop in the bucket: DIY environmentalists won't wait for others to clear the air', This Magazine, http://www.thismagazine.ca/issues/2007/09/toxicdrop.php (accessed 3 February 2012).

19. Global Community Monitor (2006), 'History of the Bucket Brigade',http://gcmonitor.org/section.php?id=136 (accessed 3 February 2012).
20. Poirier, J. (2007), 'Band to Monitor Industry', The Sarnia Observer, http://www.gcmonitor.org/article.php?id=582, 10 May (accessed 3 February 2012).
21. *Environmental Protection Act*, R.S.O. 1990, c. E-19. Standards Development Branch (2005), 'Summary of O. Reg. 419/05 Standards and Point of Impingement Guidelines & Ambient Air Quality Criteria (AAQCs)', Ontario Ministry of the Environment, http://www.ene.gov.on.ca/envision/gp/2424e04.pdf. (accessed 3 February 2012); *Bogan v. Director, Ministry of the Environment* [2007] 28 C.E.L.R. (3d) 21 (Ontario Environmental Review Tribunal).
22. The Sarnia Observer (2008), 'Localized study is complete; Aamjiwnaang test finds high levels of hazardous chemicals', copy on file with author Scott, 15 March.
23. Ontario Ministry of the Environment (2010), 'Modernization of Approval: Proposed Legislative Framework for Modernizing Environmental Approvals', Ontario Ministry of the Environment (accessed 3 February 2012).
24. *Lockridge v. Ministry of the Environment (Director)*, Notice of Application to Ontario Divisional Court for Judicial Review, Court File No. 528/10 (29 October 2010).

REFERENCES

Altman, R.G., R. Morello-Frosch, J.G. Brody, R. Ruthann, P. Brown and M. Averick (2008), 'Pollution Comes Home and Gets Personal: Women's Experience of Household Chemical Exposure', *Journal of Health and Social Behaviour*, 49(4), 417.

Bradley, A. (2008), *The Aamjiwnaang First Nation: Strategies for Environmental Justice* (unpublished, on file with author Scott and archived at Osgoode Hall Law School).

Brouwer, A., M.P. Longnecker, L.S. Birnbaum, J. Cogliano, P. Kostyniak, J. Moore, S. Schantz, and G. Winneke (1999), 'Characterization of Potential Endocrine-Related Health Effects at Low-Dose Levels of Exposure to PCBs', *Envtl Health Perspectives Supplements*, 107 (suppl. 4), 639.

Brown, P. (2007), *Toxic Exposures: Contested Illnesses and the Environmental Health Movement*, New York: Columbia University Press.

Brown, P., (1992) 'Popular Epidemiology and Toxic Waste Contamination: Lay and Professional Ways of Knowing', *Journal of Health and Social Behaviour*, 33(3), 267.

Brown, P. and E.J. Mikkelson (1990), *No Safe Place: Toxic Waste, Leukemia, and Community Action*, Berkeley: University of California Press.

Bullard, R.D. (ed.) (2005), *The Quest for Environmental Justice: Human Rights and the Politics of Pollution*, San Francisco: Sierra Club Books.

Colborn, T., D. Dumanoski and J.P. Myers (1996), *Our Stolen Future: Are We Threatening Our Fertility, Intelligence, and Survival? – A Scientific Detective Story*, New York: Dutton.

Cole, L. and S.R. Foster (2001), *From the Ground Up: Environmental Racism and the Rise of the Environmental Justice Movement*, New York: NYU Press.

Collins, L. (2001), 'Material Contribution to Risk and Causation in Toxic Torts' *J. Envtl. L. & Prac.* 11, 105.

Cranor, C.F. (2006), *Toxic Torts: Science, Law, and the Possibility of Justice*, New York: Cambridge University Press.

Fischer, F. (2000), *Citizens, Experts, and the Environment: The Politics of Local Knowledge*, Durham: Duke University Press.

Grandjean, P. and P.J. Landrigan (2006), 'Developmental Neurotoxicity of Industrial Chemicals', *The Lancet*, 368(9553), 2167.
Hajer, M. (1995), *The Politics of Environmental Discourse: Ecological Modernization and the Policy Process*, New York: Clarendon Press.
Harvey, D. (1999), 'The Environment of Justice' in F. Fischer and M.A. Hajer (eds), *Living with Nature: Environmental Politics as Cultural Discourse*, Oxford: Oxford University Press, 153.
Jackson, D.D. (2010), 'Shelter in place: a First Nation community in Canada's Chemical Valley', *Interdisciplinary Environmental Review*, 11(4), 249.
Jasanoff, S. (2002), 'Science and the Statistical Victim: Modernizing Knowledge in Breast Implant Litigation', *Soc. Stud. Sci.*, 32(1), 37.
Kuhn, S. (1999), 'Expanding Public Participation is Essential to Environmental Justice and the Democratic Decision making Process', *Ecology L.Q.*, 25(4), 647.
Kuriyama, S., C.E. Talsness, K. Grote and I. Chahoud (2005), 'Developmental Exposure to Low-Dose PBDE-99 Effects on Male Fertility and Neurobehavior in Rat Offspring', *Envtl. Health Perspectives*, 113(2), 149.
Luke, T.W. (2000), 'Rethinking Technoscience in Risk Society: Toxicity as Textuality' in R. Hofrichter (ed.), *Reclaiming the Environmental Debate: The Politics of Health in a Toxic Culture*, Cambridge, MA: MIT Press, 239.
Mackenzie, C.A., A. Lockridge and M. Keith (2005), 'Declining Sex Ratio in a First Nation Community', *Envtl. Health Perspectives*, 113(10), 1297.
Mantovani, A. (2006), 'Risk Assessment of Endocrine Disruptors: The Role of Toxicological Studies', *Ann. N.Y. Acad. Sci.*, 1076, 239.
National Wildlife Federation & Canadian Institute for Environmental Law and Policy (1991), 'A Prescription for Healthy Great Lakes: Report on the Program for Zero Discharge', Washington: National Wildlife Federation.
O'Rourke, D. and G. Macey (2003), 'Community Environmental Policing: Assessing New Strategies of Public Participation in Environmental Regulation', *J. of Pol'y Analysis & Mgmt*, 22(3), 383.
Parker, M. and G. Diamond (2005), 'Air Quality Assessment Related to Traffic Congestion at Sarnia's Blue Water Bridge', Government of Ontario, Ontario: Queen's Printer for Ontario.
Parmigiani, S., F.S. Vom Saal, P. Palanza, T. Colborn (2003), 'Exposure To Very Low Doses of Endocrine Disrupting Chemicals (EDCs) During Fetal Life Permanently Alters Brain Development and Behavior in Animals and Humans' in Richard C. Ragaini (ed.), *International Seminar on Nuclear War and Planetary Emergencies: 27th Session*, River Edge, NJ: World Scientific, 293–308.
Pellow, D.N. (2000), 'Environmental Inequality Formation: Toward a Theory of Environmental Injustice', *The American Behavioral Scientist*, 43(4), 581.
Pirk, S. (2002), 'Expanding Public Participation in Environmental Justice: Methods, Legislation, Litigation and Beyond', *J. J. Envtl. L. & Litig.*, 17, 207.
Plain, R. (2008), 'Toxic Tour', Sarnia, 12 June.
Scott, D.N. (2008), 'Confronting Chronic Pollution: A Socio-Legal Analysis of Risk and Precaution', *Osgoode Hall L.J*, 46(2), 293.
Steingraber, S. (1997), *Living Downstream: An Ecologist Looks at Cancer and the Environment*, Reading, MA: Addison-Wesley.
Tarbell, A. and M. Arquette (2000), 'Akwesasne: A Native American Community's Resistance to Cultural and Environmental Damage' in R. Hofrichter (ed.), *Reclaiming the Environmental Debate: The Politics of Health in a Toxic Culture*, Cambridge, MA: MIT Press, 93.

Tarter, J. (2002), 'Some Live More Downstream than Others: Cancer, Gender, and Environmental Justice' in J. Adamson, M.M. Evans and R. Stein (eds), *The Environmental Justice Reader: Politics, Poetics & Pedagogy*, Tucson: University of Arizona Press, 163.

van Larebeke, N.A., A.J. Sasco, J.T. Brophy, M.M. Keith, M. Gilbertson and A. Watterson (2008), 'Sex Ratio Changes as Sentinel Health Events of Endocrine Disruption', *Int'l J. Occup. Envtl Health*, 14(2), 138.

Vom Saal, F. S. and C. Hughes (2005), 'An Extensive New Literature Concerning Low-Dose Effects of Bisphenol A Shows the Need for a New Risk Assessment', *Envtl Health Perspectives*, 113(8), 926.

Welshons, W.V., S.C. Nagel and F.S. vom Saal (2006), 'Large Effects from Small Exposures. III. Endocrine Mechanisms Mediating Effects of Bisphenol A at Levels of Human Exposure', *Endocrinology*, 147(6), S56.

Wolff, M.S, (2006), 'Endocrine Disruptors: Challenges for Environmental Research in the 21st Century', *Ann. N.Y. Acad. Sci.*, 1076(1), 228.

Wynne, B. (1996), 'May the Sheep Safely Graze? A Reflexive View of The Expert-Lay Knowledge Divide' in S. Lash, B. Szerszynski and B. Wynne (eds), *Risk, Environment & Modernity: Towards a New Ecology of Risk*, London: Sage, 44.

Zilney, L.A, D. McGurrin and S. Zahran (2006), 'Environmental Justice and the Role of Criminology: An Analytical Review of 33 Years of Environmental Justice Research', *Criminal Justice Review*, 31(1), 47.

6. Whaling and dealing: aboriginal subsistence whaling, politics and poverty*

Ed Couzens

6.1 INTRODUCTION: ABORIGINAL SUBSISTENCE WHALING GENERALLY

Around the world, a number of aboriginal groups such as the Inuit/Eskimo people and the Makah Indian tribe[1] in the United States and the Chukotka people in Russia hunt and kill whales. This aboriginal subsistence whaling (ASW) is exempt from the International Whaling Commission (IWC) 1982 'moratorium'[2] on commercial whaling. The ASW exemption was placed in the 1946 *International Convention for the Regulation of Whaling*, signed at Washington, 2 December 1946 (ICRW), to preserve aboriginal cultures for which whaling was culturally significant and to alleviate poverty among those peoples. Although ASW is exempt from the moratorium, the IWC places annual quotas on aboriginal takes.[3]

Currently, there is controversy over whether four Japanese coastal communities should be classified as aboriginal subsistence whalers – at present they are not. Opponents of such recognition claim that these communities engage in commercial whaling, rather than aboriginal subsistence whaling; Japan maintains that the distinction is artificial. Japan, for instance, explained at the 46th annual meeting of the IWC that it held the view that 'its small-type whaling had the same characteristics as aboriginal subsistence whaling' and that 'hence a similar treatment should be considered' (IWC, 1994, p. 17).

According to Komatsu and Misaki, commercial whaling is 'a straightforward proposition: whaling undertaken for financial gain made through selling the catch'; and that one would presume therefore that 'it would then differ from aboriginal subsistence whaling, which you would not expect to be based upon financial transactions'. However, they contend, there is 'no IWC definition forbidding the sale of meat and other whale products from those permitted to whale under the aboriginal subsistence category' with the only rule being 'that the meat should be consumed within the region from which it was taken' (Komatsu and Misaki, 2003, pp. 111–112).

The issue is important for various reasons. Many believe that several of the species of whales (such as bowhead whales and humpback whales) taken under the auspices of ASW are endangered – with about 10 000 individual bowheads alive in the Bering-Chukchi-Beaufort Seas region.[4] On the other hand, many perceive that the communities engaging in ASW and their traditional cultures are endangered. Both might be true and, in the face of such a clash of rights and interests, reason ought to prevail. However, instead the protagonists in the fraught arena of the International Whaling Commission (IWC) have used the issue to further their own interests and political agendas to such an extent that the issue has become one of the key ones that may yet determine the future course of the IWC. This paper recounts the aboriginal subsistence whaling controversy over the course of the last 30 years where politics, rather than science and compassion, have ruled the day.

6.2 THE UNITED STATES, ASW AND THE BOWHEAD WHALE IN THE 1970s

6.2.1 The Ban at IWC 29 in 1977

At the 1977 meeting of the IWC, aboriginal taking of highly endangered bowhead whales became a contentious issue. The growing prosperity of American Eskimos had led to increased catches as there was more use being made of rifles instead of hand held harpoons (Birnie, 1985, pp. 485–486).

In 1977, all, it seems, was politics and hypocrisy. In Day's words, the bowheads 'fell to an all-time population low – perhaps 2000 to 3000 – and conservationists called for a halt to the slaughter'; but the whaling nations 'now grasped with both hands the perfect opportunity to incapacitate the American conservation effort' and 'voted for a total banning of bowheads 15–0 with one US abstention, in the IWC Scientific Committee meeting' (Day, 1992, pp. 50–54). Japan and the other whalers, he explains, then 'began a horse-trading session with the Americans – sperm whale for bowheads'. The United States 'found itself unable to argue for a moratorium on whaling' – instead finding itself, 'against its own and IWC scientific advice, fighting primarily for the highest possible bowhead quota for the Eskimos' (Day, 1992, ibid.).

The Commission agreed to give protected status to the stock and not to allow any aboriginal quota (Birnie, 1985, pp. 485–486). This ban created an awkward domestic political problem for the US with regard to its obligations to protect the cultural rights and subsistence needs of the Eskimos. The US undertook to 'implement the IWC regulation when US national legislation problems were removed, and meanwhile promised to undertake an intensive investigation of the size of the stock' (Birnie, 1985, ibid.). In fact, what happened is that the US immediately commenced efforts to change the IWC's decision.

6.2.2 The Special Meeting 1977

A Special IWC Meeting was held in December 1977. At the meeting the US requested that the Commission reconsider the earlier decision to prohibit the taking of Bering Sea bowhead whales (IWC, 1977). The Commission then agreed to a Resolution which effectively overturned the earlier decision (IWC, 1977, Appendix 2). In 1976 the Eskimos had taken 48 whales, with 43 struck and lost, and in 1977 had taken 26 with 78 struck and lost (Day, 1992, pp. 50–54).

As will be seen, the US in 2002 made a significant concession to pro-whaling countries in order to recover a similarly lost quota (or right to take). It seems indisputable that similar negotiations behind closed doors preceded the Special Meeting in 1977. International diplomacy is seldom transparent. While it is unclear what concession the US made in 1977, it has been suggested that it was probably the abandonment of support by the US for a moratorium (Day, 1992, ibid.).

6.2.3 The Bowhead Issue in 1978

At IWC 30, 1978, the US, 'supported by intensive lobbying from Eskimo observers present' sought a higher quota for 1978–79 of 27–29 whales 'for Eskimo nutritional needs' – or 32 whales (which would mean 2 per cent of the known stock) 'if cultural needs were taken into account (Birnie, 1985, pp. 500–501). The very limited 1978 quota of 18 whales struck or 12 landed under the 1977 Resolution was said to 'have caused great hardship to Eskimos' with only ten being landed and another five being struck and lost (Birnie, 1985, ibid.).

The US's research programme 'determined that the bowhead population is close to 2300 whales, or almost twice the size of our best estimate of last year, and the estimate on which the Commission based its decision last year'. Based on its new population estimates, the US argued that '[t]he risks imposed on the whale population by permitting a modest hunt are small when compared with the countervailing risks to human populations if the hunt is not permitted' (IWC, 1978a). The US Commissioner also said, later and revealingly, that, at the time of his speaking, the Eskimo advisers to their delegation had returned home from London and had indicated that:

> in light of the vote yesterday, and what they assumed would happen today, they would not comply with what the IWC has done. I mention that because that means that we may have compliance problems of a significant nature. We may have a confrontation in the United States with native peoples. ... if the [lower] figure is accepted, I foresee non-compliance and blood on all of our hands and it may not only be the blood of Eskimos but the blood of more whales than we are talking about here today if the Eskimos do not comply (IWC, 1978b, p. 7).

More diplomacy followed and, after much debate on various US proposals, the Commission adopted (9:1, with seven abstentions) a proposal that 'in 1979 hunting shall cease when either 27 have been struck or 18 landed' (IWC, 1978a, p. 26). Finally, however, at the end of the meeting, the US asked for two more bowhead whales to be added to the 1978 catch limit. The Commission adopted this change, voting 10:1, with six abstentions (IWC, 1978a, ibid.)

As would eventually happen in 2002, other states took advantage of the US's internal difficulties. Birnie argues that it was to the advantage of whaling states to accede to the US's demands for an aboriginal quota; as the concession 'undermined the US's previous efforts to press a moratorium on the IWC' (Birnie, 1985, pp. 500–501). The problem, Birnie contends, 'persisted into future meetings and enabled the USSR, Japan and other commercial whaling states to bargain for higher quotas than might otherwise have been acceptable to the US and its supporters in the Commission' (Birnie, 1985, ibid.).

6.2.4 The Bowhead Issue in 1979

In February 1979, a special Panel Meeting of Experts was convened under the IWC's auspices to consider aboriginal/subsistence whaling – and to assist the IWC Technical Committee in formulating proposals for a regime to regulate aboriginal bowhead whale hunting in Alaska and, possibly, regimes for other aboriginal hunts (IWC, 1979a, p. 1). The Panel concluded that, ideally and in 'strictly biological terms', no Bering Sea bowhead whales should be hunted at all, as the current stock was 'a small percentage of its initial size in 1850'; that there were adequate replacements, such as gray whales, walruses, seals, polar bears, caribou, birds and fish, available in the area and that the Eskimo diet would not suffer from such replacement. The Panel concluded further, on the other hand, that such a change would have a significant effect on the culture of these whaling communities (IWC, 1979a, pp. 1–2). In this regard, the Panel concluded that, although cultures are 'dynamic and resilient', natural changes are of a very different nature to 'mandated change imposed from outside'; and that any attempt to regulate behaviour from outside should, therefore, 'involve the local communities to the fullest extent possible' to achieve as much acceptance as possible (IWC, 1979a, p. 2).

By IWC 31, 1979, the bowhead whale issue arose again with the US seeking an aboriginal quota even though the Scientific Committee (SC) had advised again that no quota be allowed (Birnie, 1985, pp. 505–506). In Birnie's opinion, 'the US's need to seek a bowhead quota for the Alaskan Eskimos in spite of the SC's advice that there should be zero quotas led to other political bargains enabling the US to secure approval for an Eskimo take of 18 (26 struck)' (Birnie, 1985, ibid.).

The US Commissioner argued vigorously that in his view 'a vote for a zero quota [would be] a vote against aboriginal peoples and a vote against the bowhead whales' – his argument being that he believed that 'more bowhead whales will be killed with a zero quota than they will with a reasonable quota' (IWC, 1979b, pp. 152–153). This statement was to have a significant echo at the intersessional meeting in October 2002; when the Commissioner for Russia argued that a vote against the bowhead quota, for which the US and Russia were arguing, would be a 'vote against people' (IWC, 2002b, p. 143).[5]

The US Commissioner then argued again that '[w]e have, in addition to an endangered species of whale, an endangered stock of whale, here, an endangered culture'; and that he thought that the quota proposal then under discussion [at the time 12 whales landed, or 18 struck] was 'not only bad for [E]skimos and will not [be] complied with, and my Government will not tell [E]skimos it is fair, but … also [that it would not be] good for the whales because of what will result' – he then proposed an 18 taken and 26 struck quota instead (IWC, 1979b, pp. 159–161). The South African Commissioner then suggested that this was 'in fact more a people problem than a whale problem' and expressed concern that they would in subsequent years 'always be facing the same problem' (IWC, 1979b, pp. 162–163). The 18 taken/26 struck quota proposal was successful (the vote being 12:4 in favour) (IWC, 1979b, p. 167).

It is interesting – and illuminating – to look at the events of 1978 and 1979 from the perspective of later IWC meetings. As will be seen, in 2002 the meeting in Shimonoseki and the extraordinary meeting in Cambridge saw similar machinations, which brought ostensible opponents together. Also, there were portents that the 2007 meeting in Anchorage, Alaska, might have seen similar events[6] – and the 2012 meeting, to be held in Panama, might yet see similar.

6.2.5 The Bowhead Issue Generally

Komatsu and Misaki write that '[t]he most glaring IWC double standard, ... is the stance of the [US], which enthusiastically encourages the Alaskan Inuit whaling of the endangered bowhead whale with a five-year quota (rather than a one-year quota with greater room for scientific review). Unfortunately, it promotes the Alaskan Inuit whaling while doing everything in its power to deny the Japanese Small Type Coastal Whaling (JSTCW)[7] bid for a small one-year quota for the prolific minke whale' (Komatsu and Misaki, 2003, p. 113).

'The IWC anti-whaling bloc', explain Komatsu and Misaki, 'while approving various aboriginal subsistence submissions, has for 14 consecutive years since 1988 successfully opposed a small-scale Japanese coastal whaling minke whale quota'. They point out that the merits of the Japanese case have been recognized through a resolution 'expeditiously [to] act to alleviate the distress of the JSTCW' adopted at the 1993 IWC meeting in Kyoto, Japan (Komatsu and Misaki, 2003, ibid.).

This creates a difficult conundrum for Japan. Even though the US's indigenous whaling is hypocritical in Japan's eyes, Japan must on principle support ASW.

Norway, at the IWC, once described the bowhead whale issue as 'a difficult and contentious issue' and said that '[t]here are elements in it which strike at the heart of the conscience of scientists, and there are elements in it which are of an important political nature' (IWC 34 'Report of the Plenary Sessions' 1982, p. 172).

6.2.6 The Bowhead Issue in the early 1980s

6.2.6.1 1980

At IWC 32, 1980, according to the US Commissioner, arguing again against a zero quota, the Alaskan aboriginal take was 'an historic take that has occurred over a 4000 year period'; 'for four thousand years', he continued, 'these Eskimos have been taking whales and now some people in this Commission would stop that tradition' (IWC, 1980a, p. 25). 'In sum', he concluded, 'a zero quota will result in the extinction of this culture. It will satisfy us in no way to allow for a minority in the [US] to [cease to] engage in a cultural practice which it has engaged in for four thousand years' [sic] (IWC, 1980a, ibid.).

Australia admitted to having a 'strong sympathy for the position of the Eskimos and their desire to retain their traditions and to make their own decisions about how best to manage bowheads'; but argued that '[i]n the past the Eskimo culture [had] proved to be sufficiently resilient' and that '[t]he greatest threat to the Eskimo culture is not a transitional period of restraint in harvesting bowheads' – rather, that the pressures of a modernising world provided a greater threat (IWC, 1980a, pp. 29–30).

Eventually, a proposal was adopted (16:3, with five abstentions) providing that, in the years 1981–1983, 45 whales might be landed and 65 struck, with no more than 17 being landed in any one year (IWC, 1980b, p. 18). It is extremely curious to note that the US was one of the abstainers; but, given the apparent extent of lobbying behind the scenes, it was presumably satisfied in advance as to what the result of the vote would be. In his submission during debate on the Chair's proposal, the US Commissioner had expressed satisfaction with the figure – saying that '[i]t is my hope that this figure, which the Commission believes is correct, is one which will allow [the Eskimo] culture to survive. It is my view that it will' (IWC, 1980a, p. 175).

6.2.6.2 1981

At IWC 33, 1981, although the SC continued to recommend a zero quota for the Bering Sea bowhead stock, the Commission, without debate, continued the three-year block quota that had been agreed to in 1980 unchanged. The US apparently reported on 'the Eskimos' excellent record of compliance with a new enforcement system which the Eskimos themselves operated and stated that improved data collection indicated a stable rather than a declining population' (Birnie, 1985, p. 611).

6.2.6.3 1982

It is, of course, not unexpected that the scientific data reported by the US was favourable to its position. A clear and unfortunate strand running through the entire history of the IWC has been the production by members of scientific evidence favourable to their positions.

Japan, at this meeting, argued against the practice followed by the US of bringing representatives of the Eskimos into management, decision making and enforcement procedures; which practice Japan called effectively allowing third parties to amend the Schedule (Birnie, 1985, p. 619). Ironically, again, Japan has in more recent times brought extensive delegations to IWC meetings – including representatives from its whaling communities;[8] of course, it is unknown to what extent these representatives have influenced Japanese decision-making.

6.2.6.4 1983

The controversy continued at each successive meeting. Birnie writes that 'at IWC 35, 1983, the US three year block quota had reached an end; and that the 'SC had adopted an estimate of about 4000 whales for this stock, which therefore should be classified as Protected Stocks, with a zero catch limit' (Birnie, 1985, p. 611). The US argued in favour of a limit of 35, 'based on the needs of aborigines and conservation'. 'After many proposals and counter-proposals failed', says Birnie, 'a compromise' of a two year quota of 43 strikes for 1984 and 1985 'was agreed by consensus' (Birnie, 1985, ibid.).

6.2.7 The Bowhead Issue in the 1990s

The late 1980s and the 1990s were very quiet on the bowhead whale issue. By the time of IWC 46, in 1994, it was reported that the Bering-Chukchi-Beaufort

Seas stock of bowhead whales had been 'increasing under a regime of catches of some 15–50 animals since 1978' (IWC, 1994, p. 21).

The US asked that the total landed in the four years 1995–1998 not exceed 204, with up to 68 strikes in 1995, 67 in 1996, 66 in 1997 and 65 in 1998. Several countries expressed the desire for a more cautious approach, especially as no limit was placed on the number of whales that could be carried forward from any season, but the proposal was carried unanimously (IWC, 1994, pp. 22–23). It appears that the US has, while asking for annual quotas, adopted a policy of proposing (as compromise) totals spread over several years – initially over three years; then over four; and, as will be seen, eventually (and currently) over five.

At IWC 49 in 1997, the Russian Federation asked for an aboriginal subsistence quota of five bowhead whales from the Bering-Chukchi-Beaufort Seas stock. The US asked for a quota for its Alaskan people of 67 strikes per year, for five years – but this would be a joint US-Russian proposal (IWC, 1997, p. 27). The take of bowhead whales by the Russian Federation does not appear to be of great numerical significance. At IWC 52 in 2000, for instance, it was reported that in 1999 '48 whales had been struck, with 43 landed' from the Bering-Chukchi-Beaufort Seas stock of bowhead whales. These figures 'included one whale struck and landed by the Russian Federation' (IWC, 2000, p. 20). The Russian Federation takes far more gray whales, though.[9]

6.3 THE UNITED STATES, ASW AND THE BOWHEAD WHALE IN THE 21st CENTURY

6.3.1 IWC 54, 2002, Shimonoseki

At IWC 54 in 2002, in Shimonoseki events took a dramatic turn with respect to aboriginal subsistence whaling.

On the Bering-Chukchi-Beaufort Seas stock of Bowhead whales, it was reported by the Scientific Committee that a 'total of 75 whales was struck during the 2001 harvest and 49 (30 male and 19 female) were landed'. The low figures landed were accounted to difficult ice conditions. Off Chukotka, one female was reported to have been harvested in 2001. The SC then advised that the stock appears to be larger than at any time in the last century, and to be increasing. The Committee gave the same advice as in 2001; that it was 'very likely' that an annual catch limit of not more than 102 whales 'would be consistent with the requirements of the Schedule' (IWC, 2002a, pp. 12–15).

The US requested renewal of its ASW quota of bowhead whales, as before. In other words, the US asked for 280 whales landed, over a five-year period, with an annual strike limit of 67 and a carryover of up to 15 strikes in each year – this quota being 'shared between the Alaskan Eskimos and the Chukotka Communities in Russia'. The Russian Federation requested five landed whales per year over the five-year period (IWC, 2002a, pp. 15–16). Japan then 'commended the success of the 2001 stock abundance estimate' and noted that 'although dozens of whales had been harvested' the stock had been proved to be increasing; and that this demonstrated that 'whale resources can be used sustainably' (IWC, 2002a, p. 16).

When the US put forward its proposal for a five-year quota, Japan 'remarked that the US recognises the needs of its Alaskan Eskimos and asked whether the US could understand that the Japanese small-type coastal whalers also have needs'. Japan then remarked that it considered the bowhead stock 'to be in a very dangerous situation'; and suggested that it was not in favour of approving a five-year period quota. The US responded that it did not consider the stock to be 'in a dangerous situation' as the most recent census had given the largest ever abundance estimate (IWC, 2002a, p. 19).

After argument, the US/Russian proposed Schedule amendment was put to a vote, which ran 30:14, with one abstention; the votes in favour being short of the required 75 per cent majority. Of the countries which had voted against the proposal; Antigua and Barbuda said that it supported the right of aboriginal peoples to utilise whale resources, but that it objected to 'the discriminatory approach' of the IWC 'regarding which countries are allowed to take whales and which are not'. Mongolia, likewise, explained that it had 'voted against the double standards employed within' the IWC. St Vincent and the Grenadines argued that 'for consensus to be reached, there is a need to ensure equality of treatment'; in particular, that if a five-year block were accepted for one it should be accepted for all. The Solomon Islands spoke also of double standards, arguing that the treatment of the Japanese coastal people, and of St Vincent and the Grenadines, was unfair. St Lucia 'called for the equitable distribution of resources' (IWC, 2002a, p. 20).

A number of countries, such as Denmark, Oman, the Netherlands and New Zealand, then expressed regret as to the outcome of the vote; and as to the alleged broken agreement. New Zealand 'recalled' that this was the first time 'for many years' that an aboriginal subsistence whaling request 'had been denied'. South Africa's Commissioner 'considered' that the 'only rationale for voting against the proposal' could be that a country either 'did not understand the issue'; or that it was 'willing to sacrifice aboriginal peoples' needs for political gain' (IWC, 2002a, ibid.). The Russian Federation stated that it 'considered' that those countries which had made accusations about double standards 'were themselves guilty of applying double standards' on this issue. The US said that it was disappointed that 'some Contracting Governments' had opposed the Schedule amendment 'because of their dissatisfaction with the US's position on other issues'. Further discussions were then again postponed after the US requested another private Commissioners' meeting (IWC, 2002a, pp. 20–21).

On the third day of discussions on the issue, the US and the Russian Federation submitted a 'slightly revised' proposed Schedule amendment; but Japan considered this identical to the earlier proposal, and continued to refuse to support it. Instead, Japan proposed an amendment which would include the addition of a new paragraph permitting the taking of 25 Okhotsk Sea-West Pacific minke whales, in each of the five years under discussion, for Japan's four coastal communities. The Chair ruled that this amendment could not be done; which ruling was put to a vote and upheld (IWC, 2002a, p. 21). Antigua and Barbuda argued that Japan had been treated unfairly; as its 'coastal whaling could be classified as an aboriginal take'; Japan itself 'regretted' that its proposed amendment had not been accepted, and indicated that it could 'not support a five-year block quota over concern for the status of the bowhead stock', although a quota for one to two years 'would have been acceptable' to it. Japan indicated that it would 'now be forced to vote against' the amendment proposed by the US and the Russian Federation (IWC, 2002a, ibid.).

Japan's proposed amendment attempted to link the issues of bowhead and minke takes: a transparent political 'logrolling' manoeuvre. Obviously, the logical flaw in Japan's argument (as seen in its proposed amendment) is that Japan's purported concern for the bowhead whale stock status could hardly have been allayed by Japan's being granted a take of 25 minke whales from the West Pacific.

The US/Russian proposed Schedule amendment was then put to a vote; at which it received 32 votes in favour, 11 against and two abstentions. The amendment therefore did not receive the necessary 75 per cent, and failed. The Russian Federation then 'noted that the political games that had been played had made people forget the aboriginal peoples and their needs' (IWC, 2002a, pp. 21–22). This criticism is trenchant; however, the charge remains open that the Japanese coastal communities are victims of similar 'political games' and that the Russian Federation, and others, are guilty of hypocrisy. Mongolia, Dominica and Antigua and Barbuda had voted against the US/Russian proposal; but all took the opportunity afterwards to explain that it was not aboriginal whaling *per se* that they had voted against. Of the countries that had voted with the US and the Russian Federation, St Vincent and the Grenadines suggested that it supported both the US/Russian request and the Japanese coastal whaling request; and urged the IWC to find a 'way to grant both requests'. New Zealand argued that Japan was attempting to draw 'a moral equivalence between prosperous Japanese coastal towns and isolated Arctic communities'; a link which New Zealand argued does not exist. Denmark stressed the 'need to respect the traditional and subsistence needs' of the high Arctic people. The UK described as 'cant and hypocrisy' the conduct of those who had voted against the US/Russian proposal; and 'wondered what honour was left in the organisation'. Mexico argued that the debate had had 'nothing to do with the purpose and origins of aboriginal whaling and everything to do with politics' (IWC, 2002a, p. 22).

Something of the desperation of the US delegation after losing the vote, certainly in its allies' eyes at least, can perhaps be seen in the fact that, later, when St Vincent and the Grenadines proposed a Schedule amendment to permit it to take up to 20 humpback whales in the 'five seasons 2002/2003 through 2006/2007', the UK 'proposed to add a further amendment by including the joint US/Russian Federation request for a bowhead quota'. The US, however, indicated that it 'very much appreciated the thoughtfulness of the UK' but declined the offer (IWC, 2002a, p. 24).

Japan later in the meeting proposed again, as it had for many years, that the Schedule be amended so that 50 minke whales could be taken for its coastal communities. Japan explained that the moratorium had, in the 15 years it had been in place, 'disrupted the local marine ecosystem' in that minke whales had so increased numerically that they are currently 'depleting fishery resources' and so causing 'significant declines in the catches of local small-scale fishermen' – and thereby 'inflicting severe damage to the economy, culture and tradition of whaling communities'. The communities' cultures, said Japan, were suffering badly as a consequence of poverty and emigration (IWC, 2002a, p. 36). The Russian Federation, presumably with an eye to what had transpired earlier at the meeting, supported Japan's request (IWC, 2002a, ibid.). The vote on Japan's proposal was lost 20:21, with three abstentions, and so was not adopted (IWC, 2002a, p. 37). After the earlier events of the meeting, Japan could hardly have had any realistic hope that its proposal would be approved; but clearly felt that it ought at least to make the point of calling for a vote.

6.3.2 Reactions to the 2002 Meeting

Ultimately, then, it can be said that in the early twenty-first century, indigenous whaling quotas were a battleground in themselves. The 'scientific basis' for Japan's opposition to the US/Russian proposal was the suggestion that quotas be revised annually instead of in five-year periods. The political basis for the rejection appears to have been Japan's insistence that anti-whaling countries were guilty of 'double-standards' in rejecting Japan's coastal whaling, whilst supporting quotas for bowhead whales.

Although Japan, according to Komatsu, 'gave support, as it did previously, to the needs of aboriginal subsistence whaling as a matter of principle, it asserted that the quota should be requested on a year-to-year basis in view of the current fragile and unknown state of the bowhead population'.[10]

This does appear at first glance to have been very clever of the Japanese delegation in that it cunningly outmanoeuvred the US; and, by forcing the US later that year to call another meeting, exposed US hypocrisy. By, firstly, proposing a compromise amended proposal which would have given Japan a quota for itself and, second, not voting against the US/Russian quota at the second meeting, however, Japan also exposed its own hypocrisy. Neither side comes out of the episode with much credit (or credibility) at all.

Politics and hypocrisy were in abundance. Burns and Wandesforde-Smith comment that '[t]he bickering [in the IWC] even reached new heights in Shimonoseki when, for the first time ever in the 56-year history of the Commission, votes were forced on the renewal of catch limits for aboriginal subsistence whaling' (Burns and Wandesforde-Smith, 2002, p. 199).[11] 'Despite an effort by Japan's Fisheries Agency to put a good face on it', they write, 'Japan's defeat of a new quota for bowhead whales to be taken by Russian and American indigenous peoples in the Arctic was more widely seen as political retribution for earlier and arguably embarrassing failures of the IWC at Shimonoseki to advance Japan's agenda' (Burns and Wandesforde-Smith, 2002, ibid.).

6.4 THE 2002 SPECIAL MEETING

6.4.1 The 5th Special Meeting of the IWC, 2002

The 5th Special Meeting was held on 14 October 2002, in Cambridge. The Meeting was held at the request of the US and the Russian Federation, in order to repeat their request for a Schedule amendment to allow for the granting of an aboriginal subsistence take of bowhead whales from the Bering-Chukchi-Beaufort Seas stock (IWC, 2002b, pp. 139–140).

The Agenda for the Special Meeting saw consideration both of a proposed Schedule amendment in respect of the aboriginal subsistence hunt in the Bering-Chukchi-Beaufort bowhead whale stock; and of a proposal on Japanese coastal whaling. In an Introductory Statement, the Commissioner for the Russian Federation put the position in emotional terms; arguing that in order to save time the 'meeting should not discuss the USA-Russian proposal but accept it on the basis of consensus, and that distinguished members of delegations take the floor only if they do not agree to the possibility of a consensus on the question of whether people should eat or starve' (IWC, 2002b, p. 143).[12]

The Russian Commissioner advised also that in September 2002 a Japanese delegation had visited Chukotka; and that this delegation had seen for itself that 'there are no fruit growing in the north of my country' and that 'the whaling season is going to start in the Spring so the peoples of Chukotka cannot wait for the [June 2003] session' of the IWC (IWC, 2002b, ibid.).

The Russian Federation and the US then proposed that a five-year quota of up to 280 for bowhead whales from the Bering-Chukchi-Beaufort Seas stock be approved, until and including the year 2007; with up to 67 strikes each year, except that up to 15 strikes might be carried over each year. The proposal also suggested that the provision be reviewed annually by the Commission, in light of advice from the Scientific Committee (IWC, 2002b, ibid.).

In debate, Japan indicated that it 'recognised the commitment of the US to review the provision on an annual basis and to abide by the advice of the Scientific Committee'; these features being what distinguished the proposal from the proposal at IWC 54 in Shimonoseki. Japan indicated that while it appreciated the US's response, it did not feel that all of the questions Japan had raised at Shimonoseki had been addressed; nevertheless, Japan, although not able to join the proposed amendment, would not block consensus on the amendment (IWC, 2002b, ibid.). Norway also indicated that it would 'support the consensus adoption of the proposed Schedule amendment'; while recalling its stance that 'the Convention does not recognise the concept of aboriginal subsistence whaling' and that Norway considers the Commission's practice of 'distinguishing between commercial and subsistence whaling' to be 'artificial, illogical and morally wrong' (IWC, 2002b, p. 144).

After some debate and amendment, the proposed Schedule amendment was adopted by consensus (IWC, 2002b, ibid.).

6.4.2 Japan's Proposed Resolution

Japan then put forward a draft Resolution requesting an interim relief allocation of 50 minke whales for its four community-based whaling communities; which request, according to Japan, 'had been denied for the last 15 years'. The draft Resolution contained the following:

> ... THE COMMISSION: REAFFIRMS the Commission's commitment to work expeditiously to alleviate the distress caused by the cessation of minke whaling to the communities of Taiji, Wada, Ayukawa and Abashiri and AGREES that the most effective way of doing so would be to establish as soon as possible an appropriate catch quota for minke whales consistent with paragraph 10(e) of the Schedule; ... DECIDES that the establishment of an appropriate catch quota for minke whales for the four community-based whaling communities should be based on scientific advice of the Scientific Committee that such quota is sustainable; and FURTHER DECIDES that an appropriate amendment to the Schedule and an Action Plan to establish an appropriate catch quota of minke whales exclusively for the communities of Taiji, Wada, Ayukawa and Abashiri be considered at the 55th Annual Meeting of the [IWC]. (IWC, 2002c) Document SPEC.02/4 2002.

The draft Resolution would clearly not, by itself, have seen the allocation of a minke whale quota to the four Japanese communities – but as a symbolic step towards such allocation it would have had huge importance.

Japan then advised that it 'considered that it had made a big effort to break the impasse on this issue', noted the delicate balance within which the work had been done, and requested that the Resolution be adopted by consensus (IWC, 2002b, p. 144). In a major turnaround, the parties which supported the Resolution included the US. The US advised that it 'was able' to support the Resolution as two of its major concerns had been addressed; that Japan satisfy the provisions of paragraph 10(e) of the Schedule,[13] and that the Scientific Committee must advise that the 'catch from this stock of minke whales is sustainable' (the latter being a sub-paragraph added to Japan's draft Resolution for the first time). The US then advised that it considered Japan's draft Resolution to show 'a marked change and a positive movement towards presenting a proposal acceptable to a broad range of the Commission' (IWC, 2002b, pp.144–145). One must be somewhat cynical, of course. While countries continue to phrase their comments to seem consistent, it was very clear that deals had been concluded behind the scenes.

On being put to the vote, the Resolution failed 16:19, with two abstentions (IWC, 2002b, p. 145).[14] Certainly the most interesting aspect of this vote is that the US voted in favour; after more than a decade of opposition to such proposals. The observer is entitled, at least, to raise an eyebrow.

6.5 MORE RECENT MEETINGS

6.5.1 IWC 55, 2003

At IWC 55 in 2003, there was little debate on the issue of aboriginal subsistence whaling. It was reported by the Scientific Committee, in regard to the Bering-Chukchi-Beaufort Seas stock of bowhead whales, that it had received 'a new population estimate for 2001 of around 10 000 whales and a rate increase of 3.4% for the period 1978–2001'; and that there was, therefore, 'no reason to change its previous management advice' (IWC, 2003, p. 13). Commenting on the bowhead issue, Japan and Norway, however, called again for 'consistency in methods for both commercial and aboriginal subsistence whaling' (IWC, 2003, p. 14).

Japan, however, noted that, in the 16 years since the moratorium on commercial whaling, it had continually requested 'an interim relief allocation of 50 minke whales' for its four coastal communities. According to Japan, 'whale abundance has increased, while its coastal fisheries have become impoverished, leading to considerable discontent among fishermen over the competition between fisheries and whales'. Japan now suggested that it had decided to change its approach. Its new approach would be to promote 'community-based whaling'; with all edible parts of each whale to be used as food, and a substantive part of this to be distributed primarily among the four local communities and neighbouring areas – including the area of Kushiro, where a 'land station' would be built. This approach would, Japan argued, promote local industries, stimulate distribution of whale products and tourism, and 'reinstate traditional products associated with sales of whale meat and revitalize traditional festivals and rituals of the regions' (IWC, 2003, pp. 27–28).

In the ensuing debate, the US said that it considered the proposal to be 'for commercial whaling'. Generally, parties followed their usual positions on the issue; but the Russian Federation supported the proposal as having a 'sound scientific basis'; and because it 'complied' with principles of sustainable use, while acknowledging the 'traditional needs of the community' (IWC, 2003, ibid.). It is interesting that the Russian Federation continued to support the proposal, in the spirit of the Special (intersessional) meeting of October 2002; but that the US reverted to its longstanding position that Japanese coastal whaling could not be seen as aboriginal subsistence whaling (IWC, 2003, ibid.). On being voted on, the proposed Schedule amendment failed 19:26, with one abstention (IWC, 2003, p. 29).

6.5.2 IWC 56, 2004

In its written Opening Statement at IWC 56 in 2004, Japan appealed for 'support for our proposals for the sustainable utilization of abundant minke and Bryde's whales with scientifically calculated harvest limits and an adequate enforcement and monitoring scheme' (IWC, 2004a).

It was agreed that there would be no change to the current bowhead block quota for 2003–2007. The US and the Russian Federation commented on planned co-operative research – so that when the bowhead quota would next be reviewed, in 2007, management of the stock would be based upon the best science available at that time (IWC, 2004b, pp. 21–22).

6.5.3 Double Standards

Japan 'expressed appreciation for the active discussion in the Scientific Committee' and explained that it believed that 'the results from work on this stock should be reflected in management advice from this year onwards'. As it had the previous year, it noted what it believed to be 'double standards in the approach to management of the bowhead stock [and the stock of] western North Pacific minke whales'; and Japan then called for 'consistency in approach' (IWC, 2004b, p.24).

At IWC 55, a small group (Australia, Denmark, Russia, the US, and the Secretariat) had been charged with the review of Schedule paragraph 13, which provides for aboriginal subsistence whaling catch limits, to determine consistency. The group agreed that the words 'when the meat and products of such whales are to be used exclusively for local consumption' mean that some transactions beyond the aboriginal whaling communities under the current Schedule language are acceptable (IWC, 2004b, pp. 24–28). It was agreed by the Small Group that aboriginal communities in Chukotka have equal rights to other aboriginal communities that have Aboriginal Subsistence Whaling quotas to use the meat and products of these whale species. The Russian Federation then proposed an amendment – the effect of which would essentially be to allow the striking/taking of bowhead/gray whales accompanied by calves. The Commission eventually adopted both the report of the Small Group and the revised proposed Schedule amendment by consensus (IWC, 2004b, ibid.).

6.5.4 IWC 57, 2005

At IWC 57 in 2005, the Commission agreed that no changes were needed to ASW catch limits presently in force (IWC, 2005, p. 2).[15]

6.5.5 The Un*tied* States

The United States did not manage to put its aboriginal whaling issue to bed for good in the late 1970s and early 1980s. Not only was great damage done at the time to the country's reputation, but the controversy flared repeatedly. Friedheim argues, for instance, that the US is 'seriously pressured from both sides of the issue. It has within its voting public large lobbying organizations with a commitment to end whaling and a pro-whaling community and state delegation (Alaska) that insists that the United States accommodate their needs' (Friedheim, 2001, p. 225). Unfortunately, he explains, the US 'has a long record of establishing a principle and then either seeking exceptions to the principle for itself and its citizens or ignoring the substance of the principle when it does not suit it' (Friedheim, 2001, ibid.). This contention certainly appears to be borne out by the American experience of aboriginal subsistence whaling – *vide* the events of 1977 and 2002, in particular.

6.5.6 The Future

In international law, Japan would appear to have a reasonable case for the resumption of coastal whaling. The issue has not been discussed in detail in this chapter, which focuses on the politics surrounding the US bowhead whale quota. Increasingly, the distinction appears an artificial one designed to suit the interests of the anti-whaling bloc. On the other hand, accusations have been (and will doubtless continue to be) made that Japan is being disingenuous in seeking to equate its coastal whaling proposals with aboriginal whaling – the former having a profit motive, the latter being based on subsistence only. Further, it needs to be pointed out strongly that the communities for which Japan is claiming an 'interim relief allocation' continue to take considerable numbers of cetaceans annually – using species which are not managed by the IWC, such as Baird's beaked whale and Dall's porpoise.[16] It was therefore to be expected that, with the US/Russian Federation aboriginal subsistence whaling quota expiring, aboriginal whaling would be the issue that dominated the 2007 Meeting, in Alaska – IWC 59.

6.6 IWC 59, 2007

6.6.1 IWC 59 – Day 1

IWC 59 opened with a new temporary logo – in the shape of a bowhead whale, rather than the usual sperm whale figure of the IWC. The opening ceremonies included several pleas for recognition of aboriginal cultural whaling by persons such as Alberta Stephan, an elder of the Native Village of Eklutna; Sarah Palin, Governor of Alaska; and Ted Stevens, the US Senator for Alaska. After the opening ceremonies, which involved displays by dance groups from Barrow in Alaska, Chukotka in the Russian Federation and the Makah Tribe in Washington State, the Commission began by considering the Scientific Committee's report on the status of various stocks of large whales. The Commission was chaired by Dr William Hogarth of the US.[17]

It seemed to the present writer, observing,[18] that by putting so much emphasis on the importance to the US of obtaining its bowhead whale quota, the US and the other states in the Like-minded Group[19] were possibly playing into Japan's hands. From private conversations and preparatory negotiations attended, the writer gained the impression that there was no 'back room' deal between the US and Japan, despite the suggestions of 'assurances given'; and that the US was genuinely worried about the possibility of the bowhead quota being blocked.

6.6.2 IWC 59 – Day 2

On the second day, the Commission began considering the issue of ASW; first considering the report of its Sub-Committee on Aboriginal Subsistence Whaling. Taking into account the advice of the Scientific Committee, the

Commission then agreed on five-year renewal periods, as the usual term in recent years, for bowhead whales from the Bering-Chukchi-Beaufort Seas stock – to be taken by the indigenous peoples of Alaska and Chukotka; for Eastern North Pacific gray whales – to be taken by the indigenous Chukotkan people. The numbers decided upon were 280 bowhead whales for the period 2008–2012 (with no more than 67 whales to be struck in any one year, and up to 15 unused strikes to be carried over each year); 620 gray whales for the same period, with a maximum of 140 in any one year.[20] The catch limits for the Alaskan and Chukotkan peoples therefore remained the same as for the period 2002–2007.[21]

In debate before the decision, the US based its plea for a bowhead quota on the Scientific Committee report, and on the contention that the 'uncertainties' of 2002 have 'been dealt with'. Most countries which spoke did so in support of the granting of the quota. India did suggest that a programme to reduce aboriginal dependence on this food source was needed. Morocco and Benin, with support from Senegal, both asserted that all aboriginal subsistence whaling should be dealt with globally; and St Vincent and the Grenadines offered its support – 'as for all aboriginal subsistence whaling'.[22] Japan then stated that its policy on whaling 'is well-known – science-based and on sustainable utilisation'. Japan 'congratulated' the 'American, Japanese, Norwegian and other scientists in the Scientific Committee'. 'Based on our own policy', said Japan, 'and on the spirit of consensus' it would support the proposal; but then added the loaded remark that '[we] only ask that [the] same criteria be applied to our coastal whaling later'.[23] Iceland stated that it was 'happy' to note the 'general support for sustainable whaling'; and added, with heavy sarcasm, that it 'will be interesting to see if we'll have similar support later – or several u-turns'.[24]

The proposal was adopted by consensus – to much applause, and a feeling of palpable relief among the countries comprising the Like-minded Group. However, to this writer it seemed as though Japan had – despite apparently promising behind the scenes not to link the bowhead quota with other issues – created just such linkage very cleverly. It also seemed to this writer that, at this stage of the meeting, the Chair – who was receiving praise for the amiable tone of the meeting – was in fact handling matters fairly weakly. It was Japan's unexpected acquiescence and conciliatory tone, and the Like-minded Group's nervous anticipation of Japanese filibustering, that allowed the meeting to proceed in good spirit.

The Russian Federation then put forward its request for a quota of gray whales for its Chukotkan people; explaining that its people needed their traditional nutrition source, especially as a new problem has arisen in the last ten years – 'stinky' (or inedible) whales.[25] The US then joined Russia in the request; advising that its Makah people want 620 gray whales over a five-year period – up to 140 in each year. Japan expressed its support; suggesting that it supported 'science-based management' and that it wished the Makah good luck[26] – the Makah having taken only one whale since 1999.[27] The proposal was then adopted by consensus.

6.6.3 IWC 59 – Day 3

The third day saw the Commission consider matters related to socio-economic implications and small-type whaling; with Japan, as it had done in previous years, giving a presentation on the hardship allegedly being suffered by its four community-based whaling communities (Abashiri, Ayukawa, Taiji and Wadaura). Japan put forward a proposal that would allow a catch by these communities.[28] After some discussion, however, it was clear that there was no consensus; and the item was therefore left open.[29] In discussion, Japan's representative, Alternate Commissioner Joji Morishita, pointed out that Japan had now for 20 years been requesting assistance for its four coastal whaling communities. He described the 'history of small-type whaling' as being a 'history of broken promises'.[30] Morishita then recalled that the Commission adopted Resolutions on coastal whaling in 1993, 1995, 1996, 2000, 2001, and 2004 – all of which 'recognised the needs of the four communities and the effect of the moratorium' – but, sarcastically, suggested that in the IWC the word 'expeditiously' clearly 'has no meaning'. He referred again to a 'long, long history of broken promises'. He referred to 'commerciality' as one of the reasons given for distinguishing between small-type coastal whaling and aboriginal subsistence whaling; but pointed out that 'all activities are commercial' and that 'it doesn't make sense' that Alaskan whalers could sell products from bowhead whales. He agreed that Alaskan whaling 'should be fully supported'; but that 'we should be treated the same'. He explained that Japan was not asking for a lifting of the moratorium, nor for a specific number of whales (as they were willing to negotiate on the number); that Japan was willing to accept observers, and to 'put VMS ('vessel monitoring system') on the small vessels'. 'I kept my promises', he said, 'and supported all aboriginal subsistence whaling proposals' – as 'respect for culture and way of life'.[31] Bringing his speech toward a conclusion, Morishita said that, if the Japanese proposal was not supported, it would be 'sending a very bad message to us'; and that 'we are approaching in a spirit of compromise and willingness to talk'. 'But', he said, 'we have been waiting twenty years'; and that while Japan has 'some hope for the normalisation process' without seeing 'some tangible progress, we will have to think of alternatives'.[32]

Japan eventually withdrew the proposal before it was voted on, when it was clear that it could not be adopted by consensus.

6.7 IWC 60, 61 AND 62 AND OTHER MOVEMENTS IN 2008, 2009 AND 2010

Arising from commitments made by the Chair at IWC 59 in 2007 to continue to seek to reform the IWC, an intersessional meeting was held in London in March 2008. This meeting focused on procedural issues and on ways that negotiation might be improved within the IWC.

The IWC held its 60th annual meeting in Santiago, Chile in the last week of June 2008. The Meeting appears to have been relatively quiet, and to have reflected largely – as in 2007 – Japanese and American efforts to move toward some form of compromise. As a reflection of this Japan stated that it would not request a vote on its proposal to relieve the 'hardship suffered by' its four community-based coastal whaling communities – Japan suggesting that it would not ask for a vote 'because of the progress it saw in the discussions related to the future of the IWC'. The Chair (the US Commissioner) then 'thanked Japan for its cooperative attitude'.[33]

On other aboriginal subsistence whaling (ASW), the main issue was a proposal put forward by Denmark, on behalf of Greenland, for an annual strike limit of 10 humpback whales from 2008–2012. The Commission was divided on the issue of whether Denmark had satisfactorily documented Greenland's need for the quota. The proposal was eventually rejected (29:36, with 2 abstentions) when put to a vote.[34]

Probably the most significant result to emerge from IWC 60 was merely an agreement by all countries to continue with negotiations. In consequence, a task team of approximately 25 countries, including all of the major players, met in September 2008 in Tampa Bay, Florida, to consider steps toward a 'package deal' that might go so far as to include a limited resumption of whaling, perhaps by recognising JSTCW as having at least certain essential elements of ASW, and the bringing of small cetaceans under IWC control.[35] The Small Working Group (SWG) met in December 2008, in Cambridge, and produced a report which was presented to an intersessional meeting of the IWC held in Rome in March 2009. It is worth noting that in this report ASW does not feature as a significant issue. However, it remained 'present' as JSTCW was identified as one of three issues which the Chair of the SWG (Alvaro de Soto, of Peru) remarked on as being particularly difficult to resolve – the other two being 'special permit whaling' and 'sanctuaries'.[36] The Rome intersessional meeting itself, Chaired by the IWC Chair, instructed the SWG to continue with its work but did not make any specific recommendations.[37]

The IWC held its 61st annual meeting in Madeira, Portugal in late June 2009. A Resolution was put forward by the Chair proposing that the mandate of the SWG be extended and that 'the efforts underway should be continued for a further year and decisions taken at IWC 62'.[38] Once again, there was a proposal from Denmark that Greenland be given an ASW quota for 10 humpback whales. Data was presented from the Scientific Committee (SC) which showed that the proposed take would 'not harm the stock'. However, discussion focused on whether Greenland had adequately demonstrated its need to take these whales[39] – and the Commission eventually decided to leave the matter open beyond the meeting.[40]

In December 2009 a small Support Group to the Chair, comprising officials from 12 countries, met in Seattle in the United States. The new Chair of the IWC, Cristian Maquieira of Chile, issued a statement confirming that discussions on the future of the IWC would continue preparatory to the 62nd annual meeting, to be held in Morocco in June 2010.[41]

At IWC 62 in 2010 the US, together with Denmark, put forward a proposal which would 'remove the uncertainty' inherent in its having to renew its ASW quota every five years – but withdrew this, apparently after consultation had shown that the required support was lacking (IWC, 2010a, 'Chair's Report', p. 10). The draft proposal included a bowhead whale quota of 67 whales per year for the years 2011 to 2017, inclusive, and would have replaced ('superseded', in the language of the draft proposal) existing ASW quotas (IWC, 2010b, IWC/62/26, pp. 1 and 4). Also of interest is that the draft proposal used the term 'indigenous subsistence whaling', with which it proposed replacing the term 'aboriginal subsistence whaling' – the two terms, however, to have the same meaning (IWC, 2010b, IWC/62/26, p. 1). What this shows is that the US is once again looking to increase the time period of each renewal of its ASW quota – perhaps in the hope of effectively removing the item from the debate. One must anticipate that this proposal will resurface in years to come – in announcing its withdrawal of the proposal, the US stated that it 'remained concerned how the Commission would deal with this important issue in the future' (IWC, 2010a, ibid., p. 10).

Also in 2010, Denmark (for Greenland) again put forward a proposed Schedule amendment to allow the taking of an annual 10 humpback whales over a three-year period (2010–2012). The proposal was particularly strongly made, with Greenland's Minister of Fisheries, Hunting and Agriculture (Ane Hansen) warning that 'if the IWC could not differentiate between domestic politics and the objectives and purpose of the Convention then Greenland would question the relevancy of its continued membership of the organisation'(IWC, 2010a, 'Chair's Report', p. 18). After extensive debate, and the consideration of several revised proposals, a revised proposal was adopted (by consensus) allowing Greenland a new quota of nine humpback whales per year over the three-year period; together with a continuing quota of two bowhead whales, 10 fin whales (reduced from 19), and 178 minke whales (reduced from 200) (IWC, 2010a, ibid., pp. 17–20). The significance should not be under-recognised of this proposal being successful after having been unsuccessful in previous years – it was not a victory easily won. There is an emotional value to the adding of a new species of whale to the list of those which can be taken, and the humpback is one of the best-known of all species. At IWC 59, for instance, the Australian Commissioner argued (in opposition to a similar proposal) that the humpback whale is of particular significance to Australian people.[42] What the decision arguably testifies to is the growing strength of combined cultural and scientific arguments – Denmark having presented firm evidence that the species was not likely to be endangered by the quota.

Agreement has for so long been so rare in the IWC that for the 'warring factions' to reach consensus on an issue with emotional overtones must be of further significance – especially at a time of significant efforts to reach a compromise.

In the event, while the possibility of a 'package deal' being agreed to on essential issues had been anticipated in the lead-up to IWC 62, no dramatic compromise occurred. After extensive discussion, no consensus could be found; and the Chair (Vice-Chair Anthony Liverpool, from Antigua and Barbuda, acting as Chair) identified a 'need for a period of reflection' as being a theme which had arisen from the discussions (IWC, 2010a, p. 10). The Chair then put forward certain suggestions as to how such 'period of reflection' might be used, but this remained merely a personal suggestion and not an adopted agreement (IWC, 2010a, ibid.). There the matter rested, with discussions to resume at IWC 63 in 2011.

At IWC 63, held in Jersey, UK, the ASW issue was an undertone to the meeting.[43] While quotas and strike limits were reviewed, no changes were made to any of the limits in place.[44] However, with a view to the five-year quota revision due for IWC 64 in 2012, the Commission did agree to establish a small working group to consider unresolved issues during the ensuing year and report back in 2012.[45] On the JSTCW issue, Japan noted that 'in a spirit of co-operation' it had not sought a vote on this issue during the period of discussions on the future of the IWC; that although 'disappointed at the outcome of those discussions' in 2010, it did recognize that the process had engendered an 'improved atmosphere of discussions'; and that, consequently, it would again not seek a vote.[46]

There the matter rested – at least on the surface. However, it is important to note that the ASW issue remains a crucial one below the surface; both because it provides fuel for political manoeuvring, and because, on the other hand, it provides one of the few issues on which opposed parties are sometimes able to find agreement. Whether there will continue, in 2012, to be relative calm and continued efforts to seek consensus is as yet unknown. If not, then the ASW and JSTCW issues are likely to become contentious once again. Ultimately, both are issues which are going to need to be settled definitively.

6.8 CONCLUSION: HORSE-TRADING IN PEOPLE AND WHALES

While the last few meetings of the IWC have not been as dramatic as were the events of 2002, there have been subtle political ramifications in respect of ASW that may ultimately prove to be of great significance. One possible solution to the current impasse within the IWC might be for anti-whaling countries to recognize JSTCW as equivalent to ASW; something for which Japan has been arguing for many years. This might well enable a compromise to be reached; perhaps if Japan were to agree not to seek whales further afield. However, both ASW and JSTCW have long and contentious histories and careful future negotiation will be required. There are significant differences between ASW and JSTCW which would need to be considered carefully.

The issue highlights how difficult it can be to categorise 'traditional peoples' when it comes to poverty; how the interests of 'traditional peoples' might be recognized in international law, but be problematic to implement in practice (particularly where the natural resources concerned are, or might be, endangered); and how the rights of 'traditional peoples' can be used in international *fora* as bargaining tools, to the detriment both of the peoples themselves and of international governance generally.

This should not be taken to be a suggestion that the governments representing indigenous peoples who do, or would like to, engage in ASW are being in any way insincere in their concern for the indigenous people and their interests. Quite the opposite, in fact, as the history of ASW has seen contracting governments to the ICRW show great concern for these interests. Unfortunately, however, this concern has sometimes rendered states vulnerable on other issues and has led to the apparent sacrifice of these other issues.

The International Whaling Commission is renowned as an international instrument which is dysfunctional, in the sense that it appears to be so riven with conflict, and its parties so polarized, that agreement is nigh impossible and the Convention cannot fulfil its functions properly. While there are some indications in the past few years that the parties might be moving closer to ending the impasse through acceptance at least that certain issues must be considered essential issues and resolved rather than ignored, and there are ongoing efforts to reach compromise within the IWC, it is likely still to take many years before rapprochement is possible.

One of the aspects central to such rapprochement is bound to be the relationship between ASW and JSTCW. Unfortunately, the portents for a clear understanding of the two emerging appear slight – given the ways in which the two, ASW in particular, have been used and abused for political advantage in the last three decades. If this history is not clearly understood and recognized, then it seems likely that the peoples involved in ASW and, or, the whales which are their targets will continue to be given short-shrift for the sake of short-term political maneuvering. Poverty, culture and conservation will continue to be horses traded in a dodgy marketplace – and both indigenous peoples and whales might in the end be the poorer for it.

NOTES

* The author wishes to acknowledge the valuable comments made during the preparation of this chapter by Susan L. Smith, Professor of Law, Willamette University College of Law, Oregon; and also the careful editing comments by Yves Le Bouthillier, Professor of Law, Faculty of Law, University of Ottawa.

1. The Makah take is currently subject to domestic suspension.
2. More accurately, this should be called a 'zero quota'; but the term 'moratorium' is generally used.
3. 'Aboriginal subsistence whaling' is not in fact defined, except for the qualification that it be 'to satisfy aboriginal subsistence need'; but is clearly provided for in section 13 of the Schedule. See International Convention for the Regulation of Whaling, Schedule, http://www.iwcoffice.org/commission/schedule.htm (accessed 6 February 2012).
4. IWC, 'Whale Population Estimates', http://iwcoffice.org/conservation/estimate.htm (accessed 6 February 2012). According to the IWC, which bases its current estimate on 2001 figures, the Bering-Chukchi-Beaufort Seas stock is in the region of 10 500 (with a 95% confidence rating that the stock is between 8200 and 13 500).
5. See below, n. 11. IWC (2002b), 'Chairman's Report of the 5th Special Meeting (14 October 2002)', in Gregory P. Donovan (ed.)/IWC (2003), *Annual Report of the International Whaling Commission 2002: Covering the 2001-2002 Financial Year and the 54th Annual Meeting held in Shimonoseki in 2002*, Cambridge, UK: International Whaling Commission.
6. See below, under Sections 6.6 and 6.7.
7. JSTCW: 'Japanese Small-type Coastal Whaling'.
8. This can be seen, for instance, from the list of delegates for each party printed in every IWC Annual Report. The Japanese delegation regularly numbers more than 40.
9. Borodin, R.G., V. Yu Ilyashenko, D. Litovka, V.M. Yetylin and O.V. Yetylina (2007), 'Rationale for Needs of Aboriginal People of Russian Federation for Gray and Bowhead Whale Harvest in 2008–2012' (2007), IWC/59/ASW 3rev *Agenda items* 6.1 and 6.2 8, http://www.iwcoffice.org/_documents/commission/IWC59docs/59-ASW3rev.pdf (accessed 6 February 2012).
10. Komatsu, M. (2002) 'What Was Achieved at the Shimonoseki IWC Meeting', 26 *ISANA*, http://www.whaling.jp/english/isana/no26_01.html (accessed 6 February 2012).
11. It is uncertain what the authors mean here, given the controversy of 1977. See above, at 6.2.1.
12. See above, n. 5.
13. This being the paragraph which in 1982 established the zero quota (or 'moratorium') on commercial whaling. See above, n. 3.
14. The countries which voted in favour were Antigua and Barbuda, Benin, PR of China, Denmark, Dominica, Grenada, Rep of Guinea, Iceland, Japan, Norway, Palau, Russian Federation, St Kitts and Nevis, St Lucia, Solomon Islands, and the US. Voting against were Australia, Austria, Brazil, Chile, Finland, France, Germany, Italy, Mexico, Monaco, the Netherlands, New Zealand, Peru, Portugal, San Marino, Spain, Sweden, Switzerland, and the UK. Ireland and the Rep of Korea abstained IWC (2002), 'Voting record: Resolution no. 5, Japan proposal, IWC/SPEC.02/4'. (Electronic copy of voting records in possession of author.)
15. These catch limits include: Bering-Chukchi-Beaufort Seas bowhead whales, Alaskan

Eskimos and native Chukotka peoples – 280 whales in period 2003–2007, no more than 67 whales in a year.

16. Environmental Investigation Agency (2008), 'Japan's Dall's porpoise hunt: A quarter of a century as the largest cetacean kill in the world', http://www.eia-international.org/files/news276-1.pdf (visited 8 May 2011). Environmental Investigation Agency (2010), 'Public health threat increases as Japan's largest dolphin slaughter begins', http://www.eia-international.org/public-health-threat-increases-as-japans-largest-dolphin-slaughter-begins (accessed 15 February 2012).
17. IWC (2007), 'IWC 59 Press Release – Day 1 – Monday 28 May', http://www.iwcoffice.org/meetings/meeting2007.htm (accessed 6 February 2012).
18. The writer attended as a member of the South African delegation.
19. This being a coherent, although somewhat numerically fluid, group of anti-whaling parties – at its core being Australia, Germany, the Netherlands, New Zealand, the US and the UK.
20. IWC (2007), 'IWC 59 Press Release – Day 2 – Tuesday 29 May', http://www.iwcoffice.org/meetings/meeting2007.htm (accessed 6 February 2012).
21. IWC (2007), 'IWC 59 Chair's Summary Report of the 59th Annual Meeting (28–31 May 2007)', *Final IWC59 Chair's Summary Reportrev.doc*, 30 October 2007, http://www.iwcoffice.org/_documents/meetings/ChairSummaryReportIWC59rev.pdf (accessed 3 February 2012), pp. 2–3.
22. Couzens, E. 'Personal notes' IWC 59, 'Plenary session, Day 2, 29 May 2007'.
23. Ibid.
24. Ibid.
25. Ibid.,'Stinky' gray whales are whales which, since the late 1960s, have been caught and found to have strong medicinal smells and to cause medical problems, at least in the short term, if eaten. Despite much chemical analysis, the cause has not been ascertained to date. The numbers have increased in recent times, and it has been estimated that approximately 10% of gray whales taken are 'stinky'.
26. Ibid.
27. A small number of whales have also been taken illegally (this being domestic illegality) by Makah tribe members, with prosecutions resulting in domestic courts.
28. Above, n. 21, p. 4. Japan's proposal was to amend the Schedule to allow for the taking of minke whales from the Okhotsk Sea/West Pacific stock for each of the years 2007–2011; with the meat and products to be used for local consumption exclusively.
29. IWC (2007), 'IWC 59 Press Release – Day 3 – Wednesday 30 May', http://www.iwcoffice.org/meetings/meeting2007.htm (accessed 6 February, 2012).
30. Couzens, E. 'Personal notes' IWC 59, 'Plenary session, Day 3, 30 May 2007'.
31. Ibid., This being a strong hint that, as discussed earlier, Japan does seem to have given assurances behind the scenes that it would not seek to block the renewal of the bowhead whale quota put forward by the Russian Federation and the US.
32. Ibid.
33. IWC (2008), 'IWC 60 Press Release Day 3, 25 June 2008', http://www.iwcoffice.org/meetings/meeting2008.htm#press (accessed 6 February 2012).
34. IWC (2008), 'IWC 60 Press Release Day 4, 26 June 2008', http://www.iwcoffice.org/meetings/meeting2008.htm#press (accessed 6 February 2012).
35. IWC (2008), 'Meeting of the Small Working Group on the Future of the IWC 15–19 September 2008', http://iwcoffice.org/_documents/commission/future/ PressReleaseSep08.pdf (accessed 6 February 2012).
36. IWC (2009),'Report of the Small Working Group on the Future of the IWC', http://www.iwcoffice.org/commission/future.htm#2009 (accessed 6 February 2012).
37. IWC (2009), 'Chair's Report of the Intersessional Meeting of the Commission on the Future of the IWC', http://www.iwcoffice.org/_documents/commission/future/61-7.pdf (accessed 6 February 2012).
38. IWC (2009), 'Consensus resolution on the extension of Small Working Group on the Future of the IWC until the 62nd Annual Meeting of the Commission', http://www.iwcoffice.org/_documents/commission/IWC61docs/61-10rev.pdf (accessed 6 February 2012).

39. IWC (2009), 'Press Release Day 2, 23 June 2009', http://www.iwcoffice.org/meetings/meeting2009.htm (accessed, 6 February 2012).
40. IWC (2009), 'Press Release Day 4, 25 June 2009', http://www.iwcoffice.org/meetings/meeting2009.htm (accessed 6 February 2012).
41. IWC (2009), 'Statement by the Chair of the International Whaling Commission, Cristian Maquieira, on the Future of the IWC', http://www.iwcoffice.org/_documents/commission/future/PressReleaseDec09.pdf (accessed 6 February 2012).
42. Couzens, E. 'Personal notes' IWC 59, 2007.
43. As in 2007, the writer attended as a member of the South African delegation.
44. IWC (2011), 'Press Release – Day 3 – 13 July 2011', http://www.iwcoffice.org/meetings/meeting2011.htm (accessed 6 February 2012).
45. Ibid.
46. Ibid.

REFERENCES

Birnie, P. (1985), *International Regulation of Whaling: From Conservation of Whaling to Conservation of Whales and Regulation of Whale-Watching: Volume I*, New York: Oceana Publications.

Burns, W.C.G. and G. Wandesforde-Smith (2002), 'The International Whaling Commission and the Future of Cetaceans in a Changing World' *RECIEL* 11 (2), p.199.

Day, D. (1992), *The Whale War* (2nd edn) (Grafton).

Friedheim, R.L. (2001), 'Negotiating in the IWC Environment', in Robert L. Friedheim (ed.), *Toward a Sustainable Whaling Regime* Washington: University of Washington Press.

IWC (1977) , 'Chairman's Report of the Special Meeting, Tokyo, December 1977' (IWC Secretariat).

IWC (1978a), 'Chairman's Report of the Thirtieth Annual Meeting (26–30 June 1978)' (IWC Secretariat).

IWC (1978b), 'Report of the Plenary Sessions (26–30 June 1978)' (IWC Secretariat).

IWC (1979a), 'Report of the Panel Meeting of Experts on Aboriginal/Subsistence Whaling (5–9 February 1979)' (IWC Secretariat).

IWC (1979b), 'Report of the Plenary Sessions of the Thirty-First Meeting (9–13 July 1979)' (IWC Secretariat).

IWC (1980a), 'Report of the Plenary Sessions of the Thirty-Second Annual Meeting (21–26 July 1980)' (IWC Secretariat).

IWC (1980b), 'Chairman's Report of the Thirty-Second Annual Meeting (21–26 July 1980)' (IWC Secretariat).

IWC (1982), 'Report of the Plenary Sessions of the Thirty-Fourth Annual Meeting (19-24 July 1982)' (IWC Secretariat).

IWC (1994), 'Chairman's Report of the Forty-Sixth Annual Meeting (23–27 May 1994)' (IWC Secretariat).

IWC (1997), 'Chairman's Report of the Forty-Ninth Annual Meeting (20–24 October 1997)' (IWC Secretariat).

IWC (2000), 'Chairman's Report of the Fifty-Second Annual Meeting (3–6 July 2000)', in Gregory P. Donovan (ed.)/IWC (2001), *Annual Report of the International Whaling Commission 2000: Covering the 1999–2000 Financial Year and the 52nd Annual Meeting held in Adelaide in 2000*, Cambridge, UK: International Whaling Commission.

IWC (2002a), 'Chairman's Report of the Fifty-Fourth Annual Meeting (20–24 May 2002)', in Gregory P. Donovan (ed.)/IWC (2003), *Annual Report of the International Whaling Commission 2002: Covering the 2001–2002 Financial Year and the 54th Annual Meeting held in Shimonoseki in 2002*, Cambridge, UK: International Whaling Commission.

IWC (2002b), 'Chairman's Report of the 5th Special Meeting (14 October 2002)', in Gregory P. Donovan (ed.)/IWC (2003), *Annual Report of the International Whaling Commission 2002: Covering the 2001-2002 Financial Year and the 54th Annual Meeting held in Shimonoseki in 2002*, Cambridge, UK: International Whaling Commission.

IWC (2002c), 'Draft Resolution on Japanese Community-Based Whaling' IWC/SPEC.02/4, 11 October 2002. (Original document viewed by author, IWC Secretariat, Cambridge, UK: February 2007.)

IWC (2003), 'Chairman's Report of the Fifty-Fifth Annual Meeting (16–19 June 2003)', in Gregory P. Donovan (ed.)/IWC (2004), *Annual Report of the International Whaling Commission 2003: Covering the 2002–2003 Financial Year and the 55th Annual Meeting held in Berlin in 2003*, Cambridge, UK: International Whaling Commission.

IWC (2004a), 'Opening Statements of the Fifty-Sixth Annual Meeting (19–22 July 2004)', written Opening Statement by: Japan (IWC/56/OS/JAP). (Original document viewed by author, IWC Secretariat, Cambridge, UK: February 2007.)

IWC (2004b), 'Chair's Report of the 56th Annual Meeting (19–22 July 2004)', in Gregory P. Donovan (ed.)/IWC (2005), *Annual Report of the International Whaling Commission 2004: Covering the 2003–2004 Financial Year and the 56th Annual Meeting held in Sorrento in 2004*, Cambridge, UK: International Whaling Commission.

IWC (2005), 'Chair's Summary Report for the 57th Annual Meeting Korea, 20–24 June 2005' in Gregory P. Donovan (ed.)/IWC (2006), *Annual Report of the International Whaling Commission 2005: Covering the 2004–2005 Financial Year and the 57th Annual Meeting held in Ulsan in 2005*, Cambridge, UK: International Whaling Commission.

IWC (2010a), 'Chair's Report' in Gregory P. Donovan (ed.)/IWC (2006), *Annual Report of the International Whaling Commission 2010: Covering the 2009–2010 Financial Year and the 62nd Annual Meeting held in Agadir, Morocco in 2010*, Cambridge, UK: International Whaling Commission.

IWC (2010b), 'IWS Quotas: Submitted by Denmark and the USA', IWC/62/26, Agenda item 3, available at http://www.iwcoffice.org/_documents/commission/IWC62docs/62-26.pdf (accessed 16 February 2012).

Komatsu, M. and S. Misaki (2003), *Whales and the Japanese: How we have come to live in harmony with the bounty of the sea*, Institute of Cetacean Research.

PART III

The need for public participation in environmental issues to combat poverty

7. The role of public engagement in achieving environmental justice

LeRoy C. (Lee) Paddock*

7.1 INTRODUCTION

Over the last 25 years significant environmental inequalities have been documented in the United States. Low income communities and communities with large minority populations are often exposed to more environmental hazards – waste management facilities, air pollution, degraded water – and are more vulnerable to the impacts of environmental catastrophes – witness hurricane Katrina – than higher income or majority communities. Studies have also demonstrated that fewer environmental enforcement resources are typically deployed in these communities. One reason for this situation is that low-income communities and minority communities are frequently under-represented in government decision making. The opportunities for all members of affected communities to fully participate in governmental decision making is a problem that reaches well beyond the issue of environmental justice, but it is of particular concern in the context of environmental justice because of increased risks that many low-income and minority populations face.

Historically, the most common approaches to public engagement in government decision making in the United States often:

- occur too late in the decision making process to have a major impact on development decisions;
- do not involve genuine consultations with communities;
- fails to provide communities with the type of information and resources they need to have a real impact on decisions;
- are not designed to address cultural issues that may limit participation;
- may not take into account language and other constraints such as time, location and nature of meetings that may limit effective involvement.

This situation is beginning to change as better approaches to public engagement in government environmental decision making are increasingly recognized as an essential aspect of democratic governance and even an element of basic human rights.

This chapter reviews the progress that has been made in the last 25 years in providing the public with more 'authentic' opportunities for public engagement in government decision making, focusing particularly on public engagement as it relates to environmental justice. It provides a brief overview of the environmental justice issue in the United States, explores the importance of public engagement in environmental decision making, examines the shortcomings of many of the traditional public engagement processes still widely used in the United States and discusses the particular importance of public engagement in making progress on environmental justice. The chapter concludes with a review of some promising new approaches to public engagement at the federal, state and local levels, and a discussion of the continuing progress needed in public engagement.

7.2 ENVIRONMENTAL JUSTICE IN THE UNITED STATES

The emergence of environmental justice as an issue in the United States is often traced to 1982 protests involving a planned polychlorinated biphenyls (PCB) disposal facility in rural North Carolina at which over 500 people were arrested (Singer, 2002, p. 5). This incident sparked growing concerns, especially in the African American community, about disproportionate exposure to environmental hazards. In 1987 a study by the United Church of Christ found that three of five African Americans and Hispanics lived in communities with uncontrolled toxic waste sites (Singer, 2002, p. 7). Later, a 1992 study on environmental enforcement disparities published in the National Law Journal added additional weight to the environmental justice movement finding that 'the United States Environmental Protection Agency took 20 per cent longer to place abandoned sites in communities of color on the national priority ('Superfund') list and that polluters in those neighborhoods paid fines 54 per cent lower than those who pollute in white communities' (Lavelle and Coyle, 1992).

The US Environmental Protection Agency (EPA) began to focus on environmental justice in 1992 when it created its Office of Environmental Justice. The following year, EPA established the National Environmental Justice Advisory Council (NEJAC). This body is made up of members from community-based organizations, businesses, academic institutions, state and local governments, tribal governments, and non-governmental and environmental organizations. NEJAC was established to 'create a dialogue that can define and "reinvent" solutions to environmental justice problems'.[1]

The growing evidence of differential environmental impacts led President Clinton to issue Executive Order 12898 in 1994. This Executive Order remains the basis for addressing environmental justice at the federal level today. The order provides in pertinent part:

> To the greatest extent practicable and permitted by law … each federal agency shall make achieving environmental justice part of its mission by identifying and addressing, as appropriate, disproportionately high and adverse human health or environmental effects of its programs, policies, and activities on minority and low-income populations …[2]

Based on this Executive Order, EPA defined environmental justice as the 'fair treatment and meaningful involvement of all people regardless of race, color, national origin, culture, education, or income with respect to the development, implementation, and enforcement of environmental laws, regulations and policies'.[3] Environmental justice is directly linked to public engagement through the 'meaningful involvement' provision. Meaningful involvement requires that:

a. Potentially affected community residents have an appropriate opportunity to participate in decisions about a proposed activity that will affect their environment and/or health.
b. The public's contribution can influence the regulatory agencies decision.
c. The concerns of all participants involved will be considered in the decision making process.
d. The decision makers must seek out and facilitate the meaningful involvement of those potentially affected.[4]

7.3 THE IMPORTANCE OF PUBLIC ENGAGEMENT

> Environmental issues are best handled with the participation of all concerned citizens, at the relevant level. At the national level, each individual shall have appropriate access to information concerning the environment that is held by public authorities, including information on hazardous materials and activities in their communities, and the opportunity to participate in decision-making processes.[5]

As Principle 10 of the Rio Declaration on Environment and Development indicates, public engagement is widely seen as an essential element of environmental decision making. Building upon Principle 10, the International Union for the Conservation of Nature (IUCN), in Article 12 of its Draft International Covenant on Environment and Development, identifies public engagement as a 'right': 'All persons, without being required to prove an interest, have the right to seek, receive, and disseminate information on activities or measures adversely affecting or likely to affect the environment and the right to participate in relevant decision-making processes' (IUCN, 1995).

In the United States, President Clinton's Council on Sustainable Communities recognized the central role public engagement can play in driving sustainable development and assuring more equitable environmental outcomes. The Development Council's Sustainable Communities Task Force Report observed 'the fundamentals of sustainable communities are based in process – how people work together to build community, what information they can access, who is involved in making decisions, and how well communities work cooperatively to address shared problems that transcend their borders' (The President's Council on Sustainable Development, 1997, p. 13). While the United States has a long history of providing for public participation in government decision making, the specific nature of the public engagement process – the who, the when, the how – is of critical importance. The Sustainable Communities Report noted:

> True participation means giving people the opportunity to take part in the initial phases of planning, not just the ratifying decisions that have already been made, or commenting on plans that have already been drafted. While it is time-consuming and may not be possible in every situation, this model of decision making should be encouraged. (The President's Council on Sustainable Development, 1997, p. 15.)

Public engagement involves not only legitimacy but also the question of justice. The Report commented that 'an important component of environmental justice is the right of local residents to participate as equal partners at every level of decision making, including needs assessment, planning, implementation, enforcement, and evaluation' (The President's Council on Sustainable Development, 1996, p. 16). These findings led the President's Council on Sustainable Development to conclude that '[o]ur most important finding is the potential power of and growing desire for decision processes that promote direct and meaningful interaction involving people in decisions that affect them' (President's Council on Sustainable Development, 1997, p. 7).

During the same time frame, negotiation of the Aarhus Convention[6] focused attention on the issues of environmental impact assessment, public involvement and assuring access to justice. The Convention ties public engagement to protection of human rights:

> The Aarhus Convention is a new kind of environmental agreement. It links environmental rights and human rights. It acknowledges that we owe an obligation to future generations. It establishes that sustainable development can be achieved only through the involvement of all stakeholders. It links government accountability and environmental protection. It focuses on interactions between the public and public authorities in a democratic context and it is forging a new process for public participation in the negotiation and implementation of international agreements.[7]

These developments over the last 15 years clearly establish effective public engagement as an essential element of legitimate environmental decision making and critical to achieving more just environmental outcomes.

7.4 THE LIMITATIONS OF TRADITIONAL PUBLIC ENGAGEMENT

Public engagement is important for many reasons. Effective public engagement can:

- Create pressure for a project proposer to produce more information about the environmental impacts of a project.
- Generate information about a project based on local knowledge and expertise.
- Drive modifications in a project to address environmental concerns (not infrequently related to issues such as traffic flow, noise or odors where environmental laws are typically weak or narrowly drawn).
- Create ongoing consultative relationships between the public and the facility proposer including ongoing monitoring and reporting procedures.
- Push government agencies to more carefully consider aspects of a proposed permit including its location in communities with environmental justice concerns.
- Raise issues about past oversight of the facility or facilities owned by the project proposer (Beierle and Cayford, 2002, pp. 14–15).

Unfortunately, the principal public engagement methods used by government agencies in the United States for environmental decision making over the last 40 years – public hearings, public meetings, and notice and comment rule-making procedures – frequently do not create conditions necessary for effective or 'authentic' public engagement and therefore fail to live up to their potential for enhancing environmental outcomes and producing more just decisions. 'Authentic' public engagement 'implies more than finding the right tools and techniques for increasing public involvement in public decisions' (King, 1998, p. 317). Rather it is engagement that 'works for all parties and stimulates interest and investment in both administrators and citizens' (King, 1998, p. 317).

One study of public participation concluded that the most ineffective public participation technique is the public hearing, yet the public hearing has been the staple of administrative decision making in the United States. 'Public hearings do not work. Low attendance at public hearings is often construed [by public administrators] as public apathy or silent approval of the status quo' (King, 1998, p. 323, quoting Martin and Martin, 1991, pp. 46–63). The report explained that '[i]n actuality, low attendance is more likely to be related to the structure of public hearings. Administrators recognize that the structure of public hearings and public meetings prohibits meaningful exchange. As one administrator said, "The public hearing is not about communication, it is about convincing"' (King, 1998, p. 323).

Another study found formal public participation processes (public hearings and public meetings) were far less successful – defined as incorporating public values into decisions, improving the substantive quality of decisions, resolving conflicts among competing interests, building trust in institutions and educating and informing the public – than decisions reached through advisory committees or through negotiations and mediations (Beierle and Cayford, 2002, p. 46). Research conducted by the Environmental Law Institute revealed 'communities feel their input [in EPA proceedings] does not matter because EPA has already made its decision before it hears from the public' (Environmental Law Institute, 1999, p. 43).

To understand why the legally mandated methods of public engagement in the United States are often not effective in engaging the public it is important to review the history and context of public participation. The growth in government agency responsibility beginning in the early twentieth century led federal and state governments to employ professional managers who became experts in the mission of their agencies. These expert managers were delegated the responsibility for making decisions on behalf of the government and the people. As Beierle and Cayford note in *Democracy in Practice*, this 'managerial approach' presents '[a] fundamental challenge for administrative governance' in 'reconciling the need for expertise in managing administrative programs with the transparency and participation demanded by a democratic system' (Beierle and Cayford, 2002, p. 3).

The rapid expansion of government during the New Deal era in the 1930s and 1940s significantly increased the role of the executive branch of government and its expert managers (Beierle and Cayford, 2002, p. 3). To temper the power of expert managers who were not directly accountable to the citizenry, Congress enacted the Administrative Procedures Act (APA) in 1946[8] requiring federal agencies to use a rule-making process that allowed the public to comment on proposed rules[9] and providing the public with the opportunity to request a public hearing on adjudicatory matters such as issuing permits.[10]

Although there are now a number of legal requirements related to public involvement in administrative matters, the procedures for public involvement in agency decision making still rely on the basic APA public participation requirements enacted some 60 years ago; procedures that also serve as the model for state administrative procedural laws that require public notification only a few weeks before an agency intends to issue a permit.[11] The managerial approach to government still holds sway in most cases.

Public participation processes have four major components: (1) the issue or situation; (2) the administrative structures, systems, and processes within which the participation takes place; (3) the administrators; and (4) the citizens. Participation efforts are currently framed such that these components are arrayed around the issue. The citizen is placed at the greatest distance from the issue, the administrative structures and processes are the closest, and the administrator is the agent between the structures and the citizens (King, 1998, pp. 319–320).

The inherent clash between the managerial model for government and the principal of representative democracy remains, but citizens are increasingly reluctant to defer to expert administrators (Environmental Law Institute, 1999, p. 2). Instead, as part of a broader movement toward 'popular' democracy, citizens increasingly want earlier access to the decision making process, more opportunities to be heard and to bring local knowledge to the table, and a clearer role in decision making (Beierle and Cayford, 2002, p. 4).

This approach calls for a more authentic form of public engagement that:

> [p]laces the citizen next to the issue and the administrative structures and processes furthest away. However, the administrator is still the bridge between the two … Citizens are central and directly related to the issue; they have an immediate and equal opportunity to influence the processes and the outcomes. The administrators' influence comes from their relationship with the citizenry as well as from their expertise and position (King, 1998, p. 321).

Even though the public wants a more democratic form of engagement, many of the real world practices remain closer to the older managerial model.

> Although there is theoretical and practical recognition that the public must be more involved in public decisions, many administrators are, at best, ambivalent about public involvement or, at worst, they find it problematic … As a result, although many public administrators view close relationships with citizens as both necessary and desirable, most of them do not actively seek public involvement. If they do seek it, they do not use public input in making administrative decisions (as indicated by a 1989 study conducted by the Kettering Foundation). These administrators believe that greater citizen participation creates delays and increases red tape (King, 1998, p. 319).

In many cases, state and federal environmental laws do not compel or even encourage greater public involvement than the basic APA requirements. EPA and some states and local governments have begun to develop and deploy new, more inclusive and interactive approaches to public engagement. However, much of the public engagement in environmental permitting and other environmental agency decision making at the federal, state and local levels still use the basic APA procedures, rely on managerial expertise, and cannot be said to be 'authentic'.

7.5 PUBLIC ENGAGEMENT AND JUSTICE

The shortcomings of traditional approaches to public engagement are even more pronounced in the context of environmental justice. Environmental justice advocates have long argued that for far too many people, especially people of color and low-income people, authentic engagement in environmental decision making is illusory resulting in decisions that have historically been and continue to be inequitable. This occurs for a number of reasons, including the limited political power of low-income and minority communities, lack of resources to challenge agency actions or to acquire needed expertise, the inability to attend public meetings during working hours, limited access to information even when it is available on the internet, language limitations and cultural barriers that inhibit participation in government processes, among other issues. A number of studies emphasize the importance of 'authentic' public engagement in achieving environmental justice and therefore the need to develop techniques that overcome these hurdles.

In July 2000, the National Academy of Public Administration completed a study of 'Environmental Justice in the Permitting Process' recommending that the EPA Administrator 'adopt binding public participation requirements which ensure that permit writers will consult with affected communities "early and often"' (NAPA, 2001, pp. 17–18). The specific recommendations include:

- Contacting potentially affected community members as soon as an agency is aware that a permit application *may* be filed or that emissions at a facility *may* increase, but in no event later than immediately upon receipt of the permit application or notice that emissions could increase.
- Holding an initial hearing or informal meeting with the potentially affected communities immediately after receipt of a permit application.
- Identifying community leaders accurately.
- Developing a plan for community involvement in conjunction with the community.
- Using broadcast media or other effective means of communications to advertise the public participation process.
- Describing what the discharge/emission means to the community in lay, rather than technical, terms.
- Making technical reports accessible to the community as soon as they are available.
- Extending the 30-day comment period for complicated permits (NAPA, 2001, pp. 17–18).

The same year NEJAC adopted a Model Plan for Public Participation that included a set of 14 guiding principles (see Appendix 1).

In October 2001 the First National People of Color Environmental Leadership Summit convened by the United Church of Christ adopted 17 'Principles of Environmental Justice'. The seventh Principle focused on 'the right to participate as equal partners at every level of decision making, including needs assessment, planning, implementation, enforcement and evaluation'.[12]

In its December 2001 report on 'Environmental Justice in EPA Permitting', the National Academy of Public Administration (NAPA) in the first of three reports on environmental justice found that (1) many government officials and others believe that EPA's formal avenues for public participation are inadequate to address the concerns of disproportionately impacted communities and (2) to have an effective voice in decisions, community members need better training on participation, access to technical expertise, and earlier notice (NAPA, 2001, p. 61). The NAPA report noted '[i]mproving the capacity and opportunity for community groups to participate in the permitting process is an almost universally identified step toward achieving environmental justice. Public participation by itself is not the solution to environmental justice problems, but such problems cannot be resolved without improved public participation' (NAPA, 2001, p. 63).

These findings led NAPA to recommend that EPA:

- Expand its community technical assistant programs.
- Adopt early notice procedures.
- Provide more public involvement training to its employees and develop tools that would help EPA employees better identify the most effective approaches to public engagement for different circumstances.
- Encourage regulated facilities to work with affected communities.
- Provide better and more accessible information to communities affected by an agency decision (NAPA, 2001, p. 75).

At about the same time, the National Environmental Policy Commission found that a 'recurrent and persistent theme' in the Commission's investigations was 'the lack of community involvement and public participation in decision-making processes that significantly impact their neighborhood, family, health and environment.' (National Environmental Policy Commission, 2001, p. 41.) The Commission noted that:

> [p]ublic participation is one of the cornerstones of environmental justice. Environmental justice demands the right to participate as equal partners at every level of decision making, including needs assessment, planning, implementation,

> enforcement and evaluation. Public participation and community involvement strategies must include a proactive public involvement process that provides complete information, timely public notice, full public access to key decisions, and support early and continuing involvement of the public in developing plans, programs and research. (National Environmental Policy Commission, 2001, p. 43.)

In August 2006 NEJAC reaffirmed the importance of public engagement in achieving environmental justice observing:

> '[t]here is a distinction between public participation and meaningful involvement. Meaningful involvement requires fully informed participants from all perspectives, all armed with the capacity to participate in policy development as full partners. Moreover, the point of meaningful involvement is not only to formulate policy advice, but it must lead the way to concrete results achieving fair treatment' (United States Environmental Protection Agency, 2006, p. 4).

7.6 THE EMERGENCE OF NEW PUBLIC ENGAGEMENT TECHNIQUES

7.6.1 EPA

The increasingly clear link between authentic public engagement and environmental justice led EPA to begin to rethink its approach to public engagement in the mid-1990s. Because the environmental justice movement arose in the context of hazardous waste issues, it is not surprising that the public engagement changes at EPA began with its hazardous waste cleanup program under the Comprehensive Environmental Response, Compensation and Liability Act (CERCLA or Superfund) program and its hazardous waste management programs under the Resource Conservation and Recovery Act (RCRA).

A January 1989 management review of EPA's hazardous waste clean-up program found '[c]itizens question whether they actually influence EPA decisions, or whether EPA's community relations program is really just "sophisticated public relations." EPA managers have mixed feelings about public involvement. As mentioned previously, some are strong supporters of it; others object because of philosophy, cost and delay'.[13]

This study and other environmental justice concerns related to hazardous waste sites led EPA's Office of Solid Waste and Emergency Response to take a number of steps to address public engagement concerns. In June 1993 EPA announced a series of Superfund reforms, many of which focused on public participation. One of the key reforms was establishing 'community working groups' at several Superfund sites to provide a public forum for community concerns. EPA found that community working groups:

- Should be formed as early as possible in the site remediation process.
- The community must take the initiative in forming these groups.
- The groups must be inclusive and independent.
- Access to technical assistance is important.
- The groups are more effective than public meetings.
- The groups can give the community more influence in site-related decisions.
- Having a group involved can speed the clean-up process.[14]

Late in 1995 EPA published a new 'Expanded Public Participation' rule for RCRA-related issues. This rule requires a prospective applicant to hold an informal public meeting before submitting a RCRA permit application, and to widely publicize the meeting in a variety of media. It also requires the permitting agency to provide notice to interested parties as soon as a permit application is received and authorizes the permitting agency to require a facility owner to set up an information repository accessible to the public.[15] The new rules were followed by a RCRA Public Participation Manual that 'reflects EPA's belief that all stakeholders have a role in providing for meaningful public participation' (United States Environmental Protection Agency, 1996, p. 1–1). The RCRA Manual provided federal and state agency permitting staff with a detailed set of 'Guidelines for a Successful Public Participation Program' emphasizing early and inclusive public involvement, as well as the importance of listening and responding to public concerns, the timing and setting for public involvement and the availability of information (United States Environmental Protection Agency, 1996, chapter 2).

Based in part on the experience with the RCRA Public Participation Manual, EPA adopted in May 2003 a new 'Public Involvement Policy' that expanded the approach in the RCRA Manual to all EPA programs. In introducing the policy EPA observes that it is EPA's mission:

> to protect human health and the environment. To achieve that mission, EPA needs to integrate, in a meaningful way, the knowledge and opinions of others into its decision-making processes. Effective public involvement can both improve the content of the Agency's decisions and enhance the deliberative process. Public involvement also promotes democracy and civic engagement and builds public trust in government. (United States Environment Protection Agency, 2003, p. 1.)

The Policy ties public engagement directly to achieving environmental justice.

> This policy complements and is consistent with EPA's environmental justice efforts … Environmental justice is achieved when everyone, regardless of race, culture or income, enjoys the same degree of protection from environmental and health hazards and equal access to the decision-making process to have a healthy environment in which to live, learn and work. This includes ensuring greater public

> participation in the agency's development and implementation of its regulations and policies (United States Environment Protection Agency, 2003, p. 5).

The Policy sets out seven basic steps for effective public involvement:

- Plan and budget for public involvement activities.
- Identify the interested and affected public.
- Consider providing technical and financial assistance to the public.
- Provide information and outreach.
- Conduct public consultation and involvement activities.
- Review and use input and provide feedback to the public.
- Evaluate public involvement activities.

The Policy provides extensive guidance about how each of these steps can be carried out.

7.6.2 State Initiatives

States have also begun using advanced public engagement approaches over the last decade. NAPA, in its second study of environmental justice issues that assessed environmental justice programs in four states – California, Florida, Indiana and New Jersey – found that these four states had begun implementing a range of initiatives to enhance public engagement including:

- Developing guides to help citizens understand agency processes.
- Training citizens about how to participate effectively in agency decisions.
- Training agency staff about the value of community expertise and the need to listen to community concerns.
- Issuing public notices early in the decision-making process.
- Providing notices in more than one language.
- Writing easily understood notices, fact-sheets, and other documents.
- Publishing notices as advertisements rather than legal notices.
- Distributing notices to local institutions, such as community centers and churches.
- Building user-friendly web sites.
- Holding meetings during the evening or weekends so it is easier for citizens to attend.
- Convening small groups, not large meetings.
- Facilitating dialogues.
- Using community liaisons to establish closer ties to community leaders (NAPA, 2002, pp. 134–135).

Based on these findings, NAPA recommended that in order to achieve more just environmental outcomes states should 'involve citizens earlier in the permitting process, frequently interact with community leaders and organizations at times and places convenient to them, and expand public participation in other programs … including standard-setting, enforcement, technical and compliance assistance, research, and information gathering …' (NAPA, 2002, pp. 135–136).

The following section discusses some of the more significant steps taken by states related to public engagement in the context of environmental justice.

7.6.2.1 California

California was the one of the first states to enact environmental justice legislation. California Assembly Bill 2312 creates a grant program directed to community and grassroots organizations within environmental justice communities who seek to address the disproportionate impacts to health and the environment within these communities. Eligible grant projects will:

(1) Resolve environmental problems through distribution of information.
(2) Identify improvements in communication and coordination among agencies and stakeholders in order to address the most significant exposure to pollution.
(3) Expand the understanding of a community about the environmental issues that affect their community.
(4) Develop guidance on the relative significance of various environmental risks.
(5) Promote community involvement in the decision making process that affects the environment of the community.
(6) Present environmental data for the purposes of enhancing community understanding of environmental information systems and environmental information.[16]

California Senate Bill 32 establishes scientific peer review of screening numbers used to determine the extent of cleanup necessary to develop a previously contaminated property. The Bill requires public participation and outreach efforts to help communities understand the screening values and the steps necessary to clean up hazardous waste sites. It also requires that the California Environmental Protection Agency (CAL EPA) hold two workshops before publishing screening numbers to educate the public and other interested parties on the use and value of these numbers, as well as receive public comments on the process. Upon publication of the screening numbers, the Bill requires CAL EPA to hold three public workshops to receive further public comment. The deputy secretary for external affairs is expected to search out community-based organizations, citizen groups, and environmental organizations to participate in the workshops. Upon completion of the workshops, CAL EPA will change the screening numbers as necessary. CAL EPA will also provide a guidance document to citizens and other interested parties to inform them of the significance of the screening numbers and how CAL EPA makes determinations of the steps necessary to remediate contaminated properties.[17]

7.6.2.2 Illinois

Illinois's Interim Environmental Justice Policy contains a section titled 'Preparing for Avenues of Entry for EJ Concerns or Inquiries'. This section requires that, when an environmental justice issue is brought to the attention of the Illinois Environmental Protection Agency (IL EPA), the Environmental Justice Officer, who is the liaison for members of environmental justice communities, will be notified and will meet with members of the Environmental Justice Advisory Work Group to create the IL EPA's strategy for addressing the communities' concerns.[18]

The Environmental Justice Public Participation Policy requires that the Environmental Justice Officer oversee all aspects of environmental justice efforts for IL EPA as well as act as the liaison between environmental justice communities and IL EPA for the purpose of resolving concerns and disputes. Public participation takes two forms within IL EPA's environmental justice efforts. The first involves community outreach, which focuses primarily on providing information for environmental justice communities on permit applications and the promotion of communication between permit applicants and affected environmental justice communities. Under the Policy, communication is to be provided in plain language and published in local newspapers if necessary. Online databases are maintained to inform the public of enforcement actions and of pending permit applications.

The second form that public participation takes is in public meetings. IL EPA's Public Participation Policy encourages permit applicants to meet with community stakeholders in environmental justice areas prior to submitting a permit for approval to IL EPA including in informal settings that have been referred to as 'living room' meetings. Permit applicants are also encouraged to hold meetings with the public within 30 days of submitting an application.

Illinois's Policy focuses on waste management activities such as solid waste landfills, treatment and transfer stations, compost sites, medical waste, construction permits, joint construction and operating permits, water pollution permits and hazardous waste site remediation projects.[19]

7.6.2.3 Massachusetts

Massachusetts' Environmental Justice Policy requires that environmental justice be emphasized throughout Massachusetts' Executive Office of Environmental Affairs (EOEA). [20] The Policy requires that EOEA accomplish these goals by giving communities greater access to the decision-making process, including the environmental review process for new or modifications to pollutant sources. The Policy also encourages greater economic investment in communities with significant potential to clean up polluted sites. In addition, the Policy requires that fact sheets be made available to environmental justice communities to inform them of programs that benefit their communities and opportunities residents may have to promote environmental justice within their community.[21]

7.6.2.4 New York

New York's Commissioner Policy 29[22] requires that the New York Department of Conservation (DEC) will:

- Provide greater access to permit information through the DEC website and a toll free environmental justice hotline, including information concerning environmental justice that is given to permit applicants during the review process.
- Translate information on environmental justice into languages other than English.
- Provide guidance to permit applicants in complying with all aspects of the public participation plan to allow the permit applicant to better interact with environmental justice community members during the permit application process.
- Encourage alternative dispute resolution between permit applicants and environmental justice communities when issues arise during the permit process.
- Provide workshops to members of the community on environmental justice issues, the permit review process, and other information for how DEC identifies an environmental justice community and holds a permit review.
- Draft legislation to provide funding for a technical assistance grant program, with funds derived from the Environmental Protection Fund.

The Policy also requires permit applicants to submit an Enhanced Public Participation Plan when an environmental justice area has been identified, which must:

- Seek out impacted individuals, which include members of communities within and surrounding the proposed project, local officials and community organizations.
- Provide public notification of the proposed permit and the review process, which must be written in plain language and translated for non-English speakers when necessary.
- Create document storage locations in or near the environmental justice community to provide information on the permit application to the

public. The applicant may also additionally maintain an online database if desired.

- Contain a progress report, including any issues raised, including those that remain unresolved, and a timeline for completion of the activities laid out in the plan.
- Include written certification that the permit applicant has completed the plan as well as any updates and activities made by the applicant since initial submission of the plan. The plan must be submitted prior to a final decision on the permit by DEC.

The Policy also provides for alternative dispute resolution (ADR) when conflicts arise between community members and permit applicants. ADR may be used at any time before the final permit application decision. When issues are resolved with conditions within the authority of DEC, those conditions will be included within the permit. When the conditions resolving the issue are outside the authority of DEC, those conditions may be included in a separate private agreement between the parties.

The Policy applies to a wide range of permitting and siting activities.[23]

7.6.2.5 New Mexico

New Mexico's Environmental Justice Executive Order states:

> All cabinet level departments and boards and commissions that are involved in decisions that may affect environmental quality and public health shall provide meaningful opportunities for involvement to all people regardless of race, color, ethnicity, religion, income, or education level

and

> recognize the need to communicate in writing and orally significant public health and environmental information in languages other than English by ensuring that all publicly disseminated information, including websites, is available in Spanish and English, at a minimum, and in tribal languages and dialects as appropriate for areas of the state where these languages are spoken.[24]

7.6.2.6 Pennsylvania

Pennsylvania's Public Participation Policy[25] requires specific steps to address issues in environmental justice communities. These steps are:

- Community Outreach: The Public Participation Policy requires the Pennsylvania Department of Environmental Protection (DEP) to inform permit applicants that their application is subject to enhanced public participation. DEP will also provide information fact sheets and other information about the application and permit process as well as maintain a presence in the community, potentially through establishment of a mobile office.

- Public Information: The Policy requires that DEP utilize its e-mail notification system, eNOTICE, to inform community members about permit activities in their area. DEP staff are also encouraged to utilize other forms of communication to reach community members and the public without internet access. The policy also requires that DEP publish and distribute information and notices affecting the Environmental Justice Area in plain language and in areas noticeable to the public. These vehicles for communication include newspapers, notices to environmental groups and community centers, and community newsletters. DEP also recommends that permit applicants send information about their permit and project to residents of the environmental justice community.
- Public Meetings: The Policy requires DEP to promote pre-submission application meetings between permit applicants and community stakeholders. DEP may be present at these meetings if invited to answer questions and address concerns of the community. DEP must also schedule a public meeting within 30 days of permit submission to inform the public of environmental justice concerns and about the permit process. Applicants are encouraged to participate in the public meeting process. DEP is encouraged to make available a summary of the permit application in plain language that is easily accessible to the public. DEP may provide extended and weekend hours for viewing documents pertaining to the application, as well as keep documents in remote locations accessible by communities.[26]

Additionally, the Public Participation Policy provides a Community Involvement Checklist and a sample letter to be sent to applicants to notify them of environmental justice communities.[27]

7.6.3 The Brownfields Context

NAPA's third report on environmental justice focused on local government decision making in the context of planning and zoning. The NAPA report noted '[z]oning and land use planning have been described by some scholars as "a root enabling cause of disproportionate burdens [and] environmental injustice"' (NAPA, 2003, p. 25, citing Maantay, 2002). NAPA found that '[l]ocal governments often have broad authority for involving the public in land use planning and zoning decisions, but efforts to engage the public are not always effective in reaching residents of low-income and people-of-color communities' (NAPA, 2003, p. 22). Based on this finding, NAPA recommended:

- Local governments should engage the public in all steps of the land use process and not simply be invited to participate in public hearings after plans are essentially completed.
- Local governments should facilitate participation by translating relevant documents, using different times and places for meetings to make participation easier and taking extra steps for outreach in communities unaccustomed to participating in government decision making (NAPA, 2003, p. 22).

The case studies that were part of the NAPA study revealed several practices that facilitated public engagement in land use decision making including a neighborhood-based planning and zoning process in Austin, Texas and the use of neighborhood planning commissions in Huntington Park, California (NAPA, 2003, p. 23).

The role of local governments in public engagement has become especially important over the last decade as interest in redevelopment of old urban industrial sites has increased. Relocation of manufacturing facilities from suburban locations to areas in the south and south-western part of the country and outside of the United States from the 1960s onward resulted in thousands of acres of often abandon or under-utilized urban land. EPA estimates that there are over 450 000 such sites in the country.[28] Because these sites had been used for industrial or commercial activity at a time when hazardous waste disposal was not closely regulated, many of these old sites – now referred to as 'brownfields' to distinguish them from newer industrial facilities built on undeveloped or 'greenfields' sites – have some form of hazardous waste contamination and are almost always assumed to be contaminated until soil testing has been conducted.

Brownfields remained undeveloped for a variety of reasons including suburbanization, changes in the level of industrial activity, and the potential that a new owner would assume liability for cleanup under CERCLA and equivalent state laws. CERCLA and most of the state laws imposed strict, joint and several liability on a broad range of parties that are deemed responsible for contamination which, at least in the early years of CERCLA and the state laws, could be interpreted to include new owners and even banks. Not surprisingly, many of the brownfields sites were located in poorer communities and in communities of color.

By the early 1990s two factors drove increasing focus on redevelopment of brownfields. The first was a rapidly growing interest in urban revitalization and urban homesteading. After more than 40 years of rapid suburban growth, individuals were beginning to be drawn back to urban living and businesses saw the value of building in areas where much of the infrastructure was already in place. The second factor was the passage of brownfields laws starting with states such as Minnesota and Pennsylvania in the early 1990s and eventually including almost every state and the federal government. These laws provided a liability safe harbor for developers, owners and financiers who were not responsible for the initial contamination and who agreed to clean up the sites using a government approved clean-up plan. In addition, by the mid-1990s, the cost of cleanup had become more predictable allowing developers and financiers to make an informed business decision on expected return on investment taking into account the cost of clean-up.

The interest in brownfields redevelopment coincided with two other trends that made brownfields redevelopment a likely candidate for new forms of public engagement. The first of these was the environmental justice movement that has been outlined earlier. Since many brownfield sites are found in areas where environmental justice is likely to be a concern, the joinder of these two issues was inevitable. The second trend was a growing understanding of the limitations of traditional public involvement approaches.

One of the best early examples of how all of these factors came together to produce a new approach to public engagement designed to address environmental justice concerns is the Clearwater, Florida brownfields redevelopment program that became the basis for the International City/County Manager's Association 'Model Plan for Environmental Justice in Brownfields Redevelopment'. Urban sprawl in the densely populated Clearwater, Florida area left the city with 217 contaminated sites covering nearly 2000 acres, many of which were abandoned (Singer, 2002, p. 14). Almost 60 per cent of the over 10 000 residents of these brownfields areas were members of ethnic minorities and over 27 per cent of the residents were living below the poverty level (Singer, 2002, p. 14).

Rather than use traditional approaches to redevelopment, Clearwater, supported by an EPA Brownfields Demonstration Pilot Project grant, developed an innovative community consultation process that now serves as a model for large brownfields redevelopment projects (Singer, 2002, p. 14). The pilot project used many of the public engagement concepts that NEJAC and NAPA have recommended and follows many of the recommendations from EPA's public engagement procedures.

Clearwater created its brownfields redevelopment action agenda using a collaborative, community-based planning approach – 'In Clearwater, development of the action agenda was entirely community driven' (Singer, 2002, p. 16). The resulting Clearwater Action Agenda focuses on enhancing awareness of brownfields issues, improving the community's access to information, ensuring public participation in decision making, developing the economic base of the brownfields area neighborhoods consistent with community desires and creating a healthy and safe environment (Singer 2002, p. 35).

The Clearwater initiative was designed to simultaneously address economic, environmental and community issues. A study of the initiative indicates that the approach to engaging the community in the redevelopment process has achieved the important goal of stimulating redevelopment in a more equitable and acceptable manner. The study concluded 'Clearwater and its community groups are demonstrating the positive results of collaboration in addressing environmental justice and brownfields challenges' (Singer, 2002, p. 44).

7.7 THE WAY FORWARD

The historic public participation processes relied on in the United States for decades that interpose government agencies and processes between the citizens and the issues with which they are concerned clearly do not provide the type of public engagement needed to produce the best decisions, maximize the legitimacy of those decisions and provide the kind of access to the decision making process that the public today demands. The problems with traditional approaches to public participation are magnified in the context of environmental justice. Long-standing power imbalances combine with a wide range of other factors (such as lack of familiarity with how to effectively participate in government decision making, time and resource limitations and even language skills) to deprive people from low income and minority communities the opportunity to effectively engage in government decision making. Because authentic engagement in governmental decision making is widely recognized as a key tool for achieving environmental justice, it is critical that steps continue to be taken to open up the decision-making process to more authentic public engagement. Evolving standards of international law support the idea that authentic public engagement is more than just good practice. It is, instead, increasingly seen as a basic human right.

Over the last 20 years innovation at the federal, state and local governmental levels has produced a range of techniques that help create a more authentic public engagement process in the United States. Still, these practices remain far from uniform and frequently, even at EPA, are only provided based on agency policies that do not have the force of law. The challenge going forward is to transform these policies and practices from interesting experiments in a few programs and in a few jurisdictions to standard operating procedures for government agencies at all levels supported by appropriate legislation and regulations.

To truly engage the public in a way that is likely to produce more just outcomes, governments must:

- Provide early notice when government approvals are first sought rather than at the end of the process when a project has been fully formulated.
- Widely distribute notices through channels that will reach affected communities and in languages that are likely to be understood in affected communities.
- Encourage those seeking government approvals to first work with community members affected by the proposed action to identify concerns and help shape solutions.
- Provide communities in appropriate cases with the resources needed to consult with technical experts that represent the community interests.
- Develop and use collaborative planning and decision-making processes including community dialogues, mediation and other techniques that allow communities to be directly engaged in decisions affecting them.
- Provide easy and early access through a variety of channels such as the internet and local libraries to information about proposed permits or other proposed government actions that includes non-technical descriptions of the actions and that is available in languages spoken in the affected communities.
- Hold meetings at times, in locations, and utilizing formats that encourage community engagement.
- Identify communities that are disproportionately affected by environmental hazards and direct additional public engagement resources to these communities.
- Use communication methods such as community action panels and 'living room' meetings that directly engage community members in their own communities rather than rely on formal public meetings or public hearings.
- Utilize new communication techniques such as geographic information systems that can make complex data more easily understood.
- Actively listen to community concerns, take those concerns into account in their decisions and communicate with the community about how its concerns were taken into account in the final decision.
- Train agency staff about the value and importance of local knowledge in the agency decision-making process and actively seek out local knowledge relevant to the approval process.
- Teach government employees both about the importance of public engagement and the range of techniques available to provide opportunities for authentic engagement.
- Regularly evaluate public engagement processes and adjust the processes based on experience and feedback.

These approaches to engagement must be more than public policy statements or agency policy. They must be incorporated into statutory and regulatory requirements, and become standard operating procedures for government agencies at all levels. Only when governments routinely provide all affected persons a more authentic form of public engagement will the goal of achieving more just environmental outcomes be achieved.

APPENDIX 1

NATIONAL ENVIRONMENTAL JUSTICE ADVISORY COMMITTEE (NEJAC)

CORE VALUES AND GUIDING PRINCIPLES FOR THE PRACTICE OF PUBLIC PARTICIPATION

1. People should have a say in decisions about actions which affect their lives.
2. Public participation includes the promise that the public's contribution will influence the decision.
3. The public participation process communicates the interests and meets the process needs of all participants.
4. The public participation process seeks out and facilitates the involvement of those potentially affected.
5. The public participation process involves participants in defining how they participate.
6. The public participation process communicates to participants how their input was, or was not, utilized.
7. The public participation process provides participants with the information they need to participate in a meaningful way.
8. Involve the public in decisions about actions which affect their lives.
9. Maintain honesty and integrity throughout the process.
10. Encourage early and active community participation.
11. Recognize community knowledge.
12. Use cross-cultural methods of communication.
13. Institutionalize meaningful public participation by acknowledging and formalizing the process.
14. Create mechanisms and measurements to ensure the effectiveness of the public participation (Model Plan for Public Participation 2000, p. 13).

NOTES

* Sarah Zubair and Virginia Glasgow assisted with this article.

1. http://www.epa.gov/compliance/environmentaljustice/nejac/index.html (accessed 6 February 2012).
2. Executive Order 12898, section 1–101, available at http://www.epa.gov/compliance/ej/resources/policy/exec_order_12898.pdf (accessed 6 February 2012).
3. http://www.epa.gov/environmentaljustice/index.html (accessed 6 February 2012).
4. http://www.epa.gov/environmentaljustice/basics/ (accessed 6 February 2012).
5. http://www.wri.org/publication/content/8078 (accessed 6 February 2012).
6. United Nations Economic Commission for Europe (1998), *Convention on Access to Information, Public Participation in Decision-making and Access to Justice in Environmental Matters*, available at http://www.unece.org/env/pp/documents/cep43e.pdf (accessed 6 February 2012).
7. United Nations Economic Commission for Europe (2000), *The Aarhus Convention: An Implementation Guide*, available at http://www.unece.org/env/pp/acig.pdf (accessed 6 February 2012). Among other things, Article 6 of the Aarhus Convention provides:

   - 'Each Party shall provide for early public participation, when all options are open and effective public participation can take place.' Aarhus Convention art. 6 ¶ 4.
   - 'Each Party should, where appropriate, encourage prospective applicants to identify the public concerned, to enter into discussions, and to provide information regarding the objectives of their application before applying for a permit.' Ibid., at art. 6 ¶ 5.
   - 'Each party shall ensure that in the decision due account is taken of the outcome of the public participation.' Ibid., at art. 6 ¶ 7.

8. Administrative Procedure Act, 5 U.S.C. §§ 551–706 (2007).
9. Administrative Procedure Act, 5 U.S.C. § 553(c) (2007) (requires that after the notice the agency must give interested persons an opportunity to participate in the rulemaking through submission of written data, views, or arguments with or without the opportunity for oral presentation).
10. Administrative Procedure Act, 5 U.S.C. § 554(a) (2007).
11. See, for example, New York Administrative Procedures Act §§ 1–601 (2003); Minnesota Statutes §§ 14.001–.70 (2003).
12. www.ejnet.org/ej/principles.html (accessed 6 February 2012).
13. United States Environmental Protection Agency, *Superfund Reforms*, available at www.epa.gov/superfund/programs/reforms/byround.htm (accessed 6 February 2012).
14. Superfund Reforms, available at www.epa.gov/superfund/programs/reforms/reforms/2–5a.htm (accessed 6 February 2012).
15. 60 Federal Register 63417–63434 (December 11, 1995).
16. California Public Resources Code § 71116 (2007).
17. California Health & Safety Code § 57008(c)(1)–(c)(2)(e)(2006).
18. Illinois Environmental Protection Agency, Interim Environmental Justice Policy, available at http://www.epa.state.il.us/environmental-justice/policy.html, (accessed 6 February 2012)
19. Illinois Environmental Protection Agency, Environmental Justice Public Participation Policy, available at http://www.epa.state.il.us/environmental-justice/public-participation-policy.pdf (accessed 6 February 2012).
20. Massachusetts Office of Environmental Affairs, Environmental Justice Policy, available at http://www.mass.gov/eea/docs/eea/ej/ej-policy-english.pdf (accessed 15 February 2012).
21. Ibid.
22. New York State Department of Environmental Conservation, Commissioner Policy 29, Environmental Justice and Permitting, available at http://www.dec.ny.gov/regulations/36951.html (accessed 6 February 2012).

23. Ibid.
24. N.M. Environmental Justice Executive Order 2005–56, at 1, available at http://www.nmenv.state.nm.us/Justice/EO_2005_056.pdf (accessed 6 February 2012).
25. Pennsylvania. Department of Environmental Protection, Environmental Justice Public Participation Policy, at 5–7, available at http://www.elibrary.dep.state.pa.us/dsweb/Get/Version-48671/012–0501–002.pdf (accessed 6 February 2012).
26. Ibid.
27. Ibid., at 14.
28. http://www.epa.gov/brownfields/basic_info.htm (accessed 15 February 2012).

REFERENCES

Beierle, T.C. and J. Cayford (2002), *Democracy in Practice: Public Participation in Environmental Decisionmaking* (Resources for the Future).

Environmental Law Institute (1999), *Building Capacity to Participate in Environmental Protection Agency Activities: A Needs Assessment and Analysis* (Environmental Law Institute).

International Union for the Conservation of Nature (1995), Draft International Covenant on Environment and Development.

King, C.S. et al. (1998), 'The Question of Participation: Toward Authentic Public Participation in Public Administration', 58 *Public Administration Review* 317.

Lavelle, M. and M. Coyle (September 21, 1992), 'Unequal Justice: The Racial Divide in Environmental Law', 15 *National Law Journal* No. 3.

Maantay, J. (2002) 'Zoning Law, Health, and Environmental Justice: What's the Connection?' *Journal of Law, Medicine & Ethics*, 6 (December 22).

Martin, K.L. and J.A. Martin (1991), 'Enhancing Citizen Participation: Panel Designs, Perspectives, and Policy Formation', 10 *Journal of Policy Analysis & Management* 46–63.

National Academy of Public Administration (2001), *Environmental Justice in EPA Permitting: Reducing Pollution in High-Risk Communities is Integral to the Agency's Mission.*

National Academy of Public Administration (2002), *Models for Change: Efforts by Four States to Address Environmental Justice.*

National Academy of Public Administration (2003), *Addressing Community Concerns: How Environmental Justice Relates to Land Use Planning and Zoning.*

The President's Council on Sustainable Development (1996), *Sustainable America: A New Consensus for Prosperity, Opportunity and a Healthy Environment for the Future.*

The President's Council on Sustainable Development (1997), *Sustainable Communities Task Force Report.*

Singer, M. (2002) *Righting the Wrong: A Model for Environmental Justice in Brownfields Redevelopment* (International City County Management Association).

United Church of Christ Commission on Racial Justice (2007), Toxic Waste and Race at Twenty 1987–2007.

United States Environmental Protection Agency (1996), Office of Solid Waste and Emergency Response, *Public Participation Manual.*

United States Environmental Protection Agency (2003), Office of Policy, Economics and Innovation, *Public Involvement Policy* (May).

United States Environmental Protection Agency (2006), Office of Environmental Justice, National Environmental Justice Advisory Council, *Future Mechanisms to Enhance Stakeholder Involvement and Engagement to Address Environmental Justice* (August).

8. The right of access to information as a tool for environmental protection and poverty eradication in Mexico

Carla D. Aceves-Ávila

8.1 INTRODUCTION

Principle 10 of the *Río Declaration* states that:

> Environmental issues are best handled with participation of all concerned citizens at the relevant level. At the national level, each individual shall have appropriate access to information concerning the environment that is held by public authorities, including information on hazardous materials and activities in their communities, and the opportunity to participate in decision-making processes. States shall facilitate and encourage public awareness and participation by making information widely available. Effective access to judicial and administrative proceedings, including redress and remedy, shall be provided.[1]

The three concepts found within Principle 10, namely access to environmental information, access to decision-making processes and access to environmental justice through redress and remedy, form the basis of environmental democracy. They also constitute powerful tools for poverty eradication.

Environmental resources and the services they provide are especially important for people living in poverty since a good part of this population draws much of their livelihoods from forests, pastures, fisheries or farming. Thus, their economy as well as their quality of life is strongly linked to environmental goods and services. Also, they tend to reside in areas with stressed or low quality environmental resources such as sloped areas with greater risk of landslides, dry rivers or rivers which when flooded represent a greater hazard, and polluted areas where sectors of the population with more decision-making power as well as higher incomes would never choose to live. Therefore, the improvement of low quality environmental resources is an indirect goal of anti-poverty policies (UNDP et al., 2005, p. 9–11).

According to studies, the top four leading risk factors to health in developing countries are (1) malnutrition, (2) unsafe sex, (3) unsafe water and lack of sanitation and hygiene, and (4) indoor smoke from solid fuels. The prevalence of malnutrition is associated with food insecurity as well as with an unhealthy environment, with especially dire consequences among young children (World Bank, 2007, pp. 26–29). Thus, the reduction of environmental risk factors through access to fresh and safe water and access to safe food will contribute to the improvement of other indicators, directly influencing the quality of life.

The linkages between poverty and environmental degradation still need to be researched in more depth. Nevertheless, it is clear that poverty reduction will not necessarily lead to an improved environment unless specific environmental action is taken. At the same time, an improved environment will mitigate the effects of extreme poverty by improving health and sanitation conditions. However, this will not be possible only through public policy and legislation as these are not sufficient to change a negative or indolent attitude towards environmental protection. Caring for and nurturing of environmental resources requires an interactive approach between the State and society.

The realization of the three concepts found in Principle 10 of the *Rio Declaration* as well as the implementation of a sound public policy for poverty eradication requires a clear articulation of legal mechanisms as well as the joint engagement of the state and citizens. The mere existence of legal mechanisms for access to participation, access to justice or access to information is not effective for environmental protection or for eradication of poverty. What is also needed is the active involvement of the population through those instruments. The role of the state is strengthened when its decisions are taken on the basis of what the needs are within the households of the nation. In addition, participation of individuals is a form of validation of the state's performance since it reflects the trust that society has in it. It is the true reflection of governance.

With regard to eradication of poverty, public policy must expressly consider the needs of the vulnerable groups in order to enable and support their public participation and their access to information. Without simple access to reliable and understandable information necessary for immediate and sound decision making, no informed public participation is possible.[2] There is no decision making occurring when information about the status quo is unavailable. Also, there is no decision making when there are no choices available to decide over. Unfortunately, the poor and marginalized do not decide; they tend to live in whatever conditions are possible.

In sum, access to information represents a powerful tool for the eradication of poverty and the protection of the environment since it formally enables and protects social participation through interaction as well as making possible decision-making processes which contribute to the quality of life of the stakeholders. Access to information empowers citizens and in the case of the poor enables them to decide over their own environmental goods and services while at the same time validating State decisions though the active participation of individual stakeholders.

8.2 MEXICAN IMPLEMENTATION OF PUBLIC ENVIRONMENTAL ORDER AND PRINCIPLE 10

The three dimensions of sustainability are economic, environmental and social. They have to be considered holistically for sustainability to be achieved. According to Decleris, sustainable development rests on certain basic principles, the first one being the principle of Public Environmental Order. By its very nature, this principle is the 'province and responsibility of the state for strategic control and supervision, but it requires that all members of society including government, groups, organizations, businesses and citizens alike act in accordance with the diverse actions which depend on them' (Decleris, 2000, p. 67). Thus, the state will be responsible for creating this order through the enactment and putting into practice of an appropriate legal framework. The state will also have the responsibility of controlling, structuring and reviewing the implementation of this framework. It is also its duty to create an adequate political environment that enables and promotes participation of all groups. The accountability and transparency of state procedures promotes and strengthens credibility thus inducing public participation. Quadri recognizes that information is the 'lubricant' of every transaction or regulation and the foundation of public policy. Lack of information is cause for uncertainty and risk and also limits decision making, both for the common citizen as well as for the state (Quadri, 2006, pp. 158–159).

8.2.1 Access to Information as Public Environmental Order

In Mexico the first relevant legislation for environmental protection was the General Law of Ecological Balance and Environmental Protection (*Ley General del Equilibrio Ecológico y la Protección al Ambiente*, LGEEPA by its acronym in Spanish). Published on 28 January 1988, it has gone through several amendments since its enactment.[3] It currently includes a whole chapter on access to information and public participation, although its legal role in regards to access to information has substantially changed since its enactment as we will see later.

The LGEEPA was a pioneer law in terms of access to information. Its Article 159 *bis* states that the Mexican Federal Environmental Agency (SEMARNAT)[4] shall develop a National System of Environmental Information and of Natural Resources which shall register, organize, update, and disseminate national environmental information. The law states that this database shall be available for consultation. As we shall see later, this general provision is displaced by a specific one which may be interpreted as the Mexican equivalent of a 'Freedom of Information Act' translated as Federal Transparency and Access to Government Public Information Law (LFTAIPG for its acronym in Spanish or *Ley Federal de Transparencia y Acceso a la Información Pública Gubernamental*).[5] Given that Mexico is a Federation, the Federal law takes precedence over any state laws. Currently, Mexico has transparency laws for every state of Mexico and based on our administrative law principles, these special laws (Federal transparency legislation as well as state transparency legislations) displace the older provision in LGEEPA regarding access to information.

Access to information enables stakeholders to make informed choices and, as a result, improves the environmental performance of societies. This concept imposes on governments the duty to collect, disclose and disseminate the information. A specific request will be known under current environmental governance theory as passive access to information while information disseminated by the State without request is known as an active one.[6] Active access to information provides the opportunity for targeted parties that receive the information to make better informed choices. It also creates a sense of awareness in the population. In Mexico, the LGEEPA only requires the SEMARNAT to create a Federal environmental information system which will be discussed later. There is no clear provision in the law as to how such information is to be organized and disseminated, except for passive disclosure through the internet. In addition, the LFTAIPG as well as transparency state legislations only require the Federal or the state authorities to disclose the information that they are specifically required to disclose through a petition regulated by such laws. Thus, active access to information is scarcely used and passive access to information is not clearly regulated, as we will see below.

Timely access to accurate and meaningful information enables individuals to make informed choices and therefore to better plan their own immediate future and, in some cases, the long term. Information is essential to exercise precaution and thus prevention. It is no longer useful, no matter how accurate it is, when it comes too late to prevent damage to the environment or health. Unfortunately, accurate and timely information is costly and the state may not yet be able to provide such information.[7] This can have dire consequences during environmental emergencies and natural disasters. Rapid access to reliable information during those situations can allow individuals to make better choices as to where to go and what to do. As well *ex post* information regarding the emergency or the disaster will enable individuals to learn from the experience. For the state, *ex post* follow up and evaluation allows for a proper assessment of the damage and to better prevent or plan for future disasters or emergencies. Neither the LGEEPA nor the LFTAIPG establish in Mexico the administrative obligation to provide timely and sensible environmental information. On the contrary, through the LFTAIPG, sensitive information which might endanger the health and well being of the population may be restricted and even classified.[8]

The concept of access to information in Principle 10 of the *Rio Declaration* must be interpreted in the broadest possible sense, both in terms of accountability and quality of information.[9] For instance, the information must be accessible if requested. If it is posted through electronic media or publications it should be in plain language so that it can be easily understood.[10] It should also be regularly updated and organized in such a way that it can usefully be compared with other relevant data. Without these characteristics, the information may be useless even if available and actively disseminated by the state. In the Mexican case, neither the LGEEPA nor the LFTAIPG establish any guidelines that ensure that the available information is understandable for the general public, and even more, that it may be useful for the population that may need it the most. A great part of the available information is in technical terms which may not be useful information for the general public. In addition, accessibility to real decision-making information is limited and most SEMARNAT internet sites that provide information on 'relevant' environmental news resemble more an administrative activity environmental chronicle than a public site for environmental information data. They scarcely comply with the above and thus clearly do not meet their informative purpose.

8.2.2 Access to Decision Making as Public Environmental Order

Regarding public participation, Article 159 of the LGEEPA establishes the possibility of participation in decision-making processes through citizen organizations (generally councils) that may be composed of common citizens, representatives of public institutions, as well as social or business organizations. Whenever collective organizations issue an opinion, the Mexican Federal Environmental Agency (SEMARNAT) shall explain why it accepts or rejects such opinions. Unfortunately, open mechanisms for public participation mechanisms are still scarce as is the spontaneous participation of the public. In the case of individual participations in public consultations there is no obligation on the Federal authority to follow up on opinions or interventions expressed orally in such procedures and inform the individual participant of the integration or rejection of his or her proposal, even though there is a registration procedure previous to participation which could enable follow up.

Through a process for public participation, ordinary citizens can interact with the government in order to contribute in the decision-making process on environmental issues. This may occur for specific projects or for general environmental public policy making. Public knowledge enriches the process and can result in more effective public policy. In the case of particular projects, public participation can lead to the approval from groups and individuals directly affected. Unfortunately, Mexican environmental law does not require the active participation of citizens in relevant information and participation mechanisms such in the case of an environmental impact assessment. As an illustrative example, neither general environmental law nor the specific environmental impact federal regulation[11] requires that potentially affected population participates. Public consultation may occur in the EIA Federal procedure if a person requests it. If the regulation appears inclusive on paper, the reality is that citizens will rarely demand or take part in a public consultation process if they are not personally informed that a project could potentially affect them. Unfortunately, Mexican regulation does not require active access to information to all stakeholders interested or involved, but rather only those directly impacted by projects as owners or directly affected parties.[12] Also, there is no obligation to follow up on any citizen observations and/or suggestions unless done in writing. As follow up is only mandatory when done in writing, it limits public participation as well as the responsibility of the state to provide access to information. Environmental procedures both at a state and at a local level may still be legally approved under relative secrecy, even when projects involve public funds.

8.3 PRINCIPLE 10 AND POVERTY ERADICATION

In September 2000, the states of the world adopted the Millennium Declaration[13] which aims to reduce extreme poverty as well as achieving seven other goals with a set deadline of year 2015. Known as the Millenium Development Goals (MDGs), these targets are meant to promote development through the eradication of extreme poverty, improvement of social conditions and protection of human rights, eradication of hunger and disease, promotion of peace, and protection of the environment through global cooperation. Duraiappah identifies ten constituents for improving well-being and reducing poverty:

1. Being able to be adequately nourished.
2. Being able to be free from avoidable disease.
3. Being able to live in an environmentally clean and safe shelter.
4. Being able to have adequate and clean drinking water.
5. Being able to have clean air.
6. Being able to have energy to keep warm and to cook.
7. Being able to use traditional medicine.
8. Being able to continue using natural elements found in ecosystems for traditional, cultural and spiritual practices.
9. Being able to cope with extreme natural events including floods, tropical storms and landslides.
10. Being able to make sustainable management decisions that respect natural resources and enable the achievement of a sustainable income stream.

(Duraiappah, 2004, p. 4)

These constituents, in particular numbers two, three, four, five and nine, clearly rely and depend on public participation issues discussed in the previous section. Regarding constituent two, the guarantee of access to information means having timely and accurate knowledge of the places in which sicknesses occur, as well as adequate information for the prevention of a disease. The third constituent, being able to live in an environmentally clean and safe shelter, requires that the public be made aware of places that could be exposed to abrupt environmental changes, whether natural disasters (earthquakes, floods, geological flaws, hurricanes among others), or emergencies or disasters caused by anthropogenic activities such as exposure to hazardous activities or high level of pollution. In such cases, timely, accurate and available information is vital for the preservation of life. In terms of the fourth and fifth constituents, access to information will obviously not provide clean and safe water and clean air, but the information available will convey to the affected population what is the quantity and quality of the available resources. Given the essential role that water and air play on human health and the environment, a targeted active access to information approach is required. This is also true for the population that is to use such resources in order to prevent disease in the event of an emergency involving water or air pollution. Regarding constituent nine, the ability to cope with extreme natural events including floods, tropical storms and landslides will be increased or impaired in part through the access to timely and accurate information, evidently through an active access approach, clearly targeted to the potentially affected population. Also, prevention and future planning depend on access to adequate information for decision making. The potentiality of risk, whether environmental risk or risk to the population based on geographical, geological or other natural conditions should be at least passively disseminated by the state in order to enable adequate risk management.

Some international instruments identify and recognize the existing linkage between environment and development as well as poverty. In the *Draft International Covenant on Environment and Development*, an instrument widely consulted, article 12.3 states that: 'Parties shall ensure that all persons, without being required to prove an interest, have the right to seek, receive, and disseminate information in respect to the environment, subject only to the restrictions as may be provided by law and are necessary for respect for the rights of others, or for the protection of the environment.'[14] Thus, states shall, according to this document, guarantee at least passive access to information with respect to the environment. The *Draft International Covenant on Environment and Development* identifies specific linkages between development issues involving environmental protection and access to information, stressing the importance of public participation as well as the role of the State in guaranteeing at least passive access to information.

8.4 ACCESS TO PUBLIC INFORMATION IN MEXICO

As commented previously, the Mexican equivalent to the United States' Freedom of Information Act (FOIA)[15] is the Federal Law on Transparency and Access to Public and Government Information (LFTAIPG) enacted in 2002. Later on, a federal organ was created, the Federal Institute of Transparency and Access to Information (IFAI).[16] This is an organ autonomous from the Mexican Federal Public Administration. Its function is to review the appeals of denials of petitions for access to information against any of the federal agencies subject to the LFTAIPG. Currently, all the Mexican states have their own Law on Transparency and Access to Public and Government Information which regulates access to public information held by state government agencies. In addition, most of the states also have their local Institute of Transparency and Access to Information for local information.

8.4.1 Public Environmental Information in Mexico: Conceptual Limitations

Article 159 *bis* 3 of the LGEEPA defines environmental information as follows:

> For the effects of what is established in this regulation, the following will be deemed environmental information; any written, visual or database information in power of the environmental authorities regarding water, air, land, flora and fauna and natural resources, as well as information over the activities or measures that affect them or may affect them.[17]

On the other hand, the LFTAIPG does not make any express mention of environmental information. Apart from the provision under LGEEPA (which as mentioned, is no longer the primary legal instrument for the regulation of environmental information), there is no other reference to or definition of environmental information under the LFTAIPG. There is in fact no distinction between environmental information and any other kind of information. This omission is important since the identification of information as 'environmental' or not may be crucial to determine if access to it is possible. As commented before, under the LFTAIPG, information which may put at risk the life, safety or health of any person may be classified or reserved. Clearly, if the legislation or even regulations do not establish the link between the quality of environmental elements such as water, air, land, flora or fauna, and their effect over general human wellbeing, environmental information that may impact life, safety or health but is not directly on those elements may be genuinely withheld by Federal authorities. Also, if this ambiguity is sustained, sensible information that may impact life, safety or health clearly could result in irreversible damages on the environment. This lack of clarity as well as the absence of an administrative provision that identifies this link for the better understanding of the meaning of 'environmental information' could tacitly tolerate environmental damage based on this legal ambiguity.

Article 3 of the Mexican environmental general law (LGEEPA)[18] defines 'environment' as 'the group of natural and artificial elements or those induced by man, which make possible the existence and development of human beings and the rest of living organisms which interact in a determined time and space'.[19] This definition is broad as it comprises natural elements as well as those elements introduced by man. However, while many natural resources fall under the authority of SEMARNAT, oil and all the activities associated with its exploration and refinement, as well as the production of electricity and nuclear energy (as well as other forms of energy), are under the administrative scope of the Secretary of Energy (SENER),[20] while a large part of the land as well as agricultural activities and fisheries are under the scope of the SAGARPA.[21] Additionally, under Article 115 of the Mexican Federal Constitution,[22] urban development is locally regulated and controlled. Therefore, not all matters included within the definition of 'environment' or under 'environmental information' under Mexican federal laws will fall under the power of the same authority. 'Environmental authority' is nowhere defined whether in the environmental legislation or in the FOIAs. SEMARNAT, SAGARPA, SENER and municipalities have public information that affects or may affect water, land, air, flora, fauna or other natural resources, but may not be deemed environmental authorities with the exception of SEMARNAT as environmental protection is its main mandate. Also information regarding emergencies (whether natural disasters or local emergencies) may be dealt with by federal or local agencies, contributing to the dispersion (not dissemination) of this information.

Another obstacle to the release of information is that some of it is cogenerated by the state and a private party, or is entirely the property of the latter. No matter how sensitive for decision making the information might be, if it is deemed as 'private property' or 'personal information', it may well be treated as confidential and, as such outside the reach of the legislation. Thus, some information may be provided under Federal or state LTAIPGs but it may be incomplete and thus meaningless if key parts of the information related to health or environmental safety issues are missing. In addition, not all of the information may be held by public authorities, but rather by private parties when working as contractors for the state, thus also being deemed as personal information or private data protected under privacy or intimacy regulations. Mexican law has not yet properly addressed this situation (Hallo, 2001, p. 5). This is typically the case for waste management, whether hazardous or non-hazardous, allowing the state (or the private party) to 'legally conceal' or not disclose such information.

8.4.2 Passive Access to Environmental Information through SNIARN

In terms of national environmental information the LGEEPA created the National System of Environmental Information (SNIARN).[23] This system compiles all the public environmental information, whether gathered or generated by the SEMARNAT, and makes it available through electronic means.[24] These databases comprise most of the public environmental practice in Mexico and include:

1. the Natural Protected Areas Registry (RENANP);[25]
2. all reports of atmospheric quality (air pollution);[26]
3. all information collected through the National Register for Emissions and Pollutant Transfer (RETC);[27]
4. the National System of Information on Biodiversity of Mexico[28] whose main function is to serve as a decision-making instrument for SEMARNAT and other federal agencies;
5. the National Subsystem of Information on Wildlife;[29]
6. the System of Information on Integral Waste Management[30] which integrates information on local waste management situation, local waste inventories, and local infrastructure for waste management, as well as information on unauthorized hazardous waste sites or repositories which may have already been identified. This system is part of an integrated approach that will compile information on hazardous waste and persistent organic pollutants. This database will be created as a subsystem of information within SNIARN, but serious incompatibilities in the collection of the information, the methodology used to compile it as well as the potential inaccuracy of the information provided by waste generators have seriously limited progress in its implementation.

According to Article 109 of the LGEEPA,[31] all information contained in the SNIARN will be public and may be requested through the mechanisms provided by law. Most of this information is obtained by SNIARN through reports prepared by the state and private parties. Indeed, the greater part of this information is provided by private parties and not necessarily verified by SEMARNAT. In addition, even though SEMARNAT is the main administrative entity, the information is compiled through different specialized environmental agencies, all part of SEMARNAT, such as the National Commission of Natural Protected Areas (CONANP)[32] and the National Commission for the Knowledge and Use of Biodiversity.[33] Given that SEMARNAT neither possesses nor concentrates all the 'environmental information', SNIARN is a successful instrument for gathering the greater part of the information, but it could still be improved upon.

Besides SNIARN, there are other databases which contain environmental information in Mexico:

1. The National System of Information on Fisheries and Aquaculture,[34] the National Registry of Fisheries and Aquaculture, the National System of Information on the Fisheries and Agriculture and Food Sector,[35] all administered by the SAGARPA, as well as the National Network of Information and Research on Fisheries and Aquaculture.[36] The latter is administered by the National Institute of Fisheries and Aquaculture (INAPESCA).[37] As mentioned before, SAGARPA, Mexico's agriculture and livestock agency, is yet another federal agency that has some environmental competences over a number of natural resources such as fisheries or livestock.
2. The Public Registry of Water Rights[38] includes data on concessions, and water discharge permits. This information is compiled and administered by the National Water Commission (CONAGUA),[39] which is also part of SEMARNAT.
3. The National System of Information on water quantity, quality, uses and conservation,[40] also administered by CONAGUA and which includes information from private parties.[41]
4. The National System of Information on Biosafety[42] and the National Registry of Genetically Modified Organisms,[43] administered by the Intersecretarial Commission of Biosafety of Genetically Modified Organisms (CIBIOGEM).[44]
5. The National System of Forestry Information (SNIF),[45] with the information generated and held by the National Forestry Commission (CONAFOR), another organ of SEMARNAT.
6. The National System of Information for Sustainable Rural Development[46] which will contain economical, environmental, technological, and industrial information. This system is also administered by SAGARPA, but it may be fed through information provided by SEMARNAT through CONAFOR, among other agencies.[47]

Besides these, the federal administration developed other databases such as the National Environmental Indicators System (SIDIA)[48] and the National System of Municipal Information (SNIM).[49] There are several other local information efforts and even a few other federal ones, but they may not be permanently available, or, as currently happens in most of the databases cited, they may not be regularly updated.

These are the main systems containing environmental information as well as the main registries which hold the federal environmental information. This system provides the structures for other databases which hold (or will hold) environmental information compiled and administered by local environmental agencies that will also provide additional information for these federal data systems.

While most of the databases mentioned are passive mechanisms for access to information, there are a few examples of active access. The Metropolitan Air Quality Index or air quality monitoring program (IMECA),[50] is a permanent program that monitors air quality standards in the major metropolitan zones throughout Mexico. This program is part of the National Emissions Inventory (INEM)[51] supported by SEMARNAT and other national and international agencies. The results of air quality analysis are shown, practically in real time, through public screens in strategic places in the cities, as well as in the corresponding websites of local environmental authorities and they are later inventoried. This effort is complemented by others such as the previously mentioned RETC, and the Inventory of Greenhouse Emissions.[52]

Another example of active access to environmental information in Mexico is the Clean Beaches Integral Program launched by SEMARNAT in conjunction with the Federal Commission for the Prevention of Sanitary Risks (COFEPRIS). These results in fact integrate the National Information System of Water Quality in Mexican Beaches.[53] This program monitors the water quality in sea water in the main tourist destinations in Mexico. It measures the hazardous bacteria found in water and makes the results public and provides targeted information in case of emergency (emergencies may occur not only because of pollution but also due to rainy seasons, or marine natural events). Not permanently implemented, this program tends to be active during high tourist seasons.

As can be seen, active access represents only a minority of the information available. Besides the fact that the real decision-making information for the everyday consumer is hard to find, large amounts of relevant information are misleading because they are not updated while others require registration for consultation, some information being meaningless without a knowledge of the methodology with which it was obtained. There is no obligation to disseminate correct, complete and current information to interested parties through means accessible to them. This is unfortunate in a country in which more than seven million Mexicans do not speak Spanish but instead an indigenous mother tongue and live in poverty (Comisión Nacional para el Desarrollo de los Pueblos Indígenas, 2000).[54] Needless to say, this further aggravates their already difficult condition, hindering the possibility of participating in active decision making procedures.

Of course, this is also true of other populations living in poverty. Around 10.71 per cent of the Mexican population lived in extreme poverty in 2009. In the last two years, the number of poor (not extremely poor) increased to 19.6 per cent which is equivalent to 9 of the 32 states of Mexico.[55] The National

Institute for Statistics, Geography and Computing (INEGI) stated that only 6.3 per cent of the households in Mexico had access to internet in 2010.[56] As we have observed, the internet is a powerful tool used by the Mexican government which is still a distant reality for most Mexican households. This fact limits access to information for most Mexicans (when asked for information the state environmental authority may argue that the information is already publicly available through the internet), and it limits even more those vulnerable groups such as the poor who have no electricity, education, or knowledge of official language. Empowerment of indigenous groups as well as other vulnerable collectivities is necessary in order to fully achieve and fulfil the guarantee of access to information.[57]

In 2004, the *Instituto Federal de Accesso a la Informacion* (IFAI) made an interesting diagnosis of the right of access to environmental information in Mexico based on the LFTAIPG and the LGEEPA, concluding that there had been an enormous change in the approach to access to information over the last years, but criticizing the disorganization of the information and the lack of a regulation regarding files and archives, as well as the obscurity of the criteria for classifying and declassifying information. Possibly the greatest flaw identified was the lack of a culture of access to information (IFAI, 2004, pp. 21–35). Sadly, in 2011 the picture has not changed much regarding the disorganization of the information, as well as the lack of interest of the environmental authority to promote a better involvement of the population in decision-making processes. Information has certainly increased in quantity and certainly in potential access, but it has not in quality and certainly not in organization. A formal strategy for education and information has not yet been planned to reach vulnerable population, and a formal strategy (and policy) for organization and systematization of public environmental information has not been implemented.

Nevertheless, in 2007, the mechanism for requesting information in Mexico was identified by Rodríguez as 'much more efficient' (than the one previously in force). She stressed the fortunate fact that the LFTAIPG established 'control mechanisms in order to assure the right to access to information' through IFAI.[58] She referred to access to environmental information and she made an interesting comparison between the access to information mechanisms previously enforceable by the LGEEPA and by the LFTAIPG and the subsequent amendments to the LFTAIPG access to information procedure. However, as mentioned above, the LFTAIPG does not make any specific mention of environmental information.

The LFTAIG also contains a provision, Article 13, paragraphs one and four, on 'reserved information', referring to information that may be withheld on the grounds of compromising 'national security, national defense … put in risk life, safety or the health of any person …'.[59] A large part of the Mexican population which is vulnerable to natural disasters and/or environmental emergencies, does not have access to the internet and, as mentioned, there is no obligation from the environmental authority to follow up on active access to information procedures in case of emergencies. Information may be withheld under LFTAIPG regulation when justified by 'evidence of harm'.

While Mexican legal literature recognizes active access to information (Salazar Ugarte, 2008, p. 11), the Mexican legal framework and implementation of access to information mechanisms are not based on this approach. As mentioned previously, active access represents only a minority of the information available. Thus, even if the State is aware of environmental information that could be crucial for the involvement of citizens in the process of decision making, it has no material duty to make it known to the potentially affected parties as the regulation allows it not to release the information for up to 12 years.

Even though some environmental information instruments are of high quality, most of the information available to ordinary citizens through simple internet searches is not sufficiently clear. While technical documents are needed by professionals and researchers, it is also important to communicate effectively with the non-experts. In addition, there are currently no administrative criteria for the systematization, monitoring or the update of information available through the internet. Likewise, there are no criteria for the organization of physical archives containing past 'environmental information'. One step in the right direction would be to centralize the organization (not control) of environmental information in one entity in order to assure homogeneity.

8.5 CONCLUSION

While access to information in Mexico through LFTAIPG and IFAI is good compared to other regional efforts in Latin America, it still suffers from a number of defects, including the following:

1. The concepts of 'environment' as well as that of 'environmental information' under federal applicable laws do not encompass only the information compiled by SEMARNAT. While most of the federal environmental information can be found in SNIARN, some of it also falls under the jurisdiction of SAGARPA and SENER, as well as local authorities (at state or municipal level).
2. The information is not systematically integrated, classified or updated, making it often difficult to understand or of limited use to address environmental problems.
3. Although, there are some examples of active access to information,

Mexican law mandates only passive access to information. This is a real concern since most environmental information is now disseminated through the internet in a country in which a sizable portion of the population does not have access to this means of communication.

4. Very little of the information is available in indigenous languages even if traditionally indigenous groups are linked to environmentally vulnerable or sensitive areas.
5. A significant part of Mexico's population live in vulnerable conditions, naturally exposed to environmental emergencies. Currently, environmental information may be withheld by a public authority on the ground that it may endanger the life or health of a person as well as national security. Criteria for withholding information under this item have not yet been clearly developed under Mexican law.

In order to further improve access to environmental information in Mexico, in particular for the poor and vulnerable, the following are some of the measures that should be considered:

(a) mandate an active approach to access to information, starting with environmental emergency situations;
(b) target active access to information for vulnerable groups;
(c) provide environmental information to indigenous groups in their own languages, starting with the largest language groups and with key environmental information;
(d compile, classify and disseminate the information through environmental authorities according to clear administrative criteria, with an emphasis on the need for periodic update, clarity and identification of relevant information pertaining to environmental damage prevention, human health, environmental emergencies and natural disasters;
(e) make all the environmental information available through one main entity (presumably SNIARN) which would in turn coordinate the organization and linkage to all other bites of information for which it is not currently directly responsible. This entity would ensure that the information would be communicated in a language accessible for the ordinary citizen and in any case ensure that available technical information could be easily identifiable and thus requested by interested stakeholders or parties;
(f) make the information easily accessible in the case of passive access to information;
(g) finally, while it is important for Mexico to continue to invest in the training of environmental professionals, including legal professionals, it is also as important to build capacity among its citizens. Increased aware-

ness and better knowledge will engender greater public participation as well as a greater sense of shared responsibility over environmental issues. A true environmental democracy is based on differentiated rights and obligations, something that the Mexican population has not benefited from for a number of reasons, including marginalization, ignorance, or open distrust. The state has not sufficiently empowered citizens, notably by better following up on opinions expressed by citizens during the decision-making process.

Improved access to environmental information in Mexico requires first and foremost a transformation of attitudes. There has to be a better recognition and translation into law of the new social roles for the state and for citizens. Judges can also facilitate the transition to this new paradigm by helping to articulate the concept of environmental justice. On the other hand, failure to extend access to environmental information may greatly affect marginal and vulnerable groups and diminish the effectiveness of economic public policy linked to environmental protection and eradication of poverty.

NOTES

1. http://www.unep.org/Documents.Multilingual/Default.asp?documentid=78&articleid=1163 (accessed 7 February 2012).
2. The quality, besides the mere availability of information, is crucial. Information needs to be available (easily reachable for common people and/or free), timely, reliable, understandable, direct, and targeted when necessary in order for everyone, including vulnerable populations, to be 'empowered'.
3. *Ley General del Equilibrio Ecológico y la Protección al Ambiente*, Diario Oficial de la Federación,México, 28 January 1988, as well as its amendments. The provisions in this law address all the substantive matters regarding environmental policy, pollution prevention and pollution control. Several of its provisions deal with access to environmental information. Indeed, it was one of the first federal laws to introduce the possibility of access to information in Mexico. Several regulations were also enacted under this legislation.
4. *(SEMARNAT)* stands for *Secretaría de Medio Ambiente y Desarrollo Sustentable* which means *the* 'Secretariat of the environment and sustainable development'.
5. *Ley Federal de Transparencia y Acceso a la Información Pública Gubernamental*, Diario Oficial de la Federación, Diario Oficial de la Federación, June 11, 2002, México, as well as its amendments.
6. Sand, P.H. (2003), 'The Right to Know: Environmental Information Disclosure by Government and Industry' www.inece.org/forumspublicaccess_sand.pdf (accessed 7 February 2012).
7. For example, knowing in real time what is the air quality in a certain area requires the implementation of a system for air quality monitoring as well as the technology to organize the information, interpret it and communicate it to the affected population.
8. Article 13 of LFTAIPG establishes that 'Information dissemination of which may cause the following may be classified as reserved: I. May compromise national security, public safety, or national defense; II. May diminish the effectiveness of negotiations or of international relations, including such information which other States or international organizations communicate as confidential to the Mexican State; III. Damage financial, economical or

monetary stability of the country; IV. Place at risk the life, safety or the health of any person; or V. Cause serious damage to the activities of verification of legal compliance, crime prevention or crime prosecution, administration of justice, tax recollection, migratory control operations, procedural strategies in judicial or administrative processes while the resolutions are not final.' (Translation by the author) There are certain criteria available for discerning the circumstances under numeral I, although it is not clear. Criteria for discernment of numerals II and IV are completely obscure and clearly may impact information relating to environmental protection or damage as well as human health and safety. Even though these are 'common' provisions under other FOIAs in the world, the lack of specificity in the Mexican instruments places the individual in a greater legal danger or uncertainty.

9. In some cases, the problem is not the lack of information itself but rather the excess of disorganized technical information which does not have any meaning for the ordinary citizen or even for the State.
10. Kiss, C., E.H. Poltima , M. Struminska, and M. Ewing (2007), *Environmental democracy. An assessment of access to information, participation in decision-making and access to justice in environmental matters in selected European countries,* Access Initiative/Europe Regional Report at www.accessinitiative.org, (accessed 7 February 2012).
11. The *Reglamento de la Ley General del Equilibrio Ecológico y la Protección al Ambiente en Materia de Evaluación de Impacto Ambiental* (LGEEPA EIA Regulation), May 30, 2000; Diario Oficial de la Federación, México, specifically regulates Federal EIA procedure, although state environmental regulations may have their own EIA regulations which are applicable for the projects or activities which do not pertain to the Federal Authority but rather fall under state or municipal jurisdiction.
12. EIA procedure is regulated under the LGEEPA, above, n. 3. Even though the EIA file itself is open for consultation by any person, except such information which may be confidential or reserved by its own nature, paragraph 3 of Article 34 states that 'The Secretary [environmental ministry] **may proceed** with a public consultation upon the request of any person, under the following provisions: I.- The Secretary will publish the application for environmental impact assessment in the *Gaceta Ecológica* [internal publication with public access]. Also the promoter shall publish at its own cost, an abstract of the project being evaluated, in a local newspaper with broad circulation in the State where the project is to be completed, within five days from the presentation of the project to the Ministry; II.- Any citizen, within 10 days of the publication of the abstract of the project in the terms mentioned above, **may request that the Secretary make available to the public the EIA file in the state that is involved** (meaning the state of the Mexican Federation in which the project or activity is intended to be developed); III.- When the project or activity being evaluated may cause grave ecological unbalances or damage to public health or the ecosystems as understood in the regulation under this Law, the Secretary, in coordination with the local authorities **may organize a public meeting** during which the promoter will explain the technical aspects of the project or activity being evaluated; IV.- Any person, within twenty days that the Secretary makes the EIA available to the public, **may propose** the establishment of additional preventive or mitigation measures, as well as the observations that it deems necessary; and V.- The Secretary **will add the observations made by the stakeholders to the file** and will integrate, the process of public consultation conducted as well as the results of the observations and suggestions that were done in writing in the resolution that it dictates.' (Translation and emphasis by the author).
13. See http://www.un.org/millenniumgoals/ (accessed 7 February 2012).
14. IUCN Commission on Environmental Law, (2004) *Draft International Covenant on Environment and Development* (3rd edn), IUCN Environmental Law Programme, http://www.i-c-e-l.org/english/ EPLP31EN_rev2.pdf (accessed 7 February 2012).
15. FOIA is a world reference on access to information legislation since its enactment in 1966. It is based on balancing the confidentiality of the government information as well as the state duty to inform, and the right to know of the population. *Freedom of Information Act, 5 U.S.C. § 552 as Amended by Public Law No. 110–175, 121 Stat. 2524,* available at http://www.state.gov/m/a/ips/ (accessed 7 February 2012).

16. See www.ifai.org.mx (accessed 7 February 2012).
17. Above, n. 3. (Translation by the author).
18. Above, n. 3.
19. Translation by the author.
20. *Secretaría de Energía (SENER)* which means 'Secretariat of energy'. Unfortunately, the Mexican federal administration does not consider oil exploration and refinery, mining industry, production of electricity nor nuclear energy production as part of the environmental agenda.
21. *Secretaría de Agricultura, Ganadería, Desarrollo Rural, Pesca y Alimentación (SAGARPA)* is the ministry of agriculture, livestock, rural development, fisheries and food supply.
22. *Constitución Política de los Estados Unidos Mexicanos*, February 5th, 1917, Diario Oficial de la Federación, México; as well as applicable amendments. Please note that all Mexican Federal legislation may be found in alphabetical order on this site: http://www.diputados.gob.mx/LeyesBiblio/index.htm (accessed 7 February 2012).
23. *Sistema Nacional de Infomación Ambiental y de Recursos Naturales (SNIARN)*, which translates as the 'national system of environmental information and of natural resources'. See http://www.semarnat.gob.mx/informacionambiental/Documents/sniarn/index.html (accessed 7 February 2012). It contains four main sections: 'Statistical database', 'Geographical digital space', 'National System of Environmental Indicators', and 'Statements, Reports and Publications'. (Translation by the author). This website has grown substantially and been reorganized in the last five years, although most of the information available tends to be outdated by more than two years.
24. See Articles 159 *bis* through 159 *bis* 6 of LGEEPA. Above, n. 3.
25. *Registro de Áreas Naturales Protegidas (RANP),* natural protected areas registry. See Article 74 of LGEEPA, ibid. The RNAP is not in force anymore and the SINAP was created in turn (*Sistema Nacional de Áreas Naturales Protegidas* or National System of Protected Areas). This system is intended to be more than a registry and it compiles diverse types of information. Interestingly enough the SINAP does not register every Federal Natural Protected Area in Mexico since they have developed criteria for the registration which includes the following: richness of species, presence of endemic species, presence of species of restricted distribution, presence of endangered species, difference of species when compared to others in areas previously incorporated to the National System of Protected Areas, diversity of ecosystems within the area, presence of relictual ecosystems, presence of ecosystems of limited distribution, presence of important or fragile natural phenomenae, functional integrity of the ecosystems, importance of the environmental services the area generates, and social viability for its preservation. See http://www.conanp.gob.mx/que_hacemos/sinap.php, (translation by the author), (accessed 7 February 2012). This registry thus does not necessarily contain all Federal protected areas created up to date. The Commission for Natural Protected Areas will analyze the above mentioned criteria and thus will decide whether to include it or not on the registry, although this decision does not have any legal effect on the creation mandate of the natural protected area. 53.26% of the national area under legal protection is currently registered. The purpose of this classification of information (according to the National Commission of Protected Areas) is to homogenize information and better enable its review and comparison.
26. See Article 112, para. 6 of LGEEPA, (above, n. 3). Most of these reports are locally generated and thus locally compiled and disseminated. There are dozens of sites in which air quality may be consulted, most of them under the responsibility of the local environmental authority. There are also a few examples of joint efforts such as the Net for Technology Transfer which maintains the Center of Information of Air Pollution for the Mexico-United States Border which is part of the current Border 2012 Program, see http://www.epa.gov/ttncatc1/cica/indexs.html (accessed 7 February 2012). Even though substantial advances have been made in this regard, there is not yet one unified system of information which efficiently compiles and canalizes air pollution information at the Federal Level, nor is there yet a system (or protocol) which may be applied uniformly guaranteeing that important air pollution information or air quality information arrives timely to the citizen for appropriate prevention and decision making.

27. *Registro de Emisiones y Transferencia de Contaminantes (RETC)* which may be the closest Mexican equivalent to the United States' Toxic Release Inventory or TRI. Its purpose is to collect all information produced by registered hazardous waste generators including quality, quantity, as well as the place of final confinement, destruction or liberation (as in the case of emissions). It was created under LGEEPA but it has its own Federal regulation (*Reglamento de la LGEEPA en materia de Registro de Emisiones y Transferencia de Contaminantes*). The latest version of the RETC may be consulted at http://app1.semarnat.gob.mx/retc/. Most information is updated to 2007. However, not all the website is available, although the site was presented in 2008 (accessed 7 February 2012).
28. See Article 80 of LGEEPA. It is known as the *Sistema Nacional de Información sobre Biodiversidad de México*. Known as the SNIB for its acronym in Spanish (National System of Information on Mexican Biodiversity), see http://www.conabio.gob.mx/institucion/snib/doctos/acerca.html (accessed 7 February 2012); it has an internal policy for access to information which may be synthesized as follows: Criteria under specific agreements between the National Commission on Biodiversity for access to information as well as the legal criteria under the National Law of Author's Rights (*Ley Federal de Derechos de Autor*) and any other regulation applicable to the specific kind of information must be respected, all data will be publicly available unless there are specific data restrictions by the information provider, in any use or data application credit will be given to the author or the owner of such, users of information will be advised at all times of their duty of citing the original source of information as well as of the prohibition to redistribute the information without specific authorization, as well as the restriction to use it in activities which are detrimental to biodiversity. (Translated by the author).
29. *Subsistema Nacional de Información sobre la Vida Silvestre*. See Article 48 of the General Wildlife Law (*Ley General de Vida Silvestre)* published on 3 July 2000, Diario Oficial de la Federación, México. There is no available website or even one in construction for this purpose.
30. S*istema Nacional de Información sobre la Gestión Integral de Residuos*, See Article 37 of the *Ley General para la Prevención y Manejo Integral de los Residuos*, or General Law for the Prevention and Integral Waste Management enacted on 8 October 2003, Diario Oficial de la Federación, México. There is currently no website nor one under construction for this purpose.
31. Above, n. 3.
32. *Comisión Nacional de Áreas Naturales Protegidas*. See http://www.conanp.gob.mx/ (accessed 7 February 2012).
33. *Comisión Nacional para el Conocimiento y Uso y de la Biodiversidad*. See http://www.conabio.gob.mx/ (accessed 7 February 2012).
34. *Sistema Nacional de Información de Pesca y Acuacultura* and *Registro Nacional de Pesca y Acuacultura,* respectively. See Article 2, section XII of the General Law of Sustainable Fisheries and Aquaculture (*Ley General de Pesca y Acuacultura Sustentables)* as well as Articles 29 and 31, enacted on 24 July 2007, Diario Oficial de la Federación, México. In compliance with this mandate the National Network of Information and Research on Fisheries and Aquaculture, coordinated by the National Fisheries Institute under SAGARPA, was created. Most of its regional operational committees were created in 2011. This information network may only be consulted under registration. See http://www.registro.inapesca.gob.mx/ (accessed 7 February 2012). (Translated by the author).
35. *Sistema Nacional de Información del Sector Agroalimentario y Pesquero*. See http://www.siap.sagarpa.gob.mx/ (accessed 7 February 2012).
36. *Red Nacional de Información e Investigación en Pesca y Acuacultura*. See n. 34 above in this regard.
37. *Instituto Nacional de Pesca y Acuicultura.*
38. *Registro Público de Derechos de Agua*. See Article 3 of the Law of National Waters (*Ley de Aguas Nacionales*), enacted on 1 December 1992, Diario Oficial de la Federación, México. This registry has currently four databases which may be accessed only for information purposes (no certifications may be obtained online) through its main site: http://www.conagua.gob.mx/ocavm/Espaniol/TmpContenido.aspx?id=0367103b-671b-

4b37-b550-7da83af1fc69|Estructura%20Interna|0|4|0|0|0 (accessed 16 February 2012). The access to the Public Registry of Water Rights appears as 'under construction' and only general information about the Registry may be accessed.
39. *Comisión Nacional del Agua.*
40. *Sistema Nacional de Información sobre cantidad, calidad, usos y conservación del agua.*
41. See general information on the system is available at http://www.conagua.gob.mx/Contenido.aspx?n1=3&n2=60&n3=60 (accessed 16 February 2012).
42. *Sistema Nacional de Información sobre Bioseguridad.* See http://www.cibiogem.gob.mx/Sistema-Nacional/Paginas/default.aspx (accessed 7 February 2012).
43. *Registro Nacional de Bioseguridad de los Organismos Genéticamente Modificados.* See Articles 108 and 109 of the Biosafety Law of Genetically Modified Organisms (*Ley de Bioseguridad de Organismos Genéticamente Modificados*) enacted on 18 March 2005, Diario Oficial de la Federación, México. Registry is under the CIBIOGEM system and may be consulted at http://www.cibiogem.gob.mx/OGMs/Paginas/default.aspx. Most information is surprisingly updated to 2010. (accessed 7 February 2012).
44. *Comisión Intersecretarial de Bioseguridad de los Organismos Genéticamente Modificados.* See http://sippic.main.conacyt.mx:7777/pls/sippic/RNBIOSEG.tocAdm (accessed 7 February 2012).
45. *Sistema Nacional de Información Forestal.* See Article 39 of the General Law of Sustainable Forestry Development (*Ley General de Desarrollo Forestal Sustentable*), enacted on 25 February 2003, Diario Oficial de la Federación, México. See http://148.223.105.188:2222/gif/snif_portal/index.php?option=com_content&task=view&id=4&Itemid=59. Even though the site is still under construction, the SNIF may be consulted under nine principal categories. (accessed 7 February 2012).
46. *Sistema Nacional de Información para el Desarrollo Rural Sustentable.* The information system does not yet exist and the information available is still very limited. More information on the program for the integration of the system may be consulted at http://www.inforural.com.mx/programas.php?&id_rubrique=13&id_article=1204, (accessed 7 February 2012).
47. At this point, there is a financial program within SAGARPA, with the participation of the National Institute of Statistics, Geography and Computing (INEGI), as well as all the states of Mexico. See: http://www.inforural.com.mx/programas.php?&id_rubrique=13&id_article=1204 (accessed 7 February 2012). Information is from 2007, no official updates are available.
48. *Sistema Nacional de Indicadores Ambientales.* See http://www.semarnat.gob.mx/informacionambiental/SNIA/Pages/snia.aspx (accessed 7 February 2012).
49. *Sistema Nacional de Información Municipal.* See http://www.inafed. gob.mx/wb/inafed09/descargas (accessed 7 February 2012).
50. *Indice Metropolitano de la Calidad del Aire.*
51. *Inventario Nacional de Emisiones.* See http://www.ine.gob.mx/dica/547-calaire-inem (accessed 7 February 2012).
52. There is a document produced in August 1999 by the Climate Change Office then under the National Ecology Institute as part of the SEMARNAP , immediate predecessor of the current SEMARNAT. Such inventory contains National Inventory of Greenhouse Gas Emissions with statistics for 1990 (electronic publication available on line at http://www2.ine.gob.mx/publicaciones/libros/489/inventario.pdf (accessed 7 February 2012)). There is a second National Inventory of Greenhouse Gas Emissions with statistics for 1994–1998. The third of this kind was the Reports of the National Inventory of Greenhouse Gas Emissions 1990–2002 (electronic document available at http://www2.ine.gob.mx/descargas/cclimatico/inegei_res_ejecutivo.pdf (accessed 7 February 2012)), followed by the Fugitive Ozone Methane in the Oil, Natural Gas and Carbon Industries in Mexico 2000–2001, and finally Transportation Information 2000–2001 (all of the above available at http://cambio_climatico.ine.gob.mx/comprendercc/qsehaceparamitigarelcc/ambitonacional.html (accessed 7 February 2012). These reports have been reasonably updated, although not to 2010 for most of them. For general information regarding Greenhouse Gas Emissions Inventory, Mexico currently has the National Emissions System based on the report obligations

imposed by the RETC referred above. Unfortunately this information is only available through the internet in a site under construction, and which requires registration for login, see http://aplicaciones.semarnat.gob.mx/sine/default.asp (accessed 7 February 2012).

53. Programa Integral de Playas Limpias. It can currently be visited at http://www.cofepris.gob.mx/wb/cfp/playas_limpias (accessed 7 February 2012). The newest program in this regard, based on environmental information for beaches by SEMARNAT, was launched in December 2010 as the Water Quality Monitoring System for Priority Beaches based on those that represent the greatest profit from tourism. It can be reviewed at http://www.semarnat.gob.mx/playas/playas_prioritarias/Paginas/SistemaPlayasPrioritarias.aspx (accessed 7 February 2012). Unfortunately, as its name clearly states, it is meant for 'priority' beaches, this criteria based on those which receive more tourism. Curiously enough, international tourism tends to be the trend to follow.
54. Additional significant information may be obtained at www.inea.gob.mx (Institute for the Education of Adults) as well as www.inegi.org.mx (National Institute of Geography and Statistics), (accessed 7 February 2012). Factors such as educational level, indigenous population and income are strongly related, showing that the higher percentage of the adult indigenous population still lives in extreme poverty, does not have access to education, and thus has a limited access to information since many still cannot read. Additionally, these groups tend to live in high biodiversity areas, resulting often in poor environmental protection as well as environmental degradation.
55. See relevant information at the National Systems of Geography and Statistics http://sc.inegi.org.mx/niveles/index.jsp (accessed 7 February 2012).
56. Primary source, http://www.elsemanario.com.mx/catagories/cat_display.php?section=Politica&story_id_send=10000862 (accessed 7 February 2012), confirmed through crossed information through www.inegi.org.mx (accessed 7 February 2012).
57. See chapters 26 and 40 of Agenda 21, http://www.un.org/esa/sustdev/documents/agenda21/english/agenda21toc.htm (accessed 7 February 2012).
58. Rodríguez, P. (2007) 'El acceso a la información ambiental'. in Haight, L. and J. Fox (eds) *Derecho a saber. Balance y perspectives cívicas*, pp. 297–302.
59. See Article 14 LFTAIG, above, n. 5, as well as Zamora Etcharren, R. (2003) *Acceso a la información pública gubernamental* (Porrúa), p. 11: 'National security' is defined as 'the actions destined to protect the integrity, the stability and permanence of the Mexican State, the democratic governance, the external defense, as well as the security within the Federation, oriented to the general welfare of society, which allow the fulfilment of the ends of the Constitutional state'. (Translation by the author).

REFERENCES

Comisión Nacional para el Desarrollo de los Pueblos Indígenas (2000), 'Indicadores socioeconómicos de los pueblos indígenas de México', Federal Government, México.

Decleris, M. (2000), *The Law of Sustainable Development. General Principles. A report produced for the European Commission*, Office for Official Publications of the European Communities.

Duraiappah, A.K. (2004), *Exploring the links. Human well-being, poverty, ecosystem linkages*, United Nations Environment Programme and the International Institute for Sustainable Development.

Hallo, R. (2001), '*Proposal for a new directive on public access to environmental information: An analysis*', EEB document no 2001/004, European Environmental Bureau.

Instituto Federal de Acceso a la Información (IFAI) (2004), *El derecho de acceso a la información en México: un diagnóstico de la sociedad*, IFAI.

Quadri de la Torre, G. (2006), *Políticas públicas. Sustentabilidad y medio ambiente* Miguel Ángel Porrúa; Cámara de Diputados, LIX Legislatura; Tecnológico de Monterrey.

Salazar Ugarte, P. (coord.) (2008), *El derecho al acceso a la información en la Constitución Mexicana: Razones, significado y consecuencias*, Universidad Nacional Autónoma de México and Instituto Federal de Acceso a la Información.

United Nations Development Programme (2005), United Nations Environmental Programme, International Institute for Environment and Development, International Union of Conservation of Nature, World Resources '*Institute Investing in Environmental Wealth for Poverty Reduction*', Poverty Environment Partnership.

World Bank (2007), 'Poverty and Environment: Understanding Linkages at the Household Level', Environment Department paper 40218, World Bank.

PART IV

States' approaches to address environmental degradation and poverty

9. Embedding social justice in the design of environmental regulation[1]

Paul Martin

9.1 INTRODUCTION

Western resource management theory suggests that the optimal conservation strategy is to impose access constraints through the law, and then empower the economically competent users of constrained resources through trading and permits. This will maximise wealth (often represented as social optimality), and long-term environmental services for the majority. However, efficient conservation can embed social disadvantage for the vulnerable minority. Social cost is not an accidental 'spillover' of either environmental policing and markets, it is intrinsic. This chapter considers this issue and proposes procedural options to improve consideration of social justice in the design of environmental regulation.

For the purposes of this chapter, environmental regulation is any state imposed legal constraint for the purpose of conserving natural resources. It includes exclusion and policing, environmental property rights, and restrictive licenses to use resources. This chapter argues that regardless of the constraint type there is an inherent potential for inequity, though its extent and significance varies with the vulnerability of those affected, the nature of the constraint, and the particular circumstances.[2]

Many social liberals hold the fond belief that because disproportionate resource consumption is an attribute of the rich, conservation will naturally benefit the poor, leading to an expectation that conservation and social justice are happy companions. Unfortunately this is not intrinsically so. Environmental law can exacerbate social injustice unless conscious steps are taken to address these risks.

9.2 SCARCITY AND THE VULNERABLE

In nature, scarcity usually leads to the dominance of the powerful, adaptive and/or lucky. In human society, policy responses adjust the impact of scarcity by incorporating political and economic power, values, and sophisticated knowledge. Resource scarcity, whether natural or created through regulation, has different consequences for the strong than for the weak. Strategies intended to alleviate resource over-consumption can result in inequities that even transcend national boundaries (sadly illustrated by the so-called 'Taco riots' triggered by a doubling of corn prices due to US corn demand for biofuels production).

From first principles some broad impact patterns from different constraints can be anticipated.

1. under unconstrained consumption, as depletion is approached, access will be controlled by power, talent, luck, or (if a market emerges) wealth;
2. with an effective market, reallocation from the less economically competent (viz. less wealthy) to those more economically competent (viz. more wealthy) is achieved;
3. under a conditional (policed) constraint, lawful access is subject to conditions like limits, permits, or membership of a specified class. Depending on preconditions, wealth, sophistication and natural endowment (like location) are likely determinants of access;
4. under a policed ban on consumption, access will be constrained to those with the capacity to circumvent the constraint, using cunning, ruthlessness, and power; and
5. under voluntary constraint those who are socially responsible, or who can painlessly comply, will be those whose consumption is most affected.

Under any regulatory constraint it ought therefore to be expected that impacts may fall disproportionately on the disadvantaged. Economically efficient approaches to conservation depend upon resource reallocation to those possessing endowments of skill, wealth or position. *Ipso facto*, many environmental laws can prejudice the poor, the ignorant or the otherwise poorly endowed.

In a recent study of best practices in the design of regulation, case studies were conducted of environmental regulation of Australian farmers (Martin, Bartel et al, 2007). These highlighted many social justice issues in regulation which impact on the most vulnerable resource users. Whilst readers concerned with the environmental and social justice issues of the developing world may feel that issues of relatively well-endowed people in a rich country are trivial, they are not. For those affected, they are fundamental. Because of trade interconnectedness the solutions in a rich country often result in new social problems in less wealthy trade partners. The number of people and the depth of their plight may differ, but many of the same causes and concerns can be observed across the world.

Farmers everywhere vary in their economic and social vulnerability, and all are dependent on resource access. In Australia, as in other parts of the world, environmental regulations enforce conservation of biodiversity and water, and help control adverse impacts such as salinity and the spread of invasive flora and fauna. Many costs of this necessary protection are borne by the farm sector, but the significance of that impact varies with location and landscape, enterprise, wealth, and demographic characteristics. In some instances the resulting unfairness is substantial. This is a microcosm of the world, where heterogenous social and environmental characteristics, coupled with natural or economic endowment and luck lead to laws to protect the environment for the majority creating varying degrees of injustice to a vulnerable minority.

Many costs are necessary to effective regulation even if impacts on the vulnerable are not intended. These costs are the foregone economic opportunity, loss of amenity, risk or expenditure that are axiomatic to effective control. This restriction impacts those who would otherwise have exercised the freedoms that they lose through regulation. Exacerbated by differing vulnerabilities, inequities arise in the extent and distribution of these purposeful restriction costs. Illustrative of the mal-distribution of social costs of environmental regulation is the cost to marginal hunter communities of attempts to protect fish, whale and other fauna stocks from industrialised over-use.

The social impact of regulation can also come because laws are ineffective. Our examination of weeds regulation highlighted the social cost of instrument failure. Ill-designed and insufficiently implemented weed laws fail and lead to major control costs and production losses, substantially borne by a subset of farmers. As most weeds are escapes from non-accidental introduction, particularly from gardens or landscaping, there is a concealed transfer of wealth from the vulnerable to the advantaged.

With regard to biodiversity and native vegetation protection the cost imposts are different. Farmers protest that the regulations are restrictive, administratively slow and uncertain. The issues they complain about are a mixture of restriction, and private transaction costs. Again, the spread of impacts and vulnerability is heterogenous, but for at least some of those impacted the results can be characterised as unjust. The farmer whose parents were too concerned to conserve what they ought now finds himself compelled by legislation to continue to protect the residual native habitat, whilst his neighbour with less ethical parentage is not so constrained. Is this good social or environmental polity?

With weeds and native vegetation (and to a lesser degree biodiversity) there is an imbalance in the distribution of costs, with some farmers carrying the major burden. This can undermine the viability of farms to a level that is personally catastrophic for the vulnerable.

In our research of water markets we have seen indications of the generation of disadvantage. Australia has led the world in the creation of water property rights untied to land. This has resulted in the ability of a rights owner to permanently or temporarily trade water to suit their needs (but naturally excludes those who do not own an entitlement). Rights are designated as a percentage of the available flows, after taking into account minimal requirements of the environment. Recent droughts have led to volumetric reductions in allocations, leading to water owners who have insufficient volume selling or leasing their rights to others (creating a sufficient 'pool' to allow production by some farmers). Subsequent to creating tradeable rights, Australian governments have gone into the market to purchase water and/or land, in order to claw back water for the environment.

For owners of water rights changes in their property rights or in the volumes that can be drawn down will be reflected in changes to the economic value of the extractive right. To at least some degree there is an automatic adjustment, though this does not apply to the non-property interests of farm workers or local shopkeepers. Various forms of property right have different mechanisms for handling the distributional equity issues between water owners and users, and these give rise to different distributions of impacts.

Under a traditional riparian system, an upstream extractor has a legal obligation not to harm the downstream user. This makes the upstream user interest subservient in some ways to the downstream users. In the interests of efficiency, Australian and American governments have shifted towards allocation through administration based on plans, away from riparian traditions. They have attempted in some cases to ameliorate potential equity impacts through mechanisms such as a 'prior allocation system' under which the older right has priority over later interests, or by attempting to accommodate equity considerations in the administrative processes of water allocation. In a fully traded water rights approach, equity effects are generally considered in designing the market, by recognising special interests (for example indigenous cultural uses) or by providing allocations to those who might be otherwise impacted. Such arrangements are intended to address some of the risks of distributional inequity.[3]

As a result of market and environmental dynamics, vulnerable communities are now beginning to protest.[4] Whilst not clearly expressed by these communities (nor by researchers), they face new challenges from these forms of environmental regulation. The first is a newly created split between the interests of owners and non-owners in a region. A distressed water owner may be able to obtain compensation from selling or leasing their water right, and then possibly leave the industry with economic dignity. However, the workers on the farm and the people in the town who would otherwise have shared both the pain and the opportunity from coping with scarce (but available) water find that they now carry only the pain. Coupled with this, the ability to trade increases the volatility and unpredictability of water-related activity for these second and third order resource users. The first order user (the owner) can decide at any time, without notice, to buy or sell the water upon which his and their employment depends. Second and third order users who once had the same degree of predictability as the first order user are now dependent not only on the weather and the water regulator, but also on the water owner. Whilst arguably improving environmental management and the situation of the water owner, this environmental regulation may have inherently increased the vulnerability of many others who are dependent on the resource.[5]

Even whilst these social cost issues remain unresolved in the rich countries that have pioneered such institutional innovations, the same solutions (with their unresolved social problems) are being promoted as desirable and efficient solutions for economies with even greater social disadvantage problems (Baeur, 1997).

It is perhaps normal (but not desirable) that the impact of regulatory exclusion falls heavily on those who are disadvantaged. An inability to cope with administrative systems is more likely among the less educated; those who are poor find it harder to pay for advice, property rights or permits; and those who are least mobile are least able to find alternative ways of satisfying their needs. For some, exclusion costs are a temporary frustration, whilst for others they are fundamental to lifestyle, culture and self-worth.

9.3 ARE MARKET INSTRUMENTS MORE EQUITABLE?

In recent times we have seen increasing use of tradeable resource entitlements. The expectation is that these will be environmentally effective, and generate socially optimal outcomes. Whilst market instruments are important to achieve efficient conservation (in some settings), it is important to question the Panglossian expectation that they will consistently produce good outcomes for the underprivileged.

The principle underlying the expectation that markets will better protect the weak is a version of Coase's argument that (absent transaction costs) regardless of original allocation, free trading of resource rights will result in the social optimal allocation of those resources (Coase, 1960, p. 3). Unfortunately the economic optimum is an aggregate for society. Allocation of resources to the economically competent through trading is essential to this optimal outcome. Distributional equity is far from a 'given'.

A second point relates to assumptions about transaction costs. Transaction costs are analogous to friction in a mechanical system. They are the many impediments to the efficient trading that arise in practice (even if sometimes assumed away in theory). They include the effects of distrust and bargaining, the costs and delays of contract formation, and the problems of contract enforcement. Markets without transaction costs, like machines without friction, exist only as an ideal. Coase was explicit in identifying that these costs are keys to whether efficient redistribution will occur.

Transaction costs play a material part in determining the social and economic outcomes from regulatory constraints. If, through trading, access to natural resources shifts (for example the movement of water to the highest value use), then the theoretical ideal would be that all those affected would have ready access to information about opportunities, and would be freely able to move to where those opportunities exist. It could be argued that both their wealth and that of society would be optimised. However the real world transaction costs for (say) a poorly educated rural indigenous worker in achieving this mobility are substantial. Asymmetry of opportunity and transaction costs and impacts is emerging as a concern from water trading and buybacks affecting struggling communities in Australia. It is exacerbated by the increased separation of the interests of the water owner from the community within which they operate. Both the extent and the allocation of transaction costs impact on patterns of trading (Bromley, 1991; Martin and Verbeek, 2006), and unfortunately the disadvantaged will normally not secure the same benefits from market opportunities as the well-endowed.

The second argument suggesting that markets will be more benign for the poor is that innovation induced by economic opportunity will result in increased value from the constrained resource, and a general increase in welfare. The claim generally is made that market instruments are more likely to harness this capacity to innovate than policed controls (Simon, 1981). There are forms of the argument that legally constrained supply even without trading will also stimulate innovation (Porter et al., 1996).

Does this argument for greater efficiency through innovation suggest that the less advantaged will benefit proportionately (or ideally, super-proportionately) with others? In a technologically advanced society, valuable innovations in technology, management or commerce are often sophisticated, drawing on accumulations of specialist skills, physical capital and economic power (Marceau, Manley and Sicklen, 1997). Effective exploitation often involves capturing intellectual property, requiring expertise, capital and commercial acumen. The reward for the inventor lies in the premium for that invention (viz. a higher cost to the end-user), which is likely to be paid by all including the poor. Particularly in developing economies, alongside the economic effects of commercial innovation come power shifts, sometimes making it impossible for the poor producer to reduce dependence on the technology supplier once this dependence has been established.[6] For such reasons there is little reason to be sanguine that the economic gains from market-induced efficiency will accrue to the relatively disadvantaged.

There are opportunities for innovation, markets and other interventions to contribute to redressing disadvantage but this is not likely to be a natural result of using environmental law to constrain resource consumption. To address social inequity at the same time as improving resource conservation requires specific attention to the interests of the less advantaged, whilst improving resource sustainability for society as a whole.

Implicit in conservation strategy is a competition between the ethical imperative to avoid unfairness and the pragmatic limits to taxation that can be used to support (or compensate) the vulnerable. Governments may choose regulation to force unwilling investment, because they do not have the funds to use other methods. Whilst rarely publicly debated, this pragmatic conflict is important in practice in determining whether government will use regulation, compensate for the private cost of delivering social outcomes, or use other interventions. Regulatory processes discussed later in this chapter can ensure that distributional issues are debated by regulators, parliament and affected communities.

What regulatory approaches might advance both resource conservation and social justice? One possibility might be to avoid strategies that impose constraints on the poor. This is not likely to be generally effective as eventual resource depletion will also lead to inequities. A failure to act merely alters which generation of users (including the less advantaged) bears the cost. A 'do nothing' option does not appear to maximise social justice, or environmental sustainability.

An alternative is to avoid using market instruments, in favour of policed controls. This approach would appeal to those who mistrust the capacity of governments to constrain the excesses of entrepreneurs, or who abhor that a capitalist mechanism serves best those who command capital. However, if a well-designed and implemented trading arrangement can maximise innovation and economic performance, then there is little objective basis to believe that avoiding the market will be in the interests of either society or the disadvantaged. Other strategies to address social justice are needed.

There are theoretically possible mechanisms to address inequities. Whilst there are examples of their use they are not yet backed by a systematic understanding of how effective they are under different conditions.[7] They are not mutually exclusive, and combinations and permutations are possible. Given the limits of this paper it is only possible to touch upon their characteristics.

The first is *sui generis* rules for disadvantaged groups, which might (for example) provide them with subsidies to improve their resource access, training and support, or special allocations of use rights. A form of this is to exempt vulnerable groups from regulatory constraints. This is exemplified by indigenous hunting rights, or support to purchase fishing or water rights (which may involve creating a special class of inalienable interests).

A second approach is to compensate adversely affected groups for the added disadvantage. This may be by offsets (for example replacement lands when a national park is created), or by allocating management rights or royalties. Where a market is created a tradeable share or a percentage of the value of trades may be used to compensate for the loss of unfettered use of the resource.

A third possibility, reflecting the Coasian concept discussed above, would be to allocate tradeable entitlements to the disadvantaged group. This endowment provides the disadvantaged with market interests that they could freely hold or trade.[8]

Objections can be raised that each of these approaches carries its own inefficiencies. Some may retard efficient environment markets, or undermine efficient policing, and many carry the potential for abuse. There is no method that will be universally effective and efficient. The literature does not demonstrate a systematic approach to amelioration or avoidance of social inequities exacerbated through environmental regulation. This is an important untapped area of policy and economic research.

What is needed is a more powerful impetus for the development of reliable methods for addressing inequity. The balance of this paper suggests that by incorporating questions of social justice into emerging processes of regulatory review this impetus will be created. However, this will require modification of the existing emphasis on economic impacts of regulation, towards embracing social justice. Various economic analyses can be adapted for this purpose, which would seem to be the line of least resistance towards getting social equity considered alongside economic efficiency (without pretending that these are necessarily synergistic).

9.4 CAN BETTER REGULATORY PRACTICE IMPROVE FAIRNESS?

If potential social justice impacts from resource conservation are to be addressed, this will not occur automatically. Further, if innovative social equity strategies are not systematically developed and tested, then it is unlikely that we will see the evolution of efficient ways to protect social capital whilst conserving natural capital.

Over the last few decades, there has been a gradual development of regulatory review processes by (mostly) Western governments aiming to stimulate scientific improvement in regulation. The focus has been economic efficiency. In a small number of instances impacts upon protected interests (notably primary producers) have also been given attention. In relatively few have the concerns of the vulnerable been given particular emphasis. However, these formal regulatory design and review approaches do provide an established framework for evaluation of the social equity risks associated with environmental regulation.

Improved regulatory processes could ensure that social justice implications are debated using objective data. In a prior study we evaluated the wealth of processes literature.[9] We identified many processes involved in the creation and implementation (and subsequent refinement) of regulation, encompassing goal setting, policy formulation, resourcing, drafting, legislating, implementation plans, resourcing, implementation, evaluation and refinement. Many processes are informal, relying on interpersonal communication and bureaucratic activity rather than any transparent approach. The formal regulatory practices discussed below are at varying stages of development. Overall their use for the purposes of addressing social disadvantage issues has been limited.[10]

9.5 OPTION 1: EMBED SOCIAL JUSTICE PRINCIPLES

In some jurisdictions formal regulatory principles guide legislators. These principles come in three inter-connected forms. The first is over-arching principles for regulation in general, the second is sector or issue-specific guidelines, and the third is consultative requirements.

9.5.1 Over-arching Principles for Regulation

There is not yet an accepted standard for regulatory principles. Comparing four lists of principles of good regulation revealed that no principle was on all four (Better Regulation Task Force. United Kingdom Government, 2000; Council of Australian Governments, 2004; External Advisory Committee on Smart Regulation, Canadian Government, 2004; Organisation for Economic Co-operation and Development, 2005). 'Transparency' appeared on three of the four, and 'Effective', 'Consistent', 'Flexible', 'Reviewed' and 'Accountability' all appeared on two. Other principles were: 'Collaboration', 'Proportional', 'Internationally Compatible', 'Commitment to Reform', 'Unrestrictive of International Trade' and 'Serving Competition, Efficiency, and the Public Interest'. Some focus on strategies for regulation design. For example the guide 'Routes to Better Regulation – A guide to alternatives to classic regulation' focuses on the advantages and disadvantages of the use of contemporary regulatory design in different situations (Better Regulation Task Force. United Kingdom Government, 2005). Others attempt to cover many aspects (for example, Government of Canada, 2003).[11]

Although the concept of governing principles for regulation is increasingly accepted, there is no consensus on principles. Attention to social justice implications of regulation is minimal. Australia illustrates this, with the state of Queensland being arguably the most advanced with its 'fundamental legislative principles' in the Legislative Standards Act 1992. These suggest principles of justice, supported by a Scrutiny of Legislation Committee. In common with the international situation these principles are primarily concerned with economic efficiency. Social equity and distributional fairness are given little emphasis.

Regulation oversight bodies are often national, such as the Canadian External Advisory Committee on Smart Regulation, the United Kingdom's Better Regulation Commission, and Australia's Office of Regulation Review.[12] Thus far no international overseeing bodies have been formed, although some multinational bodies, such as the OECD and the EU, have produced design advice (for example, Rodrigues, Justino and Roda, 2000; Organisation for Economic Co-operation and Development, 2005). The emphasis is on economic rather than social concerns.

Suitable statements of regulatory principle requiring greater emphasis on reducing impacts on the vulnerable are one potential mechanism to increase attention to the social justice aspects of environmental regulation.

9.5.2 Stakeholder Protection Principles

A second version of principles is to require attention to the interests of particular groups. There are examples of attempts to incorporate vulnerable group-specific principles in some jurisdictions. The treatment of farmers as a vulnerable class is illustrative.[13]

In California, the Monterey Bay Plan Development Regulatory Coordination and Streamlining report highlighted the impact on farmers of multiple permits from several agencies, with separate fees, requirements, timelines, and contradictory mandates (Water Quality Protection Program for Monterey Bay National Marine Sanctuary, 1999). It suggests that this may not allow for sufficient flexibility in conservation and proposes to simplify permitting process, improve the effectiveness of regulations; and strengthen collaboration between regulatory agencies and landowners.

In Scotland the *Rural Development Regulation*[14] emphasises competitiveness and the role of consultation in developing effective rural regulations.

In the European Union, the Regulation on Rural Development[15] suggests integrated regulation management to improve the competitiveness of farming and forestry; provide support for the environment and the countryside; promote the diversification of the rural economy and its quality of life; and the use of 'bottom up' development strategies.

9.5.3 Stakeholder Consultation Principles

A further approach to protecting the interests of the vulnerable is through mandatory consultation. Agency theory has highlighted that where the interests of a concentrated powerful class are at risk they tend to capture the political process to protect their interest. Dreissen (2003) has illustrated this dynamic in the creation of environmental law, and has suggested that a process that empowers the 'outsiders' will be needed to achieve reform of environmental law.

Minimum requirements can ensure transparent evaluation of whether consultation has been independent, and whether the interests of the less privileged have been heard. Suggested Australian minimum standards recommend that all interested parties should have the opportunity to participate, a preliminary Regulatory Impact Statement should be available, and a mandatory minimum period of consultation (Argy and Johnson, 2003).

I believe that a range of techniques be used, such as multiple communication and feedback channels, targeted consultation with selected groups, workshops and public meetings (Regulatory Affairs Commission, 2005; Argy and Johnson, 2003). The Canadian government argues that criteria for selecting a representative range of participants for the consultation process can help ensure that all stakeholders are taken into account (Regulatory Affairs Commission, 2005). Dreissen (2003) goes further, proposing that the only way to ensure that consultative processes avoid capture by powerful interests is to elevate the role of those who wish to promote radical change to the status quo.

It seems that regulatory principles at these three levels may be viable ways to stimulate social justice evaluation of environmental regulations. Over-arching parliamentary social justice principles for environmental regulation, coupled with principles that draw attention to the disadvantaged, and mandatory consultation with vulnerable groups, would be powerful mechanisms. Coupled with disciplined impact assessment requirements (discussed below) they would provide an impetus for innovations addressing social justice in natural resource management.

9.6 OPTION 2: SOCIAL JUSTICE ASSESSMENT

Principles for the protection of vulnerable citizens can be embedded within a Regulatory Impact Assessment (RIA), which is conventionally focused on economic matters. An RIA can require that all costs and benefits be identified and communicated to all who are affected, that consultation occur, and that the resulting information be factored into decisions. An RIA, backed by specific principles such as those described above, should provide a framework for proper consideration of the interests of the disadvantaged.

A formal public statement of impacts (a Regulatory Impact Statement or RIS) encourages transparency. The OECD has suggested various regulatory review practices (Organisation for Economic Cooperation and Development, 1997) including standardised evaluation techniques and decision criteria; an RIA integrated into the review; reviews targeted at regulations where change will produce most benefits; and having all regulation updated through automatic reviews.

RIA procedures typically use economic cost/benefit assessment. Whilst the focus on economic efficiency highlights commercial considerations, it is possible for standard analytic methods to address distributional effects. This is discussed later in this chapter.

At a national level in Australia it is mandatory since 1997 to prepare an RIS for reviews of existing regulation, proposed new or amended regulation, quasi-regulation and proposed treaties involving regulation, which will directly or indirectly affect business or restrict competition.[16] The states in Australia have different regulatory impact assessment provisions, with Victoria, South Australia, and Queensland drawing specific attention to sector-specific non-commercial impact. In practice implementation at a national or state level pays scant attention to social justice, and a great deal of attention to macro-level economic efficiency.

Regulatory impact is a consequence of both design and implementation. The OECD has recommended that any review examine the regulation's enforcement and compliance, and the results achieved. The Netherlands' Table of Eleven (T11) (Organisation for Economic Co-operation and Development, 2002) highlights factors that influence the probability of breaches being detected and controlled.

There is great variation in the rigour and content of reviews across jurisdictions (Organisation for Economic Co-operation and Development, 2002). RIA and RIS requirements are a step towards transparent and rigorous regulation making. The key to their success lies (like most things in the regulatory arena) in the capacity of the regulator to implement them with integrity, which in turn reflects the skills, data and other resources, and motivation of the agency.

With regard to evaluation of regulatory social cost, the state of the art is under-developed.[17] Even accepting that legislative assessment methods are fledgling, social justice evaluations are often unconvincing because they lack precision in identification of vulnerable groups (and impacts upon them). This is arguably because commerce has been the strongest advocate for their concerns. Riding this impetus, adding consideration of social justice would seem to be a feasible path to improved evaluation of fairness in natural resource management.

9.7 OPTION 3: RE-FRAMING REGULATORY EFFICIENCY?

The goal of 'efficiency' connotes pursuit of the least costly means for achieving any given set of goals. Regulatory efficiency is measured by the relationship between regulatory costs and benefits (Sparrow, 2002). Cost-benefit assessment could enlighten decisions about the pursuit of social interests as well as economic ones. Whilst regulatory review has evolved with an emphasis on impacts on commerce, there is no intrinsic impediment to addressing social justice.

Combining concerns for parsimony with fairness would focus attention on the total cost of achieving desired outcomes, and on how costs and benefits are distributed. If laws have social goals, then these can be addressed in an economic evaluation of efficiency. In this light the considerations when judging regulatory efficiency ought to be:

1. Achieving the desired behaviour by the regulated public (benefit);
2. at minimum cost (cost); and
3. allocating costs and benefits fairly (distribution).

Efficiency evaluation requires that decision makers define their goal(s) and criteria, and then use objective approaches to compare alternatives against the stated criteria. The approach can be applied with multiple goals including contributions to social equity. Whilst incorporating social goals like distributional efficiency and minimal impact on the vulnerable will add complexity, it is methodologically feasible. The added complexity suggests only that the analysis is more likely to be realistic in addressing the competing interests within society.

The pivotal consideration is clear goal specification for both the regulation and the impact evaluation. Whilst the desirability of well-specified regulatory goals is broadly accepted, how one can distil goals from competing political considerations is a challenge that needs to be addressed. Without clarity of goals (even if these are internally inconsistent) it is difficult to apply any optimising approach to economic, social or environmental instruments.

9.8 APPLYING ECONOMIC ANALYSIS

There is a range of economic techniques for analysis of the economic impact of regulation, which can be adjusted to address social justice considerations.[18] The discussion that follows is necessarily a mere introduction to complex techniques.

9.8.1 Benefit-cost Analysis (BCA)

BCA notionally is simple. It is the calculation of the net gains (or losses) from the implementation of a policy. In practice it often involves sophisticated analyses using fiscal units to compare heterogenous non-fiscal values, which can include social justice; careful quantification of various forms of cost (only some of which are fiscal); and the adjustment of these calculations to take into account risk, timing and trade-offs.

BCA can encourage transparent debate. A statement of social principles or goals for environmental law can trigger investigation of costs, benefits and the analysis of these using BCA. However, caution is needed to ensure that any such technique is used with skill and objectivity. A guess stated to five decimal places remains a guess, and environmental or social justice 'values' are a judgement rather than a metric fact.

9.8.2 Cost-effectiveness Analysis (CEA)

Cost-effectiveness analysis is used to evaluate the least-cost approach for delivering a specified program. This technique assumes that the given program is justified, and only considers the costs of achievement. Whilst this is less comprehensive than CBA, it can help to achieve specified objectives at least cost.

In relation to environmental regulation, it would be possible to specify a particular social justice goal (for example, 5 per cent of tradeable water or biodiversity transactions benefiting traditional land owners), and use CEA as a basis for comparing the costs of achieving this goal.

9.8.3 Cost Considerations

In both techniques cost evaluation is important. Fully assessing the cost of a regulation – or any other social intervention – is complex. Simply stated, the cost of a law is the sum of financial costs, including public and private transaction costs, plus any lost social, economic or environmental opportunity or amenity. To quantify distributional effects we need to also identify to whom regulatory costs accrue, which may be the government, those being regulated, or particular members of the community; and evaluate potential unintended second-order cost effects.

Private transaction costs associated with a regulation, such as permit applications or reporting, and coping with the complexity that comes with more obligations (Productivity Commission, 2006) accrue to all whose interests may be affected by the law. These costs typically fall more heavily on those who try to comply than those who are indifferent (and who therefore do not search out their obligations, evaluate and seek permission). Transaction costs are also likely to be greater for people who are less well educated, remote, or culturally uncomfortable in dealing with bureaucracy.

The cost of regulatory failure is another consideration. The aim of environmental regulation is to protect the environment in the interests of future generations or to remediate harm done in prior times. Such intentions are good but some attempts to achieve them have failed incurring considerable social and economic costs. Invasive flora and fauna control in many jurisdictions illustrates the non-symmetrical impact of such regulatory failures.

To fully evaluate the distributional effects of cost and benefit would be an enormous task. Our literature review did not uncover this type of evaluation.[19] Methodologies for comprehensive distributional analysis of regulation are not well developed, perhaps because current impact review requirements do not demand rigorous evaluation of vulnerability.

BCA and CEA are most readily applied when the probability of an impact is high. If, for example, a new regulation will definitely prevent access by a vulnerable group then the costs and benefits to society and to that group can be evaluated using that approach. However, when a socially desirable environmental regulation may have impacts, but if the incidence and/or magnitude of these is uncertain, then risk evaluation may be more useful.

9.8.4 Risk-risk Evaluation

Regulation often has flow-on effects (or 'spillovers') on other values. The assessment of these is termed 'risk-risk analysis'.

Conventionally this is concerned with three forms of spillover. The first is *substitution*. Regulations may prohibit activities or goods but these may be replaced in ways that carry their own potential for adverse effects. For example, a regulation to prevent unlicensed fishing may result in poor families having less healthy diets, resulting in other costs to them and the community.

The second form is *compliance* referring to the inherent risks that can arise in attempts to comply with the regulation. Again using fishing as an example, if the creation of a no-fishing zone results in people having to travel further, or fish in unsafe waters, then a compliance risk is created.

The third type of risk-risk is *opportunity costs* associated with a regulation. If compliance requires a poor family to invest in obtaining a license, or in new equipment, then that time and effort is redirected from other things that may improve their welfare. The potential resultant harm is opportunity risk.

Risk-risk methods offer a basis for evaluation of the risk of social spillovers from the protection of natural resources. Whilst these methods usually address matters other than social justice, it is possible to design refinements to allow them to effectively address uncertain social consequences of environmental regulation.

9.9 CONCLUSIONS AND RECOMMENDATIONS

Perceived justice is at the heart of the legitimacy of the law, and legitimacy is important for the protection of the environment. It is in the everyday business of governing through law that power is exercised, and it is in the processes of government that the pattern of exercise is shaped. Environmental regulation imposes private cost for the public good, often upon people who (so far as they or the broader community is concerned) may not have done anything wrong. This chapter has demonstrated that the exercise of regulatory power to conserve natural resources often does have adverse effects on the vulnerable. It has demonstrated that this potential exists regardless of whether regulation is through policed constraints or market instruments.

This speaks of the need for regulatory power to be applied with a concern for potential impacts on the innocent or vulnerable. Regulatory review processes can provide a framework for creating fairer environmental laws, enabling the transparent debate about the social impacts of regulatory proposals. Formal regulatory social impact assessment, coupled with comprehensive explanation in a regulatory impact statement, would have this effect.

Most regulatory impact methods focus on economic efficiency. Few are concerned with the distributional effects of the law, or with using environmental law to address pre-existing social inequity. This chapter has demonstrated that it would take little to adjust conventional review principles and economic analysis techniques to embrace social justice.

Social justice ought be a distinct focus for regulatory review. To achieve this, the social justice goals of any environmental regulation ought to be clearly specified, in forms that are measurable. Regulatory objectives should address both environmental and social outcomes, and the acceptable levels and distribution of costs of achieving these.

Parliamentary principles for regulation should identify how the interests of vulnerable minorities ought be taken into account. There is a case in most jurisdictions for special principles to apply to particular disadvantaged people such as indigenous people, or economically marginal resource users. In Australia at least this is clearly the case.

Each regulatory intervention should be the subject of transparent scrutiny using regulatory impact assessment techniques incorporating (where appropriate) benefit/cost assessment, risk-risk assessment and genuine consultation with the less advantaged. This should ensure debate about social justice issues within environmental regulation.

Without widespread use of an accepted methodology for analysis of distributional inequities or social risk the potential to develop efficient mechanisms to reduce such problems is limited. Learning requires the accumulation (and analysis) of experience.

From the perspective of environmental lawyers, these proposals suggest some directions for research and action. They suggest the need for:

1. generally accepted convention and principles for social impact assessment within or alongside economic efficiency evaluation, of environmental regulation;
2. broadening the factors considered in regulatory impact assessment to embrace the vulnerable, as well as government and commerce;
3. refined methods for evaluation of distributional impacts, based on conventional economic analysis techniques; and
4. a 'community of practice' in social impact evaluation of regulation which will propose, model and evaluate interventions to ameliorate potential inequities.

Given the increasing pressure on our environment and increasing population, it is likely that society will demand more, rather than less, environmental regulation. If we do not develop methods for better considering the impacts of this on the innocent or the vulnerable, we risk devaluing our moral currency. Both from a philosophical perspective, and in the interests of the legitimacy of environmental law, this would be an undesirable thing. Tackling the challenge now, with integrity, would be the better path to take.

NOTES

1. The research for this paper was conducted with the support of the Cooperative Research Centre for Irrigation Futures System Harmonisation Program (www.irrigationfutures.org.au/projects.asp?ID=35 (accessed 7 February 2012); and the Australian Farm Institute and Land & Water Australia funded research 'Developing a Good Regulatory Practice Model for Environmental Regulations impacting on Farmers' Martin P., R. Bartel P. et al. available through http://lwa.gov.au/projects/3138 (accessed 7 February 2012) from which elements of this chapter have been developed.
2. Whilst this chapter focuses on the constraint aspect of natural resource law, it can be argued that there is also an inequity inherent in some forms of government incentives.
3. Thanks to Professor Mike Young, University of Adelaide, and Professor John Becker, Penn State University, and the reviewer of this paper for their helpful comments on these issues. Also to Hannah Taylor for her research assistance.
4. See for example www.abc.net.au/news/stories/2008/09/11/2361615.htm (accessed 7 February 2012) or www.abc.net.au/rn/breakfast/stories/2008/2351405.htm (accessed 7 February 2012) for illustrative stories.
5. It should also be noted that in areas importing water, some compensating gain may arise for other second or third order users of the resources.
6. For an illustrative discussion of these issues in relation to genetically improved seeds, see www.globalresearch.ca/index.php?context=va&aid=12309 (accessed 7 February 2012), or www.organicconsumers.org/articles/article_18777.cfm (accessed 7 February 2012).
7. This in itself is an important gap in our understanding of environmental law and policy, which could be addressed by strategic research.

8. The efficiency implications of such a strategy are complex, depending among other things on the extent of transaction costs. Further detailed research would be desirable to explore when such an approach will be both economically efficient and socially useful.
9. 'Developing a good Regulatory Practice Model for Environmental Regulations Impacting on Farmers', above, n. 1, from which parts have been extracted in this chapter. This chapter aims to refocus that work on social justice aspects of regulation, and to provide a more comprehensive discussion of social strategies.
10. It should be noted that in project impact assessment there are well developed methods for social impact assessment. It is anticipated that a formal requirement for social impact of regulation would lead to a cross fertilisation with this knowledge.
11. External Advisory Committee on Smart Regulation 2003, The Regulatory Process: Enabling Smart Regulation – A Dialogue with Stakeholders, Government of Canada. See http://epe.lac-bac.gc.ca/100/206/301/pco-bcp/committees/smart_regulation-ef/2006-10-11/www.pco-bcp.gc.ca/smartreg-regint/en/03/01/bk-03.html (accessed 15 February 2012).
12. Now 'Office of Best Practice Regulation'.
13. Similar approaches to the consideration of the impact of legislation on other minority groups such as the indigenous or the poor (though feminist action has elevated these concerns in legislative design) were not identified. *Sui generis* laws exempting indigenous people from regulatory constraints, or providing special interests, are, however, relatively common.
14. *(ec) No 1257/1999: Rural Development Plan for Scotland (Amended February 2005).*
15. Regulation (EC) No 1698/2005, 2005 (European Union).
16. During 2005–06 adequate RISs were prepared for 71% of the regulatory proposals that required them. (Productivity Commission, 'Regulation and its Review 2005–06', Annual Report Series, Commonwealth of Australia, 2006).
17. Again noting that there are well-developed methods in the field of social impact evaluation of projects.
18. For a recent detailed discussion of methodologies see OECD (2006), 'Cost-benefit analysis and the Environment: recent developments' (OECD).
19. However see: Holmes S. (1997), 'Some Lessons From The Use of Environmental Quasi-Regulation in North America', Staff Working Paper, Office of Regulation Review; Better Regulation Task Force (2005), 'Routes to Better Regulation: A Guide Alternatives to Classic Regulation', United Kingdom Government; Freeman J. and C.D. Kolstad (eds), (2007), 'Moving to Markets in Environmental Regulation: Lessons from Twenty Years of Experience', Oxford University Press.

REFERENCES

Argy, S. and M. Johnson (2003), *Mechanisms for Improving the Quality of Regulations: Australia in an International Context*, Staff Working Paper. Productivity Commission, Commonwealth of Australia.

Baeur, C.J. (1997), 'Bringing Water Markets Down to Earth: The Political Economy of Water Rights in Chile, 1976-95', World Development, Vol. 25, No. 5, 639.

Better Regulation Task Force (2000), *Principles of Good Regulation*, United Kingdom Government.

Better Regulation Task Force (2005), *Routes to Better Regulation: A Guide to Alternatives to Classic Regulation*, United Kingdom Government.

Bromley, D.W. (1991), *Environment and Economy* Oxford: Blackwell.

Coase, R.H. (1960), 'The Problem of Social Cost', *Journal of Law and Economics*, 3, 1.

Council of Australian Governments (2004), *Principles and Guidelines for National Standard Setting and Regulatory Action by Ministerial Councils and Standard-Setting Bodies*, Council of Australian Governments.

Driessen, D.M. (2003), *The Economic Dynamics of Environmental Law*, Cambridge, Massachusetts: MIT Press.
External Advisory Committee on Smart Regulation (2004), *Smart Regulation: A Regulatory Strategy for Canada*, Canadian Government.
Freeman, J. and C.D. Kolstad (eds), (2007), *Moving to Markets in Environmental Regulation: Lessons from Twenty Years of Experience*, Oxford: Oxford University Press.
Holmes, S. (1997), *Some Lessons From the Use of Environmental Quasi-Regulation in North America*, Staff Working Paper, Office of Regulation Review.
Marceau, J., K. Manley and D. Sicklen (1997), *The High Road or the Low Road: Alternatives for Australia's Future*, Australian Business Foundation Limited.
Martin, P., R. Bartel, J. Sindel, N. Gunningham, I. Hannam (2007) *Developing a Good Regulatory Practice Model for Environmental Regulations Impacting on Farmers*, Land & Water, Australia and the Australian Farm Institute.
Martin, P. and M. Verbeek (2006), *Sustainability Strategy,* Federation Press.
Organisation for Economic Co-operation and Development (2005), *OECD Guiding Principles for Regulatory Quality and Performance*, Organisation for Economic Co-operation and Development.
Organisation for Economic Co-operation and Development (1997), *The OECD Report on Regulatory Reform: Synthesis*, Organisation for Economic Co-operation and Development.
Organisation for Economic Co-operation and Development (2002), *Regulatory Policies in OECD Countries: From Interventionism to Regulatory Governance*, OECD Reviews of Regulatory Reform Organisation for Economic Co-operation and Development, Organisation for Economic Co-operation and Development.
Organisation for Economic Co-operation and Development (2006), *Cost-benefit analysis and the Environment: recent developments*, Organisation for Economic Co-operation and Development.
Porter, M. (1996), 'Green and Competitive: Ending the Stalemate' in Welford, R. and R. Starkey (eds), *A Reader: Business and the Environment*, Abingdon: Taylor & Francis.
Productivity Commission (2006), *Regulation and its Review 2005–06*, Annual Report Series, Commonwealth of Australia.
Regulatory Affairs Commission (2005), *Guidelines for Effective Regulatory Consultations*, Canadian Government.
Rodrigues, E.L., A. Justino and C. Roda (2000), *Economic Instruments for Sustainable Development: Improving the External and Working Environment Part III*, European Foundation for the Improvement of Living and Working Conditions.
Simon, J. (1981), *The Ultimate Resource*, Princeton: Princeton University Press.
Sparrow, M.K. (2002), *The Regulatory Craft: Controlling Risks, Solving Problems, and Managing Compliance*, Washington: Brookings Institution.
Water Quality Protection Program for Monterey Bay National Marine Sanctuary (1999), Action Plan IV: Agriculture and Rural Lands, Water Quality Protection Program for Monterey Bay National Marine Sanctuary.

10. Planning and environment in Mexico City's metropolitan zone: trying to defeat poverty

Miriam Alfie Cohen and Oscar Flores Jáuregui

10.1 INTRODUCTION

By the end of 1960, we had certainly witnessed the relentless surge of industrialization 'at all costs', limitless both in progress and expansion. Today, the constant growth of population, together with the depredation of non-renewable resources, the irrational use of energy sources and the deterioration of renewable resources, among others, mark the beginning of a new era in which human existence itself is under threat. Several writers refer to this situation as 'Socioeconomic Metabolism'; inasmuch as the consumption of energy plus the use of materials, as well as the residues produced in the process, prevent timely recuperation by nature.[1] Mainstream theories of development and underdevelopment have failed to sufficiently consider such ecological dynamics (Bunker, 1985) which are attributable to flaws in the market and in government. In the first case, the market, there is a failure to put a price on nature and to clearly delineate property rights. In the latter, the lack of governmental legislation has significant repercussions that are not easily solvable.[2]

This process of industrialization did not simply increase; its growth was poorly planned in most countries, leading to a deterioration of environmental conditions and an unequal distribution of resources within the population. The extensive growth of this new productive form, combined with the inappropriate use and intensive and systematic exploitation of natural resources, did not foresee what is today a risky future for all of us.

It is also important to stress the existing relationship between poverty and the environment. Environmental health is undoubtedly and fundamentally linked to development, equity and justice. However, industrialization and urbanization have caused deterioration of the environment and at times have also led to more poverty. Excessive consumption of non-renewable resources, erosion of land, pollution of water and air slowly diminish the quality of life of many groups within the population. The immediate results are environmental injustice, migrations, poverty and shortages. This explains why today cities and their citizens have a profound interest in, and a concern for the improvement of environmental conditions.

Most of us wish for a pollution free environment, uncontaminated water, reduction of noise, additional green zones, the protection of the habitat and living at a distance from the risks and dangers caused by contamination. In this sense, environmental health is directly related to important parameters, which allow us to measure not only the dangers to health but also, more generally, the quality of life of the inhabitants of a region, and the possibility of increasing development, diminishing poverty and speaking about environmental justice.

Given the above, this chapter focuses on the need to integrate urban planning and high-quality environmental management, emphasizing the need to draw up integral and transversal plans and programs capable of producing positive effects on health and the quality of life for the inhabitants of the Metropolitan Zone of Mexico City (MZMC).

Our approach looks into and exposes the different existing discourses in relation to poverty and the environment, highlighting the importance of local governance as a means to succeed in establishing environmental agreements to bring significant improvements for the poor.[3] We are particularly interested in analyzing the special features of the heterodox school that studies environmental risk, 'environmental agreements' and local governance as priority issues resulting in real action, plans and programs designed to confront the ecological deterioration facing highly marginal groups. Our intention is to explain how proper urban planning can provide a framework to deal with environmental and poverty problems in the MZMC.

10.2 POVERTY AND ENVIRONMENT: BETWEEN ORTHODOXY AND COMPLEXITY

The study of the relationship between poverty and the environment has been conducted through two theoretical postures: the orthodox school of thought and the heterodox or complex perspective. The orthodox posture stresses a direct relationship between poverty and environment, arguing that they are closely linked and reinforce each other. The relationship is presented as a downward spiral, in which it is assumed that the only way of avoiding environmental degradation is by combating poverty.

Since the formulation of some of the key principles of sustainable development in 'Our Common Future' (World Commission on Environment and Development, 1987), the nodal point has been the eradication of poverty with a view to achieving the international objective of sustainability.

> As indicated earlier, development that is sustainable has to address the problem of the large number of people who live in absolute poverty - that is, who are unable to satisfy even the most basic of their needs. Poverty reduces people's capacity to use resources in a sustainable manner; it intensifies pressure on the environment. Most such absolute poverty is in developing countries; in many, it has been aggravated by the economic stagnation of the 1980s. A necessary but not a sufficient condition for the elimination of absolute poverty is a relatively rapid rise in per capita incomes in the Third World. It is therefore essential that the stagnant or declining growth trends of this decade be reversed.[4]

For years, international organizations, social development agencies and national governments promoted political actions and strategies which did not take into account the different meanings that the environment entailed for the poor, and focused on macroeconomic responses, which worsen the problems. Local experiences were ignored. This approach made it impossible for the poor to create their own institutional responses to the economic, demographic and/or environmental challenges. Efforts to reduce poverty as the first step in achieving environmental conservation does not guarantee successful results when it fails to take into account the local ways of life and their needs.[5] One of the reasons for this is that policies have privileged the protection of natural resources when the quality of life of the inhabitants of a locality depends on the use, management and control of these resources.

> It is important to point out how the causes which lead to poverty and environmental degradation can be mediated by local practices. In other words, attention needs to be paid on the forms, the institutions, and the specific groups which have access, control and management of specific natural resources, as well as environmental services which are important for their well being (Forsyth, et.al., 1998, p. 28).

Contrary to the orthodox school, the heterodox one deals with the intricate relationship between local populations and resources in fragile ecosystems, where poverty and environment are key factors. Authors such as Leach and Mearns (1996), Davidson and Mayer (1992) and Martinez-Allier (1990) have clarified relevant concepts and categories, and have emphasized the impact of poverty and the environment on the less developed countries.[6] From their point of view, the changes, environmental impacts and socio-economic problems are analyzed and understood, in most cases, from the perspective of the developed countries, not from the standpoint of poor societies, poorest countries and the poorest populations within these countries.

This school puts forward the fact that any kind of relationship between poverty and environment is indirect, that environmental deterioration occupies a strategic place in relation to development and growth, and that the solution to poverty does not guarantee the protection of the environment. Analysis originating from the less favored countries and from the poorest communities is seen as a priority.

> From a historical point of view, during the last five centuries, the inhabitants of the imperialist countries have contracted a debt with the poor of the world, as a result of the diversity of mutually related processes between those that stand out: the extraction of resources (mineral, marine, forest and genetic) in the countries of the south, the consolidation of an uneven ecological interchange, as a result of which primary goods are exported without economically evaluating the social and environmental impact generated by their extraction or production; the plundering, destruction and devastation of men and culture from the colonial era; the appropriation of traditional knowledge of indigenous communities concerning seeds and medicinal plants in which modern agro industries and biotechnology find sustenance; the destruction of the best farming lands and of marine resources for exportation, weakening food self-sufficiency and the cultural sovereignty of the communities of the south (Vega Cantor, 2006, p. 10).[7]

They set out a new environmental policy, which seeks to interlink social interactions and different institutional replies to confront environmental degradation of various scales and involving different actors. The aim is to generate more representative environmental policy objectives at the local level and to promote the interests and problems of the poor with what they call 'Environmental Agreements'. Local environmental agreements imply new forms of power and bear an influence upon regional, national and global decisions. Environmental agreements foment new forms of shaping policy, where the political gap between actors is superseded, dialogue is promoted, as is the capacity to broaden local governance and increase new forms of participation in the decision making of environmental policy, the so called empowerment.[8]

The central point of their analysis revolves around the concept of 'sustainable forms of life', which implies taking into account all the capabilities (material and social), resources and activities needed to live a dignified existence. It contemplates the use, management and control of natural resources in a sustainable manner by the communities themselves.

> A way of life is sustainable when we can confront and repair the effects of environmental risks, which bring about pressures and impacts. The goal is to maintain or increase capacities and means without weakening the bases of natural resources (Leach, and Mearns, 1996, p. 14).

Given that environmental harm is more devastating for poorer communities, different movements such as Eco-socialism and Environmental Justice have emerged to combat Socioeconomic Metabolism and external factors provoked by markets and governments alike. Important manifestations of these movements can be seen in Peru, Brazil and Ecuador as well as within marginal populations in the USA.[9]

> In the countries of the South, the concept of environmental justice has not been linked as much to toxics contamination as in the United States. Rather, the focus has

> been the lack of access to and control of the natural resources possessed by the poor, as well as the problems which they undergo through environmental degradation (Milagros, 2000, p. 21).

These movements highlight the fact that multifaceted social and environmental crises can only be resolved via radical political and structural changes. Awareness of environmental problems and education based on ethno-environmental values suggest concrete strategies for political action.

The actors immersed in these mobilizations generally seek small scale changes. For instance, local communities seek to strengthen municipalities (municipal radicalism) by promoting an image of man and nature in productive harmony.

This discourse focuses on the civil rights of the poor and ethnic minorities and their exposure to contamination in their different districts, boroughs and localities. Issues such as class, ethnicity and environment merge to shape a strong movement of local groups united in networks where neither leaders nor bureaucratic structures exist.[10]

> The members of the base movements are intensely involved in local affairs, given that their health and that of their family, as well as their property, are at risk. Lois Gibbs works with a network of between 8000 and 9000 local groups which range from a dozen members to several hundred (Shabecoff, 2000, p. 36).[11]

These groups seek to create new environmental agencies in order to diminish the impact of environmental risk and promote sustainable lifestyles. This requires a redefinition of the roles played by the Nation-State and the development agencies alike. Thus, for these movements, the only kind of agencies capable of managing environmental risks are those at the local level, in such a way that the relevant problem is how to influence the access, management and control of resources.

The heterodox school has suggested the empowerment of communities and localities capable of taking charge of the use, management and control of their resources, the sale of environmental services and the need of 'Environmental Agreements' as new forms of shaping policy. This means a radical change at various levels. In the international sphere, it implies situating the environmental agenda in another perspective; while it is true that environmental risk is global, it is presented in a differentiated manner with an understanding that more vulnerable economies take the brunt of the environmental impacts.

At the national level, environmental agreements strengthen environmental policy. The inclusion of actors at the negotiating tables, observing and promoting solutions for the poor, consolidates democratic processes. And, finally, at the local level, it means the development of local communities through access to subsidies, which makes it possible to strengthen the agriculture or forest resources and as a result reduce poverty and environmental degradation.

The complex or heterodox viewpoint also emphasizes the importance of concepts such as way of life and wellbeing in defining poverty. In other words, poverty cannot be measured solely on the basis of income. The poverty index should also take into account the elements for a dignified life, including life expectancy, proper nutrition, adequate housing and good education. The authors analyze ways by which the relationship poverty-environment should be mediated by local practices, focusing in particular on ensuring that groups can access, control and administer environmental resources of vital importance for their subsistence. Innovations in groups' participation and empowerment to strengthen governance through new forms of democracy are key factors of this agenda.

> The most strident conclusion designed by this new way of thinking about environmental poverty is the need to move away from macro scales, approaches and policies towards a rigorous appreciation of people in places. This change can be justified, based on the fact that macro scales are experienced at the local level or simply because the experience of poverty and environmental problems is differentiated spatially and at the heart of every society (Chambers, 1997, p. 56).

The goal is to expand the field of politics, from a mere situation of viability of recourses, to a dynamic rapprochement where agencies, actors, empowerment and democratic consolidation are taken into account. This approach questions general and international solutions and emphasizes local policies as a guarantee of specific trajectories of change.

The heterodox school contrasts with the prevailing theoretical trends which find expression in international agreements, development agencies or the dominant environmental discourse itself. All of these have acknowledged the right to development of non-developed countries but always on the basis of an Occidental model.

10.3 URBAN PLANNING: ENVIRONMENT AND POVERTY

Adopting the approach of the heterodox school, we now examine how urban planning in general has played a relevant role since the 1960s in shaping cities. We focus in particular on the role of urban planning in fighting environmental deterioration as well as poverty.

Over the years, environmental planning at the local level has acquired greater importance, identifying problems concerning land use, invasions of protected lands, contamination and pollution caused by industry in residential areas and the dangers inflicted on the environment due to the impossibility of controlling traffic in cities. It was not until 1970, however, that environmental conditions became a key element of many governments' national and local policies.

Governments adopted over the years environmental legislations and norms as well as programs to improve the quality of air and water, and control the exposure of inhabitants to toxic and carcinogenic material. Nevertheless, in many cases these measures have not been able to deal effectively with environmental risks. Therefore, it is imperative to consider setting up transversal plans capable of putting into practice programs of environmental quality and equality for all the inhabitants, a plan based on environmental justice.

> The concept of environmental justice suggests that people of color and/or people of low income bear a disproportionate burden of pollution that is unfair and in need of change. The notion of an inequitable distribution raises difficult questions on how best to measure and address environmental inequities across space and environmental equity studies indicate racial disparities at some scales of resolution and analysis, and class-based disparities at others. With the problem of environmental inequity thus characterized by spatial ambiguity and with no indisputable rationale for favoring one scale of resolution and analysis over another, environmental justice politics are permeated by considerable debate over the nature and spatial extent of both problem and possible solutions (Kurtz, 2003, pp. 887–888).

Since the 1970s, the most significant achievement of governments in environmental matters has been to minimize 'externalities'. These are produced by the activities of one group impacting upon another, usually in a negative manner. Growth control and urban planning thus focused on density and land use. In many locations the use of industrial and urban land was separated so as not to generate negative burdens on the more sensitive sector. The central issue was to avoid environmental problems in order to improve the quality of life of urban residents and also protect rights to property.

However, this focus on control development and planning suffered from a short-term vision, inasmuch as it excluded phenomena such as the quality of water and air, the sensitive environmental areas, the generation of noise, the environmental risk and global warming. To a large extent this limited vision was due to a lack of information on environmental issues and risks, explainable in part by the limited number of trained personnel on which specialized agencies could rely.

When environmental problems and risks became evident they were tackled with specific regulations: protection of water resources, preservation of woodlands, air and water regulations, and so on. Many of these norms continue to exist and there is no integral planning program, in some cases, for the development of cities and regions.

Starting in the early 1990s, urban planning and environmental management became a priority for local governments in many countries. Today, the analysis of the interconnections between environment, poverty and planning involves three elements: scale and space; the construction of agendas; and the setting in motion of transversal and integral environmental-poverty plans.

Scale and space refer to the existing relationship between urbanization and economic growth. These two phenomena go hand in hand and are associated with the process of development. It is not possible to understand economic growth, a feature of the industrial revolution, without considering the process of urbanization and vice versa. The economic growth of the previous two decades took place in urban centers. It is significant to appreciate the manner in which urbanization and economic growth were congregated in certain regions and countries.

> The combination of urbanization and economic growth is often associated with the classical city-scale environmental problems of urban smog, polluted urban waterways and peri-urban resources degradation, which have arisen partly in response to the location of populations and economic production in urban centers. From this perspective, it might seem that the environmental impact of urbanization has been to concentrate environmental impacts spatially (Marcotullio and McGranahan, 2007, p. 2).

One of the characteristic features of economic growth and urbanization is environmental deterioration and the increases of inequalities. Today the environmental risks we are facing take different scales and magnitudes, ranging from local to global. Urbanization and economic growth are clearly associated with the classical environmental problems of the city: air pollution, shortage and contamination of water and land, deterioration of resources on the outskirts, internal migrations of poor people, production of garbage and its eventual disposal, as well as energy consumption, among many others.

Environmental problems are the result of the concentration of population growth and attraction poles, which provoke impacts that can be localized and determined by space. Scale and space also allow us to find concrete solutions to localized problems. Therefore, scale and space become key elements when one considers the possibility of establishing connections between environment-poverty and planning.

The second element to bear in mind in the relationship between planning and environment-poverty is the construction of agendas. Governance and regulation of urban environmental responsibilities have not been easy tasks under the command-control model set in motion in the 1950s. The problem is that governments did not incorporate long-term prevention in their approach.

To remedy this situation, local and national governments put into practice three kinds of agenda: brown, grey and green. The purpose of the brown agenda is to put an end to a city's sanitary problems; access to drinking water, drainage and paving is linked to health standards in an attempt to reduce the number of illnesses and deaths in low income cities. Grey agendas are concerned with the serious problems of environmental contamination caused by industrialization and the burning of fuels. As early as the 1970s governments began to implement aggressive policies to curb emissions by developing norms and specific programs. Finally, the green agenda, with a more global approach and in search of new solutions for the environmental problems, is concerned with programs including global warming, alternative energy, recycling and the reprocessing of materials.

The model implies a linear process in the development of the agenda, but a government can set in motion a brown agenda, and it can also implement a grey or green agenda. Above all, this type of model separates the intrinsic relationship between planning and the environment and limits itself to combating the effects provoked by economic, urban or population growth without putting forward an integrated plan which brings together and seeks out new solutions as well as diversifying possibilities. It is thus a question of elaborating hybrid agendas which combine the urban-spatial sphere, environmental considerations and poverty issues.

> For Mexico City environmental issues and agendas arise in a far from linear fashion. By examining the evolving agendas for water and air pollution, and how they are historically fashioned and politically situated it is necessary a robust antidote to the over-interpretation of statistical trends. Indeed, this complex and historically grounded discussion of how agendas are constructed and fought over is presented as revealing that any notion of an urban environmental transition, relevant to urban centers around the world, is simplistic and misleading (Connolly, 2006, p. 280).

In our view it is necessary to rethink the complexity of environmental issues as it requires new ways of appreciating the interaction between scales of impact and systems of governance. We also need to rethink ways in which public policies are constructed and to design new decision-making platforms regarding the environment.

The third element in the interaction between environment-poverty and planning is the construction of a public policy with a transversal and integral environmental program, produced via a process designed to compare and evaluate each decision, and incorporate the analysis of environmental assessment. This policy needs to provide for consideration of alternatives put forward by the public, other government agencies and experts. The project or program will have a transversal environmental approach in the decision making on development and increase environmental justice.

> The Environmental Agreements will try to open up negotiations with multiple actors in order to find adequate measures, so that the political proposal is a matter

of regulation in a fluent, transparent, flexible, participative and creative administration. Therefore, unknown actors and several minorities are given strength, at multiple contexts. New collective practices based on negotiation and consensus, citizen networks of interactions that operate side by side with the State on the decision making (Alfie, 2008, p. 78).

10.4 THE MZMC: MAIN ENVIRONMENTAL RISKS

The MZMC, located in the middle of what was once a lake, is a highly seismic zone and is also prone to flooding and occasional volcanic eruptions. The geo-morphological conditions of the city are responsible for the concentration of contaminants and the well-known greenhouse effect.[12] Made up of 16 *delegaciones* (the lowest tier of government in the Federal District), 37 municipalities from the State of Mexico and one more from the State of Hidalgo, it is the largest pole of attraction of economic and political activities in the country. By the year 2000, 500 of the largest companies in the country were located in the MZMC, mainly in Mexico City, which is the main internal consumer market at the national and regional level (Programa de Ordenamiento Territorial para la Zona Metropolitana del Valle de México.

This growth and economic power resulted in a significant concentration of inhabitants. Between 1980 and the year 2000, the population of the MZMC increased by more than four million, to a total of 17.9 million registered inhabitants. In 2005, this number rose to 20.3 million inhabitants.[13]

Since the 1950s, the demographic growth rate of the outlying municipalities began to surpass that of the Federal District (DF), transforming the State of Mexico into a pole of attraction for incoming inhabitants. This was caused by the industrial de-concentration from the capital, the construction of industrial parks and cities and the offer of cheap land in the municipal zones themselves. A key factor in this extension of urban conglomerates is the highway and transport network, which makes mobility between both zones much easier (Negrete, 1993).

The deterioration and neglect of the central zone is one of the most serious problems of current urbanization, based in the inappropriate use of the infrastructure of the city's urban, economic and cultural patrimony. The results, among many others, are the proliferation of an informal economy which deters investment and flaws in the real estate market, inasmuch as the land in this zone becomes more expensive due to the pressures of more profitable uses (services).[14]

What cannot be denied is the fact that the MZMC has grown in an anarchical fashion. The extension of the urban mass has led to isolation, segregation, deterioration and disintegration. In a study carried out in 2002 on poverty in the MZMC, the authors point out that since the implementation of focalized programs to fight poverty, the poor of the DF have suffered from a lack of attention from a federal government tolerant of urban poverty.[15] The same study, using information from the 2000 census, shows that one in every six poor and one in every eight extreme poor in the country live in the MZMC. Poverty in the MZMC increased and intensified between 1984 and 2000. Thus, the DF has the most polarized social structure, with a bigger proportion of indigents and non-poor, and therefore, the lowest proportion of non-indigent poor.[16]

The social impact of poverty has had environmental costs and repercussions on the inadequate use, management and control of natural resources. Prominent among these are land conservation and green belts with constant arrival of poor people who demand services, scarcity and contamination of water, deterioration of air quality and inadequate final disposal of waste, among many others.

Today, the only significant territory available in the DF with which to pursue horizontal urban expansion is the so called preserved land.[17] This reality causes a strong tension between value of use and value of exchange and the subsequent degradation of environmental services. An indicator of such pressure is revealed by the fact that 76 per cent of new housing built in the DF between 1980 and the year 2000 (377 000 units) is located in the seven *delegaciones* with conservation land rights (Gobierno del Distrito Federal, 2000).

The majority of these settlements are irregular, with high environmental impact due to their location in ravines, high surcharge zones, and so forth. Almost all of them expand permanently via 'ant-like' invasions, as it is known in Mexico, increasing the tension between the urban-rural frontiers and intensifying the effects of overflow from the rural settlements. The irregular settlements have an impact on the environment, not only due to the change in land use and contamination, but because they require services, water and energy to sustain their growth. This generates inequality that can be seen and measured as environmental injustice.

With regard to water, it was estimated in the mid-twentieth century that the available sources of water without risk to the ecosystem of the Basin of Mexico were sufficient for a population of eight million. This limit was exceeded over 40 years ago (Garza, 2000). Nonetheless, both supply and demand continue to grow, which has meant injecting 60m3/s into the drinking water network, while a growing deficit of 7m3/s is forecast (Universidad Nacional Autónoma de México, 2003). Drinking water resources for the DF are equivalent to 351 liters daily per person, this usage being one of the highest in the world. What is paradoxical and points to serious management problems is the inequality of access (45 126 dwellings and 120 000 inhabitants are without water service) and the over-exploitation of aquifers while 37 per cent of drinking water is lost in leaks. Moreover, only 68.8 per cent of homes receive water on a daily basis and for the entire day.[18]

In the MZMC, the government has an available yearly inventory of emissions of contaminants. The major contribution of contamination comes from mobile sources (84 per cent). The inventory of emission of contaminants enables us to estimate that the daily demand for energy via the number of vehicles in circulation approaches 4.5 million liters of diesel, 18 million liters of petrol and 700 thousand liters of LPG ('Liquid Petroleum Gas').[19]

This is equivalent to 47 per cent of the total energy consumed in the MZMC. Although anti-contaminant programs have been put into practice and efforts made to regulate vehicle emissions, the environmental quality of the MZMC continues to present problems originating from vehicles with emissions of particles smaller than 10 micrometers. The government of the city has recognized the impact that this problem can cause in the deterioration of health (respiratory diseases) and the quality of life for the inhabitants of MZMC (Secretaría del Medio Ambiente del Gobierno del Distrito Federal, 2000).

Regarding solid residues, it is estimated that every inhabitant generates an average of more than 1.2 kilos of garbage daily, equivalent to 21 544 tons a day or 7.9 million tons a year. This immense volume, in addition to growing at a daily rate, represents an increase in waste that cannot be recycled or which is not biodegradable (Gobierno del Distrito Federal y Agencia de Cooperación Internacional del Japón, 1999).

As we can see from the above, the environment-poverty panorama in the MZMC is a high-risk issue requiring immediate and urgent action and needs to be tackled by the different local governments.[20]

10.5 THE POVERTY AND ENVIRONMENTAL POLICIES OF RECENT MZMC GOVERNMENTS

There are different local plans for fighting environmental deterioration and poverty. However, these local plans did not address environment and poverty as a common unit.

Although the current elected government of the DF, headed by the PRD (Party of the Democratic Revolution), has promoted plans and programs against poverty that do strive to break with focalized politics, these have not succeeded in building a unique plan of guaranteeing the quality of life and full human development of the inhabitants of the MZMC. The political opposition has harshly criticized these programs.[21]

The role of local governments cannot be limited to administering social policies defined by national governments. Instead, they should promote a social-economic policy of sustainable human development in the local field

(Bodemer, Corragio and Ziccardi, 1999). This ambitious objective, given the high levels of urban poverty and social exclusion in our cities, not only supposes the availability of substantial resources but also a profound institutional reform to create a governmental structure capable of putting into practice the reforms needed.

In Mexico City, the political democratization processes for the local governments have not been accompanied by a reform of old organizational structures. These are, in general, focused on sectors, highly centralized, extremely bureaucratic and provide few real opportunities for citizens' participation (Sánchez Mejorada, 2008). With the arrival of the PRD as the first elected government of Mexico City in 1997, expectations were high regarding the possible course social and environmental policies could take.[22] Thus, during the administration of Cuauhtémoc Cárdenas (1997–1999), the Social Development Secretariat (SDS) was oriented toward the promotion of a social policy aimed at the reconstruction of the social tissue heavily damaged during the economic crisis of 1995. Different NGOs were involved in the decision-making processes, particularly in reproductive health programs. As well, the Urban Development and Housing Secretariat promoted participative planning processes for 31 Partial Programs of Urban Development in districts meant to address urban and social conflicts (Zicardi, 2003).[23] The Cárdenas administration also created the Institute of Housing and designed a policy of popular housing with the participation of NGOs, professional representation organizations (such as the Association of Architects) and urban social organizations of the popular sectors.

During the second elected PRD government, social policies and programs of the Government of the DF were revised by Head of Government Andrés Manuel López Obrador (2000–2005) and his team.[24] This new team decided to emphasize territorial integration in social programs which gave birth to the Integral Territorial Program for Social Development. This program privileged a territorial criterion in defining its areas of action but it was designed and put into practice by the central apparatus of the Government of Mexico City, under the main responsibility of three secretariats (Social Development, Health and Urban Development and Housing) and the participation of a few other secretariats (Economy, Tourism, Environment and Public Work). There was scarce participation by the Delegaciones, the level of government closer to citizens.[25] This resulted in a segmented or *sectorialized* policy, which meant a failure to put together a metropolitan planning agenda that responded 'to the root' of the poverty questions and environmental risks associated with the pattern of urban growth and the available natural resources.[26]

The Social Policy has become one of the main political platforms of the PRD. The third elected government, headed by Marcelo Ebrard, (2006–2012), has inherited the bases of the López Obrador administration and has assumed entirely the programs adopted by its predecessor, with the objective of extending coverage thereof. Thus, for this new government there are three important programs: the social welfare policy, the economic promotion policy and finally the urban and territorial policy.[27]

Social assistance programs include the following: school breakfasts, school supplies and textbooks, assistance for the homeless, elderly persons, single mothers and children, addiction prevention, medical assistance, assistance and prevention of intra-family violence, scholarships, integral women's health, food and medical aid both in hospitals and in residences for the elderly. In the sphere of economic promotion, it is worth noting the productive credits and/or micro-credits, training and employment programs, scholarships for unemployed workers and support to handicapped people.[28]

As far as urban and territorial policy goes, a key element has been the promotion of the housing program through the expansion and rehabilitation of housing in owned lots of land and renewals of common areas in housing projects. Another important program is the Neighborhood Improving Program, inasmuch as the design and execution of projects therein is carried out in a decentralized manner, allowing delegaciones and neighbors' committees an important space for participation.[29]

With regard to the environment the priorities of local governments have been air, water and land conservation. The first elected government of the DF inherited a consolidated Environmental Industry (low emissions, alternative energy, control programs, and so on), together with the recently adopted DF Environmental Law (*Ley Ambiental del Distrito Federal*). Likewise, it took up again the environmental platform of the Integral Program against Atmospheric Contamination designed in 1990 and continued with the program of vehicle verification and control of pollutant emissions.

The period from 2000–2006 is remembered for the controversial decision to add a 'second floor' to the city's ring road. In environmental terms it turned out to be a very bad decision as it encouraged the use of private transport. During this administration, the Law of Solid Residues of the DF was adopted (*Ley General de Residuos Tóxicos del Distrito Federal*), but no action has been taken in this matter since its publication. However, it is also fair to point out that during the aforementioned administration, the Environmental Office and Territorial Organization of the DF[30] responsible for overseeing the fulfillment of environmental standards was created. In addition, thanks largely to the pressure of organized civil society, the Metro bus network project was initiated as a clean, collective, modern and safe mode of transport.

During the current administration of Marcelo Ebrard, the most important institutions for environmental management in the DF should harmonize perspectives and interests. The first 'Green Consultation' was carried out with society at large and the Green Plan adopted.[31] As well, the Metro bus and other means of transport such as the tram, the subway and the bicycle were encouraged.

The Green Plan turned out to be too ambitious, given the actual capacities of the local government. It has left aside certain themes such as auditory contamination, the integral recovery of land conservation and several of the principal strategic actors required for appropriate environmental management, such as the PAOT and the political municipalities of the DF.

Prominent among the challenges to resolve is the city's deep drainage system which is on the verge of collapse, the need for new sanitary filler in view of the depletion of the city's western outer edge, and the avoidance of human settlements in protected zones.

As one can see, both social and environmental plans in the MZMC exist separately. By failing to join needs or problems, these two policies remain totally disconnected from each other in their formulation and implementation by local government of the DF.

10.6 THE CHALLENGES: INTERCONNECTING PLANNING ENVIRONMENT AND POVERTY IN THE MZMC

To combine urban planning and quality environmental management in the MZMC requires putting into practice a transversal program which crosses all economic activities; fomenting social participation and triggering co-responsibility in decision making, what we called the Environmental Agreements.

What is needed is a process that brings to the table all actors involved: the social (NGOs, social movements), private (citizens, entrepreneurs) and public sectors (multilateral cooperation agencies, international agencies), not to mention the government. All need to work together to develop platforms that commit them to taking real and specific actions to face environmental-poverty risks, strengthening new forms of making policies which can be constructed from the bottom-up, promoting cooperation networks and providing opportunities for public policies of environmental orientation in governance.

In specific terms the policies to be constructed should bear in mind scale and space, as this makes it possible to better define the problems and solve them. The MZMC has to be seen from a holistic viewpoint which includes the use, control and management of natural resources, contaminant sources, new technological processes, and action programs to attack the problems of environmentally vulnerable zones.

In our view, some of the measures that should be considered in an environmental policy for the MZMC include the following: validating the dispositions contained in the General Law of Ecological Equilibrium and Protection of the

Environment (*Ley General de Equilibrio Ecológico y Protección Ambiental*, LGEEPA) in order to oblige contaminant companies to internalize costs per emissions; establishing environmental-poverty funds; including environmental effects in national accounts; introducing environmental costs via reliable indicators in the Gross Domestic Product; creating mechanisms and fiscal incentives which reward sound environmental management. To put in practice a heterodox approach, which deals with the intricate relationship between population and resources in fragile ecosystems, where poverty and environment are key factors, is what is needed to deal with the environmental deterioration in the MZMC.

It is important to take into account the participation and empowerment of the communities directly affected by environmental problems and to create effective and open communication channels with the inhabitants. There is also the need to develop programs that achieve environmental services, and bring local authorities, and decentralized agencies of multilateral cooperation (PNUMA, World Bank) closer to private individuals and citizens in multilevel networks in order to ensure viable policies.

Planning, environment and poverty can no longer be viewed as three separate action zones. What is needed is the creation of hybrid agencies that combine central aspects of city needs, environmental pressures and fighting poverty. It is no longer a question of separate agendas seeking to solve a specific type of environmental or poverty problem, but rather the construction of agendas capable of being converted into actions to give rise to sustainable development.

Thus, the new programs of territorial regulation would combine policy analysis (the normative technical part) with the process of policy making (degrees of consensus, alternatives, and courses of possible action). The setting in motion of these elements could not only help to combat the causes of environmental degradation but also in establishing a better quality of life in the MZMC.

One of the additional tasks for the current Government of the Federal District is to carry out an institutional reform which, among other things, promotes the updating of the administrative apparatus, the decentralization of resources down to the delegaciones, metropolitan coordination with the authorities of the metropolitan municipalities of the Estate of Mexico and a more intense participation of citizens in the design, implementation and evaluation of universal public policies.

10.7 CONCLUSION

The poorest countries as well as the poorest actors will be more sensitive and vulnerable to the perverse effects of environmental degradation.

Environmental risk is closely linked to social risk, given the fact that the loss of resources, the impossibility of controlling them, and the lack of relevant legislation, can produce significant disruption in governance. The inability to see solutions to environmental problems within the poor communities clouds the possibilities of confronting the imminent environmental risks in a different and maybe more responsive way.

To view nature as an object, alien and manipulable, where human beings are in control, dominating it, making it their own, is a highly questionable view today. In reality, society and nature are linked in an indissoluble relationship where distinction between object and subject of the action becomes highly complicated. From the human and non-human agents, active-passive, society-nature, subject-object dichotomies emerge the difficulty to establish the contours and frontiers between the external and the internal, between the remote and the near. Social and political actions cease to be over-determined; this is the case of the poverty-environment relationship.

The heterodox school has brought into the discussion the possibility of the empowerment of communities and localities capable of taking charge of the use, management and control of their resources, as well as the sale of environmental services and the need for 'Environmental Agreements'. These can enable new ways of shaping transversal policies where the gap between actors is closed and dialogue is promoted. Increasing new forms of participation in the decision making of environmental policy and fomenting local governance to broaden democratic consolidation are part of a new project.

This hybrid agenda, where nature ceases to be the object of control, is converted into a field of original experiences where co-responsibility and new forms of environmental governance in environmental affairs becomes a priority in all spheres and at all levels.

The task of citizens in building hybrid metropolitan planning agendas is an essential one. In other words, public function should not only be seen as the mere execution of vertically designed plans by the central administration, but as the appropriation of public spaces by citizens on the bases of the permanent exercise of political and civic rights: the right to access information, to association, to monitor and watch over the different programs, including the allocation of funding for each of them. The proper implementation of these elements may lead not only to combatting the damages caused to the environment, but also to establish a better quality of life and equity in the MZMC.

NOTES

1. The concepts of socioeconomic metabolism (which basically encompasses consumable materials, processing, the remains of societies, and its corresponding energy production and

colonization of nature (activities which deliberately alter the natural systems with a view to render them more useful to society), constitute attempts at relating the notion of 'sustainable growth' to fundamental characteristics of society, from a historical perspective. These concepts can be useful in identifying and applying objectives and strategies for sustainable development. The analysis of metabolism and the colonization strategies of different types of societies differ depending on their modes of production, their technologies and their life styles, and offer a useful framework in approaching the socioeconomic and cultural reasons for environmental problems. Independently of demographic growth, the scale of metabolism per capita of industrial societies should be tackled with strategies of 'sustainable development'. We can only develop these strategies adequately if we understand the economic, technological and cultural variables of industrial societies as this influence upon this metabolism. See Campbell, S. and S. Fainstein (2007), *Readings in Planning Theory*, Oxford: Blackwell; Huang, S., et al. (2007), *Socioeconomic metabolism in Taiwan: Energy synthesis versus material flow analysis*, Institute of Urban Planning, National Taipei University.

2. Actions of one or various persons can affect a third party as external factors. According to several economists, these external factors can provoke flaws in the market when price mechanisms fail to consider the 'total social costs' and the 'total social benefits' of production and consumption. In such a situation, the private optimum obtained at a produced quantity level by the producer, or at a consumer level is greater than the social optimum. This results in a conclusion opposed to that of Adam Smith and the liberal economists, according to which the individual, in pursuing his own well-being or promoting his own interests will promote those of society in a more effective manner than when the government directly attempts to promote them. According to mainstream economics, another market flaw takes place in the case of so called 'public goods'. These public goods are very positive external factors. They are not produced by the market in light of their non-profit making nature. In other words, the market will not provide consumers with such goods and the government should therefore produce them so the public at large may have access to them.
3. In Spanish the word 'gobernaza' (governance in English) does not exist; in fact, several writers like us have adopted it as a neologism to highlight the importance which this concept has acquired since the 1980s in political science and political sociology. Certain writers refer to 'good government' as a synonym for 'gobernaza'.
4. United Nations (1987), *Gathering a Body of Global Agreements*, NGO Committee on Education, http://www.un-documents.net/index.htm (accessed 8 February 2012).
5. The World Bank recognizes that the visible outlook at the end of the 1990s could be described as 'the bottleneck of progress', a result of the East Asia crisis, the increase of poverty in India, famine in Sub-Saharan Africa, and impoverishment in Europe and Central Asia. In the words of Michael Walton, director of the Program for the Reduction of Poverty and Economic Management of the World Bank, 'we do not have a global poverty estimate for the close of the decade, but if the percentage of poor people has not varied during that period – 30% survive on less than a dollar a day, - we would have been obliged to reach the conclusion that the number of persons relying on a survival amount of less than a dollar has increased from 1,300 million in 1993 to approximately 1,500 million in 1999.' The World Bank (2002), *Linking Poverty Reduction and Environmental Management – Policy Challenges and Opportunities*, World Bank, 69.
6. Juan Martinez-Allier analyzes the phenomenon in Latin America, using the term environmentalism of the poor.
7. Author's translation.
8. The *Report on Human Development of the United Nations Development Program*, UNDP, 1997, 123, distinguishes three perspectives on poverty: income, basic needs and capacities. Income: from this standpoint poverty is associated with monetary inability to satisfy life's most pressing elements, that is to say, a person is considered poor only when his income level is below the defined poverty line. The poverty line is frequently defined in terms of possessing income sufficient enough to buy a determined quantity of food. The satisfaction of needs depends exclusively on income and on private consumption and, in general, the real satisfaction and lack of satisfaction of these needs are not taken into account. The problem

of poverty would seem to depend entirely on the absence of income, when in reality poverty is also the product of other factors.

Basic Needs: this concept of privation goes much beyond the lack of private income. Poverty is perceived as the privation of the material means to satisfy human needs in an acceptable measure, including foodstuffs, basic health and education services, as well as other essentials which it is the community's obligation to provide to prevent people from becoming poor. It also recognizes the need for employment and participation.

Absence of capacities: in this criterion poverty represents the absence of certain basic capacities. It refers to the fact that the operational aspects pertaining to this analysis can vary from the physical kind, such as being well fed, dressed and adequately housed, as well as avoiding preventable mortality, to more complex social achievements such as being able to take part in the life of the community. The criterion of capacity combines the concepts of absolute and relative poverty, in that the relative privation of income and products can bring about an absolute privation of minimal capacity.

9. Two actions characterize the discourse of Environmental Justice: the NIMBY (not in my backyard), has been transformed into NIABY (not in anybody's backyard), and in LULUS (locally unwanted land uses).
10. Certain groups and environmental NGOs on the border shared by Mexico and the US have adopted this theme; worthy of note are the prominent Mexican groups: *Factor X* and *Cañón del Padre* in Tijuana, *Justicia Ambiental* in Ciudad Juarez, and *Pastoral Juvenil Obrera* in Matamoros.
11. Gibbs's involvement in environmental causes began in 1978 when she discovered that her 7-year-old son's elementary school in Niagara Falls, New York was built on a toxic waste dump. Subsequent investigation revealed that the entire neighborhood, Love Canal, had been built on top of this dump. With no prior experience in community activism, Gibbs organized her neighbors and formed the Love Canal Homeowners' Association. She led her community in a battle against the local, state, and federal governments. After years of struggle, 833 families were eventually evacuated, and the cleanup of Love Canal began. In 1980, Gibbs formed the Citizens' Clearinghouse for Hazardous Waste, later renamed the Center for Health, Environment and Justice (CHEJ), where she currently serves as Executive Director. CHEJ is a grassroots environmental crisis center that provides information, resources, technical assistance and training to community groups around the nation. CHEJ seeks to form strong local organizations in order to protect neighborhoods from exposure to hazardous wastes. See Alfie, M. (2005), *Retos, Riesgos y Opciones en la Era de la Globalización* UAM-A, Pomares.
12. Mexico City is one of the world largest metropolitan areas in the world, housing nearly 21 million inhabitants within the Valle de Mexico. The Valle de Mexico occupies 1300 km^2 at a nominal elevation of 2240 m above mean sea level, and is bordered on the east and west by mountains that rise 1000 m above the valley floor, with low points to the north and south. At 2240 the atmospheric pressure is roughly 25% lower than at sea level. The Metropolitan Area of Mexico City, also called *Zona Metropolitana de la Ciudad de México*, lies in a high altitude basin almost completely surrounded by hills, mountains (including dormant/active volcanoes where seismic activity is frequent; the area is well known as an '*earthquake zone*') but with an opening to the north that extends over 4 km^2 and is located 19°3´ north latitude and 99°1´ west longitude.

    More than 20% of Mexico's entire population lives in the Valle de Mexico, and more than 30% of the country's industrial output is produced within its environs. More than three million vehicles travel on its streets daily. See Yip, M. and P. Madl (2003), *Air Pollution in Mexico City: Project-Study paper*, University of Salzburg, 53.
13. Consejo Nacional de Evaluación de la Política de Desarrollo Social (CONEVAL) (2005). http://www.coneval.gob.mx/coneval2/htmls/medicion_pobreza/HomeMedicionPobreza.jsp, (accessed 15 February 2012)
14. Mexico City's real estate market has been somewhat spared from the global downturn, largely because the market is predominantly local. It is also cash-based, because there is no formalized mortgage market in Mexico. From 2001 to 2007, prices citywide climbed about 7% a year. Today, prices in Coyoacán, Polanco and other affluent neighborhoods start at

$200 a square foot and quickly go up from there. The real estate industry is not regulated in Mexico, and there is no formal licensing of real estate agents.

15. Boltvinik, J. and R. Estévez (2002,), 'Magnitud de la pobreza en la ZMCM', *La Jornada.* (27 November), 5. The poor of the Federal District (DF) suffer not only from negligence but also from legal discrimination. The *delegaciones* of the DF do not receive, unlike the municipalities of the State of Mexico forming the MZMC along with them, federal contributions, which includes among others, the FAIS (Fund of Contributions for Social Infrastructure), the most important program against poverty in the country. It is worth noting that all municipalities in the country benefit from this scheme. Federal contributions are determined by the Law of Fiscal Coordination (LCF), and are known as 'Tagged resources', whereas Federal Participations refer to transferred resources which do not have a specific expenditure destination, and so can be used for any government function.
16. For Boltvinik and Estevez, ibid., poverty in the MZMC in 2000 is calculated using the database of the extended questionnaire of the 12th Census of Population and Housing, in relation to calculations derived from other sources: the National Survey on Households' Income and Expenditure and the National Survey on Urban Employment, as well as the tendencies of the evolution of poverty. Thus, in the MZMC poverty has a floor of 56.5% and a ceiling of 72.3%.
17. From an ecological perspective, preserved lands shelter natural ecosystems with more than 1800 species of wild flora and fauna; nearly 2% of the biological world richness and 11% of the national biological richness. Within this context the Federal District occupies twenty-third place for the number of endemic vertebrate species in Mesoamerica and twenty-fourth place for state endemic species. In addition, several natural processes take place on preserved land, through which different environmental strategic goods and services are provided. These are considered convenient for the Federal District's sustainability and the level of the quality of life of the inhabitants and refer mainly to climatic regulations through the capture of Carbon Dioxide (CO_2) since, on average, the zones that compose this type of land have a capacity of 90 ton/ha for the capture of carbon. From the preservation of hydrological cycles, this land provides 57% of the water consumed by the city, providing a flow of over 19m3/s. It also contributes to the decreasing of atmospheric pollution by retaining suspended particles and it plays a major role in preserving biological diversity along with the recreational possibilities and scenic value that forest ecosystems provide, as well as for ecoturistic activities (Gobierno del Distrito Federal, 2008).
18. INEGI. (2000), Estados Unidos Mexicanos, XII Censo General de Población y Vivienda, www.inegi.org.mx/sistemas/mexicocifras/ (accessed 15 February 2012).
19. Centro de Información Ambiental de la Ciudad de México (1998), (accessed 8 February 2012).
20. According to estimates by the Consejo Nacional de Evaluación de la Política de Desarrollo Social, above, n. 13, in 2005, 5.4% of the population in the DF lived under basic needs, 10.3% had stages of absence of capacities and 31.8% were in patrimonial poverty.
21. The elected governments of the DF, since 1997, have tried to give their own imprint to social policy. Universality of coverage is their principle which opposes focalism, since focalized policy is for small groups and universal policies are for all. Universal coverage policies protect the extreme poor, the poor and those at risk of falling into poverty. A focalized policy, on the other end, only tries to mend the fiercest costs of economic policy among the extreme poor. The second fundamental characteristic of the social policy of the Government of the Federal District (GDF) is the recognition of permanent rights. It is not a question of temporary policies that can be implemented and removed at will by the person in office, but rather of rights stated in laws which offer recourses to citizens. They are not, then, altruistic concessions of the governing party but social obligations of the state. Thus, for instance, pensions for the elderly, free school supplies or free medication are already enshrined in the law of the DF and have a spending line in the budget. See Secretaría de Desarrollo Social (GDF) (2007), *Informe de trabajo 2007*, (accessed 8 February 2012)
22. Engineer Cuahutémoc Cárdenas became Mexico City's first chief of government in 1997, after the Federal Electoral Reform of 1996 which instituted the direct election of a Chief of Government of the DF. Since 2000 the Heads for the offices of the different *delegaciones* are also directly elected.

23. Cuahutémoc Cárdenas left the city government to be nominated once again by PRD as its candidate for the presidency of the Republic in the 2000 election. Previously authorized to do so by the Legislative Assembly, he appointed Rosario Robles in his stead, who was then Government Secretary. During her brief administration there were virtually no changes of the government's social policies.
24. López Obrador stepped aside from city government to be nominated by the PRD as its candidate for the presidency of the Republic in the 2006 election. He appointed Alejandro Encinas, after being authorized to do so by the Legislative Assembly, to finish his term in office.
25. Currently, the 16 delegaciones receive around 26% of the total budget of the government of DF, a percentage that has not varied significantly despite the process of political democratization of the city government. This means that although the delegaciones are the territories where a large part of the population's civic life actually takes place, their resources are extremely limited. At this level, governments try to prioritize the introduction and preservation of basic urban infrastructure (water supply, drainage, road pavement). See Secretaría de Desarrollo Social (GDF) (2007), Informe de trabajo 2007, http://www.sds.df.gob.mx/ (accessed 8 February 2012).
26. Local communities have no control over the management of natural resources. The two important cases are the delegación Iztapalapa with a water scarcity problem and the delegación Xochimilco with an invasion of dangerous species in its lake. See Centro de Información Ambiental de la Ciudad de México (1998), http://www.sma.df.gob.mx/ceina/ (accessed 8 February 2012).
27. The assistencialist policy of Andrés Manuel López Obrador can be synthesized in a phrase incorporated in his governmental discourses: 'For the well being of all, the poor first.'
28. By the month of September 2007, the total number of direct beneficiaries who received the equivalent of half the then valid minimum wage in the DF was 412 350. The amount received has increased each year, starting at 600 pesos monthly in 2001 to 758.55 pesos in 2007. See above, n. 21.
29. The program is coordinated by the Social Development Secretariat, along with the Secretariats of Works and Services and Urban Development and Housing. Its main objective is to develop and integrate a sustained and participative process for the improvement of public spaces in the different neighborhoods, towns and districts within the Federal District, particularly those that present the highest rates of social conflict, urban degradation or are classified as centers of medium, high and very high marginalization. In the initial phase, social, civic, and communitarian organizations were summoned to participate along with groups of organized neighbors and academic institutions. The projects selected will be carried out by the neighbors themselves, under the supervision of the organization and the Social Development Secretariat.
30. Procuraduría Ambiental y de Ordenamiento Territorial, PAOT, synchronism in Spanish.
31. The Government of the City has formulated a mechanism to make the call 'Green Consultation', through which citizens were asked their views on issues related to transport, water and environment. Here are some of the questions: Should city taxis using petrol be replaced by other vehicles using cleaner engines?; Should the City's school transportation be mandatory for private schools?; In order to reduce traffic and pollution should each particular car stop running one Saturday a month?; Do you agree to increase green areas?; Do you agree to constructing 500 wells, water absorption, four treatment plants and two gaps?; Do you want the invasion of land of environmental value and the destruction of forests to be treated as a felony?

REFERENCES

Alfie, M. (2008), 'Gobernanza: Respuesta a las transformaciones del Estado-Nación o concepto clave para la reconstrucción de la política', in *Tensiones políticas de la Modernidad*, Mexico: UAM-A, Porrúa.

Bodemer, K., et al. (1999), 'Las políticas sociales urbanas en el inicio del nuevo siglo', *Red URBAL Políticas Sociales Urbanas,* n. 5, 36.
Bunker, S.G. (1985), *Underdeveloping the Amazon: Extraction, Unequal Exchange, and the Failure of the Modern State*, Chicago: University of Illinois Press.
Chambers, R. (1997), *Whose Reality Counts?* London: Mediate Technology Publications.
Connolly, P. (2006), 'Fixing Environmental Agendas in Mexico', in G.M. Peter and J. Marcotullio (eds), *Scaling Urban Environmental Challenges. From Local to Global and Back*, London: Earthscan.
Davidson, J. and N. Mayer (1992), *No time to waste: Poverty and the global environment*, London: Oxfam.
Forsyth, T., et al. (1998), *Poverty and Environment: Priorities for Research and Policy - an Overview Study*, Falmer, Sussex, UK: Institute of Development Studies.
Garza, G. (2000), *La Ciudad de México en el Fin del Segundo Milenio*, Mexico: COLMEX.
Gobierno del Distrito Federal (2000), *Estrategia para el Desarrollo Territorial del Suelo de Conservación del D.F.*, GDF.
Gobierno del Distrito Federal y Agencia de Cooperación Internacional del Japón (JICA) (1999), *Estudio sobre el manejo de residuos sólidos para la Ciudad de México*, GDF.
Kurtz, H.E. (2003), 'Scale frames and counter-scale frames: constructing the problem of environmental injustice', *Political Geography* 22, 77.
Leach, M. and R. Mearns. (1996), *The lie of the land: Challenging received wisdom on the African Environment*, Oxford: James Currey.
Marcotullio, P.J. and G. McGranahan (2007), *Scaling Urban Environmental Challenges. From Local to Global and Back*, London: Earthscan.
Martínez-Allier, J. (1990), 'Ecology and the poor: A neglected dimension of Latin American History', *Journal of Latin American Studies* 23, 621.
Milagros, C. (2000), 'Justicia Ambiental, Luchas Comunitarias y Política Pública', *Revista Administración Pública*, 31 (32), 326.
Negrete, M.E. (1993), 'Migración', in G. Garza (ed.), *La Ciudad de México en el Fin del Milenio*, Mexico: GDF, COLMEX.
Sánchez Mejorada, C. (2008), *De Actores y Programas Sociales en la Ciudad de México*, Mexico: Secretaría de Desarrollo Social.
Secretaría del Medio Ambiente (SMA), I. N. d. E., Geografía e Informática (INEGI) (2000), *Estadísticas del Medio Ambiente del Distrito Federal y la Zona Metropolitana*, SMA.
Shabecoff, P. (2000), *Earth Rising, American Environmentalism in the 21st Century*, Washington: Island Press.
Universidad Nacional Autónoma de México (2003), *Programa Universitario de Estudios sobre la Ciudad de México. Actualización del Programa de Ordenamiento del Valle de México,* Coordinación de Humanidades, Mexico: UNAM.
Vega Cantor, R. (2006), 'El interminable saqueo de la naturaleza y de los parias del sur del mundo', *Revista Herramienta* 31, 156.
World Commission on Environment and Development (1987), *Our Common Future*, Oxford: Oxford University Press.
Zicardi, A. (2003), *Planeación Participativa en el Espacio Local: Cinco Programas Parciales de Desarrollo Urbano en el Distrito Federal*, Mexico: UNAM.

PART V

The role of environmental courts in the fight against poverty and environmental degradation

11. The 'greening' of justice: will it help the poor?

George W. (Rock) Pring and Catherine G. (Kitty) Pring

> Improving, facilitating and expanding individual and collective access to law and justice supports economic and social development. Legal reforms give the poor the opportunity to assert their individual and property rights; improved access to justice empowers the poor to enforce those rights. Increasing accessibility to courts lessens and overcomes the economic, psychological, informational and physical barriers faced by women, indigenous populations, and other individuals ... New legislation, subsidized legal services, alternative dispute resolution, citizen education programs, court fee waivers and information technology are other means to improve access. (The World Bank, 2011)[1]

'Greening' – the integration of environmental, social and cultural values into financial enterprises, industry, communities, markets and other institutions – is a central goal of sustainable development (Werksmann, 1996; World Bank, 2000; Nanda and Pring, 2003, pp. 22–27). Now, in numerous countries around the world, another important institution is greening – the judiciary.

Specialized environmental courts and tribunals (ECTs) are springing up in dozens of countries. These are judicial and administrative bodies specifically authorized to adjudicate and decide disputes primarily concerning the environment, natural resources, land use and/or related issues. The University of Denver Environmental Court and Tribunals (ECT) Study, as of the start of 2012, has identified over 465 ECTs in 46 different nations and over 50 per cent of these have been created in just the last five years. This first-ever global multidisciplinary comparative study of ECTs examines how they can improve access to justice for those involved in environmental disputes, as prescribed by the Rio Declaration,[2] Aarhus Convention,[3] and other international legal instruments (Pring and Noé, 2002, pp. 44–50).

The ECT Study published its findings in *Greening Justice: Creating and Improving Environmental Courts and Tribunals* (Pring and Pring, 2009, hereafter *Greening Justice*; see also Pring and Pring, 2010; Pring and Pring, 2011). The book is based on interviews with over 200 ECT experts – justices, judges, prosecutors, government officials, private-sector attorneys, non-governmental organizations (NGOs) and academics. It identifies the 12 'building blocks' which control the success of ECTs and the 'best practices' for ECTs in providing access to justice (*Greening Justice*, 2009, pp. 19–87).

The UN Millennium Development Goals (MDG) have made eradicating poverty the world's top development priority.[4] Given the MDG and this IUCN-AEL book's timely focus on poverty, one must ask the question: Can specialized ECTs really help the poor? The answer is a qualified 'Yes'. The study finds ECTs which incorporate *six particular building blocks* out of the 12 do enhance environmental justice for those living in poverty, better than the general courts have or can. This is a crucial finding, since the poor are typically the most exposed to and most impacted by environmental harm, yet least empowered to protect their own health, welfare and future sustainability or to seek justice (UNDP, 2005).[5] This chapter first provides an overview of the ECT phenomenon, then outlines the 12 ECT building blocks and concludes by analyzing the six which have the most relevance for providing access to justice for the poor.

11.1 OVERVIEW OF ECTS

Specialized 'environmental' adjudication bodies[6] first appeared in the early 1900s.[7] For example, Denmark created a Nature Protection Board in 1917 and Sweden created specialty Water Courts in 1918, but few followed. The 1970s 'environmental movement' generated new environment, natural resources and public health laws around the world, and some countries, states and local jurisdictions created specialized ECTs as part of this reform. The next wave of ECTs came in the 1990s and 2000s, prompted in large part by increasingly complex environmental laws and issues.

ECTs can now be found on every inhabited continent; in every major legal system; in large countries and small; and in developed, developing and even least developed nations (see the list in *Greening Justice*, 2009, pp. 106–109). Belgium, Chile, China, England and Wales, India, Kenya, Peru and South Africa have all authorized ECTs since *Greening Justice* was published in 2009. Other jurisdictions have been busy reforming and improving the ECTs they already have. Historically, Australian states and New Zealand have been the leaders in ECT creation, but in the last decade ECTs have spread in South and East Asia, Africa, Western and Eastern Europe, Latin America and North America.[8]

Governments create ECTS in response to internal and/or external pressures. The pressures can come from NGOs, academics, judges, government officials, or the media. Generally, a charismatic, credible advocate takes the lead in urging the creation of an ECT. The most frequent reasons found in the ECT

Study (*Greening Justice*, 2009, pp. 13–16) and mentioned in the literature[9] are:

1. *Efficiency*: Decrease time necessary for decisions.
2. *Economy*: Decrease costs for all concerned with more efficient handling of cases.
3. *Expertise*: Obtain higher quality decisions from judges more expert in complex environmental laws, scientific-technical questions and value-laden issues than general jurisdiction judges.
4. *Access to justice*: Improve access to justice for business, government and the public by having an identified forum to handle environmental complaints.
5. *Case processing*: Improve case processing and reduce backlog of undecided cases in the general court system.
6. *Commitment*: Demonstrate government's commitment to protection of the environment, sustainable development, compliance with international treaties and agreements, etc., by creating a visible court symbolic of that commitment.
7. *Flexible solutions*: Open up more flexible ways to solve environmental problems, including alternative dispute resolution (ADR), collaborative planning and decision-making, hybrid civil-criminal prosecution, creative sentencing and enforcement options, court appointed special commissions and facilitated settlement agreements.
8. *Public Participation*: Encourage greater public participation and support for the decision-making process through more open standing, use of community expert committees, etc.
9. *Public confidence*: Increase public confidence in the government's environmental and sustainable development efforts by having a transparent, effective, expert decisional body.
10. *Increase administrative accountability*: Make the government more conscientious and transparent in making decisions which affect the environment, because government's decisions are open to scrutiny and legal challenge.

Certainly, there are counterarguments against specialized courts, although the Study found this a minority view. Anti-ECT arguments include the existence of other fields with legal and factual complexity, resistance to fragmenting the judicial system, reluctance to set environmental law apart from other relevant issues, preference for incremental reforms in the general judicial system, doubts about sufficient caseload, concerns about added costs, etc. (*Greening Justice,* 2009, pp. 17–18).

Interest in specialized ECTs has grown dramatically in the last 10 years and a number of jurisdictions are now considering establishing an ECT or reforming their existing general court structure to provide such specialization. The United Nations Environment Programme (UNEP) has been a leader in promoting ECTs. As an example, UNEP's Experts Group on Access to Environmental Justice in the Caribbean noted in 2007 that 'consensus [has] emerged on the need for the establishment of specialized and independent courts or specialized environmental divisions of the … judicial system'.[10]

What was found lacking, at the start of the ECT Study in 2007, was any in-depth comparative analysis of all the different existing ECT models or any practical guidance on how to create (or improve) an ECT. Some individual ECTs had been analyzed in depth, including the well-known examples in Australia's State of New South Wales[11] and in New Zealand (Birdsong, 2002), but their models were not necessarily appropriate for all jurisdictions. There also were studies assessing the desirability of establishing ECTs in particular jurisdictions, such as England (Woolf, 1992)[12] and Scotland.[13] However, these too focused primarily on English common law and European examples, not necessarily appropriate for all jurisdictions.

A multidisciplinary decision-making framework that could work for a broad range of legal cultures was needed, focused on national and subnational ECTs.[14] What emerged from the several years of library, media and online research and the worldwide interviews was a logical framework of design factors that result in an effective and efficient ECT.

11.2 THE ECT 'BUILDING BLOCKS'

Twelve design factors for ECTs – 'building block' decisions – were identified as a result of the Study. The options or alternatives within each factor should be evaluated by any jurisdiction considering creating or reforming a specialized ECT. Not all 12 factors have a direct impact on access to environmental justice for those living in poverty, but six certainly do. This section describes the 12 factors, with an asterisk by those directly and positively affecting the poor. The following section discusses how those six asterisked factors can make a profound difference in the environmental justice that an ECT provides those living in poverty.

11.2.1 Type of Forum[15]

ECTs can be structured in many ways, varying chiefly in independence, jurisdiction, competence and cost:

1. *Specialized Court*: This model is an actual 'court' in the judicial branch of

government, with judges expert in environmental law. It is created by legislation, is independent of the executive and legislative branches of government, has a separately identified budget and gives judges security of tenure. Typically, these judges do not hear other types of cases (examples include New South Wales, Australia; New Zealand; State of Vermont, USA).

2. *Specialized Green Chamber*: A general judicial court can designate within itself a chamber, panel, or bench consisting of a judge or judges assigned to hear environmental cases. This 'green bench' can be formally designated or an ad hoc assignment. It does not require special legislation to be created or a separate budget (Netherlands, Finland, Thailand).
3. *Tribunal*: This catch-all term covers options that are not judicial branch courts yet are specialized bodies in the executive or administrative branch of government empowered to make binding decisions in environmental cases. Tribunals are usually created by authorizing legislation, have approved annual budgets and may or may not have enforcement powers. Their membership can include a mix of judges, lawyers and laypersons, even in some cases all laypersons (Ireland). Tribunals' independence varies but there are basically three models, ranging from most to least independent as follows:
   - Independent Tribunal – answerable directly to the head of government, not housed inside another executive branch agency and definitely operating outside of the environment agencies whose decisions, permits, plans and actions they are reviewing (Ontario, Canada; Tasmania, Australia; New York City, USA);
   - Quasi-independent Tribunal – housed in an executive branch agency, but a different one from the agencies it is reviewing (such as an Attorney General's Office, or the Office of Administrative Law Judges serving the US Environmental Protection Agency (USEPA));
   - 'Captive' Tribunal – housed within the environmental regulating agency whose decisions they review (Austria, the USEPA's Environmental Appeals Board, Kenya National Environmental Tribunal).
4. *Other Dispute Resolution Bodies*: In addition to the court-tribunal adjudicative models, there are other types of government entities that function as environmental dispute resolution bodies. Examples include:
   - Environmental Prosecutors – Environmentally trained prosecutors and technical staff can significantly improve efficiency, competence, coverage and credibility of the enforcement process. Some countries provide environmental prosecutors with civil power in addition to traditional criminal power, particularly useful in juris-

dictions where NGOs and other potential citizen/community groups are weak or unlikely to bring ECT cases (Brazil).

- Environmental Ombudsman – An ombudsman is an office or individual empowered by law to investigate environmental complaints, intercede with the government or private sector on behalf of complainants and advocate for their rights. Some are even given standing and funding to bring lawsuits in court (Austria, Hungary) while, at the other extreme, some are given little to no power to make a difference (Kenya).
- Environmental Commissions – Special commissions or committees can be appointed by a court to investigate environmental problems and make recommendations to the court. Some are purely advisory (Philippines), while others are given virtually judge-like power (India).
- Environmental Mediation Bodies – Some countries appoint environmental tribunals and give them limited or no decision-making or enforcement power, relying on them instead to use forms of ADR to seek solutions to environmental problems (Japan, South Korea).

11.2.2 Legal Jurisdiction[16]

A crucial factor is what laws are placed under the ECT's jurisdiction or control. The majority of ECTs deal primarily with environmental laws and issues such as pollution permits, environmental quality and natural resources development. Some expand beyond these to include endangered species, parks and recreation, health and safety, etc. Some provide an even fuller range of issues, adding land use, sanitation, building codes, noise, transportation, fire regulations and so on. (New York City). Some deal only with land use laws and not environmental laws (Ireland). Still others may deal with only one issue, such as environmental impact assessments (Kenya National Environmental Tribunal). Naturally, the more comprehensive the ECT's jurisdiction, the better 'problem solver' it can be.

11.2.3 Court Level and Appeals[17]

ECTs can exist at any step in the adjudication ladder – the internal agency level, trial court, intermediate appeals court and/or the supreme court level.

1. *Internal Agency ECT*: An ECT can be placed inside the environmental or other regulatory agency. There it can serve either as (a) the body that makes the agency's initial decision (to issue a permit, enforce a violation, approve a plan and so on) or, more often, (b) the body to which such a

bureaucratic decision can be appealed inside the agency (USEPA, for example, has both tiers). This 'first instance' ruling usually can be appealed to a judicial branch trial or appeals level court for a 'second instance' review.

2. *Trial Court ECT*: Most common is an ECT at the trial level. These can be either of two kinds: (a) second instance review, where the ECT hears appeals of agency decisions and rulings, with appeals of this going to an intermediate appeals court for a final ruling (third instance review), but typically not on to the supreme court; or (b) first instance fact-finding, where the ECT hears new case filings that are not appeals of agency decisions, such as one neighbor suing another for pollution, property damage, noise, etc., with appeals also going to an intermediate appeals court (second-instance review), then possibly the supreme court (third instance).
3. *Appeal Court Level ECT*: In a few instances, an agency decision can be appealed directly to the intermediate appeals court, bypassing the trial court level. This usually occurs only when the agency is viewed as having a very trustworthy, competent and objective internal adjudication process that is as good as a trial court could provide (USEPA).

11.2.4 *Geographic Coverage[18]

If the ECT jurisdiction is large or travel is difficult, its geographic coverage needs careful evaluation. Distance can easily disenfranchise the poor. ECTs have responded to this challenge of distance by creating online filing procedures (New South Wales), traveling courts (Brazil; Queensland, Australia; the Philippines), on-site hearings (Vermont), testimony by teleconferencing and video conferencing (New Zealand).

11.2.5 Case Volume[19]

Legal jurisdiction (11.2.2 above) and court level (11.2.3 above) primarily control the caseload of the ECT. We found volume as low as six or seven cases per year (Trinidad & Tobago) – making it difficult to justify a specialist court – to over 700 000 per year (New York City), requiring hundreds of administrative law judges (ALJs).

11.2.6 *Standing[20]

Standing (*locus standi*, the legal rules controlling who can file or participate in a case) is a critical factor. Standing rules vary widely in ECTs and can be a very significant barrier to anyone's access to justice, but particularly for the poor. Standing is designed to limit court relief to those with a 'personal stake' in a controversy 'capable of judicial resolution'.[21] That is, it is a policy decision that access to the courts should be limited to those who have a genuine interest, prejudiced by the opposing side, which a court order can redress.

Standing can make the courthouse doors range from very open to extremely narrow. At the least, ECTs should have powers to dismiss groundless or frivolous lawsuits. However, care must be taken not to exclude important constituencies with a real stake (such as the poor, indigenous peoples, communities, NGOs and so on) or important societal values (such as endangered species, protection of old growth timber, climate change, etc.). Interestingly, ECTs with the most open standing (Canada, India, New South Wales, the Philippines, Queensland) have had very few problems with frivolous lawsuits because judges have power to dismiss cases and because litigation is expensive. These jurisdictions have found that suppressing the filing of legitimate grievances can be counter-productive, leading to societal distrust and unrest and that open access to justice is a good safety valve.

11.2.7 *Costs[22]

The costs of litigation are perhaps the biggest barrier to environmental justice. Costs add up quickly for court fees, lawyers' fees, expert witness expenses, security of costs for injunctions, risk of countersuits, and the loss of time, employment, income and other out-of-pocket expenses. An even bigger economic chilling factor is the so-called 'English Rule' that the unsuccessful party must pay all of the litigation costs of the winner ('costs follow the event'), regardless of how meritorious the action was. Australian citizen groups, communities and environmental NGOs are reluctant to bring litigation in the general courts because they apply the English Rule. The Environmental Defense Organization (EDO) in Sydney reports that a community non-profit organization lost a legitimate law-reform case and had to declare bankruptcy to avoid hundreds of thousands of dollars of debt. The 'American Rule' is the reverse: US judges have no power to engage in such cost-shifting without special legislation (for example penalizing 'groundless-frivolous' litigation). To counteract this chill of bankrupting costs, several Australian ECTs by rule make it clear that they do not follow the English Rule, realizing its negative impact on access to justice.

11.2.8 *Expert Evidence[23]

Environmental principles and problems are becoming increasingly complex, requiring expert scientific and technical expertise in addition to legal understanding. ECTs have been particularly innovative in assuring that they have the needed scientific-technical expertise available. Some ECTs hire and rely on their own independent experts using budgeted judicial funds (Ontario, Canada), while others rely solely on the expert witnesses presented by the parties (the so-called 'battle of the experts') (USEPA, Vermont); or on experts working for the government agency (New York City); or solely on the record of the preceding decision maker or court (Tasmania, Australia; Finland; most appellate level courts).

There are ECTs that appoint scientists and other technically trained specialists as actual judges or decision makers, with equal weight given to their opinions as to the legal judges on the panel (Sweden has a lawyer and a chemical engineer as judges on one panel). Others maintain lists of volunteer experts in various disciplines in academia, think tanks, consulting firms and so on, on whom the ECT can call (Denmark, Belgium) and still others appoint special commissions of experts to investigate and report their recommendations back to court (India).

To avoid the bias experts paid by the parties can have, several ECTs make them swear to take no instructions from the parties or their lawyers, to be objective and to serve as 'officers of the court' not advocates for a party – or be found in contempt of court (New South Wales). That same ECT also requires parties' experts to focus only on issues of professional disagreement, possibly putting both sides' experts on the witness stand together and having them respond directly to each other's points of disagreement (New South Wales). A few employ 'trial de novo,' starting over with testimony repeated from the same or different experts (Vermont). In ECTs where the decision makers can rely on objective testimony from their own experts or can effectively manage the parties' experts, access to justice is more affordable and reliable and decisions do not rest on which party can pay for the most persuasive or voluminous expertise.

11.2.9 *Alternative Dispute Resolution (ADR)[24]

ADR is the cutting-edge trend in ECTs, particularly those that define their role as 'problem solving', rather than only applying the legalistic 'rule of law' like an uncreative umpire. Mediation is most widely used – a trained, neutral facilitator to support communication and develop acceptable options between the parties (Tasmania, Vermont, New Zealand). Restorative justice is a new approach being seen in some criminal cases – cooperative sessions engaging not just the accused and the victims, but community representatives as well and focused on the harm to the victims and society rather than just penalizing the wrong-doer (New Zealand). Ombudsmen are utilized in some jurisdictions (Austria, Hungary, Kenya) – individuals or commissions separate from the ECT and the agency who negotiate the interests of the public and may have standing to represent concerned parties in court. Jurisdictions with a more traditional focus on 'rule of law' (Sweden, Finland, Denmark) generally do not use ADR, except for judge-supervised settlement conferences. Reversing that, the ECTs in a few countries (Japan, South Korea) appear to use mediation almost exclusively rather than adjudication.

11.2.10 Judicial Competence[25]

ECT judges range from those with no specialized environmental law training or interest to judges with extensive environmental law training, expertise and commitment. They can range from those assigned without choice to those who are carefully selected based on their competence and willingness to serve. Some jurisdictions have an insufficient number of cases to justify a specialized judge, so they use generalist judges for the ECT, sometimes holding it on a set day of the week. Generally, those interviewed felt that judges who were highly trained, experienced and motivated and who served full time were clearly preferable. A trained decision maker can provide informed decisions and faster decisions, resulting in shorter trials and reduced costs.

11.2.11 *Operational Tools[26]

Many ECTs have developed and employ new operating tools for increasing their effectiveness and efficiency, some quite alien to the traditional court system. These include:

1. *Case Management*: Rigorous case management is a hallmark of some ECTs. Case management is accomplished by a combination of (a) an assigned staff case manager who is the initial and on-going point of contact for the litigants during the adjudication process plus (b) a computer data management system (see 11.2.11(2) below). The case manager explains court processes, reviews the case record, may recommend or actually conduct mediation, may have the power to hold scheduling (directions) hearings, assures that parties are noticed in advance on all deadlines, monitors filings with the ECT and may draft decisions for the judge(s). The scope of authority given the case manager depends on the judge and the training and expertise of the case manager. Lawyers or non-lawyers can act as case managers, depending on scope of authority assigned.
2. *Information Technology (IT)*: Computer data management systems are being developed by ECTs that can track and time every step in the cases by filing date, type, assigned judge, specific dates and deadlines, time to a final decision, outcome (including sentencing details), court costs and compliance with court orders. In addition, IT is used to support video tele-

conferencing of hearings and off-site expert testimony (New South Wales), immediate transfer of verbal testimony on the record via a Word document to a judge in another locality (New Zealand), historical analysis of sentencing for violations to establish sentencing guidelines when they are not set by statute and to evaluate court performance over time. IT can allow filings to be made online and provide websites giving the public access to information about procedures, costs and decisions. Needless to say, only the best funded ECTs reach this level.

3. *Scheduling Hearings*: To prevent delay, some ECT judges regularly require scheduling (directions) hearings to establish and monitor firm court filing and hearing deadlines. Directions hearings keep cases moving and prevent inaction and routine requests for postponement.
4. *Traveling Courts*: To make the ECT more accessible for litigants and the public and to allow judges to see the physical sites in issue, many courts travel out of the court seat for investigations and hearings. One creative judge in the Amazonas State of Brazil has a van with a miniature courtroom in the back, complete with judge's bench, witness chair, counsel table and seating.
5. *Simplified Rules of Procedure*: Streamlining the process, using simplified rules of procedure, is also being done by a number of ECTs. Rules of evidence in particular are being analyzed to improve the quality of the fact record, focus only on the issues in dispute and to save court, litigant and expert witness time and expense.

11.2.12 Enforcement Tools[27]

Without adequate powers to enforce its decisions, an ECT cannot ensure compliance with its decisions. The majority of ECTs in the Study were civil, non-criminal courts and their enforcement tools included settlement conferences, mediation, monetary penalties, cease and desist orders, community service, new permit conditions, remand back to the agency for reconsideration and/or required remediation and closure. ECTs lacking cease and desist powers, that is preliminary or temporary injunction power at the outset of the case, often could not prevent the environmental harm or damage from happening during the pendency of the case.

ECTs with criminal powers can employ these non-criminal enforcement tools as well as prison sentences and fines (even for government officials who are found negligent (Costa Rica)). Criminal enforcement is most effective in cultures where there is a great social stigma attached to a person or corporation accused of crimes (Belgium, Brazil). The size of the fine permitted by law is also an important consideration; if the fine is not large enough to act as a strong deterrent, it is wholly ineffective.

11.3 ECT 'BUILDING BLOCKS' INCREASING LOW-INCOME ACCESS TO ENVIRONMENTAL JUSTICE

While all 12 ECT 'building block' factors described above have bearing on improving access to environmental justice for the poor, six in particular stand out as crucial. The six are (4) geographic coverage, (6) standing, (7) costs, (8) expert evidence, (9) alternative dispute resolution, and (11) operational tools.

11.3.1 Geographic Coverage

The distance between the ECT and a plaintiff's community, particularly a rural community, can be a nearly insurmountable barrier to access to justice for those who cannot afford to travel long distances or to pay the expenses of a stay in the ECT's city or to take time off from work, children and other responsibilities. The solution is simple: Take justice to the people.

One solution is to have multiple ECTs that are regionally distributed. Where this is not possible budgetarily or where this would still not provide proximity in large jurisdictions, ECTs have developed creative ways to bring the court to the people. The judge of the environmental court in the huge Brazilian state of Amazonas has a 'travelling courtroom' housed in a bus in which he commutes to remote areas of the Amazon. Planning and Environment Court judges in Queensland, Australia, faced with thousands of miles between the site of a conflict and the state capital, take to the air and fly to court hearings in remote sites. In Ireland, hearings are often held in local hotels and halls at the site in issue, providing access to those most affected by the decision. In the small US state of Vermont, the two environment court judges have 'divided' the state and use a variety of other courthouses and halls to hold hearings in addition to the main ECT outside the state capital. New York City's ECT has offices and hearing rooms in each of the city's five districts, and the Philippines has designated 117 environmental courts throughout the nation, again bringing the court to the people. Other techniques for making environmental justice more physically accessible include night courts, tele-conference or video-conferencing testimony and arguments, even written or email submissions.

11.3.2 Standing

Some ECTs' standing rules are much more restrictive than necessary to assure non-frivolous litigants and, as a result, are particularly exclusionary for low-income persons. For example, some ECTs give standing solely to those owning real property within a prescribed distance (possibly only a few hundred meters) of the activity complained of (Ireland). Some limit standing to those who can prove actual impacts on their own property, lives, or health. Other ECTs reject those who did not participate in the administrative proceedings leading up to the lawsuit, regardless of lack of notice or insufficient funding (a problem in administrative law in the US). Sweden's environmental law, for a time, disqualified NGOs from having legal standing to appeal government decisions affecting the environment unless they had over 2000 members, a requirement met by only two NGOs in the country. In 2009 the European Court of Justice (ECJ) ruled this violated EU law.[28] Still more outrageous, Bangladesh allows litigants access to its ECT only after they have applied for and received permission to sue from the national environmental agency (even when that agency's decisions are the subject of the lawsuit)! Excessively strict or illogical standing requirements have a disproportionately exclusionary effect on the poor, who lack funds to participate in the first rounds of agency decision-making, or to hire lawyers to challenge standing requirements in court, or to pay for experts to prove their injuries. Such a 'closed court house door' also excludes issues that may be of great importance and have a disproportionate impact on those living in poverty, such as slum conditions, water and air pollution, toxic dumping, public health and physical security.

Countries with a constitutional provision that provides a right to a healthy environment (such as Austria, Belgium, Brazil, Finland, India) have more open standing than countries that rely on environmental legislation, which can be interpreted restrictively by the courts (USA). India is at an extreme, allowing any person to complain of a violation of his/her constitutional right to a healthy environment and to do so without a lawyer, merely by sending an email or letter to India's highest court! Thousands take advantage of this ease of access, resulting in an overburdened Supreme Court attempting to hear factual cases as if it were a trial court, a standing approach that goes too far the other way.

Providing standing for environmental NGOs (ENGOs), whose lawyers are familiar with the courts, procedures and issues, increases access to justice for some poverty groups. However, the historical mission of ENGOs has generally not been the protection of the disadvantaged, but the protection of the environment. Only recently have some ENGOs taken on the mantle of 'environmental justice' and human rights, in addition to environmental protection. ENGOs all suffer from financial constraints and staffing limitations, requiring them to carefully choose cases based on the ability to establish an important precedent, to make a major impact on the environment and to be 'marketable' for fundraising, so that they can raise the money required for the very expensive costs of litigation that may go on for years. Environmental attorneys willing to serve the poor for free (such as law school clinics) contribute to environmental justice for the poor, but they are few and far between.

11.3.3 Costs

The costs of litigation are the biggest deterrent to seeking justice for everyone, especially for the poor. Court fees are just a small part of the expense of litigation, but recognizing that even these can be prohibitive for low-income litigants, some ECTs have substantially reduced filing fees and other court costs (even providing 'no-cost' filing) or created a fund to assist litigants below the poverty level with their court costs. A truly intimidating and unnecessary economic deterrent, however, is the so-called 'English Rule' or 'loser pays', discussed above, which requires the losing side to pay all of the expenses of the winning side in litigation. Australian citizen groups, communities and environmental NGOs are frankly reluctant to bring litigation in the general courts because they apply the English Rule. To counteract this chill of bankrupting costs, several Australian ECTs by rule make it clear that they do not follow the English Rule (except for groundless or abusive lawsuits), realizing its negative impact on access to justice. Establishing a legal principle that parties each bear their own costs of litigation, absent gross misconduct or groundless-frivolous actions, protects low-income litigants from the risk of huge legal awards in the event they do not prevail in court.

Jurisdictions with strong specialized environmental prosecutors, such as Brazil, also help hold costs down for low-income and NGO plaintiffs. Prosecutors can increase access to justice by aggressively pursuing actions that negatively impact communities or groups who are often too impoverished and unempowered to represent themselves. These legal challenges have no direct cost for the impacted individuals because the prosecutors are paid government employees. For example, in Brazil, the Parana State environmental prosecutor's office has pursued litigation against the government itself, challenging its plans to construct a dam that would wipe out the homes and livelihoods of hundreds of people living in and adjacent to the dam site. In Amazonas State, prosecutorial actions have been brought against the timber industry and wildlife poachers.

However, environmental prosecutors are not a panacea for protecting low-income communities, as Brazil also illustrates. With some of the strongest environmental protection legislation in the world, but a huge landmass and some of the worst environmental problems, the prosecutors are hampered by size of caseload, lack of sufficient investigative and monitoring personnel, lack of aggressive local enforcement once verdicts have been handed down and lack of both sufficient prosecutors and judges to handle all the violations. In addition, some prosecutors feel their existence discourages the development of NGOs that could bring environmental actions.

11.3.4 Expert Evidence

Scientific and technical expert studies, field work, evidence and testimony are necessary in many ECT cases, constituting another of the prodigious cost barriers to access to justice. The need to retain experts can make litigation wholly prohibitive for low-income individuals and groups, if not represented by a prosecutor or NGO with access to free or reduced-fee experts. ECTs are experimenting with many different approaches for overcoming the 'experts hurdle' for impoverished litigants. In the New South Wales ECT, experts are sworn in as 'friends of the court' and instructed by the judge to testify as if they were not paid by a particular side, on penalty of perjury. They also may be instructed to discuss their testimony together, identify those issues where they are in professional disagreement and then present to the court only evidence that is in professional contention (New South Wales). In the words of Michael Rackemann, Judge for the Planning and Environment Court of Queensland, 'the management of experts from [an early stage] assists in narrowing the scope of the trial reports and testimony and in improving the quality and helpfulness of the analysis. These approaches save court time and reduce costs for all parties'.[29]

Other ECTs hold down expert costs by having science and engineering experts serving as co-judges (Sweden), calling on experts from the environmental agency (NYC and many others), recruiting volunteer experts in the community (Belgium, Denmark), relying on scientific institutes (Japan), or by having a legislatively or judicially created fund to pay the expert fees of indigent litigants with legitimate claims. Ontario, Canada had such intervener funding for several years, but it was allowed to lapse when the political climate changed. Some appellate ECTs rely completely on the record of the agency below, which eliminates expert witness fees for litigants, but removes the possibility of challenging the agency experts or introducing new expert testimony. Referral to mediation, which occurs in many ECTs, can eliminate the need for expensive experts, but may result in uninformed agreements if experts are not present at the mediation.

The 'precautionary principle' (Nanda and Pring, 2003, pp. 38–39) can actually serve as a cost-saving device for low-income litigants. Scientific uncertainty is a major impediment in proving many environmental cases and the party with that burden of proof faces significant expense at best, or a losing case at worst. The precautionary principle can be invoked to shift the burden of proof from the complainant to the developer or other entity proposing a change in the status quo. Interestingly, in Queensland, the burden of proof is always on the developer, whether it is a developer's appeal against a permit refusal or an environmentalists' appeal against an approval. Thus, the developer must produce sufficient evidence to satisfy the court that its proposal should proceed, reducing the cost burden on the party challenging the proposal.

11.3.5 ADR

ADR techniques are a very positive development in ECT practice. ADR can enhance access to justice for all parties, particularly for the impoverished, by reducing costs, speeding the process, assuring a more 'level playing field' and developing a wider range of creative solutions than are available from a judge.

The ADR process most widely employed is mediation – use of a trained neutral to serve as a non-judgmental catalyst who assists the parties in developing and agreeing on a solution. This can enhance access to justice for the poor in several important ways. First, mediation may allow parties to participate without expensive attorneys or experts. The danger, of course, is that unrepresented parties may not know or understand the issues, their legal rights, or the consequences of an agreement and might settle for a solution that may not be sustainable or in their long term best interests. This can be ameliorated by allowing their advocates, NGO representatives, or attorneys to participate in the mediation to assure equity and protection of the legal rights of the parties. Second, trained mediators who are also attorneys with knowledge of environmental law or who are staff or members of the ECT can help 'level the playing field' and assure that agreements are both fair and legal. Third, mediation allows parties to generate creative options – solutions that may not be available to the judge. For instance, a mediated agreement for the development of a mine in an impoverished rural area could include typical court-ordered modifications to location, access, size, noise, remediation, etc., but – with mediation – could also include major investments by the mining company in a safe community water supply, schools, hospitals, employment and other infrastructure for the residents that would improve living conditions and support positive sustainable outcomes.

The cost of ADR is typically much less than litigation and can be subsidized in various ways to aid low-income litigants. The Netherlands ECT received a grant to pay the costs of private mediators; while the grant was in place over 50 per cent of parties chose to mediate and 50 per cent of those were successful in reaching an agreement without court intervention. However, when funding ran out and parties had the choice of paying for mediation or going straight to court, only 10 per cent chose mediation and a majority of those did not reach a satisfactory agreement. Evaluation indicated that parties were unwilling to pay for mediation plus litigation if mediation was unsuccessful, when they could go straight to court and obtain a judicial order. In Vermont, cases appropriate for mediation are referred to private mediators in the community, who may charge up to $1500 a day, with parties splitting the costs, which many find cost-effective in lieu of a trial. In Queensland, Australia, the ECT has hired a full-time attorney-mediator who mediates cases when the court directs based on initial judicial review of the allegations. In Australia's island state of Tasmania, where mediation has been so successful it is now mandatory, the ECT registrar is a highly trained and effective mediator; that ECT is now training members of the ECT as mediators. In yet another approach, professors at a leading Brazil university have created a nonprofit environmental mediation center which provides mediation services free to impoverished communities – even helping villagers caught illegally manufacturing sugarcane alcohol (cachaca) to avoid criminal prosecution and receive a government license.

Another ADR approach that can enhance access to environmental justice is the ombudsman – a government-appointed official or tribunal that provides a check on government and others by investigating and acting on complaints reported by individual citizens and groups – often enhancing or replacing an ECT. In Austria, each district has an environmental ombudsman who has the authority to investigate and respond to complaints, both against the government and private business interests. The Austrian ombudsmen have standing and budget to file in court representing the complainant(s), costing the parties nothing and providing a professional evaluation of the merits of the case and the options prior to litigation. In Kenya, a Public Complaints Committee theoretically acts as an environmental ombudsman, but has no litigation authority and is very underfunded and understaffed and so is less effective.

'Collaborative decision making' (CDM) is a newer ADR approach that brings government and civil society stakeholders together with a facilitator to participate collectively in open discussions in which they share information and power as they take joint responsibility for making decisions, resolving issues and reaching solutions. CDM is gaining favor with US government agencies as a way to involve impacted communities in evaluating a proposed development, negotiate alternatives before permits are granted and save costs.

'Restorative justice' (RJ) is another ADR process being experimented with in several criminal-jurisdiction ECs (New Zealand, New South Wales). It can also benefit those living in poverty. After a guilty verdict or plea, RJ brings together the perpetrator, victims and community members in facilitated sessions that focus on repairing the harms to the victims and society, rather than just punishing the wrong-doer.

The most common ADR approach – standard negotiation between parties without a formal neutral intermediary – is still relied on extensively by ECTs and can produce 'win-win' outcomes. For example, on one of Fiji's Yasawa Islands, a small resort developer successfully negotiated with the local fishing village to stop over-fishing the resort's lagoon and dive sites in return for training and employing village residents to work at the resort, bringing tourists to the village to participate in kava ceremonies and purchase handicrafts and providing a motorboat 'school bus' to take the village children to and from school on another island.

ADR has been opposed by some US environmental groups, over feelings that compromise is inappropriate in environmental conflicts and that many environmental issues are not amenable to mediation. Some still have these concerns, which have been partially ameliorated in jurisdictions where ECTs are known to carefully analyze the appropriateness of cases, issues and parties for ADR as opposed to trial.

11.3.6 Operational Tools

Courts which have adopted strong case management tools help increase access to justice, especially for poorer or unrepresented parties, by assuring that cases move in a timely way, that parties have access to court procedures and receive all notices, that experts are managed expeditiously, and that cases are monitored to ensure compliance with court directions. In some jurisdictions, a case manager also educates parties (particularly unrepresented parties) about how to file a case, what to expect from the judicial process, what will be required of them and what the costs will be. ECT case managers can evaluate cases for the appropriateness of mediation and can ensure that cases do not get 'lost' in the system. Introduction of sophisticated computer databases, in conjunction with case management techniques, has greatly increased both the efficiency and effectiveness of ECTs. Information technology, scheduling hearings and travelling courts, as described above, can greatly increase the effectiveness, efficiency and reach of ECTs, thereby helping hold down costs for parties.

ECTs that simplify their rules of procedure – covering such matters as filing, discovery (information exchange), hearing procedures and evidence rules – greatly improve access to justice, particularly for the less empowered. For example, some ECTs provide simple forms, allow filings online and permit testimony in writing. Some permit *pro se* representation (not requiring attorneys) and provide case management assistance to help litigants. Some have also introduced less formal, less intimidating court proceedings. Rules which streamline the presentation of expert testimony by requiring experts to focus testimony only on those issues in dispute simplify proceedings and reduce both time and cost for litigants.

11.4 CONCLUSION

The University of Denver ECT Study finds that creating and improving specialized ECTs can enhance access to environmental justice for the impoverished – the very people whose health, livelihoods, living conditions and futures may be most impacted by environmental change and who may be least able to protect themselves, their families and their communities. The ECTs that appear to have had the largest positive impact in this arena are those where the 12 building blocks have been structured with a sensitivity to the issues of poverty – in particular the six crucial factors of geographic coverage, standing, costs, expert evidence, ADR and operational tools – as described above.

NOTES

1. The World Bank (2011), 'Access to Justice for the Poor', http://go.worldbank.org/MHG1Y94BM0 (accessed 16 April 2012).
2. http://www.unep.org/Documents.Multilingual/Default.asp?documentid=78&articleid=1163 (accessed 16 April 2012).
3. http://live.unece.org/env/pp/treatytext.html (accessed 16 April 2012).
4. United Nations (UN) (2011), 'Millennium Development Goals: A Gateway to the UN System's Work on the MDGs', http://www.un.org/millenniumgoals (accessed 16 April 2012).
5. Leatherman, C. (2008), 'The Poverty Question: What Does Poverty Mean for Conservation?' *Nature Conservancy Magazine,* pp. 42–51.
6. We use 'court' to indicate a true judicial branch body and 'tribunal' to indicate collectively all other governmental organs (typically less formal administrative bodies) that are empowered to resolve environmental disputes.
7. Scottish Government (2005), 'Environmental Courts – Experience in Other Countries', http://www.scotland.gov.uk/Resource/Doc/921/0017251.doc (accessed 16 April 2012).
8. Interestingly, the US has resisted creating an environmental court at the national level (Whitney, 1973). Nevertheless ECTs proliferate in the US, including national environmental tribunals within executive branch agencies like the US Environmental Protection Agency and the Department of the Interior, one state environmental court (Vermont), and numerous local-level ECTs (such as New York City and Memphis, Tennessee).
9. See, for example, in the References at the end of this chapter, Birdsong; Shelton and Kiss; and Woolf; Scottish Government, above, n. 7; Preston, The Hon. B.J. (2007), 'The Land and Environment Court of New South Wales: Moving Towards a Multi-Door Courthouse', http://lawlink.nsw.gov.au/lawlink/lec/ll_lec.nsf/pages/LEC_speeches_and_papers#preston (accessed 16 April 2012); Stein, Paul L. (2000), 'Down Under Perspective of the Environmental Court Project', http://www.lawlink.nsw.gov.au/lawlink/supreme_court/ll_sc.nsf/pages/SCO_speech_stein_270600 (accessed 16 April 2012).
10. United Nations Environment Programme (UNEP) (2007), 'Experts Group on Access to Environmental Justice in the Caribbean SIDS [Small Island Developing States]: Conclusions' (Barbados, 10–11 December 2007) (copy with authors).
11. See Stein as well as Preston, above, n. 9.
12. See also Macrory, R. and M. Woods (2003), 'Modernising Environmental Justice: Regulation and the Role of the Environmental Tribunal', http://www.ucl.ac.uk/laws/environment/tribunals/ (accessed 16 April 2012).
13. Scottish Executive Environment and Rural Affairs Department Environment Group (2006), 'Strengthening and Streamlining: The Way Forward for the Enforcement of Environmental Law in Scotland', http://www.scotland.gov.uk/Publications/2006/11/22152827/0 (accessed 16 April 2012).
14. International or multinational ECTs are not a focus of this study, since they are presently not a particularly promising terrain. The International Court of Justice established a special chamber to deal with environmental matters in 1993, but it has not been used in the Court's

several important environmental cases. Sands, P. (2008), 'Litigating Environmental Disputes: Courts, Tribunals and the Progressive Development of International Environmental Law', paper at the Organization for Economic Co-operation and Development (OECD) Global Forum on International Investment VII (27–28 March 2008), www.oecd.org/dataoecd/45/7/40311090.pdf (accessed 16 April 2012), p. 4. The Permanent Court of Arbitration, an intergovernmental organization (IGO) of over 100 member states, has developed a 'unified forum' for arbitrating environmental and natural resources disputes, but has handled few (www.pca-cpa.org) (accessed 16 April 2012). There is also the NGO International Court of Environmental Arbitration and Conciliation, which has done little business (http://www.unep.org/dec/onlinemanual/Compliance/NegotiatingMEAs/DisputeSettlementProvisions/Resource/tabid/660/Default.aspx) (accessed 16 April 2012). Canada, Mexico, and the USA have created a Commission for Environmental Cooperation (CEC) under the North American Agreement on Environmental Cooperation (the 'Environmental Side-Agreement' of the North American Free Trade Agreement (NAFTA)), and that international body is authorized to hear citizen submissions on NAFTA governments' failures to enforce environmental laws, but it has no enforcement powers (www.cec.org) (accessed 16 April 2012). There are calls for the creation of an International Environmental Court, for example by the NGO International Court of the Environment Foundation (www.icef-court.org) (accessed 16 April 2012).

15. For a more in-depth discussion, see *Greening Justice*, 2009, pp. 21–26.
16. Ibid., pp. 26–28.
17. Ibid., pp. 28–30.
18. Ibid., pp. 30–31.
19. Ibid., pp. 31–33.
20. Ibid., pp. 33–40.
21. *Sierra Club v. Morton*, (1972) 405 U.S. 727,732.
22. Above, n. 15, pp. 40–54.
23. Ibid., pp. 55–61.
24. Ibid., pp. 61–72.
25. Ibid., pp.72–75.
26. Ibid., pp. 76–79.
27. Ibid., pp. 79–87.
28. Case C-263/08, *Djurgården-Lilla Värtans Miljöskyddsförening v. Stockholms kommun genom dess marknämnd*, 2009 E.C.R. I-09967 (Oct. 15, 2009), http://eur-lex.europa.eu/LexUriServ/LexUriServ.do?uri=CELEX:62008J0263:EN:HTML (accessed 16 April 2012). The ECJ ruled (at para 52) that this high requirement for standing violated European Council Directive 85/337/EEC on public participation in environmental decision-making procedures. After the ECJ judgment, the Swedish Supreme Court set aside that country's rule on NGO standing and remanded the case back to the Swedish Environmental Court of Appeal. Since 1 August 2010, the Swedish Environmental Code now allows any organization with 100 members or more to appeal decisions on permits and related issues.
29. Email from Michael Rackemann, Judge, Planning and Environment Court of Queensland, Australia, to authors (28 March 2009) (on file with authors).

REFERENCES

(For a comprehensive list of references see *Greening Justice*, pp. 95–105.)

Birdsong, B. (2002), 'Adjudicating Sustainability: New Zealand's Environment Court', *Ecology Law Quarterly* 29: 1–69.

Nanda, V.P. and G. Pring (2003), *International Environmental Law & Policy for the 21st Century*, Ardsley, NY: Transnational Publishers Inc.

Pring, G. and C. Pring (2009), *Greening Justice: Creating and Improving Environmental Courts and Tribunals*, World Resources Institute/The Access Initiative. The book is downloadable (1.5 MB) without charge at www.accessinitiative.org/resource/greening-justice or www.law.du.edu/ect-study.
Pring, G. and C. Pring (2010), 'Specialized Environmental Courts and Tribunals at the Confluence of Human Rights and the Environment', *Oregon Review of International Law*, 11: 301–329; copy at www.law.du.edu/ect-study.
Pring, G. and C. Pring (2011), 'Increase in Environmental Courts and Tribunals Prompts New Global Institute', *Journal of Court Innovation*, 3:11–21; copy at www.law.du.edu/ect-study.
Pring, G. and S.Y. Noé (2002), 'The Emerging International Law of Public Participation Affecting Global Mining, Energy, and Resources Development', in D. Zillman, A. Lucas, and G. Pring (eds), *Human Rights in Natural Resources Development: Public Participation in the Sustainable Development of Mining and Energy Resources*, Oxford: Oxford University Press, pp. 11–76.
Shelton, D. and A. Kiss (2005), *Judicial Handbook on Environmental Law*, UNEP.
United Nations Development Programme (UNDP), et al. (2005), *World Resources 2005: The Wealth of the Poor – Managing Resources to Fight Poverty*, Washington: World Resources Institute.
Werksmann, J. (ed.) (1996), *Greening International Institutions*, London: Earthscan.
Whitney, S.C. (1973), 'The Case for Creating a Special Environmental Court System', *William and Mary Law Review*, 14: 473.
Woolf, H. (1992), 'Are the Judiciary Environmentally Myopic?' *Oxford University Journal of Environmental Law*, 4:1.
The World Bank (2000), *Greening Industry: New Roles for Communities, Markets and Governments*, Oxford: Oxford University Press.

12. The resolution of urban housing development disputes as a mechanism for poverty alleviation: a case study of Kenya's National Environment Tribunal

Albert Mumma

12.1 INTRODUCTION

Historically, in the urban areas of Kenya, demand for housing has always outstripped supply, creating an acute shortage of habitable dwellings, overcrowding and extensive slums and informal settlements. For instance, during the 1970s, an average of 25 000 housing units were constructed annually, compared to the 50 000 that were required. In the 1990s, the average number annually was 112 000 compared to a demand of 560 000. Currently, the average annual urban housing demand is estimated at 150 000 units but only an estimated 30 000 to 50 000 is expected to be constructed, representing an estimated 20 per cent of the total number of new urban households required (Ministry of Lands and Housing, 2004, pp. 2–3).

Consequently, more than half of the poor urban dwellers in Kenya live in slums and other unplanned settlements, with limited access to basic sanitation, potable water, garbage collection and security of tenure. Some of these slums, such as the Kibera slums in Nairobi, which has a population of over half a million residents, are among the largest urban slums in the world. This situation is likely to be aggravated by the population trends which show that Kenya is expected to be a predominantly urban country by 2030; by then more than half the population will be residing in urban areas (Ministry of Lands and Housing, 2004, pp. 2–3).

This housing deficit arises from a combination of factors including the low level of investment in the sector, rapid urbanization arising from rural-urban migration, inaccessibility to land and housing finance, stringent planning regulations, restrictive building standards, the high cost of infrastructure and a high level of urban poverty. An appropriate and well enforced Government policy on urban housing is required to address these issues.

The strategy of successive Governments in Kenya has been to put in place a policy and a legal framework that would facilitate an increase in the stock of affordable housing available to the poor and middle income urban dwellers in line with the Millennium Development Goals,[1] amongst other international instruments. The country's 2020 vision for housing and urbanization is 'an adequately and decently housed nation in a sustainable environment', while the medium term goal for 2012 is to increase the annual production of housing units from the current 35 000 annually to over 200 000 (Ministry of Planning and National Development, 2007, para. 5.5)

The country's current National Housing Policy is intended to arrest the deteriorating housing condition and bridge the shortfall in housing stock. The aim is to minimize the number of people living in shelters that are below habitable living standards and curtail the mushrooming of slums and informal settlements, especially in the major towns. The objective of this policy is to facilitate an annual output of 150 000 housing units annually in urban areas capable of housing 750 000 households, if a unit houses several households. (Ministry of Lands and Housing, 2004, para. 3.2). The achievement of this ambitious target is constrained by, *inter alia*, the lack of a comprehensive land use planning and management policy, which has led to the proliferation of substandard settlements, and inadequate infrastructure, services and open spaces. The housing policy paper recognizes that:

> The opening up of new land for housing development or the upgrading of existing informal settlements require installation and maintenance of infrastructure such as water, sewerage, roads, electricity, social services and security. Infrastructural facilities therefore form a major and vital component of shelter provision (Ministry of Lands and Housing, 2004, para. 3.3.2).

Inadequate infrastructure has not only been a key limiting factor in the private sector's efforts to develop additional housing units but also the main bone of contention in the disputes that have arisen between developers and residents regarding urban housing developments. In an attempt to overcome 'restrictive and outdated' physical planning laws and policies and infrastructural constraints, developers have resorted increasingly to unconventional architectural plans and designs, which, while appearing to comply with the letter of the law, have sought to maximize the number of housing units to be built on a particular plot of land.

The efforts and maneuvers by the developers to maximize the use of limited physical space have not escaped the watchful eyes of resident associations, particularly within affluent neighbourhoods where there is a strong desire to maintain the 'single dwelling' character of the area. These residents typically have objected to these developments on the ground that an increase in the number of residents of the area consequent upon the proposed housing developments will overwhelm the already strained physical infrastructure and amenities such as sewerage systems, road networks, water supplies and security. In many instances these objections have led to appeals lodged with the National Environment Tribunal for determination.[2]

Against this background, this chapter discusses the resolution of urban housing development disputes as a mechanism for the alleviation of poverty in urban areas. The focus of the chapter is on the National Environmental Tribunal's decisions on disputes arising from proposed urban housing projects in and around the city of Nairobi in Kenya. The chapter argues that an analysis of these decisions shows that the National Environment Tribunal (NET) has been able to provide access to environmental dispute resolution which is expeditious and cost effective and, through this, it is enabling the country to enhance the stock of urban housing available for urban dwellers in and around the city of Nairobi.

The majority of the disputes have concerned urban housing units targeting the middle income category. However, the ruling of the Tribunal in one instance in which a housing project was designed specifically for the poor slum dwellers, the *Jamii Bora Decision*,[3] continues to cause ramifications within the country's environmental and wildlife conservation movement. It has made a meaningful contribution to the jurisprudence on the interface between environmental protection and the alleviation of poverty in urban areas.

The chapter comprises three parts. Section 12.2 discusses NET's jurisdiction over housing disputes and highlights several shortcomings in the prevailing legal and regulatory frameworks governing the housing sector in Kenya which undermine the effective resolution of environmental disputes arising from housing projects. Section 12.3 looks at the nature of housing development disputes which have come before the NET and argues that NET's jurisprudence has been able to strike a balance between the provision of housing and the conservation of the environment. The last section focuses on procedural issues, in particular *locus standi*, time and costs. These factors can undermine access to justice. To address them, various states have established quasi-judicial tribunals as a mechanism to enhance access to justice, particularly for the poor. The chapter argues that in handling these issues, NET has enhanced the avenues for cost effective and expeditious resolution of housing development disputes in Kenya.

12.2 THE JURISDICTION OVER HOUSING DEVELOPMENT DISPUTES

Two regulatory frameworks govern disputes over housing projects in Kenya: the Environmental Management and Coordination Act, 1999 (EMCA),[4] which sets up the NET and the Physical Planning Act, of 1996,[5] which creates an *ad hoc* dispute resolution body known as the Physical Planning Liaison Committee.

The NET is established under s. 129 of EMCA. It is established as a quasi-judicial tribunal with the mandate of determining appeals from the decisions of the National Environment Management Authority (NEMA). NEMA is established by the same Act as a licensing and regulatory agency. Its principal regulatory instrument is the environmental impact assessment (EIA) licence. Under s. 58 of the Act, every person proposing to undertake a development activity (described as a 'project proponent') is required to seek an EIA licence from NEMA. Failure to seek the EIA licence or to comply with the licence conditions is an offence liable to be punished under the Act. NET's mandate is to determine appeals from the decisions and enforcement actions of the NEMA.

NET comprises five members, three of whom (including the Chairman) are lawyers while the other two are environmental scientists. Following its establishment in 2003 NET formulated its rules of procedure, the National Environment Tribunal Procedure Rules as required by the Act, and in 2005, it commenced hearings. By the end of 2010, 50 appeals had been filed. Of the appeals filed, three-quarters concerned urban housing projects, most of them in Nairobi. In a few cases, the appeals have not been disposed of because the respondents opted to challenge NET's jurisdiction to determine the appeal through judicial review proceedings and obtained stay orders pending the determination of the judicial review proceedings.

The Physical Planning Act requires a developer to seek planning permission from the relevant physical planning authority before undertaking a development, and where the planning permission is granted, the developer is required to comply with its conditions. Persons who are aggrieved by the decisions of the planning authorities regarding planning permissions may appeal to the Physical Planning Liaison Committee, for which provision is made by the Physical Planning Act.

Planning permission is considered in the context of the applicable land use plan for the area, and, *inter alia,* deals with:

- the location of the development (that is, zoning);
- the land use conditions governing the land in question;
- the allowable proportions of the housing units in that locality and on that land; and
- the availability and adequacy of amenities such as infrastructure, potable water supply and sewage disposal.

Under the Physical Planning Act, an environmental impact assessment of the proposed development is not a mandatory requirement. Section 36 of the Act leaves it to the discretion of the physical planning authority to decide whether or not the proposed development raises issues which require that an EIA report be submitted, and to date, no physical planning authority has put in place systems for environmental impact assessments of proposed developments before granting planning permissions. Planning permissions therefore are granted without taking account of the potential environmental impacts of the proposed development.

The Physical Planning Act stipulates that the local authority is the physical planning authority for its area. The local authority is established under the Local Government Act, Chapter 265.[6] It is a legal entity which is distinct and separate from the EIA licensing authority, NEMA. Appeals from its decisions on planning permissions are determined by the Physical Planning Liaison Committee, which is also distinct and separate from the NET. Consequently, the two systems which regulate housing developments in Kenya – the physical planning laws and the environmental management laws – are established as distinct and separate regulatory frameworks.

In numerous instances, parties who are aggrieved by physical planning permissions granted to housing developers have appealed to NET. In the majority of cases, the appellants have pointed to irregularities in physical planning permissions which, they have argued, vitiate the planning permissions granted. In a few instances the appellants have argued that the physical planning permissions were granted without taking into consideration the potential environmental impacts of the proposed housing developments.

The fact that aggrieved parties have opted to appeal to NET and not the Physical Planning Liaison Committee is testimony to the widely held perception that the latter is not a suitable dispute resolution mechanism. The likely reason for this is that the Physical Planning Liaison Committee – which comprises the relevant public officers from the Government departments whose mandates relate to physical planning developments – is not a standing appeal body, but rather is constituted as and when appeals are filed. Consequently, its sittings take time to convene. By default therefore NET has become the appeal forum of choice for parties aggrieved by physical planning decisions. NET's jurisdiction to entertain appeals on physical planning decisions has, however, been challenged by those against whom such appeals have been lodged.

When faced with challenges to its jurisdiction to determine appeals based on irregularities arising from the decisions of physical planning authorities, NET's approach has been to allow the appeal to proceed. The NET has ruled consistently that it does not sit on appeals from the decisions of physical planning authorities and therefore has declined to dismiss the appeals on the ground that the physical planning permission granted to the development is flawed.[7] However, it has, at the same time, ruled that, where the implementation of the development activity on the basis of the planning permission will lead to adverse environmental impacts, it has the jurisdiction to deal with the appeal.

In the *Nakumatt Decision*, the second respondent proposed to develop a housing estate in an area designated for light industrial development. The appellant, which operates a commercial storage facility in the vicinity of the proposed housing estate which services its chain of supermarkets, objected to the housing development on the basis that it was incompatible with the use of the area. Its concern was that the use of the neighbouring property for residential purposes would introduce a land use conflict with the appellant's use of its land for light industrial purposes since incoming residents would object to the noise, air pollution and other disturbances caused by the appellant's activities arising, for instance, from the movement at night of delivery trucks. In support of its objections the appellant pointed to the fact that the area in question was designated under the physical planning laws as an industrial area, and that, therefore, a residential estate should not be constructed within it.

From an examination of the City Council's physical planning policies, the Tribunal found as a fact that an area designated for light industrial activity could also be used for residential purposes. The Tribunal ruled that:

> in deciding on the nature of likely impacts of a proposed development, account must be taken of the status of the environment within which the proposed development will be undertaken. *That status is not determined by the fact alone that the area is designated as an industrial area or even as an area of mixed development. Such a designation is only indicative of the nature of environmental considerations that might arise.* It is still crucial that the actual status of the environment in the locality be ascertained. (Emphasis added)[8]

Since, from the evidence that was adduced, it was shown that the quality of the air and the extent of traffic noise and other potential environmental impacts would be within prescribed environmental limits, there was no reason to refuse to issue an EIA licence for the housing development. Therefore, the Tribunal upheld NEMA's decision to grant an EIA licence to the housing project. Similar considerations arose in the case of the *Elgon View Estate* decision.[9]

In that appeal, residents objected to the grant of an EIA licence for the development of a light industry (a metal fabricating workshop) in Elgon View Estate in Eldoret (which is Kenya's fourth largest town) on the grounds that, if allowed, the industry would interfere with the residents' quiet occupation of their residences, as it was likely to make a lot of noise and emit fumes. The residents faulted the grant by the Council of planning permission for the development. They argued that the area where the workshop was supposed to be built was purely a high class residential area. If the proposed industrial development activity was implemented, other industries were likely to come up in the vicinity thereby changing the character of the neighbourhood.

However, the Tribunal ruled that, from the evidence that was adduced, the operations of the development in question would not cause noise, traffic, air pollution, water pollution and aesthetic deterioration in excess of the normal standards for an area used for human habitation. The sound-proofing measures which had been adopted, consisting of double glazing and other noise containment measures, were effective in containing the noise pollution and other potential disturbances. The Tribunal also found as a fact that there would not be adverse impacts to water quality, as the facility would not discharge effluent into the ambient environment. Traffic movements too were not likely to exceed those for which the access road had been designed.

Accordingly the Tribunal affirmed the grant of the EIA licence to the developer. The Tribunal did not think that the concerns related to the location of the industrial workshop in a high class residential area on their own were sufficient to defeat the proposal in the absence of actual environmental impacts arising from the operations of the workshop.

12.3 STRIKING A BALANCE BETWEEN ENVIRONMENTAL PROTECTION AND HOUSING PROVISION

The Tribunal's decision in the *Jamii Bora* case[10] provides the best illustration of the Tribunal's role in contributing to the alleviation of poverty through the provision of housing in the urban context. In a decision considered particularly controversial, the Tribunal overturned NEMA's decision refusing to grant an EIA licence for the project.

This project concerned a proposal to construct 2000 housing units intended to house about 10 000 people who were members of a non-governmental organization, the *Jamii Bora Charitable Trust*, which was founded to alleviate and relieve poverty and enhance the living conditions of the people of Kenya through the provision of self-help, credit, savings and other schemes. The organization's 100 000 or so members reside within the slums of Nairobi. The housing project was conceived to assist the members to move out of the slums into secure housing in a good and well managed environment.

The project, known as *Kaputiei New Town*, consisted of low cost housing units, a light industrial zone, a business and commercial centre, educational facilities, infrastructure, an administrative centre and all the amenities normally found in a town, including utilities and services such as water and sewerage services, garbage collection and disposal, street lighting, recreation, a worship centre and a cemetery. The members of the savings and credit organization would purchase the housing units on a mortgage basis, relying on their membership of the organization as the guarantee for the repayment of the mortgage, in an arrangement typical of micro-finance facilities elsewhere in the world.

The project's proposed location was a 293 acre piece of land in Kaputiei, in the Kajiado District, about 60 kilometres to the south of the city of Nairobi. The location falls within the ecological zone known as the Athi Kapiti Plains, which is significant as a wildlife dispersal zone. It is bordered to the north by the world famous Nairobi National Park, and serves as a wildlife dispersal zone for the wildlife of this national park. Historically the area was occupied predominantly by the pastoralist and nomadic Maasai, but in more recent times, on account of its proximity to Nairobi, the population has become more mixed as satellite towns have sprung up to meet the housing demands of Nairobi residents.

Members of the local community, Government agencies, such as Kenya Wildlife Service, and wildlife non-governmental organizations expressed strong opposition to the project. Their reasons ranged from cultural to demographic to environmental considerations. They argued that people from the slums of Nairobi had cultural and social attributes that were different from the local Maasai and that to introduce them into the area would adversely affect the local culture and lifestyle, the local political equation, the local security and the local environment. In its ruling, the Tribunal rejected these arguments, pointing out that 'views which are not founded on pertinent environmental concerns should not be allowed to influence the outcome of an EIA licence application'.[11]

The principal environmental concern cited was that the proposed project lies within the wildlife migratory corridor and dispersal area, and that it would adversely affect the continued use of the area as a wildlife habitat. The evidence adduced showed that the Athi Kapiti Plains serves as a wildlife habitat within which the wildlife of Nairobi National Park disperse. Additionally, two wildlife species, in particular the zebra and wildebeest, migrate seasonally to a calving zone to the southern part of the area and it was said that the proposed housing project lies within the migratory corridor. The evidence showed that the maintenance of the ecological integrity of Nairobi National Park depends on the continued access by the wildlife to the Athi Kapiti dispersal area. The objection to the project was based on the concern that it would block the wildlife migratory corridor and threaten the continued use of the area by wildlife as a dispersal area, leading ultimately to the demise of Nairobi National Park.

The project proponent, on the other hand, argued that given the dramatic changes that were already occurring in the Athi Kapiti ecosystem area, this housing project would not, on its own, materially affect the status of wildlife in the area in ways that could not be managed through appropriate mitigation measures. They produced evidence which showed that, in the years since independence in 1964, the seven Maasai Group Ranches, which formerly owned the land in the area on a communal basis, had sub-divided the land and disposed of it to individuals who were mostly non-Maasai immigrants and that, presently, there were approximately 42 000 individual land tiles in the Athi Kapiti ecosystem area. These sub-divisions were followed by changes of the use of the land from nomadic pastoralism to industrial, commercial and residential uses. Indeed, there were already six other towns of a comparable size that had sprung up in the area. Unlike the proposed Kaputiei New Town, these other towns were unplanned and lacked basic amenities such as sewerage systems and garbage disposal arrangements. The sub-divisions, land use changes and unplanned urban settlements were taking place in a policy vacuum since a land use plan for the area had yet to be developed.

In its ruling the Tribunal rejected the argument that this particular development would spell the end of the ecosystem as a wildlife habitat. The Tribunal held that it had not been demonstrated that there would be any less risk of interference with the dispersal area arising from the unplanned settlements and conversion of the use of the area from nomadic pastoralism to commercial farming and industrial and residential use within and around the unplanned towns that had sprung up in the area. The Tribunal stated that:

> the threat to the viability of the wildlife habitat arises not from any *one* development, spontaneous or unplanned, but from the absence of an enforceable land use plan for the area which has allowed uncoordinated and unplanned sub-divisions and conversions of land use to take place on individual plots without being accompanied by the development of the necessary common infrastructural and utility services.[12]

Significantly, on the pertinent issue regarding the pressing demand for housing, particularly among the poor urban slum dwellers, the Tribunal ruled that:

> the proposed town offered an opportunity to find ways of meeting the pressing demands for new housing by residents of Nairobi within a framework that provides systems for mitigating the potentially adverse environmental impacts arising from human settlement within the ecosystem. It is much to be preferred to spontaneous unplanned settlements which are going on unchecked within the ecosystem.[13]

This effort to find a balance between the pressing need for housing and environmental protection can be seen in the other cases which have come before the Tribunal.

In the *Tony Mzee* decision,[14] neighbours objected to the construction of eight maisonettes on a piece of land lying within an area zoned for single residential dwelling for each 0.05 ha plot of land. NEMA's approval of the development had stipulated that the development should adhere to the 0.05 ha minimum for one dwelling unit specification, 0.35 per cent maximum permitted ground coverage and 0.75 per cent permitted plot development ratio specifications for residential development in Zone 5 of the City of Nairobi. According to the neighbours, the City Council's approval of the construction of eight units on this piece of land breached the physical planning laws and policies. They argued that, given that the plot in question was only 0.2835 ha in size, in effect, the approvals which the developer obtained authorized the construction of only four to five maisonettes. Therefore this development, which was of eight maisonettes, was unlawful.

In the evidence the architect explained that the eight units were designed in such a way that the physical structures (that is, the 'footprint' of the houses on the land) comprised of only four units. However, internally, the houses were designed in such a way that they constituted accommodation for eight (rather than four) families. Because the proposed development was for eight units in Zone 5 within which the recommended specification per single dwelling is 0.05 ha, the City Council had required the developer, as a condition of granting approval, to construct a sewer line as the method of waste water disposal, instead of resorting to septic tanks, which is the standard method of waste water disposal in the area neighbouring this development. Given the City Council's planning guidelines, without a sewer line, approval could only be granted for the construction of four to five units on this 0.2835 ha plot. Approval for the construction of a sewer line was granted on 25 August 2005 and this was followed, on 18 October 2005, with an approval for the construction of the eight maisonettes.

In upholding the grant of the EIA licence for the construction of eight housing units, the Tribunal observed that:

> the lack of access to sewerage facilities is the principal reason for the limitations imposed on the density of housing development in this zone. Therefore, with the installation of this sewer line, there is no environmental reason against this development since the Tribunal accepts that a well functioning sewerage facility would adequately meet the requirements for the disposal of waste water arising from 8 or more maisonettes on land the size of this plot.[15]

In the *WE CAN DO IT and Kyuna & Shanzu Residents Association* decision,[16] two neighbourhood associations challenged the grant of an EIA licence to construct 23 houses on a two acre piece of land which, they argued was contrary to the physical plan for the area, which was zoned as a low density housing area. They argued also that, given the physical planning restrictions applicable in the area, the plot of land in question could only accommodate 16 housing units. Services like water and electricity to the area were already strained and would be strained further if this kind of development was allowed. Additionally, there would be an increase in traffic movement and pollution. The developer pointed out that a change of use had been obtained allowing the construction of multiple dwellings on the plot of land and that there was a nine inch sewer line which would satisfactorily carry away liquid waste. The architect explained that, by adding a studio to the top floor of the houses, the developer had been able to provide a floor area for the use of the occupants that was comparable to similar houses in the neighbourhood while utilizing a smaller land area. In this way they were able to accommodate 23 units on this piece of land. The Tribunal upheld the grant of the EIA licence, satisfied that adequate measures were in place to deal with the anticipated environmental impacts of converting this plot to a high density use.

In the *Phenom* decision,[17] the Tribunal upheld a condition imposed by NEMA to the EIA approval restricting the construction of a proposed seven-storey housing block to only four storeys. The appeal had been filed by the developer against the said condition but in the course of the appeal the local residents' association was joined as interveners. The residents objected to the proposed development on the grounds that it fell within an area zoned for only four floors; the roads in the area would not sustain the increased traffic; the developer had not obtained permission to change the use of the plot of land from single dwelling to multiple dwelling; and the construction of 26 units in this area would negatively impact on the value of the properties in the area. The developer explained that the structure had been designed in such way that advantage would be taken of the slope of the land to construct two of the floors below the surface so that from the ground level only the four floors above the surface of the ground would be visible. In its ruling the Tribunal upheld the interveners' objections observing that the 'developer failed to produce any credible evidence that it had obtained approval for change of use from single dwelling to multiple dwelling which is a requirement of the law'.[18]

12.4 PROCEDURAL MATTERS

An important rationale for the establishment of administrative tribunals is that, unlike the regular courts, they can better facilitate cost-effective and expeditious access to justice. This is particularly so for the poor, who face significant constraints in accessing the mainstream courts for redress. An examination of the rulings of the NET on issues regarding *locus standi*, time and cost, reveals that it has been able to provide a cost effective mechanism for the determination of environmental disputes, particularly in regard to housing in Nairobi.

12.4.1 Locus Standi

Section 129 of the EMCA gives a right of appeal against the decisions of NEMA. But it does so in two ways. Section 129(1) provides a right of appeal to project proponents and developers who are aggrieved by NEMA's decisions on the applications which they have made for EIA licences as well as by conditions imposed by NEMA on EIA licences. Section 129(2) on the other hand states simply that where NEMA or its Director General, Committees or officers have made a decision, such a decision may be appealed against to the NET. Nothing is said specifically about appeals by third parties. However, in the National Environment Tribunal Procedure Rules, provision is made for third parties to participate in appeals before the NET as 'interveners'.

In several instances, appeals against NEMA's decisions have been filed by third parties, often resident associations and neighbourhood groups who object to the grant of an EIA licence for a proposed housing development. In a number of instances the *locus* of such groups to file appeals before the NET has been challenged by the respondents. NET's position has been that, whereas under s. 129(1) only a project proponent or a developer may file an appeal, s. 129(2) does not restrict the right of appeal, and third parties may therefore file an appeal. NET has articulated this position in, for instance, the *Tony Mzee* decision.[19]

In the *Malindi Green Town Residents Association* decision, the High Court held that third parties do not have *locus* to file appeals before the NET and that they may only come before NET as interveners. Regarding s. 3 of the EMCA, which eliminates the requirement to demonstrate *locus standi* to file appeals, the High Court held that s. 3 provided a right to file proceedings in the High Court but not a right of appeal to the Tribunal.[20]

In its judgement, the High Court did not make a distinction between s. 129(1) and s. 129(2) and therefore a question mark remains regarding whether the Tribunal is correct in its position that under s. 129(2) any person may appeal against NEMA's decisions. Additionally, it can be argued that where a member of the public has participated in the public consultation with respect to an application for an EIA licence by submitting comments, then such a third party would probably be considered a person aggrieved by the decision of NEMA on the application and would be entitled to lodge an appeal in the Tribunal against the decision. In *R v. The National Environment Tribunal ex parte Ol Keju Ronkai Limited*,[21] the High Court stated as follows:

> There is no dispute that the first Interested Party did not participate in the EIA study process for the development in question, in NEMA's process of approval of the development or complaint to the PCC. It cannot be said that it was aggrieved by the entire process which led to the issuance of the licence as it did not participate in it and no decision was made against it that would have led to a challenge by way of

> an appeal to the Respondent. There is no way one can read section 129 to make the 1st Interested Party 'an aggrieved party'.[22]

12.4.2 Time

As stated previously, among the principal justifications put forward for the establishment of administrative tribunals is their ability to dispose of disputes speedily. Section 129 provides that appeals shall be lodged within 60 days from the date of the decision being appealed against. This time limit is also stipulated in the National Environment Tribunal Procedure Rules, 2003. Once an appeal has been filed, the Tribunal has been able to dispose of the majority of appeals, including oral hearings, within six months of the filing. This is quite expeditious when compared to the High Court in which the average time for the determination of disputes is between three and four years.

A number of cases have been filed out of time, and the Tribunal has been faced with an application to extend time for the filing of the appeal.

In the *Pharmaceutical Factory* decision,[23] the appellant applied for an extension of time for filing the appeal on the basis that NEMA's failure to publish a notice in the Gazette and in the local newspapers informing the public of the proposal to set up a factory in the neighbourhood meant that the neighbours did not get to know of the grant of the EIA licence until after the time for the filing of the appeal had lapsed. The Tribunal agreed that, in the absence of public notice of the EIA licence application, the appellants would not have known of the grant of the EIA licence in time to be able to lodge an appeal against it within the prescribed period. The Tribunal therefore exercised its discretion under Rule 7 of the Tribunal Procedure Rules to allow the appeal to be filed out of time. The Tribunal made a similar ruling in the *Beth Mugo decision*.[24]

But in the *Lavington Residents Association decisions*[25] the Tribunal struck out appeals filed after the construction of the housing units, to which the residents association objected, had been completed. The Tribunal pointed out that the residents could not have failed to know that the housing units were being constructed, and, consequently, there was no justifiable reason for the inordinate delay to file the appeal, which could have been done as soon as the construction commenced.

The Tribunal's approach therefore has been to look beyond the legal requirement of 60 days to determine whether in fact the members of the public had an opportunity to file the appeal on time but did not.

12.4.3 Costs

Section 129 of EMCA provides that the Tribunal may award costs in an appeal. Rule 39 of the National Environment Tribunal Procedure Rules, however, stipulates that the Tribunal may not award costs except in respect to appeals or responses which are vexatious or frivolous or where the appellant or respondent has been wholly unreasonable in filing or in maintaining the appeal or the response.

Accordingly, the Tribunal does not normally award costs. In one of the *Lavington Residents Association decisions*,[26] the appellant applied to withdraw an appeal that had been filed out of time. The Tribunal rejected an application by the second respondent for costs, pointing out that the appellants had withdrawn the appeal as soon as they realized that the appeal was out of time. In the circumstances the Tribunal could not impute bad faith in filing the appeal to the appellants and therefore an award of costs was not justified.

In the *A.K. Filing Station* appeal,[27] the appellant had lodged an appeal against a stop order issued by NEMA requiring it to stop operating a petrol filling station without the required licences and permissions. Despite the stop order, the petrol station did not cease operations and it continued to operate throughout the period of the hearing of the appeal. The Tribunal ruled that an appeal filed in defiance of a stop order, and with no intention of complying with a stop order, is vexatious. Accordingly, the Tribunal awarded costs against the appellant.

Having awarded costs, the Tribunal had to assess the amount. Given that the Tribunal has not yet made rules on costs, the Tribunal had no clear criteria for assessing the amount of costs to be awarded. This can only be remedied by making rules on costs, which the Tribunal needs to do urgently. As regards this particular appeal, the Tribunal based its assessment of costs on the scale set out in the Advocates Remuneration Order for matters filed in the High Court.

12.5 CONCLUSIONS

Through its decisions, the National Environment Tribunal has endeavoured to strike a balance between the imperative to promote the development of much needed housing in Nairobi and environmental conservation. This review of its decisions has demonstrated that in the process it has made significant contribution to the alleviation of poverty through the development of housing units in Nairobi and its environs, albeit principally within the middle income category of housing.

The fact that the majority of housing construction disputes that have come before the NET have dealt with housing projects for the middle income housing sector is a reflection of the fact that most of housing development projects which are being undertaken are aimed at the middle income market. The housing units are being constructed by private developers for sale to this category of urban dwellers. Only a few housing units are being constructed by the Government or by other public entities, such as local authorities or state corporations.

Providing middle income housing through private investment does increase the overall stock of housing available in Nairobi but it does little to alleviate the acute housing shortage facing the urban poor, particularly those living in the urban slums. It is also an indication that the strategy adopted by the Government to implement its policy on housing is not catering for the urban poor. Therefore the Government's housing policy is not likely to achieve its objective of providing housing for the urban poor. It is in this context that the NET's decision in the *Jamii Bora* decision, the only decision which dealt with a housing project specifically for the slum dwellers, is particularly significant.

In the course of the review of NET's decisions, two issues have come up which require further development of the law under which the NET operates.

First, it has been argued that the Tribunal should be given original jurisdiction over environmental disputes, such as that given to the High Court. The reason for this proposal is the belief that the Tribunal has the expertise required to determine environmental disputes and giving it original jurisdiction would enhance its contribution to the determination of environmental disputes. Indeed s. 162(2) of the new Constitution of Kenya, which was adopted on 27 August 2010, provides that Parliament shall establish a court with the status of the High Court to hear and determine disputes relating to the environment and the use and occupation of, and title to, land. It is still not clear what NET's future role will be, if any, once that court is established.

In considering NET's future role, sight must not be lost of the fact that the reason for the success so far of the NET has been its character as an administrative tribunal which is able to focus on its mandate. A court with original jurisdiction over all environmental disputes will not have the same ability to provide a quick appeal mechanism from the administrative decisions of the NEMA. Consequently, there would still be need for an administrative tribunal, more so if the locus before such a tribunal is limited to persons directly involved in the application for an EIA licence.

What might be considered however is to further enhance the subject matter jurisdiction of NET, while retaining its character as an administrative tribunal. Presently, the Forest Act, 2005, has enhanced the Tribunal's subject matter jurisdiction by stipulating that disputes arising under that legislation are to be determined by the National Environment Tribunal. The Physical Planning Act, Chapter 286, should also be amended to bring physical planning disputes under the mandate of the National Environment Tribunal.

A second issue, which merits consideration, is the fact that EMCA does not give the NET the power to enforce its own orders. Under s. 129, failure to obey the orders of the NET is a criminal offence liable to be punished by the imposition of a fine or imprisonment or both. The prosecution for the offence has to be brought by the Attorney General. This means that in case of a refusal to comply with the NET's orders, the NET would have to refer the matter to the Attorney General to prosecute. This is unlikely to prove effective in practice.

Additionally, and far more serious, the NET does not have the power to punish for contempt. This lacuna in the law manifested itself in the case of the *A.K. Filing Station* appeal.[28] Although the NET awarded costs, the appellant ignored the award and did not pay the costs, and further compounding the problem, the NET lacked the powers to enforce the award by punishing the contempt. The option available to the beneficiary of the award is to file proceedings in the High Court for enforcement orders. This situation, which is similar to that prevailing with respect to other administrative tribunals, does not augur well for the standing of the NET, and could undermine the gains that have been made by the NET in establishing itself as the forum of choice for the resolution of housing development and other environmental disputes. It is important that steps be taken urgently to amend the law to give to the NET the power to enforce its own orders.

NOTES

1. http://www.un.org/millenniumgoals/ (accessed 8 February 2012).
2. Out of the 50 appeals which had been filed with the National Environment Tribunal as of December 2010 approximately three-fourths relate to urban housing projects.
3. *Jamii Bora Charitable Trust & Another v NEMA & Another*, Gazette Notice No 4944, the Kenya Gazette, Vol. CVIII, NO 46, 30 June 2006, at p. 1375.
4. http://www.vertic.org/media/National%20Legislation/Kenya/KE_Environmental_Management_Act.pdf (accessed 8 February 2012).
5. http://www.kenyalaw.org/Downloads/Acts/Physical%20Planning%20Act%20%28Cap.%20286%29.pdf (accessed 8 February 2012)
6. http://www.marsgroupkenya.org/pdfs/Oct_07/Acts/Local_Government_Act.pdf (accessed 8 February 2012).
7. See for instance *Jamii Bora Decision. Ibid.; Nakumatt Holdings Ltd v NEMA and Great Properties Ltd*, Gazette Notice No 9947, the Kenya Gazette, Vol. CVII No 85, 9 December 2005, at p. 3027; *Tim Busienei & Others v NEMA & Mechai International*, Tribunal Appeal No 10/2006 (*The Elgon View Residents Association Appeal*).
8. *Nakumatt Holdings Decision, ibid.*
9. Above, n. 7.
10. Above, n. 3.
11. Ibid., para. 28.
12. Ibid., para. 70.
13. Ibid., para. 67.
14. *Tony Mzee & 22 Others v NEMA & Others*, NET Appeal No 18/2007.
15. Ibid., para. 12.
16. *WE CAN DO IT & Kyuna and Shanzu Residents Association v NEMA and Houses & Plots Ltd,* NET Appeal No 9/06.
17. *Phenon Ltd v NEMA and Riverside Gardens Residents Association*, NET Appeal NO 04/05/05.
18. Ibid., para. 45.

19. Above, n. 14, para. 13.
20. *R v National Environment Tribunal, NEMA and Malindi Green Towns Residents Association ex parte Overlook Management Ltd and Another,* High Court Misc Application No 391 of 2006.
21. Nairobi High Court Misc. Civil Application JR ELC No 111/2008 (not yet reported).
22. Ibid., at pp. 20–21.
23. *Mahinda Gatigi & 13 Others v NEMA & Universal Corporation Ltd*, NET Appeal No 15/07 (*The Pharmaceutical Factory case*).
24. *Hon Beth Mugo & Others v NEMA and Silver Crest Enterprises*, NET Appeal No 23/07.
25. *Lavington Residents Association v NEMA & Drake Lines Ltd*, NET Appeal No 11/06; *Lavington Residents Association v NEMA & Noorani Mohamed Hussein*, NET Appeal No 12/06; *Lavington Residents Association v NEMA & Camelot Investments Ltd*, NET Appeal No 13/06; *Lavington Residents Association v NEMA & Dyke Holdings Ltd,* NET Appeal No 16/07.
26. *Lavington Residents Association v NEMA & Dyke Holdings Ltd,* NET Appeal No 16/07.
27. *Adnan Karama Petroleum Ltd T/A as A.K. Filling Station v NEMA*, NET Appeal NO 3/05, Kenya Gazette 3346 of 5 May 2006.
28. Ibid.

REFERENCES

Ministry of Lands and Housing (2004), *National Housing Policy for Kenya*, Sessional Paper No 3, Republic of Kenya.

Ministry of Planning and National Development (2007), *Vision 2030*, Republic of Kenya.

PART VI

Global challenges: international mechanisms to address poverty and environmental degradation

13. Linking climate change mitigation and poverty reduction: continued reform of the clean development mechanism in the post-Kyoto era to promote sustainable energy development on the African Continent

Daniel Behn

13.1 INTRODUCTION

There is concern from a human development perspective that demands to reduce global greenhouse gas (GHG) emissions will unjustly deprive developing countries of the same opportunities for industrialization already afforded to the developed world. Humanitarians argue that such a limitation could inequitably deny the developing world from achieving the economic development needed to free its populations from extreme poverty. Yet choices to eradicate extreme poverty or solve the global climate change problem need not be mutually exclusive.

Central to both pursuits is the access to, and use of, energy in all of its forms. The links between human development and access to energy are well-documented.[1] Equally documented are the links between fossil fuel consumption and the emission of carbon dioxide (CO_2) into the atmosphere.[2] One way to pursue both objectives is through global policies that encourage the development of sustainable energy in the developing world. This is particularly important on the African continent where access to energy is limited and extreme poverty is widespread.[3] In compelling humanity to embrace such an approach, an opportunity has emerged in the twenty-first century to both eradicate extreme poverty and stabilize the planet that we collectively inhabit.

There are internationally agreed upon targets for extreme poverty reductions and GHG emission reductions: the Millennium Development Goals

(MDGs)[4] and the Kyoto Protocol[5] respectively. Implicit in the achievement of the MDG's targets is a drastic reduction in energy poverty in the poorest parts of the world.[6] On the other hand, the achievement of the targets set by the Kyoto Protocol requires a global reduction in GHG emissions – the unwanted by-product of fossil fuel based energy production. While the industrialized world focuses on reducing energy consumption, the developing world is focusing on increasing energy production. Despite these policy agendas aimed at both curbing extreme poverty and GHG emissions, the industrialized countries of the world continue to burn fossil fuels at unsustainable rates while 1.6 billion people still have no access to electricity – including 85 percent of the rural population on the African continent.[7]

To exacerbate such inequity, the effects of global climate change – primarily caused by the industrialized world – will be borne disproportionately by the poorest populations in the world. While the industrialized world should arguably bear most of the cost for mitigating global GHG emissions, acknowledgement that they also bear the duty to financially and technically assist the poorest countries in their efforts to adapt to the future impacts of climate change has been slow to come. However, recent progress in this regard has been substantial.[8] The announcement of the development of a robust 100 billion dollar a year Green Climate Fund indicates that the post-Kyoto era appears to be aimed at remedying some of these key energy poverty issues.[9]

Overall though, the seemingly obvious links between climate change, energy use, and extreme poverty are not explicitly integrated into either the MDGs or the Kyoto Protocol. Implicitly however, the past ten years has seen the development of a potentially transformative approach for addressing both energy poverty and climate change. Dubbed the 'Kyoto surprise,' the Clean Development Mechanism (CDM) appeared late in the negotiations of the Kyoto Protocol as a market-based innovation linking sustainable development with the task of reducing GHG emissions through an endorsement of carbon emission trading between developed and developing countries (Yasmin, 1998, p. 115).

Coupled with the Joint Implementation mechanism (JI), the Kyoto Protocol embraces these so-called flexible mechanisms as a way for industrialized countries to meet their GHG emission reduction targets by investing in GHG emission reducing projects in developing and transitional economies (Wright, 2007). However, the development process of the CDM has been guided by a 'learn-by-doing' approach and as such has experienced a number of significant initial growing pains.[10] And while the CDM has arguably only provided marginal sustainable energy development benefits during the first compliance period of the Kyoto Protocol (2008 through 2012), the post-Kyoto framework should continue to embrace the CDM; albeit with a continued focus on reforming the CDM towards the provision of specific sustainable development benefits to the poorest countries of the world – particularly the least developed countries (LDCs) on the African continent (Subbarao and Lloyd, 2011).

This chapter aims to identify the limiting factors of the current CDM and to advocate for a mechanism in the post-Kyoto era that will provide LDCs with improved opportunities for pursuing sustainable energy development strategies. Section 13.2 will outline the structures and function of the CDM as implemented during the first compliance period. Sections 13.3, 13.4, and 13.5 will identify and analyze the operational and institutional deficiencies that have emerged in the implementation of the CDM. Section 13.6 will propose a reform agenda for the CDM in the post-Kyoto era; a modified framework and set of rules better designed to facilitate sustainable energy development in African and other slow developing countries.

13.2 GOALS AND STRUCTURE OF THE CDM

There is a broadening scientific consensus that the anthropomorphic activity over the preceding two centuries, primarily from the uninhibited use of inexpensive fossil fuels, has led to greatly increased GHG concentrations in the earth's atmosphere.[11] Projections hold that these increased concentrations of industrial gases in the atmosphere will warm the earth's surface temperature, and in turn, lead to a rise in sea levels, changes in crop patterns, and increasingly extreme weather conditions.[12] The most significant global response to climate change is manifest in the Kyoto Protocol: a binding commitment by the industrialized nations of the world (except the United States (US)) to reduce GHG emissions to approximately 5 per cent below 1990 levels (Gerrard, 2007, p. 38). To achieve such targets, the Kyoto Protocol embraces a market-based cap-and-trade approach to GHG emission reductions.

Under such a cap-and-trade system, industrialized nations with Kyoto Protocol commitments (Annex B countries) can use a variety of means by which to meet their target reductions in the first compliance period (Gerrard, 2007, pp. 42–50). The Kyoto Protocol includes a number of flexible mechanisms aimed at reducing the cost of compliance for Annex I countries (industrialized countries that are party to the United Nations Framework Convention on Climate Change (UNFCCC)).[13] One such mechanism, the CDM, allows developed countries to invest in GHG emission reduction projects in developing countries. The investing country can then use the resulting earned emission credits to meet its own GHG emission reduction commitments.[14] The CDM's innovation, however, comes not in its endorsement of a carbon trading system, but rather in its requirement to bring sustainable development benefits to developing countries. The investors in such projects, either a government agency or private corporation, earn Certified Emission Reductions (CER): a form of carbon credit that an investor can either sell or use to meet a portion of its own emission reduction obligations under the Kyoto Protocol.[15]

The objectives of the CDM under Article 12 of the Kyoto Protocol are twofold. First, the CDM seeks to provide a market-based mechanism through which governments and private sector entities in developed countries can invest in projects that will enable them to reduce global GHG emissions at a lower cost per ton of CO_2 emitted.[16] Second, the CDM is a device to assist developing countries in achieving their sustainable development objectives (Wara, 2008, p. 1765).

The CDM emerged late in the Kyoto Protocol negotiations as a compromise designed to promote cooperation between developing and developed countries. The Brazilian delegation had proposed the establishment of a fund under the Kyoto Protocol that would compel developed countries to finance adaptation projects in developing countries (Yamin, 1998, p. 115). While the proposed fund did not succeed, the resulting CDM incorporated design elements to achieve a similar objective.[17] Promoted under the Kyoto Protocol as a means to meeting the overall objectives of the UNFCCC, the CDM provides the potential for win-win opportunities: developed countries can stabilize their GHG emissions, while at the same time encouraging sustainable development in developing countries (Wara, 2008, pp. 1765–1766).

Developed countries benefit from the CDM in two ways. First, they can use the mechanism as an alternative mode of compliance when they are unable to meet commitment targets by regulating their domestic industries. Second, they are able to reduce the compliance costs of meeting their domestic obligations because GHG emission reductions are often achievable at a much lower marginal cost in developing countries (Wara, 2008, p. 1765–1766). There are two key limitations, however. One is that CDM projects must adhere to a supplementarity principle: all CDM projects must be supplemental to domestic efforts to meet Kyoto Protocol commitments.[18] CDM projects are likewise limited in that they cannot receive financing through a diversion of Official Development Assistance (ODA) funds already targeted for other programs. Essentially envisioned as a market-based program, primary funding of CDM projects should originate in the private sector.

For the developing world, the CDM was envisioned as a tool for promoting investment and technology transfer opportunities, while at the same time, enabling Non-Annex I countries (non-industrialized countries that are party to the UNFCCC) to achieve some of their sustainable development objectives.[19] By encouraging sustainable development, the CDM could theoretically provide Non-Annex I parties with financial incentives for low carbon intensity development in the hope of nudging them onto a more climate friendly trajectory. In hosting CDM projects, developing countries could potentially attract much needed foreign direct investment (FDI) in energy and infrastructure development, reap associated local air quality and health benefits, gain access to low-cost or no-cost technology transfers, promote institutional capacity building, improve land use, support rural development, and help promote sustainable energy development.[20]

Operationally however, the flexible mechanisms permitted under the Kyoto Protocol were little more than an empty shell after the landmark UNFCCC Conference of the Parties (COP) in Kyoto, Japan in 1997 (Lecocq and Ambrosi, 2007, p. 136). It was not until 2001 at the UNFCCC COP in Bonn, Germany that negotiation of the actual framework for international emissions trading under the CDM and the JI took place. The following year, at the COP in Marrakesh, Morocco, the parties agreed to a rulebook for the operational modes and modalities that would regulate the project cycle under the CDM and JI.[21] While the rulebook provided much needed guidance in the implementation of the flexible mechanisms under the Kyoto Protocol, its specific requirements have arguably hindered the effectiveness of the CDM in achieving some of its goals (Timilsina, 2009).[22]

As per the Marrakesh Accords, the CDM is a project-based system that accomplishes its objectives through an individually approved and validated project cycle. Each project's proposal starts with a Project Design Document (PDD), which includes *inter alia*, a description of the project, the baseline and monitoring methodologies,[23] and the environmental impacts of the project (Lecocq and Ambrosi, 2007, pp. 137–138). The PDD must explain in detail how future emission reductions from the project will be voluntary,[24] real,[25] additional,[26] and not induce leakage.[27] All four of these concepts require definition of a hypothetical baseline of emissions. This baseline represents the timeline of emissions that would have occurred absent the subsidy provided by the CDM project.[28]

Once finalized, both the host government (the Non-Annex I country) and the sponsoring government (the Annex I country) must approve the PDD. In order to participate in CDM projects, each developing country must establish a Designated National Authority (DNA) that is responsible for approving projects and verifying that the projects contribute to sustainable development.[29] If approved, the DNA of both the developing country and the developed country must issue a Letter of Approval (LoA) stating that participation in the CDM is voluntary and will contribute to the host country's sustainable development objectives. The PDD and the LoA must then be validated by an independent third party (typically an auditing company), the Designated Operational Entity (DOE) (Lecocq and Ambrosi, 2007, pp. 137–138). By validating the project, the DOE determines that all parties approve the project, and that it correctly applies the selected baseline and monitoring methodologies.[30] The PDD and LoAs then go to the CDM Executive Board (CDM EB), who registers the project and monitors its progress (Lecocq and Ambrosi, 2007, pp.

137–138). After becoming operational, the CDM EB is responsible for issuing the earned CER credits, and depositing them into the account of the project participant. CER credits are equal to the GHG emission reduction of one ton of CO_2 equivalent, and are a fungible commodity tradable interchangeably with other Kyoto Protocol allowances (CER credits, Emission Reduction Units (ERUs), and Assigned Allocation Units (AAUs)).

13.3 SUSTAINABLE DEVELOPMENT AND THE CDM

A measurement of the exact sustainable development indicators as they relate to CDM projects remains a challenge. However, the initial operation of the CDM as implemented under the Kyoto Protocol, the Bonn framework, and the Marrakesh rules has not resulted in the significant development of sustainable energy projects on the African continent or other slow developing countries (Fenhann and Staun, 2010; de Lopez, 2009; Timilsina, 2010). Though the CDM has proven successful as a means for reducing global GHG emissions at a lower cost than would be possible for developed countries domestically, the CDM has not effectively promoted energy development aimed at reducing extreme poverty.[31] Fortunately, the CDM EB is acutely aware of this criticism; and is currently working on remedying many inadequacies as they relate to the limited popularity of sustainable energy projects in LDCs.[32] One key initiative currently being developed is to provide special loans and assistance to LDCs that have registered fewer than ten projects.[33]

As of 15 May 2011, the CDM EB has registered 3100 projects with more than 6200 projects in the pipeline.[34] Of the projects currently registered globally, the majority of CDM projects are concentrated in Latin America and Asia with only 61 registered projects on the African continent.[35] Further, of the projected CER credits that will be issued worldwide from CDM projects through the end of the first commitment period, only 25 per cent will come from renewable energy projects.[36]

On the other hand, 25 per cent of expected CER credits after the first commitment period will come from projects aimed at the capture and destruction of industrial gases that are the unwanted by-product of nylon-22 and Teflon® production.[37] These so-called hydrofluorocarbon-23 (HFC-23) and nitrous oxide (N_2O) abatement projects have produced a large number of CER credits in India and China.[38] Unfortunately, these projects have severely undermined the credibility of the CDM process by creating false credits at inflated costs with no sustainable development benefits (Wara, 2008, pp. 1768–1770). It can be noted, however, that the inadequacies related to CDM abatement projects have largely been resolved and will not feature prominently in the future development of the CDM.[39] As recently as 2008, it was predicted that abatement projects would account for over 50 per cent of all the expected CER credits to be issued during the first commitment period (Wara, 2008, pp. 1768–1770). The fact that this number is currently down to 25 per cent indicates great progress in the promotion on non-abatement type projects throughout the world.

It was initially predicted that the operation of the CDM would result in a significant percentage of projects that have substantial sustainable development benefits: renewable energy, fuel switching, waste heat capture, and demand-side energy efficiency. However, CER credits issued to date have come from a less than optimal percentage of sustainable energy projects.[40] However, this too is changing. Recent increases in demand-side efficiency projects, wind energy projects, and biomass energy production indicate concerted efforts by the CDM to remedy many of the initial barriers to entry that these types of projects faced.[41] However, it remains the case that CDM projects remain disproportionately absent from the African continent (Timilsina, 2010; Byigero, 2010). The reason for the CDM's limited influence in Africa is likely the result of both CDM operational deficiencies and institutional governance deficiencies among LDCs in Africa. In order to make the CDM work as a tool for promoting sustainable energy development with poverty reduction benefits on the African continent, both deficiencies need correction.

13.4 OPERATIONAL BARRIERS

Turning first to the operational deficiencies of the CDM itself, both procedural and substantive barriers currently limit the effectiveness in bringing the CDM to the poorest regions of the world. These operational deficiencies are broadly classifiable into two categories: (1) inadequacies of the market-based approach and (2) inadequacies of specific substantive and procedural requirements. The first category includes the low-hanging fruit problem, the inadequate definition of sustainable development under the CDM, and the problems associated with using market mechanisms in environmental management. The second category includes problems relating to the additionality and baseline requirements, limitations on land use, forestry, and carbon sink projects, the registration of small-scale projects, the cumbersome and costly requirements of CDM project registration, and the uncertainty of the post-Kyoto framework for CDM-type projects.

While the market-based approach to addressing global climate change appears to have permanently seeped into the consciousness of the world's policy makers, it likewise has begun to appear that the same market-based approach has the potential to broaden development inequities between the global North and the global South (Nygard, 2009, p. 36). Instead of promoting projects that result in the greatest benefit to the greatest number of people, the CDM has rewarded green entrepreneurs who have manipulated the CDM in order to reap massive windfall profits from industrial gas abatement projects that have provided few, if any, sustainable development benefits.[42] CDM projects with the greatest sustainable benefits are often costly, and the use – or misuse – of the CDM to procure CER credits at the lowest possible cost (the low-hanging fruit issue) has prevented the promotion of costlier or riskier sustainable projects in Africa.[43] The low-hanging fruit issue states that developed country entities or foreign investors will first sponsor projects that are the most profitable, thus leaving the developing countries with only more expensive measures when they have to meet their own emission reduction commitments in the future.[44] However, it appears that CDM projects have now picked almost all the lowest-hanging fruit and there is a decided increase in projects with more limited profit margins.[45]

Another operational barrier to the promotion of CDM projects is the vagueness of the sustainable development requirement. Currently, any project that is found to reduce GHG emissions meets the sustainable development requirement. While the definition of sustainable development is malleable, it certainly requires more than climate change mitigation practices.[46] By requiring a stricter definition of the sustainable development requirement, the CDM could mitigate some of the market-based issues addressed above.

Under the current market-based regime, CDM projects with substantial sustainable development benefits will appear prohibitively costly when forced to compete with projects that provide windfall profits at low or no-cost to the investor (such as industrial gas abatement projects) (Wara, 2008, p. 1765). Using a cost-minimizing marketable rights approach to sustainable energy development – when no factor other than CO_2 emission reductions are taken into account – leads to distortion of the projects selected (such as low-hanging fruit projects), which may be far from the best projects to undertake in terms of sustainable development more broadly conceived.

The second category of deficiencies is describable as follows: in order to assure that CDM projects actually result in emission reduction benefits, the CDM implementing rules contain both substantive and procedural requirements that have interfered with creating more CDM projects. One such issue is the additionality requirement, which – as currently defined under the CDM – limits the possibility of projects on the African continent. Reductions in emissions must be in addition to any that would occur in the absence of the CDM project (the business-as-usual scenario) (Nelson, 2004, p. 636). Using this baseline approach rewards investors for cleaning up older fossil fuel based energy systems, but almost completely excludes projects that avoid future emissions through new renewable energy projects. Furthermore, this approach has limited the types of land use projects permitted under the CDM; only projects for reforestation and afforestation[47] are authorized under the current modalities (Ellis and Kamel, 2007, p. 36).[48]

For Africa, the inclusion of projects that avoid deforestation could have a significant impact in both preserving forests and promoting projects that reduce the use of unsustainable biomass fuelwood through fuel switching projects (Laurance, 2007, pp. 20–24). Hence, an additionality requirement that is determined in terms of GHG emissions avoided instead of GHG emissions reduced could be possible. Under such an avoidance approach, investors would be rewarded for promoting projects that entirely bypass fossil fuel based energy development (so-called leap-frogging) (Laurance, 2007, pp. 20–24). However, such an avoidance approach represents a fundamental reality – if we give developed countries credit for assisting avoiding future emissions in developing countries and give them permission to continue to emit based on those credits, we have not reduced emissions at all. Therefore, a better solution may be to include a separate mechanism in the post-Kyoto agreement that rewards investors and states who avoid increasing emissions through poor land use choices, deforestation, and fossil fuel based energy development. Such a mechanism would encompass both the North and the South, but place substantial responsibility on the North to finance the incentives used to encourage nations in the South to make better land use decisions, avoid deforestation, and leap-frog over fossil fuel technologies.

The required costs and cumbersome processes of CDM registration further hinder CDM projects. The current CDM process encourages large-scale projects that can quickly reap CER credits at the lowest possible cost. Small-scale renewable energy projects or small-scale carbon sink projects do not fare well under the current CDM process (Fenhann and Staun, 2010). While there have been attempts to increase awareness of CDM opportunities in Africa through such initiatives as the Nairobi framework[49] and the Africa Carbon Forum,[50] the CDM process remains a challenge for countries on the African continent (Timilsina, 2010). For small-scale projects, the cost and time required to register a CDM project is often prohibitive (Sum Low, 2006, pp. 76–80).

The CDM process requires vast documentation, technical and scientific expertise, costs ranging from 30 to 250 thousand dollars, and times ranging from nine months to a year.[51] There have been some recent attempts to remedy this problem by allowing the bundling of small-scale projects and allowing for programmatic CDM projects (called Program of Activity (PoA) projects).[52] Under the bundling approach, registration of multiple small-scale projects – such as decentralized renewable energy projects in rural areas – are combinable, thus making the CDM registration process more feasible.[53] Likewise, PoA projects allow developing countries to earn CER credits for programs (as opposed to individual projects) for reducing GHG emissions.[54] These programmatic and bundling ideas have the potential to improve the administration of the CDM dramatically (Subbarao and Lloyd, 2011).

Finally, while the current operational guidelines of the CDM do permit the issuance of CER credits beyond the Kyoto Protocol's first compliance period, such credits could become valueless without future commitment periods that embrace a CDM-type program (Ellis and Kamel, 2007, pp. 40–41). While the 2007 Bali COP decided on a road map for post-Kyoto negotiations,[55] the 2009 Copenhagen COP[56] and the 2010 Cancun COP[57] have failed to produce binding commitments for a second commitment period. As such, many projects that have long life spans – carbon sink projects and large-scale renewable energy projects – will not earn CER credits until after the first commitment period has concluded (Ellis and Kamel, 2007, pp. 40–41). However, the inclusion of a CDM-type program is likely in any future agreement, and therefore difficulties associated with post-Kyoto credits should disappear as soon as a long-term global agreement is adopted.[58]

Despite the fact that a binding second commitment period has not emerged, the continued reform, modification, and improvement of the major problems identified in the current CDM program is ongoing and promises to result in a more equitable distribution of projects, especially on the African continent. Therefore, while the current CDM has not been effective as a means for promoting sustainable energy development and poverty reduction on the African continent, the CDM concept remains visionary, and if properly reformed, promises to be a powerful development tool in the post-Kyoto era.

13.5 INSTITUTIONAL BARRIERS

Beyond the operational deficiencies of the CDM, other institutional issues play a significant role in limiting the proliferation of CDM projects in Africa. Many of the problems plaguing development in Africa are not specific to the CDM, but rather are institutional challenges for all development sectors (Winkelman and Moore, 2011, p. 1132). Economic development on the African continent has been a vexing issue for decades. Weak and corrupt institutions, high population growth, declining external resource flows, growing external debt, inadequate social development, lack of infrastructure and environmental constraints, high rates of poverty, low standard of living and disease pandemics present countries in Africa with some of the most daunting challenges of any region on earth (Nelson, 2004, pp. 616–618).

Many of these problems have the potential to deteriorate further in the coming decades as Africa begins to feel the impact of global climate change: water and food shortages, mass migration, the creation of climate change refugees, resource wars, drought, flooding, desertification, and sea level rise (Nelson, 2004, pp. 616–618). Despite the African continent's minimal contribution to the global warming problem, scientists expect the effects of global climate change to affect Africa disproportionately (Sum Low, 2006, pp. 76–80). Current projections indicate that developing countries face 75 to 80 per cent of the potential damage from climate change.[59]

From an institutional perspective, the barriers to the successful implementation of CDM projects on the African continent are dividable into two categories: (1) climate change-related problems and (2) economic development-related problems. In terms of economic development challenges, Africa is plagued with a high-risk environment (weak rule of law traditions, high levels of graft and corruption, and poor governance standards) that limits the amount of FDI flowing onto the continent (Nelson, 2004, p. 634). Since the funding of CDM projects comes primarily from private investment, such a limitation is important.

A further economic-related barrier stems from the mismatch between the climate-focused priorities of the CDM and the economic development-focused priorities of LDCs on the African continent. Climate change-related challenges include the lack of capacity and technical knowledge needed to adapt to climate change, the problems created by the limited involvement of Non-Annex I countries in the UNFCCC decision-making process, and the disconnect between GHG reduction priorities of the developed world and the energy development priorities of countries in Africa.[60] The African continent, despite its abundance of natural resources, accounts for only 2.5 per cent of the world's economic activity (Nelson, 2004, p. 634). Some non-governmental organizations hold that it is Africa's very low levels of energy consumption (2–3 per cent of the world's energy consumption) that are both the cause and consequence of underdevelopment (Nelson, 2004, pp. 634–635). Bringing energy to African populations, sustainable or not, is an exceedingly difficult problem.

The African continent continues to have the lowest rate of FDI globally: an acknowledged necessity for financing energy projects in the poorest regions of the world (Udombana, 2002, p. 304). While global strategies to increase FDI and improve governance in less developed countries is beyond the scope of this chapter, there are modifications to the CDM that might be able to increase FDI flows in developing countries: investment incentives and protection mechanisms, vehicles for technology transfer, and information dissemination about emerging carbon trading markets.[61]

Another barrier to the promotion of CDM projects on the African Continent stems from a mismatch between the priorities of the CDM and the development priorities of countries in Africa. The CDM focuses on GHG emission reductions through two major categories of projects: (1) GHG capture of industrial and agricultural gases, and (2) the promotion of clean technologies that either clean up or replace dirtier fossil fuel based energy production systems (Ellis and Kamel, 2007, pp. 11–12). With few such opportunities in Africa, the majority of eligible CDM projects do not address the African continent's need for projects that both increase access to energy and adapt to future climate change problems (Byigero, 2010). Further, the primary development agenda for countries in Africa remains food, water, and energy security – as the majority population on the continent is still living in poverty (Nelson, 2004, p. 625).

While the MDGs do not deal specifically with energy development and climate change, the achievement of the MDGs in Africa will require both climate change adaption and increased access to sustainable energy (Subbarao and Lloyd, 2011, p. 1600). To date, Africa has experienced little industrial development compared to the rest of the world. As there is a perceived historical relation between fossil fuel consumption and prosperity, the African continent is still awaiting its industrial revolution. From the African perspective, access to energy, sustainable or not, is high on the development agenda (Nelson, 2004, p. 625). Without strong incentives to develop along a sustainable energy path, Africa's future industrialization could follow the same unsustainable fossil fuel model that is now challenging the developed world.

The CDM, primarily a GHG reduction mechanism, is ill equipped to incentivize the development of a sustainable energy system for an entire continent. Further, as environmental restrictions become more limiting in the developed world, an increase in the dumping of polluting technologies in Africa is likely to produce leakage. Therefore, policies to disincentivise the promotion of fossil fuel based energy systems on the African continent are important and can benefit both the developing and developed world in long-term global efforts to adapt to climate change.

Another institutional barrier preventing the utilization of the CDM on the African continent is the limited role that Non-Annex I countries play in the development of the global climate change regime. The UNFCCC continues to promote a posture of common, but differentiated responsibilities for members of the convention.[62] While such an approach is crucial in setting GHG emission reduction commitments under the Kyoto Protocol, it has created considerable difficulties in developing a comprehensive global regime to address climate change.

Developed countries (primarily the US) have always criticized the Kyoto Protocol's refusal to set GHG emission reduction commitments for emerging or transitional countries such as India and China (Gerrard, 2007, p. 21). While the rejection of the Kyoto Protocol by the US is proving to be an unsophisticated and detrimental approach, the LDCs appear to support the US point of view; however, for completely different reasons. Under the current regime, countries with no commitments play a limited role in the decision-making process (Nelson, 2004, p. 636). Likewise, Non-Annex I countries are restricted in their participation in the market for trading carbon emission credits.

One possible approach to this problem is to allocate emission rights among all states on a per-capita basis (Nelson, 2004, p. 636). The per-capita approach reflects the view that all of the world's population has an equitable right to share equally in the use of the atmosphere. Under such an approach, developed countries currently overusing their share of the atmosphere's assimilative capacity will gradually reduce emissions while the underdeveloped regions of the world would increase their emissions until they reach a comparable state of economic development (Nelson, 2004, p. 636).

A final institutional hurdle to the promotion of CDM projects on the African continent is its extensive use of unsustainable biomass as a primary energy source. The population on the African continent is as diverse and complex as any region of the world; however, the majority of the population is rural, agrarian, and pre-industrial. As mentioned, energy infrastructure is almost nonexistent in rural areas on the continent. What infrastructure does exist is crumbling and unreliable (Nelson, 2004, pp. 625–626). The primary energy source for Africa's rural population is biomass – such as fuelwood and agricultural and animal residues (Bluemel, 2007, p. 675). While biomass energy provides about 11 per cent of the global primary energy supply, the share of biomass in primary energy consumption on the African continent is around 70 per cent (Bluemel, 2007, p. 675). Since the CDM is primarily concerned with reducing GHG emissions, it fails to address many of the land use issues that would be required to disincentivise the destruction of forests for fuelwood (Ellis and Kamel, 2007, pp. 11–12).

Considering that 70 per cent of the energy in Africa comes from unsustainable biomass consumption, any mechanism for promoting sustainable energy development in African needs to include provisions for promoting alternatives to such use (Lecocq and Ambrosi, 2007, pp. 147–148). One of the major problems of current patterns of unsustainable biomass use is its low conversion efficiency. Domestic use of fuelwood has a conversion rate of about 10 per cent (Bluemel, 2007, p. 675). Such inefficiency creates social development problems as children and women in rural areas on the African continent can spend up to seven hours a day collecting fuel for cooking.[63] Further, smoke from the burning of biomass on open fires kills an estimated 2.5 million women and children annually, with such prolonged smoke inhalation being a major factor in the contraction of acute respiratory infection.[64] Providing fuel switching to cleaner and more efficient energy sources could transform rural Africa. Not only would the development of simple renewable decentralized energy systems provide the rural poor with a greatly enhanced standard of living, it would also reduce the amount of fuelwood harvested from forests. However, under the current CDM, sustainable biomass projects have been few in number.[65]

13.6 OVERCOMING OPERATIONAL AND INSTITUTIONAL BARRIERS

In order for the CDM to become an effective tool for promoting energy development on the African continent, three post-Kyoto scenarios seem feasible. The first scenario keeps the basic CDM framework in future commitment periods, while reforming the current regime's shortcomings (Wara, 2008, p. 1765). A second approach is to abandon the market-based approach and adopt a fund-based approach best exemplified by the Montreal Protocol's Multilateral Fund.[66] A fund-based approach has the potential to encounter problems similar to those currently challenging the CDM. However, it could increase the efficiency of the flexible mechanisms, increase the ability to target projects that create tangible sustainable development benefits, and increase the ability for implementing projects that are necessary (such as renewable energy projects on the African continent), but not economically feasible under a market-based system.

Despite the potential advantages of a fund-based program, it has been assumed that the post-Kyoto framework is likely to be market-based (Ellis and Kamel, 2007, pp. 40–41). Yet, recent developments in a fund-based approach have been significant.[67] The World Bank Group's Clean Technology Fund and the Strategic Climate Fund,[68] the proposed Green Climate fund currently being developed by the UNFCCC COP,[69] the UN Adaptation Fund,[70] and the various national climate funds that individual developed countries have established constitute a serious trend away from purely market-based solutions to climate change. Statements that the CDM will continue to function, coupled with the recent proliferation of climate funds, indicates that a hybrid approach is actually emerging. This third scenario appears more and more likely to represent the path that the global community takes in its efforts to curb climate change.

Regardless of what approach becomes dominant in the post-Kyoto era, the continued reform of the CDM in the short-term remains important. From the macro level, increasing FDI flows to Africa in the coming years is important (Ellis and Kamel, 2007, pp. 16–17). In Africa, access to project financing limits the potential of CDM projects specifically, and sustainable development projects generally.[71] The future of any CDM-type program in Africa will require increased levels of FDI, and developed countries can encourage these increases through various investment incentives and guarantees. More specifically, there are a number of CDM-based methods that could be pursued.

One approach could be to create a quota system that caps the number of projects in individual countries (Nelson, 2004, p. 635). By limiting the number of projects in faster developing countries (such as China, Brazil, and India), the CDM could compel investment in higher risk environments (such as LDCs) (Schatz, 2008, pp. 708–709). A quota system would likely limit the number of low-hanging fruit projects. This limitation on the number of low-cost projects would have the potential to compel investment in more expensive sustainable energy projects.

Another approach could be to include a mechanism allowing for a full menu of emission reduction strategies in slower developing countries but limit the strategies given to faster developing countries. Likewise, the CDM could be modified in a manner that sets the value of CER credits on a sliding scale: for example, a CDM project in a faster developing country might receive 0.5 times emission reductions, while LDCs receive full credit. Along these lines, the current CDM strategy to promote projects in LDCs includes the aforementioned policy to provide incentives, assistance, and loans to countries that have registered fewer than 10 projects.[72]

The future success of a CDM-type program on the African continent will also require the allowance of GHG avoidance projects, not just GHG reduction projects. Such an outlook will allow a variety of projects that create incentives to make better land use choices. This will require a new definition of sustainable development under the CDM; a definition that would encompass a full range of mitigation and adaptation projects that currently do not fit neatly into the clean development box: reforestation and afforestation projects, livestock projects, land use projects, hydropower projects, gas capture, and industrial gas reduction projects. Further, in order to promote long-term renewable energy projects and true carbon sink projects through the CDM, the international community must agree to binding future commitment periods in an effort to provide certainty in the long-term viability of a global carbon market.

The CDM to date has had considerable success in providing low-cost GHG reduction opportunities to developed world countries. However, critics of the CDM hold that even this aspect has been a failure. A 2007 study found that a major class of CDM projects (HFC-23 abatement projects) paid as much as 50 times more for its GHG emission reductions than the costs alone would warrant, with the excessive profits ending up with the factories and the carbon traders (Wara, 2007, p. 595). Such projects have severely undermined the promotion of the CDM as a legitimate tool for achieving sustainable development objectives. The success of any future CDM-type program will require improvement to the substantive requirements of sustainable development in order to mandate that the developed world help pay for projects that promote climate change adaptation, but also provide economic and social development benefits to local populations in the poorest regions of the world.

13.7 CONCLUSION

As the global climate change regime ramps up in coming years, it is important that efforts to promote sustainable energy development on the African continent likewise increase in scope. Arguably, we all bear a moral and financial duty to prevent slow developing countries from the suffering caused by the historically inequitable distribution of the world's resources. If developed properly, the CDM still has the potential to bring much needed capital and technical expertise to Africa.[73] By helping LDCs adapt to climate change, the global community has the opportunity to reduce poverty and reduce GHG emissions at the same time. Yet, there is certainly the possibility that, absent specific reforms to the CDM, a market-based approach to climate change will only continue to address the problems facing the African continent inadequately.

NOTES

1. Gaye, A. (2007), *Human Development Report 2007/2008 – Fighting Climate Change: Human Solidarity in a Divided World*, United Nations Development Programme, http://hdr.undp.org/en/reports/global/hdr2007-8/ (accessed 9 February 2012).
2. *Fourth Assessment Report* (2007), United Nations Inter-governmental Panel on Climate Change, http://www.ipcc.ch/pdf/assessment-report/ar4/syr/ar4_syr.pdf, p. 4 (accessed 9 February 2012).
3. *The Millennium Development Goals in Africa: Progress and Challenges* (2005), United Nations Economic Commission for Africa, http://www.uneca.org/mdgs/MDGs_in_Africa.pdf, p.8 (accessed 9 February 2012).
4. *The Millennium Development Goals Report 2010* (2010), United Nations Department of Economic & Social Affairs, http://www.un.org/en/mdg/summit2010/pdf/MDG%20Report%202010%20En%20r15%20-low%20res%2020100615%20-.pdf (accessed 9 February 2012).
5. The *Kyoto Protocol to the United Nations Framework Convention on Climate Change* (1997), 37 I.L.M. 22, http://unfccc.int/resource/docs/convkp/kpeng.pdf, 11 December (accessed 9 February 2012).
6. The eight Millennium Development Goals: (1) Eradicate extreme poverty and hunger, (2) Achieve universal primary education, (3) Promote gender equality and empower women, (4) Reduce child mortality, (5) Improve maternal health, (6) Combat HIV/AIDS, malaria, and other diseases, (7) Ensure environmental sustainability, and (8) Develop a global partnership for development.
7. Practical Action (2009), *Energy Poverty: The Hidden Crisis*, http://practicalaction.org/docs/advocacy/energy_poverty_hidden_crisis.pdf, p. 3 (accessed 9 February 2012).
8. Murray, J. (2010), *Cancun Green Fund to Dominate Global Climate Finance*, Business Green, http://www.businessgreen.com/bg/news/1931989/cancun-green-fund-dominate-global-climate-finance 13 December (accessed 9 February 2012).
9. Bird, N., et al. (2011), *Design Challenges for the Green Climate Fund: Briefing Paper – Climate Finance Policy Briefs*, Overseas Development Institute, http://www.odi.org.uk/resources/download/5256.pdf (accessed 9 February 2012).
10. Gillenwater, M. and S. Seres (2011), *The Clean Development Mechanism: A Review of the First International Offset Program*, Pew Center for Global Climate Change, http://www.pewclimate.org/docUploads/clean-development-mechanism-review-of-first-international-offset-program.pdf, p. 2 (accessed 9 February 2012).

11. Above, n. 2, p. 4.
12. Ibid.
13. *The United Nations Conference on Environment and Development: Framework Convention on Climate Change* (1992), S. Treaty Doc. No. 102-38, 31 I.L.M. 849, http://unfccc.int/resource/docs/convkp/conveng.pdf, 9 May (accessed 9 February 2012). Annex I countries (industrialized countries): Australia, Austria, Belarus, Belgium, Bulgaria, Canada, Croatia, Czech Republic, Denmark, Estonia, Finland, France, Germany, Greece, Hungary, Iceland, Ireland, Italy, Japan, Latvia, Liechtenstein, Lithuania, Luxembourg, Monaco, Netherlands, New Zealand, Norway, Poland, Portugal, Romania, the Russian Federation, Slovakia, Slovenia, Spain, Sweden, Switzerland, Turkey, Ukraine, the United Kingdom, and the United States of America.
14. Fenhann, J. and M. Hinostroza (2011), *CDM Information and Guidebook: Third Edition*, United Nations Environment Programme CD4CDM Project, UNEP Risø Centre on Energy, Climate, & Sustainable Development, http://cd4cdm.org/Publications/cdm_guideline_3rd_edition.pdf, pp. 64–68 (accessed 9 February 2012).
15. Ibid.
16. All six major GHGs can earn CER credits; each credit represents the equivalent of one ton of CO_2 emitted.
17. Although it can be noted that the emergence of the recent Green Climate Fund indicates that the adaptation fund approach has merit, albeit almost 20 years after it was initially proposed by the developing world.
18. Kamel, S. (2007), *Guidebook to Financing CDM Projects,* United Nations Environment Programme, CD4CDM Project, UNEP Risø Centre on Energy, Climate, & Sustainable Development, http://cd4cdm.org/Publications/FinanceCDMprojectsGuidebook.pdf, p. 20 (accessed 9 February 2012).
19. Gunther, M. (2008), *Carbon Finance Comes of Age*, CNN Money, http://money.cnn.com/2008/04/15/technology/Gunther_carbon_finance.fortune/index.htm, 17 April, p. 1 (accessed 9 February 2012).
20. Venema, H. and M. Cisse (2004), *Seeing the Light: Adapting to Climate Change with Decentralized Energy in Developing Countries*, International Institute for Sustainable Development, http://www.iisd.org/cckn/pdf/seeing_the_light_dre.pdf, pp. 11–14 (accessed 9 February 2012).
21. *The Marrakesh Accords* (2001), Report of the Conference of the Parties on its Seventh Session, http://unfccc.int/cop7/documents/accords_draft.pdf, 10 November (accessed 9February 2012).
22. Above, n. 10, p. 29.
23. Each project must establish a clear baseline of anthropomorphic GHG emissions that would occur under a business as usual scenario.
24. Voluntary emission reductions are those not already compelled by national or provincial laws or regulations.
25. Real emissions are those monitored with sufficient care as to insure that they actually occur (in order to prevent false credits).
26. Additional emissions (the requirement of additionality) are ones that are in addition to any that would have occurred absent the CDM subsidy.
27. Leakage of emissions occurs when emission reductions that would have occurred absent the CDM subsidy move to another location because of the subsidy.
28. Wilder, M., et al. (2004), *Legal Issues Guidebook to the Clean Development Mechanism,* United Nations Environment Programme, CD4CDM Project, UNEP Risø Centre on Energy, Climate, & Sustainable Development, http://cd4cdm.org/Publications/CDM%20Legal%20Issues%20Guidebook.pdf, p. 50 (accessed 9 February 2012).
29. LDCs with weak governance and under-developed institutions have had difficulty establishing DNAs. This problem has been a particular challenge for countries on the African continent.
30. DOEs, which are paid for by the project proponent, have conflict of interest issues relating to its potential to aid and abet in the strategic manipulation of baselines – which could lead to issuance of false credits.

31. Wilder, M., et al. (2006), *The Clean Development Mechanism: Special Considerations for Renewable Energy Projects*, Yale-REIL-REEEP Roundtable on Renewable Energy & International Law, Yale University Center for Environmental Law & Policy, http://www.reilproject.org/Publications/REIL_CDM_Paper.pdf, p. 8 (accessed 9 February 2012).
32. For a prospectus on the current CDM reform agenda, see *The CDM Annual Report* (2010), Report to the Conference of the Parties Serving as the Meeting of the Parties to the Kyoto Protocol, Sixth Session, Cancun, Mexico, http://unfccc.int/resource/docs/2010/cmp6/eng/10.pdf, 29 November (accessed 9 February 2012).
33. Ibid., p. 49.
34. See, UNEP Risø CDM/JI Pipeline Analysis and Database – May 2011 Update: http://cdmpipeline.org/ (accessed 9 February 2012).
35. Ibid.
36. The renewable-type projects currently registered include biomass power, landfill gas capture, hydropower, reforestation/afforestation, fossil-fuel switch programs, geothermal power, wind power, and solar power.
37. *See*, UNEP Risø CDM/JI Pipeline Analysis and Database – May 2011 Update: http://cdmpipeline.org/ (accessed 9 February 2012).
38. Godoy, J. (2009), *Wanted – A Truly Clean Development Mechanism*, InterPress Service, http://www.ipsnews.net/news.asp?idnews=46699, 2 May (accessed 9 February 2012); *Indians Make Cool £300 Million in Carbon Farce* (2007), The Sunday Times, http://www.timesonline.co.uk/tol/news/uk/article1687531.ece, 22 April (accessed 9 February 2012).
39. Above, n. 10, pp. 29–31.
40. For an analysis of current CDM projects by type, see UNEP Risø CDM/JI Pipeline Analysis and Database – May 2011 Update: http://cdmpipeline.org/ (accessed 9 February 2012).
41. *The CDM Annual Report* (2010), Report to the Conference of the Parties Serving as the Meeting of the Parties to the Kyoto Protocol, Sixth Session, Cancun, Mexico, http://unfccc.int/resource/docs/2010/cmp6/eng/10.pdf, 29 November (accessed 9 February 2012).
42. Above, n. 10, pp. 30–31.
43. Olhoff, A., et al. (2007), *CDM Sustainable Development Impacts*, United Nations Environment Programme, CD4CDM Project, UNEP Risø Centre on Energy, Climate, & Sustainable Development, http://cd4cdm.org/Publications/CDM%20Sustainable%20Development%20Impacts.pdf, pp. 6–10 (accessed 9 February 2012).
44. van Steenberghe, V., et al. (2005), *Should Developing Countries Participate in the Clean Development Mechanism Under the Kyoto Protocol? The Low-Hanging Fruits and Baseline Issues*, CORE Discussion Paper No. 2005/23, http://ssrn.com/abstract=880384, p. 15 (accessed 9 February 2012).
45. Above, n. 10.
46. The most commonly accepted definition originates from the Brudtland Commission: 'sustainable development is development that meets the needs of the present without compromising the ability of future generations to meet their own needs'.
47. *New CDM Afforestation/Reforestation Projects Approved* (2009), Green Collar, http://greencollarclimate.com.au/news/new-cdm-afforestationreforestation-projects-approved/, 5 April (accessed 9 February 2012).
48. Only 1% of current CDM projects are for LULUCF (land use, land use change, and forestry) project types (as of 15 May, 2011). There are currently a number of LULUCF-related challenges: projects are limited to reforestation and afforestation projects, projects only produce temporary CER credits since carbon sequestered in forests can be re-emitted, and CER credits earned from LULUCF projects are redeemable for only one percent of an Annex I countries emission reductions.
49. *The Nairobi Framework: Capacity for Carbon Market Development in Sub-Saharan Africa – An Inter-Agency Program Proposal* (2006), Report of the Conference of the Parties on its Thirteenth Session, http://cdm.unfccc.int/Nairobi_Framework/NF_partner_agencies.pdf, 17 November (accessed 9 February 2012).
50. Africa Carbon Forum website: http://africacarbonforum.com/2011/english/index.htm (accessed 9 February 2012).

51. Above, n. 14, pp. 40–46.
52. Hinostroza, M, et al. (2009), *A Primer on CDM Programme of Activities*, United Nations Environment Programme CD4CDM Project, UNEP Risø Centre on Energy, Climate & Sustainable Development, http://cd4cdm.org/Publications/PrimerCMDPoA.pdf (accessed 9 February 2012).
53. Ibid., p. 13.
54. Examples of CDM Program of Activity (PoA) projects include programs for increasing energy efficiency in homes, domestic biogas programs, or small-scale fuel switching programs that provide cook stoves in regions currently using unsustainable biomass (fuel-wood) as a primary energy source for cooking. As of May 15, 2011, 86 PoA projects have been registered. *See,* UNEP Risø CDM/JI Pipeline Analysis and Database – May 2011 Update: http://cdmpipeline.org/ (accessed 9 February 2012).
55. *The Bali Action Plan* (2007), Report of the Conference of the Parties on its Thirteenth Session, http://maindb.unfccc.int/library/view_pdf.pl?url=http://unfccc.int/ resource/docs/ 2007/cop13/eng/06a01.pdf, 15 December (accessed 9 February 2012).
56. *The Copenhagen Accords* (2009), Report of the Conference of the Parties on its Fifteenth Session, Draft Decision -/CP.15, http://unfccc.int/resource/docs/2009/cop15/eng/l07.pdf, 18 December (accessed 9 February 2012).
57. *The Cancun Adaptation Framework* (2011), Report of the Conference of the Parties on its Sixteenth Session, http://unfccc.int/resource/docs/2010/cop16/eng/07a01.pdf#page=4, 15 March (accessed 9 February 2012).
58. *CDM Post-2012 Frequently Asked Questions* (2010), Climate Connect, http://www.climate-connect.co.uk/Home/sites/default/files/Post%202012%20FAQs%20CDM.pdf (accessed 9 February 2012).
59. *World Development Report 2010: Development and Climate Change*, The World Bank Group, http://siteresources.worldbank.org/INTWDR2010/Resources/5287678-122601452 7953/WDR10-Full-Text.pdf (accessed 9 February 2012, p. 5.
60. This is particularly a problem regarding the CDM's limited capacity to deal with Africa's use of unsustainable biomass (fuelwood, charcoal, and agricultural and livestock residues) as a primary energy source.
61. Seres, S. (2009), *Analysis of Technology Transfer in CDM Projects*, United Nations Framework Convention on Climate Change, http://cdm.unfccc.int/Reference/Reports/ TTreport/index.html (accessed 9 February 2012).
62. Above, n. 5.
63. *Sustainable Energy for Poverty Reduction: An Action Plan* (2002), Intermediate Technology Development Group, http://www.itdgpublishing.org.uk/docs/advocacy/itdg-greenpeace-study.pdf (accessed 9 February 2012).
64. Ibid.
65. *See,* UNEP Risø CDM/JI Pipeline Analysis and Database – May 2011 Update: http://cdmpipeline.org/ (accessed 9 February 2012).
66. *The Multilateral Fund for the Implementation of the Montreal Protocol* (2007), Secretariat of the Multilateral Fund for the Implementation of the Montreal Protocol, http://www. multilateralfund.org (accessed 9 February 2012).
67. At both the 2009 UNFCCC COP in Copenhagen, Denmark and the 2010 UNFCCC COP in Cancun, Mexico, the development of a robust Green Climate Fund has been progressing. The Copenhagen Accord that was signed at the Copenhagen summit calls for the development of a Green Climate Fund that will facilitate the financing of adaptation and mitigation in the developing world. The 2010 Cancun summit focused on making the Green Climate Fund operational and the success of the 2011 UNFCCC COP in Durban, South Africa will likely be measured in terms of the Fund becoming a reality. The Fund aspires to secure 100 billion US dollars a year by 2020, but the details remain largely undeveloped as of mid-2011.
68. World Bank Group Climate Investment Funds website: http://www.climateinvestmentfunds. org/cif/ (accessed 9 February 2012).
69. Above, n. 57.
70. United Nations Adaptation Fund website: http://www.adaptation-fund.org/ (accessed 9 February 2012).

71. Dupasquier C. and P. Osakwe (2005), *Foreign Direct Investment in Africa: Performance, Challenges, and Responsibilities*, United Nations Economic Commission for Africa, Africa Trade Policy Centre, Working Paper No. 21, http://www.uneca.org/atpc/Work%20in%20progress/21.pdf (accessed 9 February 2012).
72. Above, n. 41.
73. Dechezleprêtre, A., et al. (2007), *The Clean Development Mechanism and the International Diffusion of Technologies: An Empirical Study*, Fondazione Eni Enrico Mattei, Note di Lavoro Series, http://hal.inria.fr/docs/00/39/71/98/PDF/10509.pdf (accessed 15 February 2012).

REFERENCES

Bluemel, E. (2007), 'Biomass Energy: Ensuring Sustainability through Conditioned Economic Incentives', *Georgetown International Law Review*, 19, 673.

Byigero, A., et al. (2010), 'CDM in Sub-Saharan Africa and the Prospects of the Nairobi Framework Initiative', *Climate Policy*, 10, 181.

de Lopez, T., et al. (2009), 'Clean Development Mechanism and Least Developed Countries: Changing the Rules for Greater Participation', *Journal of Environment & Development*, 18, 436.

Ellis, J. and S. Kamel (2007), *Overcoming Barriers to Clean Development Projects*, Organization for Economic Cooperation & Development Report, COM/ENV/EPOC/IEA/SLT(2007)3.

Fenhann, J. and F. Staun (2010), 'An Analysis of Key Issues in the Clean Development Mechanism Based on the UNEP Risø Clean Development Mechanism Pipeline', *Carbon Management*, 1, 65.

Gerrard, M. (2007), *Global Climate Change and U.S. Law*, New York, American Bar Association, Section of Environment, Energy, & Resources.

Laurance, W. (2007), 'A New Initiative to Use Carbon Trading for Tropical Forest Conservation', *Biotropica*, 39.

Lecocq, F. and P. Ambrosi (2007), 'The Clean Development Mechanism: History, Status, and Prospects', *Review of Environmental Economics & Policy*, 1, 134.

Nelson, P. (2004), 'An African Dimension to the Clean Development Mechanism: Finding a Path to Sustainable Development in the Energy Sector', *Denver Journal of International Law & Policy*, 32, 615.

Nygard, J., et al. (2009), *Clean Development Mechanism in China: Ensuring a Sustainable Approach*, Washington D.C.: World Bank Publications.

Schatz, A. (2008), 'Discounting the Clean Development Mechanism', *Georgetown International Environmental Review*, 20, 703.

Subbarao, S. and B. Lloyd (2011), 'Can the Clean Development Mechanism (CDM) Deliver?' *Energy Policy*, 39. 1600.

Sum Low, P. (ed.) (2006), *Climate Change and Africa*, Cambridge: Cambridge University Press.

Timilsina, R., et al. (2010), 'Clean Development Mechanism Potential and Challenges in Sub-Saharan Africa', *Mitigation & Adaption Strategies for Global Change*, 15, 93.

Udombana, N. (2002), 'How Should We Then Live? Globalization and Africa's Development', *Boston University International Law Journal*, 20, 302.

Wara, M. (2007), 'Is the Global Carbon Market Working?' *Nature*, 445, 595.

Wara, M. (2008), 'Measuring the Clean Development Mechanism's Performance and Potential', *UCLA Law Review*, 55, 1759.

Winkelman, A. and M. Moore (2011), 'Explaining the Differential Distribution of Clean Development Mechanism Projects Across Host Countries', *Energy Policy*, 39, 1132.

Wright, D. (2007), *The Clean Development Mechanism*, Saarbrücken, Germany: VDM Verlag Dr. Mueller e.K.

Yasmin, F. (1998), 'The Kyoto Protocol: Origins, Assesment, and Future Changes', *Review of European Community and International Environmental Law*, 7, 113.

14. Poverty and the loss of cultural heritage sites

Stefan Gruber*

14.1 INTRODUCTION

The connections between poverty and environmental degradation are numerous (Klugman, 2002). For example, unsustainable farming practices and overgrazing often cause soil erosion and even desertification. Deforestation destroys whole landscapes to gain arable land, produce firewood or timber for exports. Droughts are worsened by unsustainable water use and the overexploitation of ground water. Overfishing and the use of illegal fishing methods, such as the use of explosives, deplete fishing grounds. The impacts of climate change are likely to exacerbate the situation further as the world's poor are expected to be particularly affected by the related changes in the environment and availability of resources (Brainard et al., 2009). Those effects have in common that environmental resources are depleted beyond a sustainable level, thus exceeding the capacity of the natural environment to maintain ecological and human communities. While poverty often forces communities to overexploit local environmental resources in order to sustain themselves, they also destroy their source of income and that of future generations, which ultimately causes further poverty in addition to the potential collapse of ecosystems and other serious environmental damage. That phenomenon has been called the 'Poverty-Environment Nexus' (Hughes et al., 2009, p. 144ff; Jalal, 1993, p. 9ff; Jehan and Umana, 2003).

This chapter examines how poverty, in addition to the depletion of environmental resources, often further leads to a significant drain on the cultural wealth of societies. The effects of poverty and lack of resources not only cause damages to ecosystems but also in many cases to the human environment. It highlights the links between the loss of cultural heritage sites and poverty and examines how the law can assist in breaking this chain.

In order to analyze those issues adequately, it is necessary to explore an appropriate definition of poverty in this context. To set a minimum of income per day or month that marks the poverty line, as most governments do, is in itself not so meaningful, but gives a useful and sometimes shocking insight into what politicians regard as being 'poor'. Various approaches define poverty inter alia by referring to material needs, economic circumstances, or social relationships (Spicker, 2007, p. 3ff; Bass, et al., 2005, pp. 11, 12). None of those approaches seem to be really satisfying, as all of them appear to miss crucial components. Poor parts of the population are not a homogeneous group and especially when assessing their relationships to the environment, their locations, individual levels of poverty and relevant competing groups are of great importance (Ambler, 1999, p. 5). While an accurate definition of poverty is not the main issue here,[1] it is nevertheless important to bear in mind the many different components of poverty. This chapter focuses on the effects of activities motivated to meet basic needs of the population, consequences from inequality, such as pressure from wealthier on poorer parties, lack of resources to maintain heritage structures, and impacts of non-monetary poverty.

14.2 EFFECTS OF POVERTY AND THE LOSS OF CULTURAL HERITAGE SITES

Cultural and natural heritage share a range of similarities, which are reflected in the concepts behind the Convention concerning the Protection of the World Cultural and Natural Heritage (World Heritage Convention) of 1972.[2] While formally defining cultural and natural heritage separately, the World Heritage Convention nevertheless treats them equally and lists a range of heritage sites for both their cultural and natural values.[3] Cultural and natural heritage have in common that they are non-renewable resources, and many approaches and mechanisms for their protection are similar. Some heritage structures can be reconstructed after their destruction, but this will in many cases inevitably lead to the loss of their integrity and authenticity. Both features are very important for the concept of cultural heritage,[4] which plays an important part in manifesting the diversity among states, ethnic communities, and other culturally distinct groups (Francioni, 2004, p. 1210). Of further importance in that context is the connection between tangible and intangible cultural heritage, as acknowledged by the Convention for the Safeguarding of the Intangible Cultural Heritage (Intangible Cultural Heritage Convention) of 2003.[5] That applies inter alia to intangible features and cultural spaces associated therewith[6] which is of particular significance in the context of inhabited heritage properties where the local population forms part of the site.

Cultural and natural heritage sites represent vital elements of the human environment. The interaction between human communities and those sites contribute to the collective memory of humankind, help in understanding its diversity, and assist in ensuring the survival of cultural identities and traditions (Boer and Gruber, 2012). The cultural and natural aspects of heritage sites are often impossible to separate, as, on the one hand, humankind is a part of nature and on the other, human cultural artefacts, as expressed in building materials, structures, and personal property such as artworks, are drawn from, shaped by or influenced by the natural environment. Recognizing the integrated nature of these cultural and natural elements and granting them legal protection contributes to the richness of human societies. While this chapter focuses primarily on the legal and policy links between protection of the cultural environment and human poverty, the natural foundation of much of the cultural environment should not be forgotten.

The effects of poverty on cultural heritage sites are very diverse. They reach from problems created by the lack of resources for management, preservation works, and proper protection against intentional destruction, gentrification and the destruction of old city centres, to urbanization and the loss of cultural landscapes and cohesion of rural communities.

14.2.1 Lack of Resources and Management Problems

Difficulties with conserving heritage sites due to lack of funds and resources are not only a problem of individuals, but especially of governments and local authorities. Despite poverty conditions, many regions are often significantly rich in heritage sites. One of their most severe problems is the lack of staff, funds, and specialist training.

While facing numerous other challenges related to development, authorities in many regions do not have the means to assign sufficient personnel to heritage protection.[7] Various sites remain unrecognized or unregistered, and thus excluded from any protection measures. Even if funds are available, there are often insufficient personnel to carry out surveys and expeditions in more remote areas. This applies for example to the prehistoric rock paintings in Namibia, which have been significantly damaged by vandals, or by hikers who use the sites as shelters and light fires overnight for warmth and cooking.[8] Other examples are found in China, with its vastness, its sheer number of heritage sites, and their often remote locations (Gruber, 2007, p. 283). When heritage sites are discovered in remote locations, it is difficult to implement effective protection measures without sufficient resources being available (He, 2000).

Identification of sites and implementation of comprehensive protection measures are often also difficult because of inadequate staff education. Many staff in poor or remote regions have not had the benefit of higher education, nor do they have any relevant education in their areas of work (He, 2000). Identification and conservation of heritage sites are highly specialized tasks, which cannot be adequately carried out without the necessary expertise. Heritage sites must be dated, put in historical context and, most of all, recognized as being of heritage value. Only after those tasks are carried out reliably can decisions be made about the most suitable protection methods and conservation techniques. The decision making and carrying out of necessary works are not possible without proper education and training.

Inappropriate conservation works constitute another serious threat to heritage structures as they can harm them permanently (Stille, 2002, p. 67ff). Building materials and structural techniques that were used centuries ago differ significantly from today. Much of the specific knowledge of the original architects and artists has been lost, and even if it can be researched, long and intense training is required to master the techniques that were originally used. Due to lack of funds, many restoration works are carried out by using industrial-quality paint and concrete as those materials are not only cheaper, but also decrease the cost of labour and do not require highly developed technical skills.

In addition to staff training, it is equally important to educate the population in heritage-rich areas. It is essential to convince them of the value of their heritage sites and the necessity of their protection. By involving the locals and fostering their pride in their heritage, the best long-term results can be achieved, as their support is indispensable. The most effective protection can be generated if they recognize heritage as being part of their own cultural wealth. Furthermore, destruction of heritage is more likely to be reported and pressure by the community might be put on offenders in order to stop their activities. Support from the local community is especially important regarding the identification of heritage sites in remote areas because they are not only often aware of their existence and locations, but they can also easily access the sites. However, they often lack the necessary expertise to identify sites as heritage and be aware of their importance.

14.2.2 Deliberate Destruction of Heritage Sites

Deliberate destruction poses another serious threat to cultural heritage sites. Some of those cases are also connected to insufficient numbers of personnel and funds. This applies especially to cases where local development projects threaten heritage structures. As many threats remain undiscovered until it is too late, protection measures can rarely be taken in advance. In some cases, lack of monitoring is exploited by construction companies, which tear down heritage structures before heritage protection agencies learn of those activities. Once the structures are destroyed, the development can often be carried out with no further obstruction. Sometimes the local authorities even tolerate such actions because they are dependent on the development companies' investments and contributions of local government taxes in their municipalities for building projects (Gruber, 2007, pp. 282–283).

In some cases, heritage sites are even used as supplies for building material, which still occurs, for example, with sections of the Great Wall. Farmers have destroyed some sections to gain building materials for local construction companies as this saves them transportation charges.[9] Another well-known example of such practice is the Colosseum in Rome, one of the undisputed masterpieces of Ancient Roman architecture and nowadays one of Italy's most famous tourist attractions. However, large parts of the Colosseum have been torn down over several centuries when it was used as a quarry for the construction of new buildings until Pope Benedict XIV declared it a sacred site in 1749 and prohibited any further destruction (Hopkins and Beard, 2005).

Many government officials, lawyers, and citizens lack the necessary knowledge of heritage protection law and sometimes even awareness of wrongdoing regarding the destruction of heritage structures. Besides strengthening legal protection mechanisms, it is crucial to provide training to and raise awareness among, judges, prosecutors, and government officials, while communicating relevant laws among locals in areas with many heritage sites. Furthermore, prosecutions of offenders should be circulated in such regions to make the locals more sensitive to the importance of heritage protection provisions and to the seriousness of related offences (Gruber, 2007, p. 295).

14.2.3 World Heritage Convention

Of all international legal instruments to assist states in protecting their cultural and natural heritage sites, the World Heritage Convention is the most important one. It seeks to establish 'a system of international co-operation and assistance designed to support States Parties to the Convention in their efforts to conserve and identify that heritage'.[10] The World Heritage Convention defines cultural heritage as monuments, groups of buildings and sites which are of outstanding universal value[11] from the point of view of history, art, or science.[12] Maintaining the integrity of that outstanding universal value and identifying such sites are the key obligations of the States Parties under the Convention.[13] After being identified and nominated by the State Party in control, appropriate heritage sites may be inscribed on the World Heritage List[14] by the World Heritage Committee.[15]

The World Heritage Convention recognizes specific threats from poverty, noting that 'cultural heritage and the natural heritage are increasingly threatened with destruction not only by the traditional causes of decay, but also by changing social and economic conditions which aggravate the situation with even more formidable phenomena of damage or destruction'.[16] This applies equally to threats created by the lack of funds, economic despair, impacts from social inequality, and rapid social changes that leave parts of the population destitute.

Although it provides no specific enforcement mechanism, the World Heritage Convention leaves no doubt concerning the obligations of the States Parties:[17]

> Each State Party to this Convention recognizes that the duty of ensuring the identification, protection, conservation, presentation and transmission to future generations of the cultural and natural heritage referred to in Articles 1 and 2 and situated on its territory, belongs primarily to that State. It will do all it can to this end, to the utmost of its own resources and, where appropriate, with any international assistance and co-operation, in particular, financial, artistic, scientific and technical, which it may be able to obtain.

The duty to protect heritage of outstanding universal value does not depend on its actual inscription on the World Heritage List. States Parties are also obliged to protect properties of outstanding universal value, which may have been identified, but have not yet been nominated for inscription. They are also required to create tentative lists of sites for possible future nominations for inscription.[18] Thus the 'outstanding universal value' required by the Convention does not flow from any inscription as such, which is why even a refusal by the World Heritage Committee does not lower the importance of the site once a State Party has identified that value.[19] However, the State Party is eligible for international assistance under the Convention once the property is listed.

That provision is probably the most relevant in relation to poverty-related threats, as States Parties can request international assistance[20] if they cannot adequately protect their World Heritage properties themselves. In such cases, other States Parties are expected to help with the identification, protection, conservation and presentation of the cultural and natural heritage if the States Parties on whose territory it is situated so request.[21] The World Heritage Fund[22] established by the Convention can provide assistance for staff training, studies, and supply of equipment and experts concerning the artistic, scientific and technical problems raised by the identification, protection, conservation, presentation and rehabilitation of World Heritage.[23] Funds can also be provided as low-interest or interest-free loans or in very exceptional cases as non-repayable subsidies. However, only a part of the funds needed shall be provided by the international community as the State Party concerned is expected to contribute as much as it can unless its resources are not sufficient.[24]

Apart from providing monetary, logistical, and scientific support to countries that lack the necessary funds, the World Heritage Committee has two options to address threats to World Heritage properties. In the case of a very serious threat, it may decide to either inscribe the property on the List of World Heritage Sites in Danger[25] or, if the damage already done proves to be too serious, to delete the site from the World Heritage List entirely.[26] The List of World Heritage in Danger includes World Heritage Sites that are 'threatened by serious and specific dangers'[27] for which assistance has been requested. Such a request does not necessarily have to come from the State Party itself (Vrdoljak, 2008, p. 228). The in-danger listing may even be undertaken without the consent of the State Party (Boer, 2008, pp. 100–101).[28] In any case, the State Party is obliged to cooperate and meet all requests of the World Heritage Committee once a plan of immediate measures has been drawn up.

One case where inscriptions on the World Heritage List and the List of World Heritage in Danger took place at the same time was the protection of Angkor in Cambodia.[29] The Angkor Archaeological Park stretches over some 400 square kilometres and contains the remains of several capitals of the Khmer Empire from the ninth to the fifteenth century.[30] The sites include the Temples of Angkor Wat and the Bayon Temple, as well as numerous other temples and monuments. All Angkor sites have suffered severely from looting, abandonment, and armed conflict over many years. Until recently, Cambodia had not been able either logistically or financially to secure the conservation of those sites and it was obvious that it needed decisive international support to secure their survival.

Because of the unique situation in Cambodia at that time, the World Heritage Committee decided to waive some of the procedural requirements for the inclusion of new World Heritage sites in order to secure an enhanced protection of the temples as quickly as possible, while stressing that the actions were not to be taken as a precedent for future nomination processes. This is why the Committee decided to conduct in-depth studies over three years to decide after that period if Angkor should remain on the World Heritage List. On the recommendation of ICOMOS[31] the Committee requested the Cambodian authorities to take specific actions in order to improve the situation promptly, including the enactment of adequate protective legislation, the establishment of an effective national protection agency, the creation of adequate boundaries and buffer zones, and the coordination and monitoring of the conservation initiatives.

The Cambodian efforts led to the establishment of the Authority for the Protection and Management of Angkor and the Region of Siem Reap (APSARA).[32] Its areas of responsibility focus on the protection of the monuments and buffer zones, the coordination of any projects related to the sites of Angkor, funding and financing activities, and efforts to reduce local poverty. The decisive international assistance from UNESCO and individual States Parties proved to be successful and also included several engineering and reconstruction projects. After the situation improved significantly, Angkor was removed from the List of World Heritage in Danger in 2004,[33] although issues of protection of both the monuments themselves and their associated intangible heritage remain.

14.3 THE EFFECTS OF GENTRIFICATION

The protection of heritage sites that are inhabited and form part of peoples' daily lives poses a very different set of challenges. Cultural heritage sites are not necessarily archaeological sites, but are often part of communal life. When people form part of heritage sites, the protection of those sites proves to be even more complicated. In such cases, it is the interaction between such sites and the local population that makes them so precious.

The main threat to such sites, apart from the lack of funds and availability of experts for their preservation, is posed by significant economic inequality within societies. Such inequality often leads to gentrification, when new residents from a higher social class with better incomes replace the poorer original residents of an area. Without the original inhabitants the sites often lose a significant part of their integrity.

14.3.1 Demolition of Old City Centres

One of the most serious issues related to gentrification is the destruction of old city centres and the removal of their inhabitants. The most prominent example is the still ongoing destruction of the Hutongs in Beijing, which consist of narrow alleyways and courtyard houses. They were built around the Forbidden City during the Yuan, Ming, and Qing Dynasties. Though they are regarded as the 'heart of Beijing', their area has been significantly cut down despite numerous activities for their conservation by several non-governmental organizations.[34] Support came from the World Heritage Committee, which noted that the destruction of the Hutongs might have an impact on Beijing's World Heritage sites, and recommended their protection as buffer zones.[35]

However, development pressure has proved to be too strong over the past decade, and most parts of the Hutong areas have been destroyed and replaced by uniform housing projects. Quarters that used to host numerous Chinese teahouses, theatres, and traditional shops now consist of similar-looking shopping malls and office buildings.

Despite a protection plan by the Beijing municipal government from 2002 to protect 25 historic areas, the demolition mostly continued. It is planned to develop some of those areas in a traditional style, but once the original buildings are replaced, their originality and integrity cannot be recovered. Even the quarters that will be spared demolition face serious threats. As the houses were built over the last few centuries, they often lack water pipes, toilets, and heating systems. To install them afterwards is not only expensive, but also often has a significant impact on the building substance and its integrity (Gruber, 2007, p. 280).

Those developments are accompanied by the process of gentrification, and the original residents are pushed to poorer outskirts away from the city centres as a result. Especially now that some of the surviving Hutongs have been renovated and upgraded, they are becoming status symbols for China's growing upper class and wealthy investors.[36] In many cases, residents are offered only insufficient compensation by developers to afford to move and are left in half-demolished areas.[37] Many old residents have even been evicted by force with only little compensation[38] though the situation seems to have slightly improved recently. Many of the houses have been occupied by the same families for several generations, but once the inhabitants are forced to leave, they usually cannot even afford to stay in that part of the city with the little compensation that they are paid. That applies not only to new housing but also to renovated Hutongs in areas where houses have not been torn down. Renovated Hutongs which used to house large families of different generations who took part in the quarter's life are often inhabited afterwards by only one wealthy couple or a nuclear family and transformed from an open house into an enclosed area. After that kind of transformation, the house is virtually lost for the quarter's community.

With the eviction of the original inhabitants not only the character of those quarters is lost, but a whole way of living dies as well. Old traditions and communal life are no longer present when the original residents are replaced. The Hutongs and the associated culture are unique (Meyer, 2008). The inhabitants of such old quarters are part of the area's heritage and as they are forced to move away, the quarter loses its soul. The majority of the residents are very aware of the fact that they are living in a neighbourhood worthy of heritage protection and have a clear idea of the responsibility of the government to protect the Hutongs.[39] However, they themselves do not figure in the official preservation plans.

Apart from Beijing's Hutongs there are of course many other examples of cities where urban heritage is increasingly threatened by gentrification, such as Kyoto, Shanghai, and even a number of American cities (Atkinson and Bridge, 2005). Conserving and restoring old city centres while keeping the original inhabitants in place is easier in cities where the property market is less robust. In Lebanon's West Bank, for example, several city centres are being restored by the Lebanese authorities with the assistance of the United Nations Development Programme (UNDP).[40] Historic buildings are upgraded, repaired, and rebuilt where damaged. After the works are completed, the families who own the buildings either move back in or they rent the buildings to other local families with the authorities acting as agents.

Apart from enacting protection plans and related heritage conservation provisions, it is crucial to ensure the acknowledgment of existing property rights and the right to remain resident. The law and existing rights of people must not be sacrificed for short-sighted development projects. If the authorities and courts do not protect the property rights of owners and residents, they lose a significant part of their legitimacy. Furthermore, regulations that only focus on structures without including the residents are pointless, as they miss a crucial part of the issue. The original way of living in city quarters is as much part of a city's heritage as the traditional inhabitants and the buildings that they inhabit. Effective protection plans therefore have to include provisions that ensure the support of the original owners of buildings and the inhabitants that form an active part of the city's cultural life. Considerations of social impact and equity must be compulsory components of any development regulations and impact assessments. Once the original population is replaced through gentrification, the process is irreversible.

14.3.2 Competition with Internal Migrants

Cultural heritage is also under threat where established communities are faced with competition from richer internal migrants. Minorities are especially affected by such developments.

For example, after the ancient town of Lijiang in the Yunnan Province was inscribed on the World Heritage List in 1997 as 'an exceptional ancient town set in a dramatic landscape which represents the harmonious fusion of different cultural traditions to produce an urban landscape of outstanding quality',[41] its popularity as a tourist destination increased drastically. However, the increasing number of tourists brought not only many positive developments for the local population (Su and Teo, 2009), but also attracted numerous merchants and internal migrants from other provinces, which quickly turned the central square of the town from a place for daily life into a tourist market.[42] The traditional life of the local Naxi people was deeply disturbed by those developments, which threatens some of the very features for which Lijiang has been inscribed on the World Heritage List. The former functioning economic system of this area was also challenged as the local population could not compete with the newly arrived merchants. The number of the original residents began to drop dramatically until a large number was replaced by people from other areas. Most of the originality of the former communal life in that ancient city was lost due to those massive social transformations.[43]

Similar developments can be witnessed in Hoi An in Vietnam, which was inscribed on the World Heritage List in 1999.[44] A study under the umbrella of UNESCO Bangkok from 2008 reported that the World Heritage label of Hoi An led to such an increase in the price of land that the purchase of property is now hardly affordable to any local residents. The old quarter of the town has lost many of its original residents while properties have been bought up by wealthy investors from Hanoi, Ho Chi Minh City and Da Nang and transformed for tourism purposes. Many of the often poor fishing households have been removed from the beaches and dune land around Hoi An – in many cases without appropriate compensation – to create space for resort and hotel development (Hoi An Centre for Monuments Managements and Preservation, 2008, p. 57).

Another example on a larger scale is the situation in Tibet and especially its capital, Lhasa. Due to a constant stream of largely Han Chinese migrants from other provinces of China, they have come to be in control of most of the key businesses and other important economic matters. Tibetans thus find it more difficult to find higher employment in Lhasa unless they speak Chinese.[45] It is becoming obvious that the Tibetans cannot compete with the Han Chinese migrants in economic terms, partly because all key positions in the local government are occupied by Han Chinese. This has also left its mark on the appearance of the city. Many traditional Tibetan quarters and squares have been redeveloped, while the drain of Tibetan cultural heritage is becoming more and more evident (Nyimaa, 2008) despite the efforts of the Chinese authorities to protect Tibet's culture.[46] That development is accelerated by the high-speed Qinghai Tibet Railway to Lhasa which is expected to carry even more internal migrants, in addition to Chinese and foreign tourists, to Tibet than ever before.

The only way to reduce impacts such as those mentioned is by regulating the migration into communities that exist mainly independently and cannot compete economically with internal migrants. Restrictions can range from regulating influx to controlling any movement of visitors. For example, in Australia, permits are required to enter specified Aboriginal areas which cover a considerable part of several regions.[47] Impacts on Aboriginal communal life from outside are sought to be limited to a minimum through these means. However, such restrictions are suitable only for a very limited number of cases where the local community has to be protected from external impacts. Generally, less strict regulations are desirable, but where restricted access is seen to be appropriate, regulations often do not exist at all.

Heritage protection regulations in historic cities and minority areas should include provisions for the protection of the inhabitants as well as for heritage structures. This applies especially to cases where existing communal structures are threatened by business operations from other regions. If poorly regulated, tourism sometimes not only provides new sources of income for local communities, but it can also disturb formerly functioning local economic systems. Such small economic systems as the one in Lijiang are very sensitive to social transformations within the community (Gruber, 2007, p. 286). However, related effects can be reduced by controlling internal migration and limiting the numbers of migrants. Internal migration could be further managed by focusing on skilled migration which allows people to settle within the community only if they have skills or a business that is of advantage to the area. Furthermore, influx should be controlled in areas of minorities in order to not jeopardize the cultural integrity of the community.

14.4 CULTURAL LANDSCAPES AND URBANIZATION

Another development proving to be destructive to cultural heritage sites is urbanization.[48] Urbanization is often fuelled by poverty, as 'cities concentrate poverty, but they also represent the best hope of escaping it'.[49] Since 2008, for the first time in human history, more than half of the world's population is living in urban areas, with the process of urbanization constantly accelerating.[50]

Urbanization is especially a threat to cultural landscapes which, according to the Operational Guidelines for the Implementation of the World Heritage Convention (Operational Guidelines), are the 'combined works of nature and of man … They are illustrative of the evolution of human society and settlement over time, under the influence of the physical constraints and/or opportunities presented by their natural environment and of successive social, economic and cultural forces, both external and internal'.[51] Though there are several categories of cultural landscapes[52] this chapter only refers to rural landscapes that were physically transformed by human activity (Head, 2000, p.13) in order to gain control over ecological processes to cultivate the land (Müller, 1997, p.333).

The population of rural areas often needed to develop specific techniques and talents in order to adapt to the local ecological conditions and to enable cultivation. This resulted in the development of highly specialized skills and a very close relationship between the people and their environment (Müller, 1997, p. 15). This applies, *inter alia*, to many of Asia's terraced landscapes, which were created to gain arable land and to enable rice growing and other agriculture.[53] For example, major parts of China consist of mountainous areas, which are difficult to cultivate and scarcely provide enough food to sustain the population. The local people have managed to survive in many of those areas only by transforming the landscape to meet their needs. Resources always had to be used as effectively as possible to sustain the communities, because arable land was and is still rare and valuable in China. Over generations, the local farmers discovered the best ways to cultivate their local paddocks, including companion planting, which created very individual ecological habitats (Müller, 1997, p. 336). Those habitats also attract diverse animal species that only exist in their proximity and became a significant part of the areas' biodiversity.

This interdependence often creates a strong bond between the population and the landscape. However, the local population must constantly maintain the landscape in order to conserve flora and fauna, prevent soil erosion and secure ecological stability. Without constant field work and preservation measures, cultural landscapes can be lost in a short time, which has a severe impact on both the local ecology and the cultural heritage of the region

(Gruber, 2007, p. 287ff.). This also applies to the strong regionalization of rural architecture and the customs and similar intangible heritage of the local residents in remote areas, which determines the cultural identity of the local population and has spawned an enormous cultural diversity (Müller, 1999, p. 222).

One of the areas where a specifically important set of cultural landscapes is threatened is the Rice Terraces of the Philippine Cordilleras which are located in Ifugao province and consist of the Hungduan and central Mayoyao terrace clusters, the Nagacadan terrace cluster of Kiangan, and the Bangaan and Batad terrace clusters in the municipality of Banaue. The terraces are around 2000 years old and are situated between 700 m and 1500 m above sea level.[54] The terraces were inscribed on the World Heritage List in 1995 as an outstanding example of living cultural landscapes which 'illustrate the traditional techniques and a remarkable harmony between humankind and the natural environment'.[55]

One of the reasons for the inscription of the Rice Terraces of the Philippine Cordilleras on the World Heritage List is that they are illustrative of an extraordinary continuity and persistence of cultural traditions as the applied farming and conservation techniques remained nearly unchanged for 2000 years. The conservation culture of the local farmers 'evolved through centuries of trial and error' as they 'continuously responded to the ever-changing challenges over time' (Save the Ifugao Terraces Movement, 2008, p. 16). The World Heritage Committee states that '[m]aintenance of the living rice terraces reflects a primarily cooperative approach of the whole community which is based on detailed knowledge of the rich diversity of biological resources existing in the Ifugao agro-ecosystem, a finely tuned annual system respecting lunar cycles, zoning and planning, extensive soil conservation, and mastery of a most complex pest control regime based on the processing of a variety of herbs, accompanied by religious rituals.'[56] The interaction of tangible and intangible heritage in this case is further reflected by the inscription of the Hudhud Chants of the Ifugao on the Representative List of the Intangible Cultural Heritage of Humanity in 2008 which are, *inter alia*, practiced during the rice sowing season and harvest time.[57]

Sadly, this remarkable landscape is now regarded as severely threatened and has been inscribed on the List of World Heritage in Danger since 2001.[58] The main threat comes from the decline of the numbers of local farmers as their constant maintenance work and knowledge is crucial to the preservation of the Rice Terraces. Poverty and lack of prospects are increasingly leaving their marks on this cultural landscape. Many of the younger people in the region do not see a sustainable future in farming, leave the area and move to a city in order to seek higher-paid jobs somewhere else. Ironically, even the hospitality industry in that major tourist destination, which relies heavily on the terraces, is causing a continuous drain on the numbers of young local farmers. As a result of the lack of maintenance work, the steps of the terraces have begun to erode and the complex ecosystem is out of balance.

Urbanization and the exodus of people from rural communities exact a heavy toll on cultural landscapes all around the world. That development is additionally fuelled by commercialization and economic influences on rural areas by the expansion of metropolitan areas, which have serious impacts on fragile rural economies (Gruber, 2007, p. 287). Poverty and inequality force more and more people to leave the area of their forebears and to give up significant parts of their heritage. When farmers leave their home areas in order to find other means to support their families, it often also weakens the regional communities. This applies even more to minorities, as they usually live in homogenous groups. If minorities merge into metropolitan areas, their traditions and ways of living can hardly survive. The percentage of the rural population has been declining over the last few years, which is a development that especially applies to Eastern Asia (Forbes and Lindfield, 1997, p. 12ff.). Once they leave their home areas, rural-urban migrants often become part of the growing urban poor and are used as a cheap labour force.[59]

In order to provide effective protection of cultural landscapes, it must be realized that the local population is often a part of the landscape itself. The Operational Guidelines state that the concept of cultural landscapes 'embraces a diversity of manifestations of the interaction between humankind and its natural environment'.[60] This means that the landscape is as dependent on the local population as the local population is dependent on the landscape. When the close relationship of the people with the landscape and their knowledge gathered by their forebears over many centuries fades, not only a significant part of their intangible heritage will be lost, but the tangible heritage is also jeopardized. Consequently, the Save the Ifugao Terraces Movement argues that the sustainable management of the Ifugao Rice Terraces is all about safeguarding a conservation culture which 'existence depends heavily on the survival of the living repositories of indigenous knowledge'. Safeguarding and sustaining that culture and knowledge resources means 'sustaining the well-being of the direct managers of the landscape' (Save the Ifugao Terraces Movement, 2008, p. 16).

Conserving cultural landscapes is a difficult task as they not only require protection against environmental degradation and development pressure, but the local population must also be in a position to sustain themselves without being in significant economic disadvantage to other parts of the country. Laws that only regulate the availability of a specific amount of arable land often prove to be ineffective in this context. It is not sufficient to designate areas as farmland without ensuring the survival of the local communities. Therefore, land use laws and resources laws, among others, must ensure sustainable access to resources and reduce competition. Further, it is crucial to minimize development pressure in heritage-rich cultural landscapes. This could be done by establishing large and connected protected areas with buffer zones and migration corridors for wildlife. Finally, it must be recognized that local populations regularly form part of cultural landscapes and must therefore be included in relevant management plans by cultural heritage conservation regulations. Ecosystems and the human population often benefit from the same protection measures, such as the prevention of further soil degradation, sustainable use of resources, and the protection of water supplies (Munasinghe and Swart, 2005, p. 242).

Our understanding of heritage conservation law must be expanded to meet those challenges in an effective way while applying regulatory instruments from other areas in an integrated fashion. Relevant provisions include inter alia land use, water, and environmental impact assessment regulations. In some cases even economic regulations can be utilized as part of heritage law when they contribute to the support of people in heritage-rich landscapes. Supporting the indigenous populations is an important aspect of securing the survival of cultural landscapes. This is even more necessary when new anthropogenic threats emerge or environmental factors such as climate change place additional stresses on them (Gruber, 2011). If agricultural production further declines because of climate change, whole cultural landscapes could be lost in remote areas that are difficult to cultivate. A slight change of temperature, rainfall or extreme weather events can permanently harm those ecosystems and make agriculture more difficult. If the fields can no longer sustain the local farmers, they will be forced to abandon those areas, which would inevitably mean the end of those ecosystems.

One of the possible ways of assisting such communities is to help them with developing additional ways to create income. Further activities might include the introduction of enhanced land and resource management and the development of pricing and marketing policies to reduce economic inequality. A crucial component of that approach must be considerations of social impact and equity.

14.5 CONCLUSION

Poverty contributes to the loss of cultural heritage sites in many ways. This applies not only to cases where authorities lack funds and staff for their conservation, but especially to all situations where people interact with heritage sites in their daily lives. Whenever people are forced by poverty or economic pressure to leave their homes, their exodus has a significant impact on their areas and the remaining parts of their communities.

In order to break the link between poverty and the destruction of heritage sites, far-reaching actions are needed. First of all, they must include the strengthening of heritage protection agencies and the introduction of more extensive protection schemes and provisions. International assistance by wealthier nations and stronger solidarity are also essential components of that process. Furthermore, education of staff and private persons promises long-term results as their knowledge can be used in further training and make protection measures much more effective. The same applies to specialized training for prosecutors and judges, and an increased distribution of relevant regulations.

In addition, new concepts are needed for the protection of rural cultural landscapes and other inhabited heritage sites. Impact assessments must include considerations of equity and social impact. Existing inhabitants must be included and involved in protection plans and should be seen as part of the sites rather than as potentially disruptive elements, while acknowledging their property rights and rights to remain resident. Furthermore, legal provisions from different areas of law must be used in a holistic way to enhance the protection of heritage and decrease poverty.

By fighting poverty, the task of conserving cultural heritage becomes much easier. When people are not forced to act out of economic despair, they are far more receptive to the concept of heritage conservation. Ultimately, cultural poverty can be as devastating to a nation as monetary poverty because culture is the connecting link within all societies.

NOTES

* The author would like to thank Emeritus Professor Ben Boer for his invaluable comments and generous assistance in the revision of this chapter.

1. Overviews to that debate can be found in Spicker (2007) and the various essays in S. Jenkins and J. Micklewright (2007), *Inequality and Poverty Re-Examined*, Oxford: Oxford University Press.
2. Convention concerning the Protection of the World Cultural and Natural Heritage, opened for signature 16 November 1972, 1037 UNTS 151 (entered into force 17 December 1975). See http://whc.unesco.org/archive/convention-en.pdf (accessed 10 February 2012).
3. Besides 704 cultural and 180 natural properties, there are also 27 mixed cultural / natural properties among the 151 States Parties inscribed on the World Heritage List. The World Heritage List can be accessed at http://whc.unesco.org/en/list (accessed 10 February 2012).
4. The importance of authenticity and integrity is underlined by the Operational Guidelines for the Implementation of the World Heritage Convention (Operational Guidelines), UNESCO Doc WHC. 08/01 (January 2008), paras. 78–95.
5. Convention on the Safeguarding of the Intangible Heritage, opened for signature 3 November 2003, 2368 UNTS 1 (entered into force 20 April 2006). See http://portal.unesco.org/en/ev.php-URL_ID=17716&URL_DO=DO_TOPIC&URL_SECTION=201.html (accessed 10 February 2012).
6. Ibid., Art. 1.
7. Ringa, M. (2009), 'Heritage of Alms – Sad Plight of Sub-Saharan States', *AllAfrica*, 12 October 2009 http://allafrica.com/stories/200910120117.html (accessed 10 February 2012).

8. See the national report on Namibia in ICOMOS (2003), *Heritage at Risk: ICOMOS World Report 2002/03 on Monuments and Sites in Danger*, http://www.international.icomos.org/risk/2002/namibia2002.htm (accessed 10 February 2012).
9. 'China's Great Wall under Threat', *Daily Times*, 13 September 2004 http://www.dailytimes.com.pk/default.asp?page=story_13–9–2004_pg9_1 (accessed 10 February 2012).
10. World Heritage Convention, above, n. 2, Art. 7.
11. The term 'outstanding universal value' is defined in Operational Guidelines, above, n. 4, paras. 49–53.
12. World Heritage Convention, above, n. 2, Art. 1.
13. Ibid., Arts. 4, 5.
14. Ibid., Art. 11(2).
15. Ibid., Art. 8.
16. Ibid., Preamble.
17. Ibid., Art. 4.
18. See Operational Guidelines, above, n. 4, paras. 62–76.
19. *State of Queensland v. Commonwealth of Australia* (1989) 167 CLR 232.
20. World Heritage Convention, above, n. 2, Arts. 19–26.
21. Ibid., Art. 6(2).
22. Ibid., Arts. 15–18.
23. Ibid., Art. 22.
24. Ibid., Art.25; Operational Guidelines, above, n. 4, para. 233.
25. World Heritage Convention, above, n. 2, Art. 11(4); see also Operational Guidelines, above, n. 4, paras. 177–191.
26. This has happened only twice to date. In an unprecedented decision the World Heritage Committee deleted the Arabian Oryx Sanctuary in Oman from the World Heritage List after the State Party planned to reduce the Sanctuary by 90%. The World Heritage Committee was 'convinced that as a result of the reduction of the Sanctuary under Omani Law, the property has deteriorated to the extent that it has lost its Outstanding Universal Value and Integrity'. See World Heritage Committee (2007), *Decisions Adopted at the 31st Session of the World Heritage Committee (Christchurch, 2007)*, UNESCO Doc WHC-07/31.COM/24, Decision 31COM 7B.11. The second site was the Dresden Elbe Valley in Germany. The property had been inscribed on the List of World Heritage in Danger since 2006 after the local government decided to build a four-lane bridge across the river valley, spoiling the cultural landscape's original features of outstanding universal value. After continuous appeals by the World Heritage Committee remained ignored, the site was delisted in 2009. See World Heritage Committee (2009), *Final Decisions of the 33rd Session of the World Heritage Committee (Seville, 2009)*, UNESCO Doc WHC-09/33.COM/20, Decision 33COM 7A.26.
27. World Heritage Convention, above, n. 2, Art. 11(4) mentions several examples, such as 'the threat of disappearance caused by accelerated deterioration, large-scale public or private projects or rapid urban or tourist development projects; destruction caused by changes in the use or ownership of the land; major alterations due to unknown causes; abandonment for any reason whatsoever; the outbreak or the threat of an armed conflict; calamities and cataclysms; serious fires, earthquakes, landslides; volcanic eruptions; changes in water level, floods and tidal waves'.
28. Ibid., Art. 11 (4) states that 'the Committee may at any time, in case of urgent need, make a new entry in the List of World Heritage in Danger and publicize such entry immediately'.
29. See World Heritage Committee (1992), *Report of the Rapporteur of the 16th Session (Santa Fe, United States of America, 7–14 December 1992)*, UNESCO Doc WHC-92/CONF.002/12, Decisions 16COM X.A, 16COM X.E.
30. Details on the World Heritage site of Angkor are available at http://whc.unesco.org/en/list/668 (accessed 10 February 2012).
31. International Council on Monuments and Sites.
32. For further information, see http://www.autoriteapsara.org (accessed 10 February 2012).
33. See World Heritage Committee (2004), *Decisions Adopted at the 28th Session of the World Heritage Committee (Suzhou, 2004)*, UNESCO Doc WHC-04/28 COM/26, Decisions 28COM 15A.23.

34. See for example the activities of the project *Friends of Old Beijing* under the umbrella of the *Beijing Cultural Heritage Protection Center*. Further information can be found at http://en.bjchp.org/?page_id=275 (accessed 10 February 2012).
35. World Heritage Committee (2003), *Decisions Adopted by the 27th Session of the World Heritage Committee in 2003*, UNESCO Doc WHC-03/27.COM/24, Decision 27COM 7B.43; World Heritage Committee (2004), *State of Conservation of Properties Inscribed on the World Heritage List*, UNESCO Doc WHC-04/28.COM/15B, Report 54; World Heritage Committee, above, n. 34, Decisions 28COM 14B.30, 28COM 15B.54.
36. Ouroussoff, N. (2008), 'Lost in the New Beijing: The Old Neighbourhood', *The New York Times*, 27 July 2008, AR1.
37. Qian, Y. (2009), 'Hutong Homeowners in Deadlock', *China Daily*, 19 November 2009, p. 25 http://www.chinadaily.com.cn/metro/2009-11/19/content_8999787.htm (accessed 10 February 2012).
38. See, for example, Human Rights Watch (2004), Demolished: Forced Evictions and Tenants' Rights Movement in China http://china.hrw.org/timeline/2004/demolished (accessed 10 February 2012).
39. Beijing Cultural Heritage Protection Center (BCHPC) (2007), 'Old Beijing in the Eyes of Its Local Residents: Survey Report on the "Cultural Heritage Protection" Awareness of Old Beijing Local Residents' http://en.bjchp.org/?p=105#more-105 (accessed 10 February 2012); BCHPC (2008), "Friends of Old Beijing" Period Research Results – Resident Interviews' http://en.bjchp.org/?p=310 (accessed 10 February 2012).
40. For a detailed coverage of those projects, see UNDP / Programme of Assistance to the Palestinian People (2004), *Focus 2004 Vol.1 'Cultural Heritage'*, http://www.papp.undp.org /en/newsroom/publications/pdf/focus/04v1.pdf (accessed 10 February 2012).
41. World Heritage Committee (1998), *Report, World Heritage Committee, Twenty-first session, Naples, Italy, 1–6 December 1997*, UNESCO Doc WHC-97/CONF.208/17, Decision 21COM VIIIC; see further, ICOMOS (1997), *Advisory Body Evaluation of the Old Town of Lijiang* http://whc.unesco.org/archive/advisory_body_evaluation/811.pdf (accessed 10 February 2012).
42. World Heritage Committee (2008), *Mission Report - UNESCO WHC-ICOMOS Reactive Monitoring Mission to the Old Town of Lijiang, China (10–19 January 2008)*, UNESCO Doc WHC-08/32.COM.
43. See the national report on China in ICOMOS (2000), *ICOMOS World Report 2000 on Monuments and Sites in Danger* http://www.international.icomos.org/risk/world_report/2000/china_2000.htm (accessed 10 February 2012).
44. World Heritage Committee (2000), *Report of the Rapporteur of the Twenty-third Session Marrakesh, Morocco 29 November–4 December*, UNESCO Doc WHC-99/CONF.209/22, Decision 23COM VIII.C.1.
45. Generally on the protection of minority languages in China, see Tsung, L. (ed) (2009), *Minority Languages, Education and Communities in China* Basingstoke: Palgrave Macmillan.
46. A discussion of China's efforts to protect Tibetan culture can be found at The State Council Information Office, China (2009), 'Protection and Development of Tibetan Culture', *Chinese Journal of International Law* 8(1), 233.
47. See for example related information by the Central Land Council of the southern half of the Northern Territory in Australia at http://www.clc.org.au/Permits/permits.html and the Northern Land Council which covers inter alia Arnhem Land at http://www.nlc.org.au /html/permits.html (accessed 10 February 2012).
48. The United Nations Population Fund (UNFPA) defines urbanization as '[t]he process of transition from a rural to a more urban society. Statistically, urbanization reflects an increasing proportion of the population living in settlements defined as urban, primarily through net rural to urban migration. The *level* of urbanization is the percentage of the total population living in towns and cities while the *rate* of urbanization is the rate at which it grows'. See UNFPA (2007), *State of World Population 2007: Unleashing the Potential of Urban Growth* (UNFPA), p. 6.
49. Ibid., p. 1.

50. Ibid.
51. Operational Guidelines, above, n. 4, para. 47.
52. For definitions of landscapes designed and created intentionally by man, organically evolved landscapes, and associative cultural landscapes, see Operational Guidelines, ibid., Annex 3 (Guidelines on the Inscription of Specific Types of Properties on the World Heritage List), para. 10.
53. World Heritage Committee (1995), *Report of the Regional Thematic Study Meeting 'Asian Rice Culture and its Terraced Landscapes', Manila (Philippines), 28 March–4 April 1995*, UNESCO Doc WHC-95/CONF.203/INF.8.
54. Details on the World Heritage site of the Rice Terraces of the Philippine Cordilleras are available at http://whc.unesco.org/en/list/722 (accessed 10 February 2012).
55. World Heritage Committee (1996), *Report of the Rapporteur of the 19th Session of the Committee (Berlin, Germany, 4–9 December 1995)*, UNESCO Doc WHC-95/CONF.203/16, Decision 19COM VIIIC.1.
56. World Heritage Committee (2009), *Decisions Adopted at the 32nd Session of the World Heritage Committee (Quebec City, 2008)*, UNESCO Doc WHC-08/32.COM/24Rev, Decision 32COM 8B.73.
57. Details on the inscription of the Hudhud Chants of the Ifugao on the Representative List of the Intangible Cultural Heritage of Humanity are available at http://www.unesco.org/culture/ich/index.php?lg=en&pg=00011&RL=00015#identification (10 February 2012).
58. World Heritage Committee (2002), *Report of the 25th Session of the World Heritage Committee (Helsinki, Finland, 11–16 December 2001)*, UNESCO Doc WHC-01/CONF.208/24, Decision 25COM X.3.
59. See case studies from Calcutta, Phnom Penh and Hanoi in Forbes and Lindfield, 1997, pp. 71, 72.
60. Operational Guidelines, above, n. 4, Annex 3 (Guidelines on the Inscription of Specific Types of Properties on the World Heritage List), para. 8.

REFERENCES

Ambler, J. (1999), *Attacking Poverty While Improving the Environment: Towards Win-Win Policy Options*, UNDP.

Atkinson, R. and G. Bridge (eds) (2005), *Gentrification in a Global Perspective: The New Urban Colonialism*, London: Routledge.

Bass, S., et al. (2005), 'Introduction', in S. Bass, et al. (eds), *Reducing Poverty and Sustaining the Environment: The Politics of Local Engagement*, London: Earthscan, p. 1.

Boer, B. (2008), 'Article 3: Identification and Delineation of the World Heritage Properties', in F. Francioni and F. Lenzerini (eds), *The 1972 World Heritage Convention: A Commentary*, Oxford: Oxford University Press, p. 85.

Boer, B. and S. Gruber (2012), 'Heritage Discourses' in K. Rubenstein and B. Jessup (eds), *Environmental Discourses in International and Public Law*, Cambridge: Cambridge University Press, 375.

Brainard, L., A. Jones and N. Purvis (eds) (2009), *Climate Change and Global Poverty: A Billion Lives in the Balance?* Washington D.C.: Brookings Institution Press.

Forbes, D.K. and Lindfield, M. (1997), *Urbanisation in Asia: Lessons Learned and Innovative Responses*, Australian Agency for International Development.

Francioni, F. (2004), 'Beyond State Sovereignty: The Protection of Cultural Heritage as a Shared Interest of Humanity', *Michigan Journal of International Law* 25, 1209.

Gruber, S. (2007), 'Protecting China's Cultural Heritage Sites in Times of Rapid Change: Current Developments, Practice and Law', *Asia Pacific Journal of Environmental Law* 10(3&4), 253.

Gruber, S. (2011), 'The Impact of Climate Change on Cultural Heritage Sites: Environmental Law and Adaptation', *Carbon and Climate Law Review* 2/2011, 209.

He, S. (2000), 'The Mainland's Environment and the Protection of China's Cultural Heritage: A Chinese Cultural Heritage Lawyer's Perspective', *Art Antiquity and Law* 5(1), 19.

Head, L. (2000), *Cultural Landscapes and Environmental Change*, London: Hodder Arnold.

Hoi An Centre for Monuments Managements and Preservation (2008), *IMPACT: The Effects of Tourism on Culture and the Environment in Asia and the Pacific: Cultural Tourism and Heritage Management in the World Heritage Site of the Ancient Town of Hoi An, Viet Nam*, UNESCO Bangkok.

Hopkins, K. and M. Beard (2005), *The Colosseum*, Cambridge, Massachusetts: Harvard University Press.

Hughes, B., et al. (2009), *Reducing Global Poverty: Patterns of Potential Human Progress*, vol. 1, Denver: Pardee Center for International Futures, University of Denver.

Jalal, K.F. (1993), *Sustainable Development, Environment and Poverty Nexus*, Asian Development Bank.

Jehan, S. and A. Umana (2003), 'The Environment-Poverty Nexus', *Development Policy Journal* 3, 53.

Klugman, J. (ed.) (2002), *A Sourcebook for Poverty Reduction Strategies*, vol. 1, World Bank.

Meyer, M. (2008), *The Last Days of Old Beijing: Life in the Vanishing Backstreets of a City Transformed*, New York: Walker & Company.

Müller, J. (1997), *Kulturlandschaft China: Anthropogene Gestaltung der Landschaft durch Landnutzung und Siedlung* [Cultural Landscape China: Anthropogenic Creation of Landscapes though Land Use and Housing Development] Darmstadt: Justus Perthes Verlag.

Müller, J. (1999), 'Die traditionelle Ländliche Architektur Chinas in ihrem landschaftlichen Kontext' [China's Traditional Rural Architecture in its Regional Context], *Die Erde* 130, 205.

Munasinghe, M. and R.J. Swart (2005), *Primer on Climate Change and Sustainable Development: Facts, Policy Analysis and Applications*, Cambridge: Cambridge University Press.

Nyimaa, T. (2008), 'The Chinese Development of Tibet: Lhasa in Transformation', *Forum for Development Studies* 35(2), 257.

Save the Ifugao Terraces Movement (2008), *IMPACT: The Effects of Tourism on Culture and the Environment in Asia and the Pacific: Sustainable Tourism and the Preservation of the World Heritage Site of the Ifugao Rice Terraces, Philippines*, UNESCO Bangkok.

Spicker, P. (2007), *The Idea of Poverty*, Bristol: Policy Press.

Stille, A. (2002), *The Future of the Past – How the Information Age Threatens to Destroy Our Cultural Heritage*, New York: Picador.

Su, X. and P. Teo (2009), *The Politics of Heritage Tourism in China: A View from Lijiang*, London: Routledge.

Vrdoljak, A. (2008), 'Article 13: World Heritage Committee and International Assistance', in F. Franciono and F. Lenzerini (eds). *The 1972 World Heritage Convention: A Commentary*, Oxford: Oxford University Press, p. 219.

15. Chartering sustainable transnational corporations

Susan Lea Smith

15.1 THE CHALLENGE OF CREATING SUSTAINABLE TRANSNATIONAL CORPORATIONS

Transnational corporations, like any other corporation, are legal fictions recognized by the government to serve the public interest.[1] They are recognized as legal entities,[2] granted rights such as freedom of speech and due process as if they were persons,[3] given privileges such as limited liability to induce investors to private capital, and endowed with perpetual existence,[4] a benefit not yet received by mere mortals.

As a result of this remarkable set of legal policies, transnational corporations have been able to aggregate unprecedented, almost unimaginable amounts of extremely fluid and geographically mobile capital. Just the 300 largest global corporations hold 25 per cent of the entire world's productive assets.[5]

The magnitude of operations of these corporations is difficult to comprehend. Wal-Mart's 2007 revenues were $378.8 billion, more than the entire gross domestic product of countries such as Austria, Greece, Denmark, Iran, South Africa, Argentina, or any of 150 other countries. Its revenues are equivalent to those of the 25th largest country in the world. ExxonMobil's 2007 revenues were $371.8 billion, more than the gross domestic product of 155 countries, equivalent to the 27th largest country in the world.

Transnational corporations, by virtue of their wealth, their control of physical capital and real property, and their ability to generate jobs, have unparalleled political power in virtually all nations in which they operate. Impelled by World Bank and IMF policies designed to attract private capital to, and stabilize fiscal and monetary policy in, developing countries,[6] these countries face extreme and almost irresistible pressures to adopt corporate friendly policies. Developing countries are compelled to participate in free trade agreements, liberalize their governments' fiscal and monetary policy, privatize government-owned industries, minimize social and environmental regulation, and change their governments' corporate governance model towards a shareholder dominated system.[7] Developed nations face the same pressures, relaxing regulatory standards and ignoring corporate violations due to the political and economic clout wielded by transnational corporations as well as the present threat that they will simply transfer their businesses elsewhere.[8]

At the same time, throughout the world, transnational corporations have caused irreparable environmental damage and enormous social dislocation, and have been implicated in murder, torture, and other human rights abuses.[9]

Regardless of self-serving corporate claims about corporate social responsibility and sustainability,[10] it is widely understood that most transnational corporations have long recognized a single formal responsibility – maximizing quarterly corporate profits and dividends.[11] And, to a great extent, corporate directors and managers have long operated most transnational corporations as if they had a single informal goal – maximizing economic benefits to management. The most recent example is the extraordinarily high compensation that Lehmann Bros. awarded its executives even as the firm was headed into bankruptcy. Even if miraculously a transnational corporation chooses to depose quarterly corporate profits and executive compensation as the twin pinnacles of corporate concern, it faces falling stock prices and risks becoming the target of a hostile takeover – all due to the financial system that we have built.[12]

Yet, inexplicably, we are surprised or disappointed when our aggregated, fluid, geographically mobile capital is deployed by transnational corporations to conduct their business in an unsustainable manner that contributes to corporate profits, but exacerbates global poverty, destroys the environment, and abuses workers.

For more than a century, we have fought to tame the savage beast. We have used tort law to compensate victims of corporate misbehavior. We have enacted substantive environmental, health, and safety legislation to rein in the most egregious corporate labor practices and environmental pollution. We have attempted to encourage corporate self-discipline through creation of voluntary industrial standards. We have encouraged market discipline of transnational corporations through third party certifications of environmentally sound and fair trade products to enable responsible purchasing. We have created social choice mutual funds, responsible investing principles, and responsible lending practices. We have valiantly educated our children to value the earth and the diverse people that inhabit it – and then sent them off to work and live in societies dominated by transnational corporations that manifest precious little regard for either the earth or its people.

And yet, after all of our noble and worthwhile efforts, we stand upon the precipice of global warming, confronting a series of climate tipping points – where continued emission of greenhouse gasses will dramatically raise sea level, drowning whole nations and vast cities, and will cause extinction of many of earth's plants and animals. In the midst of this global crisis,

ExxonMobil, the world's second largest transnational corporation has continued to fund organizations devoted to denying the scientific consensus about the human role in global warming and exaggerating the cost of effectively addressing global warming, and joined in making policy suggestions to dilute the effectiveness of government policies to address global warming.

And yet, we witness oppressive working conditions in the factories that supply transnational manufacturers and retailers – in Asian sweatshops and in maquiladoras of Mexico and Central America – that build products for Sony, Mitsubishi, RCA and others, and supply products to Wal-Mart, the world's largest transnational corporation.

And yet, we are artfully seduced through billion dollar advertising budgets to ever greater, orgy-like, consumption of the products of transnational companies, even though it is clear that they add little, if any, more happiness to our lives.

And yet, we fight or endure oil wars, waged for the rights of transnational oil companies to access the Middle East's black gold. And those companies pay bribes to drug-runners and terrorists to access South America's wealth.

And yet, we rely upon trickle-down economics, touted by neo-liberal economists funded by transnational companies, to alleviate the horrors of extreme poverty.

In part, we have failed to create a more sustainable world because we have been unwilling to plunge a sword into the heart of the beast: the mindless aggregation of virtually all of our social wealth in service of the transnational corporation goal to become bigger in order to maximize ever-increasing profits. Through our inventive collection of corporate social responsibility devices, we have at best played with the fringes of the beast's mane. We must find a way to transform transnational corporations in a more profound manner.

I offer the ideas in this chapter as a preliminary step towards creating sustainable transnational corporations. Although environmental law professors have contributed many ideas that have improved the environment and made sustainability a global concept, we have not found a means to fundamentally redirect corporate efforts towards creating ecologically sustainable and socially just societies. That is a responsibility we must now undertake.[13]

This chapter explores a recent innovative legislative attempt in the United States by the state of Oregon to encourage more sustainable corporate behavior through changing corporate charter laws.[14] Oregon now permits corporations to file corporate charters that enable them to be what I call 'sustainable corporations'. Corporations may elect to incorporate a provision in their charter that expressly allows the corporation to make business decisions consistent with a sustainable triple bottom line, considering environmental and social responsibility in addition to corporate profits and shareholder gains.

Section 15.2 describes Oregon's unique provision to allow sustainable corporation charters, its legislative history, and its effects in the context of

Oregon corporate law.[15] Section 15.3 critiques the Oregon legislation as a model of sustainable corporation chartering. While Oregon achieved its extremely modest goal of allowing corporations to act sustainably, it too failed to strike at the heart of unsustainable corporate behavior. Nonetheless, Oregon's sustainable corporate charter legislation can be a useful stepping stone, serving to highlight the possibility that corporate charters can serve as a means to begin encouraging sustainable corporate behavior by transnational and other corporations.[16] Section 15.4 suggests an alternative approach to chartering sustainable transnational corporations, building on the Oregon model.[17] Finally, section 15.5 canvasses various means to embed sustainable corporation charters in international law or to otherwise harmonize national laws with such a requirement.

15.2 THE OREGON MODEL FOR CHARTERING SUSTAINABLE CORPORATIONS

15.2.1 The Corporate Law Context: State Law Determines Corporate Structure and Governance of US Corporations

Corporations in the United States are structured primarily by two sets of laws, one public and one private.[18] The corporate law of the state in which the corporation is incorporated or chartered (sometimes called the 'home state'), establishes certain requirements regarding corporate charters and bylaws, purposes and powers, shares and distributions, shareholders, directors and officers, offices and agents, records and reports, conversions, mergers and acquisitions, and dissolution. The home state's corporate law then allows the corporation to elaborate and detail its own structure and governance mechanisms through its corporate charter (sometimes known as articles of incorporation) and through its prime internal directive – the bylaws adopted by the board of directors.

15.2.2 Chartering a Corporation under Oregon Corporate Law

Oregon corporate law is no exception to the general American rule. It contains skeletal structural provisions generally consistent with the corporate law of other American states. Like corporations in those states, Oregon corporations are given the ability to elaborate their corporate structure and governance mechanisms through their corporate charter and/or bylaws.

For example, in the Oregon corporation code, the corporate charter is required to include a bare minimum of vital information.[19] The statute then outlines several optional provisions that the charter may include, such as the name and addresses of the initial directors, the purposes for which the corporation is organized, provisions regarding managing the business and regulating the affairs of the corporation, provisions concerning the powers of the corporation, directors and shareholders, and the par value for authorized shares or classes of shares,[20] and any provision required or permitted to be set forth in the bylaws.[21] There are two other permissive provisions of relatively recent vintage: provisions with respect to limiting directors' personal liability[22] and Oregon's sustainable corporation provision.[23] The directors' personal liability provision has been widely adopted by American states. The sustainable corporation provision, on the other hand, is unique.

15.2.3 Oregon's Sustainable Corporation Charter Provision

In 2007, the Oregon legislature enacted House Bill 2826, amending the Oregon corporation code to expressly allow Oregon corporations to include in their corporate charter a sustainable corporation provision – so that they may conduct their business in an environmentally and socially responsible manner. The genesis of this modest change in Oregon corporate law is worth a short digression.

15.2.3.1 The origin of Oregon's legislation

H.B. 2826 is the brainchild of one of Oregon's sustainability gurus: Dick Roy. A corporate lawyer for over 20 years with a large, prestigious Portland law firm, Roy abandoned corporate firm life in 1993 to become a full-time volunteer activist. His primary role has been conducting educational seminars, explaining sustainability and urging individuals, businesses, and governmental organizations to voluntarily adopt sustainable practices. In the course of that mission, Roy founded the Northwest Earth Institute, the Oregon Natural Step Network, the Sustainable Investment Institute, and Oregon Lawyers for a Sustainable Future. Acting in conjunction with the latter group's corporate governance committee, Roy secured bi-partisan introduction of H.B. 2826.

In a public hearing on the legislation, Roy opined that the triple bottom line that the legislation embodied 'is now a common framework for the operation of businesses with a focus on financial, environmental, and social considerations'.[24] Roy argued that the legislation achieved three objectives: (1) it provides an option for the directors and shareholders of a corporation, acting cooperatively, to call for the corporation to be operated 'in an environmentally and socially responsible manner in pursuing the triple bottom line'; (2) it dispels a common misunderstanding that business corporations cannot pursue any objective other than increasing revenues and profits; and (3) it aligns Oregon's corporate law with Oregon's statutory goal of sustainability.[25]

One of the witnesses in public hearings on H.B. 2826 was Jeffrey Wolfstone, a corporate law partner in the large Portland law firm of Lane Powell PC.[26] Wolfstone at the time was serving as General Counsel of Nau, Inc. a start-up outdoor apparel company that had elected to expressly authorize consideration of environmental and social responsibility.[27] Wolfstone brought Nau's mission statement[28] and rules of corporate responsibility[29] to the attention of the Legislature, noting that Nau's corporate responsibility rules 'are 'baked in' to Nau's corporate DNA and can be changed only with a 75 per cent shareholder vote'.[30] He commended the legislation because it allowed companies to make an 'affirmative choice whether, and the extent to which, to expressly embrace environmental and social responsibility by corporate charter'.[31] He suggested that allowing companies to take an enlightened view of their role and responsibilities was consistent with the state's ambitious agenda to serve as a leader in environmental sustainability.[32]

There was a surprising amount of resistance in the Legislature to this modest amendment of Oregon corporate law. The measure passed by a vote of 38–18 in the House and 17–11 in the Senate. From discussions in committee, legislators opposing the bill seemed to be suspicious of any legislation with the word 'environmental'. They also argued that if the bill did not change the ability of corporations to act in an environmentally and socially responsible manner under existing law, then the bill must not be necessary.[33]

15.2.3.2 The legislative solution

Oregon's sustainable corporation provision is remarkably simple. It allows a corporation to include in its charter '[a] provision authorizing or directing the corporation to conduct the business of the corporation in a manner that is environmentally and socially responsible'.[34] The incorporators can choose whether to include the provision in the corporate charter. Additionally, they can choose whether to 'direct' that the corporation conduct business in an environmentally and socially responsible manner or merely 'authorize' it to do so.

15.2.3.3 The effect of the provision in the context of Oregon corporate law

Although this sustainable corporation provision is unique in American corporate law,[35] Oregon's provision grants directors of Oregon corporations little, if any, power or protection beyond those enjoyed by corporate directors of corporations incorporated in other American states. As in other American states, Oregon corporate law has long contained provisions that likely would have been interpreted to empower Oregon corporations to act in an environmentally and socially responsible manner. First, every corporation has the purpose of engaging in any lawful business, unless it expressly chooses a narrower purpose.[36] Second, every corporation has the same powers as an individual to do all things necessary or convenient to carry out its business and affairs.[37] Third, every corporation has specific power to make donations for the public welfare or for charitable, scientific or educational purposes.[38] Fourth, every corporation has specific power to transact any lawful business that will aid governmental policy.[39] Finally, every corporation has specific power to make payment or donations, or to do any other act not inconsistent with law, that furthers the business and affairs of the corporation.[40] With those broad purposes and powers, along with the protection of the business judgment rule, corporate directors in Oregon were already well-protected from claims that a corporate decision made to conduct the business in an environmentally and socially responsible manner was improper because it somehow impaired corporate profits and thus shareholder gains.[41]

One of the most important aspects of American corporate law that serves to protect the ability of corporate directors to run corporations in an environmentally and socially responsible manner is 'the business judgment rule'. This rule is a self-imposed limit by courts on their review of decisions by corporate boards of directors. It provides that courts will not second-guess the business decisions of corporate boards of directors. Typically, the rule is interpreted to protect disinterested directors from personal liability to the corporation and shareholders so long as they act on an informed basis and in good faith, honestly believing that the decision is in the best interest of the corporation.

One reason that Oregon needed a sustainable corporation charter provision was the lack of Oregon case law on application of the business judgment rule,[42] due to the fact that Oregon never served as the corporate home to a sizable number of large corporations.[43] Another reason was never discussed during consideration of the legislation; application of the case law of other states regarding the business judgment rule is perhaps a bit problematic. In enacting a new corporation code during the 1980s, Oregon opted to adopt explicit standards of conduct for directors rather than codify the business judgment rule. These standards of conduct largely parallel the business judgment rule, but differ in two respects. First, they establish substantive standards that courts may use to judge director conduct. Second, those substantive standards deviate from the business judgment rule, as interpreted in other American states, in certain respects.

As with other states applying the business judgment rule, Oregon requires directors to discharge their duties 'in good faith, with the care an ordinarily prudent person in a like position would exercise under similar circumstances and in a manner the director reasonably believes to be in the best interests of the corporation'.[44] In meeting that duty of care, Oregon allows a director, in making a decision, to rely on specific types of information provided by corporate officers and employees, professionals and experts, and board committees that the director reasonably believes are competent[45] – unless the director has knowledge that makes reliance unwarranted.[46] So long as the director acts in accordance with these standards, the director cannot be held liable.[47] To this extent, the Oregon standards of conduct for corporate directors parallel interpretations of the business judgment rule common in other states. However, the Oregon standards of conduct differ in their treatment of conflicts of interest or violations of the duty of loyalty. Apparently, a director who meets the standards of conduct, which embody the common law duty of care, are not liable for acts taken or omitted as a director, even if the director is not disinterested.[48] More importantly to directors who might consider environmental and social responsibility in their day-to-day decisions as directors, the Oregon standards of conduct provide extra protection for directors with respect to major corporate decisions such as mergers, acquisitions, and asset sales. The Oregon standards of conduct explicitly state that, in making such major decisions, a director may give due consideration, in determining what are the best interests of the corporation:

> to the social, legal and economic effects on employees, customers and suppliers of the corporation and on the communities and geographical areas in which the corporation and its subsidiaries operate, the economy of the state and the nation, the long term as well as short term interests of the corporation and its shareholders, including the possibility that these interests may be best served by the continued independence of the corporation, and other relevant factors.[49]

Given the fact that the Legislature specifically included those considerations with respect to major corporate decisions, but not all corporate decisions, the courts might interpret Oregon's corporation code to limit directors' ability to consider such broad factors in making day-to-day business decisions. Since many of the same broad factors are implicated in making corporate decisions in an environmentally and socially responsible manner, directors of Oregon corporations had a little more doubt than directors of most large corporations about their power to make such decisions.

However, the Oregon sustainable corporation charter provision, when combined with the business judgment rule and the statutory standards of conduct for directors, effectively put any such doubts to rest.[50]

15.3 LIMITATIONS OF OREGON'S LEGISLATION AS A MODEL FOR CHARTERING SUSTAINABLE TRANSNATIONAL CORPORATIONS

The Oregon corporate charter law is undoubtedly an innovative device to explicitly protect corporations, corporate directors and corporate managers who undertake sustainability activities either as a strategy to improve the firm's long-term financial performance or out of a commitment to sustainability. However, it falls short as a model for creating sustainable corporations for four primary reasons.

First, it is voluntary and most corporations, particularly large established corporations, are unlikely to choose to become chartered as a sustainable corporation. Second, even if a corporation chooses to become chartered as a sustainable corporation under the Oregon model, it is not committed to acting in a sustainable manner. Third, even if a corporation were committed to acting in a sustainable manner by its corporate charter, corporate law principles severely limit the enforceability of that commitment and the remedies available for violation of that commitment. It is necessary to at least consider changing those corporate law principles. Finally, even if all corporations were required to be chartered as sustainable corporations and that charter effectively required them to act in a sustainable manner, the sustainable corporate charter approach will not work unless it is adopted as a requirement on a uniform and international basis, because of the likelihood that other states and other nations will not change their corporate law to incorporate the sustainable corporation model, and will instead continue to 'race to the bottom' in terms of their corporate law.

15.3.1 Adoption of a Sustainable Charter is Voluntary

The first arguable weakness of the Oregon model is that Oregon law makes adoption of a sustainable corporate charter voluntary rather than mandatory. While some corporations may adopt a sustainable corporate charter based upon the founders' commitment to sustainability, many will not. Most corporations will only adopt a sustainable corporate charter if the corporation perceives that (1) operating as a sustainable corporation generally provides enhanced financial performance; (2) there is strategic value in establishing the corporation in a genuinely sustainable niche;[51] or (3) the corporation needs to adopt a sustainability charter as a superficial gambit for purposes of public, investor, and consumer relations.

The empirical data on whether corporations indeed achieve improved financial performance from embracing corporate social responsibility is mixed at best.[52] Certainly, most corporations can obtain immediate improvements in financial performance from reducing their environmental impacts to some extent – adopting operational practices and making capital investments that increase energy and material efficiency and reduce waste.[53] However, those gains are far more limited than the improvements that are necessary to achieve ecological sustainability and alleviate the conditions underlying extreme poverty.

Certainly some corporations can move beyond standard efficiency and waste reduction practices into a genuinely green, socially responsible niche. However, only so many corporations can occupy that niche in a given industry until sustainability becomes a matter of compliance, not corporate grace. A corporate sustainability consultant estimated at one point that the green niche might amount to less than 10 per cent depending on the industry.[54]

The final self-serving reason for corporations to adopt a sustainable corporate charter, to 'greenwash' their image, obviously impairs sustainability rather than helping achieve it. To the extent that corporations mis-characterize themselves as acting sustainably, they impair the comparative advantage of corporations that truly seek to act in a sustainable manner.

15.3.2 A Sustainable Corporation Charter Does Not Commit the Corporation to Act Sustainably

The second arguable weakness in the Oregon model is that, once a corporation adopts a sustainable corporate charter, it is explicitly allowed to make decisions with ecological sustainability and social equity in mind, but it is not required to do so. A permissive charter adds little encouragement, if any, for corporations to act sustainably. To effectively create a corporate 'triple bottom line', either the charter requirement, another aspect of other corporate law such as director standards of conduct, or the corporate bylaws must *require* the corporation to act sustainably.

15.3.3 Lax Standards of Director Conduct and the Business Judgment Rule Allow Corporate Directors and Managers to Make Environmentally and Socially Irresponsible Decisions without Providing an Adequate Remedy

A third arguable weakness of the Oregon model is that, through lax standards of director conduct and/or the business judgment rule, corporate directors and managers can nonetheless still make environmentally and socially irresponsible decisions – and corporate law generally provides no remedy for such decisions.

As a conceptual matter, it is difficult to imagine what decision rule the corporate directors must obey with a sustainable corporation charter provision. Are they supposed to make a decision in the best interests of the corporation, taking environmental and social factors into account? Are they supposed to act in the best interests of the corporation, subject to the constraint that the corporation must be environmentally and socially responsible? Are they supposed to determine the most environmentally and socially responsible course of conduct, assuming that is in the best interests of the corporation? Various corporate boards would likely interpret their decision rule differently if the question was ever addressed, although in all likelihood they would adopt the least restrictive alternative, which is mere consideration of environmental and social effects. In reality, the answer to this conceptual issue does not matter because the decisions of the director will be protected by the business judgment rule.

As discussed above, the business judgment rule is interpreted to protect disinterested directors from personal liability to the corporation and shareholders so long as they act on informed basis and in good faith, honestly believing that the decision is in the best interest of the corporation. This means that even though a corporation has a corporate charter provision that requires the directors to operate the business in a socially and environmentally responsible manner, no court will review the directors' decisions to see whether in fact the corporation is operating in a socially and environmentally responsible manner – nor will it care how the directors have interpreted the decision rules established by the charter. At most, the court will look to see whether the directors had sufficient, reliable information in front of them to evaluate the social and environmental impacts of their decision. Essentially, the business judgment rule at most requires that directors have some 'mini-NEPA' analysis in front of them when they make business decisions.

15.3.4 The Race to the Bottom by Other States and Nations with Respect to Corporate Governance Discourages Other Jurisdictions from Adopting Oregon's Model for Chartering Sustainable Corporations

The final difficulty with the Oregon model, or any compulsory model adopted in an isolated way by individual states or nations, is that there tends to be a race to the bottom with respect to corporate chartering and other aspects of corporate law. Jurisdictions tend to compete to provide 'corporate-friendly' corporate law – in terms of leniency and flexibility for the corporation and in terms of stability and predictability in interpretation.

15.4 CHARTERING SUSTAINABLE TRANSNATIONAL CORPORATIONS

This section identifies some of the key questions that must be answered in designing substantive sustainable corporation charter requirements. The questions identified and the tentative answers advanced are an illustrative, not comprehensive, analysis of what it would mean to charter sustainable transnational corporations. Hopefully, this analysis will spark discussion of the basic concept and inspire more thorough and detailed analysis.

15.4.1 Create an Enforceable Commitment to Environmentally and Socially Responsible Corporate Conduct

One key design parameter of any system to charter sustainable transnational corporations is whether adopting such a charter should be optional or mandatory. The optional nature of the Oregon charter law is a critical weakness of the Oregon model if one is truly hoping to transform transnational corporate conduct. The sustainable corporation charter law must be directive. Corporations must be required, not merely permitted, to incorporate sustainability into their corporate charters. And the sustainability provision in those charters must create a corporate commitment to act sustainably, not just authority to act sustainably.

A legal provision to incorporate sustainability into the 'corporate DNA' might be as simple as 'The charter shall set forth a provision directing the corporation to conduct the business of the corporation in a manner that is environmentally and socially responsible.'

The rationales for requiring transnational corporations to be chartered as sustainable corporations are straightforward. First, a sustainability directive in a corporate charter makes sustainability part of the corporation's mission. Like criminal law, its power in transforming the corporation lies less in the threat of internal discipline of employees or external enforcement action, than in shaping the preferences of those within the corporation toward acting in an environmentally or socially responsible manner. Culture change gurus may argue that policies voluntarily adopted by the corporate directors and managers are more powerful in shaping preferences. Whether that is true remains to be seen: the empirical results of voluntary corporate social responsibility efforts are remarkably difficult to measure. But both the scholarly literature and my own experience as an environmental crimes prosecutor suggest that white-collar criminal law certainly has a powerful preference-shaping function despite its harsh, compulsory nature. Apparently, the British Parliament agrees because, in 2007, it enacted the Corporate Manslaughter and Corporate Homicide Act,[55] making it easier to convict corporations whose negligent behavior results in death.

Second, a mandatory sustainable corporation charter requirement recognizes the reality that transnational corporations face cutthroat competition for capital and corporate survival. Unless it is a requirement and not an option, those transnational corporations opting to be sustainable corporations may not face a level playing field in the capital markets due to shareholder resistance.[56] Additionally, the cost impacts of operating in an environmentally and socially responsible manner are not necessarily small. Indeed, the circumstances in which market discipline has required sustainable conduct by transnational corporations can truly be counted on two hands.[57]

15.4.2 Limit the Mandatory Sustainable Corporation Charter Requirement to Transnational Corporations

A second key design parameter is who should be regulated? Should all corporations be required to be chartered as sustainable corporations, all transnational corporations, or some small set of transnational corporations?

One important axiom for regulatory system design is the fewer the number of regulatory targets, the easier it is to create, administer, and enforce the regulatory requirements. That axiom is counterbalanced by the desire to reach as many regulatory targets as possible in order to maximize the impact of the regulatory system. Fortunately, in this case, one can maximize the impact of the sustainable corporation charter requirement by hitting a remarkably small number of regulatory targets. David Weissbrodt,[58] in discussing international human rights standards for business, noted the enormous impact of transnational corporations:

- transnational corporations hold 90 per cent of all technology and product patents.
- transnational corporations are involved in 70 per cent of world trade.
- transnational corporations directly employ 90 million people, including 20 million in developing countries.
- transnational corporations produce 25 per cent of the world's gross domestic product.
- The 1000 largest transnational corporations account for 80 per cent of the world's industrial output.

Even a sustainable corporation charter requirement restricted to transnational corporations is certain to have a very dramatic global impact.

The obvious difficulty in limiting the requirement to transnational corporations is creating an appropriate definition of transnational corporations[59] so that crafty corporate lawyers cannot help transnational corporations evade the requirement by restructuring the corporation's businesses. While detailed consideration of this jurisdictional issue is far beyond the scope of this chapter, initially the jurisdiction of the international regulatory agency might be focused on corporations who: (1) have direct investment in a foreign country or equity investment in a foreign company; (2) buy a significant portion of a foreign company's products, (3) have a significant market share of a product in a foreign company; or (4) have structured their business so that they avoid jurisdiction of the international regulatory agency. Mere import from foreign suppliers or export of products to foreign countries would not qualify a corporation as transnational unless they meet conditions (2) or (3).

15.4.3 Allow Corporations to Define Environmentally and Socially Responsible Corporate Conduct that goes Beyond Compliance

Another key design parameter is who should define what constitutes environmentally and socially responsible corporate conduct? Should the corporate law define it? Should the courts define it? Should the corporate directors define it?

15.4.3.1 Options for defining environmentally and socially responsible corporate conduct

If corporate law defines the standards of environmentally and socially responsible corporate conduct and the courts enforce that law, then the sustainable corporation charter requirement simply transforms corporate law into environmental law[60] and the effects would go far beyond the old saw of corporate law that corporations, like any other person, are obligated to comply with law. Similarly, if the courts are permitted to define what constitutes environmentally and socially responsible corporate conduct and enforce that standard, the courts essentially become the corporate directors of all transnational corporations. On the other hand, if the corporation itself defines those standards, it can define them in any manner, as loosely or strictly as it chooses – which is perhaps functionally equivalent to the status quo.

Another alternative to defining standards of environmentally and socially responsible conduct may be more attractive: allow the corporation to design its sustainability strategy specifying such standards, but provide parameters for that design as well as strict monitoring and reporting requirements. This alternative might be termed the 'guided corporate judgment' approach.

15.4.3.2 The guided corporate judgment approach

If corporations are to define 'environmentally and socially responsible conduct' or 'contributing to ecological sustainability and social well-being' in corporate sustainability strategies – using a guided corporate judgment approach – the law imposing a corporate sustainability charter requirement needs to have several features.

First, it should include implementing provisions, along with the sustainable corporation charter requirement, that:

1. require compliance with international law, the home state's law, and all laws of the host nations in which the corporation operates that concern sustainability;
2. require the corporation to adopt, periodically review, and revise a corporate sustainability strategy to assure that the company conducts its business in an environmentally and socially responsible manner;
3. identify specific aspects of sustainability to be addressed by the strategy; and

4. require the corporation to monitor and report, subject to independent audit, compliance with international and national sustainability related laws, with any non-binding national or international sustainability-related standards,[61] and with the corporate sustainability strategy.

Second, the implementing provisions should require that the corporate sustainability strategy:

- define for corporate purposes what constitutes environmentally and socially responsible conduct;
- identify specific operational indicators of sustainability for all aspects of sustainability, including economic prosperity, ecological sustainability, and social well-being, required by the implementation law;
- identify all international, national, and state sustainability-related laws applicable to the corporation's various operations;
- identify all non-binding international and national sustainability standards applicable to the corporation's various operations; and
- create a plan to implement the strategy, selecting available resources and well-defined programs, projects, and processes to be used to implement the strategy.

This guided corporate judgment approach to creating sustainable transnational corporations allows the corporation to tailor its strategy to its individual situation and encourage innovative ideas and approaches to sustainability. Yet, it also provides a means for national governments, labor organizations, environmental organizations, investors, consumers and the public to compare sustainability commitments being made by various transnational corporations. Those groups become more able to monitor and compare the corporations' compliance with sustainability-related law and non-binding voluntary standards as well as the corporations' progress in meeting their sustainability commitments.

A guided corporate judgment approach allows the corporation, corporate directors and managers to avail themselves of the business judgment rule with respect to the charter's directive to conduct the business in an environmentally and socially responsible manner. It allows them freedom regarding the details of the sustainability strategy they adopt and their implementation of the strategy.

To be clear, this suggestion should be sharply distinguished from the arguments made by Braithewaite,[62] Sigler and Murphy,[63] and others to substitute voluntary compliance and incentives for effective regulation.

15.4.4 Create a Strong Enforcement Mechanism for the Sustainable Corporation Charter Requirement and Implementing Provisions

Any regulatory system is only as effective as its enforcement mechanism. The governmental entity administering the sustainable corporate charter requirement and its implementing provisions must be required to take enforcement action against any transnational corporation upon receiving credible information that the corporation has neglected its duties. A transnational corporation should be subject to enforcement action if:

- it fails to register a conforming charter;
- it fails to prepare a conforming sustainability strategy;
- it fails to comply with international and national laws respecting sustainability; or
- it fails to accurately monitor and file accurate reports about its compliance with law, voluntary non-binding standards and its own sustainability strategy.

Significant sanctions should be imposed on any transnational corporation committing these violations: administrative penalties on the order of 10–50 per cent of annual profits, total or partial suspension of the privilege of transacting business on a transnational basis for a period of time, or the transnational corporate death penalty – permanent cancellation of a corporation's transnational corporation charter, which forbids that corporation from ever transacting transnational business.

15.4.5 Apply the Sustainable Corporation Charter Requirement and Implementing Provisions on an International Basis

Some commentators suggest that environmentally and socially irresponsible behavior by transnational corporations can be effectively regulated through extension of extraterritorial regulatory jurisdiction by home states or nations and development in host nations of democratic governments willing to protect their citizens.[64] For a variety of reasons, reliance on home and host nations is ill-advised.

On a pragmatic level, the track record of home and host nations lends little empirical support to this theoretical possibility. Furthermore, the miserable track record in controlling environmental, labor, human rights, and corruption should be expected given the incentives of both host and home nations: both home and host nations have enormous economic stakes in retaining transnational corporation operations in their countries. In addition to the probable ineffectiveness of these approaches, imposing the substantive environmental, labor, human rights, and corruption standards of home states on host countries through extraterritorial jurisdiction raises significant questions of whether those standards are culturally, socially, and politically appropriate. Finally, decades may pass before the citizens of some host states are protected from the abuses of transnational corporations, given the difficulty of host nations developing and enforcing their standards against transnational corporations.

Relying on home states or nations to impose and enforce sustainable corporation charter requirements is even more problematic because, unlike industrial or headquarters operations, transnational corporations can literally change their corporate home by filing a piece of paper. The ease of corporate flight makes it virtually certain that no mandatory sustainable corporation charter requirement will ever be effectively implemented unless it is implemented on an international basis.

In summary, adoption of a sustainable corporate charter requirement, in accordance with the design suggestions made above, strikes an appropriate balance of corporate freedom with corporate accountability in meeting the triple bottom line. In the final analysis, such a requirement might well accomplish redirection of a substantial percentage of our global wealth from merely making corporate profits towards achieving a broader set of social purposes, including economic prosperity, ecological sustainability, and social well-being.

15.4.6 Preserve National Control of Corporations

Home nations – or, in the case of the United States, home states – should continue to charter corporations to do business, imposing whatever requirements they deem appropriate. In order to make the international requirements effective, national or state requirements should be pre-empted only if they are inconsistent with the international requirements. The international sustainable corporation requirements should be a floor, not a ceiling, on home nation regulation of their corporations.

15.5 DESIGNING AN INTERNATIONAL STRUCTURE TO CHARTER SUSTAINABLE TRANSNATIONAL CORPORATIONS

This section discusses some of the key aspects of designing an international structure to charter sustainable corporations on an international basis. Some of the key parameters in that design are:

1. whether to impose the international requirement through uniform national laws and remedies administered on a national basis or through international laws and remedies administered by an international agency;
2. whether to create a separate independent international body or create an agency within an existing international body;
3. how to integrate the requirements and remedies that are created regarding transnational corporations with other international rights and remedies regarding environmental protection, fair labor practices, human rights, and corruption.

15.5.1 Choosing International or National Implementation of the International Sustainable Corporation Charter Requirement

There are at least two means to implement an international requirement that transnational corporations obtain a sustainable corporation charter in order to operate on a transnational basis. First, national governments could agree to impose sustainable corporation requirements upon transnational corporations through uniform or harmonized national or state laws. This is a common device used to impose international law on private regulated parties through enforceable national and state laws. The Montreal Protocol on Substances that Deplete the Ozone Layer (16 September 1987),[65] for example, was implemented through the provisions of Title VI of the Clean Air Act,[66] and implementing regulations promulgated by the U.S. Environmental Protection Agency. Second, national governments could create an international body to charter sustainable transnational corporations, directly imposing liability for violations of that body's implementing regulations. Although international law has been slow to create individual liability for violations of international law and international norms,[67] the International Criminal Court does provide at least one example of international law directly applied to non-governmental actors (known in international circles as 'non-state' actors). The jurisdiction of the ICC, however, extends only to natural persons, including corporate officers, but not to 'legal persons' such as corporations.[68]

Creation of an international regulatory body under the auspices of the United Nations with jurisdiction over transnational corporations appears to be a far superior approach to establishing internationally applicable sustainable corporation charter requirements. The alternative, amending national and state corporate laws on a global basis in order to impose identical sustainable corporation charter requirements would consume significant amounts of time and resources. In that process, variations in requirements imposed by national and state corporate laws would undoubtedly appear and national governments would need to determine whether those variations were nonetheless consistent with the international agreement. Lax consistency determinations or lack of enforcement would become back-door approaches for national and state governments to engage in a race to the bottom. We have seen such problems arise in a similar context. Under the Pelly Amendment to the Magnuson-Stevens Fishery Conservation and Management Act, the U.S. Department of Commerce has had the authority to impose trade sanctions against nations that permit violations of international or multilateral fisheries agreements or endangered species agreements.[69] However, Commerce has been reluctant to exercise this authority – one explanation is that those sanctions might violate the U.S. obligations under the General Agreement on Tariffs and Trade. Another, more plausible explanation is that the United States has been reluctant to impose trade sanctions on important trade partners such as Japan for fear of provoking a trade war.

15.5.2 Other Issues

Many other issues are raised in designing an appropriate international structure to charter and regulate transnational corporations. How should the agency be structured – internally and externally in terms of integration with other international organizations? How should the sustainable corporation requirements and remedies be integrated with laws and standards administered by other organizations? How can democratic control of the agency be assured? How can agency capture be prevented? This chapter merely raises these issues. Resolution of these issues, and a multitude of other issues not yet raised, is an endeavor that is worthy of our collective attention and best efforts.

15.6 CONCLUSION

It is time for fundamental transformation of the role of transnational corporations. The truth of human nature is that we are both generous and greedy. Yet, the business structures we have created give expression only to the greedy side of our nature, throwing our societies severely out of balance. We must find a means to reincorporate the generous, altruistic part of our nature into corporations.

Corporate social responsibility must no longer be a small set of voluntary add-on activities undertaken only to the extent that they serve corporate profits by associated cost-savings and public image polishing. Instead, the commitment to act in an environmentally and socially responsible manner must be baked into the corporate DNA by requiring transnational corporations to incorporate sustainability into their corporate charter and assure their operations contribute to alleviating poverty, promoting social well-being, and achieving ecological sustainability as well as providing financial profit for corporate investors and managers.

In order to operate on a transnational basis, corporations should be required to secure a sustainable corporation charter from an international regulatory body. A corporation with a sustainable corporation charter should be required to comply with international and national laws regarding ecological sustainability, fair labor practices, human rights, and corruption. It should adopt, periodically review, and revise a corporate sustainability strategy, prepared in conformance with standards prescribed by the international agency. Subject to independent audit, it should monitor and report on its compliance with international and national sustainability related laws, non-binding national and international sustainability-related standards, and its own corporate sustainability strategy.

The international agency should be empowered to punish violations of these requirements by significant administrative penalties, partial or total suspensions of permission to operate, and ultimately by dissolution as a transnational corporation. Member nations must also agree to suspend or bar operations by any transnational corporation that ignores the chartering requirements or fails to comply with international sanctions assessed by the agency – and to impose trade and economic sanctions upon nations who fail to become party to the agreement establishing the international requirements for sustainable transnational corporations.

It is essential that we no longer grant the privilege of operating on a transnational basis to corporations willing to wreak ecological havoc, engage in unfair labor practices, commit human rights abuses, and encourage official corruption. Transnational corporations can be transformed so that they promote economic prosperity, ecological sustainability, fair labor practices, human rights, democratic governance and the rule of law – providing we insist they do so as a condition of engaging in global operations. Properly structured, a sustainable charter requirement can harness more fully the wealth and entrepreneurial creativity of these organizations in furtherance of our social goals. This, after all, is the justification for creating corporations in the first place.

It is time that we compel this transformation to occur. This may be the last opportunity for many years to achieve this transformation since no doubt many transnational corporations will resist such a change. However, history teaches when windows of opportunity for making significant legislative change appear, reforms otherwise unimaginable in the normal course of business can occur.

We must make the most of this opportunity, for the sake of our children and our children's children.

NOTES

1. 'The objects for which a corporation is created are universally such as the government wishes to promote. They are deemed beneficial to the country, and this benefit constitutes the consideration, and in most cases, the sole consideration of the grant.' Trustees of *Dartmouth College v. Woodward* [1819] 17 U.S. 518, 637.
2. As Chief Justice Marshall said in Dartmouth College, ibid., p. 636.

   A corporation is an artificial being, invisible, intangible, and existing only in contemplation of law. Being the mere creature of law, it possesses only those properties which the charter of its creation confers upon it either expressly or as incidental to its very existence. These are such as are supposed best calculated to effect the object for which it was created. Among the most important are immortality, and, if the expression may be allowed, individuality – properties by which a perpetual succession of many persons are considered as the same, and may act as a single individual.

3. *Citizens United v. Federal Elections Comm'n* [2010] 130 S.Ct. 876.
4. Above, n. 2.
5. See Weissbrodt, D. (2008), International Standard-Setting on the Human Rights Responsibilities of Business, *Berkeley J. Int'l L.* 26, 373, at p. 378. This capital has produced simply stunning, corporate profits. ExxonMobil had the highest profits in history, earning $40.6 billion in 2007, exceeded only by its rate of profits the following year, which included the onset of the 'Great Recession' in the fall of 2008. Along with the rest of the world suffering through the recession, ExxonMobil profits suffered a substantial decline in 2009 to $19 billion. However, unlike the rest of the world, ExxonMobil profits rebounded in 2010 to over $30 billion. http://www.nytimes.com/2011/02/01/business/01oil.html (accessed 10 February 2012). Based on first quarter 2011 earnings, ExxonMobil stands to make over $40 billion in 2011, thanks to high oil prices fueled by the supply disruptions associated with the Libyan civil war. http://www.marketwatch.com/story/exxon-mobil-profit-to-rise-on-100-oil-2011–04–25?siteid=rss&rss=1 (accessed 10 February 2012).
6. *See* Roodman,D. (2006) 'Creditor Initiatives in the 1980s and 1990s' C. Jochnich and F.A. Preston (eds) *Sovereign Debt at the Crossroads: Challenges and Proposals for Resolving the Third World Debt Crisis*, Oxford: Oxford University Press, for a brief history of the 'structural adjustments packages' (SAPs) forced on developing countries by international financial institutions (IFIs) such as the World Bank and the International Monetary Fund. In 1999, the IFIs disavowed the structural adjustment strategy and replaced structural adjustment packages with Poverty Reduction Strategy Papers (PRSPs). Marshall, A., J. Woodroffe, P.E Kjell (2001), 'Policies to Roll-back the State and Privatise?' World Development Movement, http://cloud2.gdnet.org/cms.php?id=research_paper_abstract&research_paper_id=3268 (accessed 10 February 2012).

   However, IFI critics argue that little has changed. Hardstaff P. and T. Jones (2006), 'Out of Time: The case for replacing the World Bank and IMF' [2006] World Development Movement http://www.wdm.org.uk/sites/default/files/outoftime14092006.pdf (accessed 17 February 2012).
7. For example, after the 1997 Asian financial crisis, the International Monetary Fund, the World Bank, and the US government considered South Korea's insider model of corporate governance to be the root cause of the crisis. They made financial assistance to South Korea conditional on South Korea dismantling its insider, stakeholder model of corporate governance. See Dignam A. and M. Galanis (2008), 'Corporate Governance and the Importance of Macroeconomic Context' *Oxford J. Legal Stud. 28, 201,* at pp. 240–241, citing Alan Greenspan, Testimony before the Committee on Banking and Financial Services, US House of Representatives (30 January 1998); Ouattara A., Globalization, Lessons from the Asian Crisis and Central Bank Policies, Reunion des Gouverneurs des Banques Centrales des Pays Francophones Ottawa (23 June 1998), http://www.imf.org/external/np/speeches/1998/062398a.htm (accessed 10 February 2012). Singh, A., A. Singh and B. Weisse, Corporate Governance, Competition, The New International Financial Architecture and Large

Corporations in Emerging Markets, ESRC Centre for Business Research, University of Cambridge Working Paper No. 250 (2002), http://ideas.repec.org/p/cbr/cbrwps/wp250.html (accessed 10 February 2012).

8. Weissbrodt, D., above, n. 5, p. 375 , citing Grossman C. and D.D. Bradlow (1993), 'Are We Being Propelled Towards a People-Centered Transnational Legal Order?' *Am. U. J. Int'l L. & Policy* 9, 1, at p. 8.
9. Transnational corporations have been accused of a remarkable litany of abuses in several dozen, currently pending, lawsuits brought under the federal *Alien Torts Claim Act (ATCA)*, American state tort law, and international law. Only one corporate ATCA case has gone to trial: defendant Drummond Co. was found not liable by the jury in a case that charged Drummond with aiding and abetting the murder of three Columbia trade union leaders at Drummond's coal mining operations. The labor union leaders were pulled off buses chartered by Drummond and killed by paramilitary groups. Rio Tinto is accused of violating international law in its mining operations in Bougainville, Papua New Guinea. Chevron Corporation is accused of agreeing to attacks upon Nigerians by Nigerian military and police. Government contractor CACI is accused of torturing Iraqi nationals held in US military prisons in Iraq. Blackwater USA, a private security firm, is accused of extrajudicial murders and war crimes in Iraq. Chiquita Brands International is accused of providing material support to the United Self-Defense Forces of Columbia (AUC), a paramilitary group murdering Columbian nationals. Yahoo!, to protect its access to China, provided the Chinese with the identity of e-mail users who were then accused of anti-government speech, leading to their arrest, detention and torture by the Chinese government. Exxon Mobil is accused of providing material support to and directing Indonesian security forces' violent attacks and torture of Acehnese villagers in order to secure its natural gas extraction and processing facility in Aceh. DynCorp is accused of spraying toxic fumigants on Ecuadoran nationals. Occidental Petroleum is accused of severely contaminating land and rivers in the Amazon region of Carijano, Peru, causing widespread lead and cadmium poisoning of local residents. See Altschuller, S., D. Feldman and L. Blecher, 'Corporate Social Responsibility' (2008) *Int'l Law* 43,489.
10. I was recently a victim of the most self-serving protestations imaginable. ExxonMobil hired a public relations firm to connect ExxonMobil's former general counsel and current head of public affairs with influential bloggers in hopes of resurrecting ExxonMobil's reputation as a responsible player in the climate change arena. In one of several conference calls, he indicated that ExxonMobil was no longer in the business of funding organizations devoted to denying global warming science, citing the fact that ExxonMobil no longer supported Competitive Enterprises Institute. The truth of that corporation's 'philanthropic' efforts turned out to be otherwise.
11. See a similar argument made in Kelly M. and A. White (2008), 'Corporate Design: The Missing Organizational and Public Policy Issue of Our Time' *New Eng. L. Rev.* 42, 761

    Until recently, academic commentators decried this tendency of corporations to serve as profit-maximizers and to put private interest above public interest. However, during the last 30 years, a wave of conservative, free market advocates have regarded corporations as good citizens only if they strive to maximize profits. William Meade Fletcher, 5 Fletcher Cycl. Corp. 2096.30. The wave of corporate scandals in the beginning of the twenty-first century, starting with WorldCom, Enron and others, has created well-founded skepticism about corporate management's loyalty to corporate investors. For example, Enron's managers were making ill-gotten gains for investors as well as themselves, even as corporate managers were lying to investors and inducing their independent accountants to lie as well. This led to enactment of the Sarbanes-Oxley Act of 2002, Pub. L. 107–204, 116 Stat. 745, which is designed to protect investors by improving the accuracy and reliability of corporate disclosures.

    The adverse effects of some of these early scandals reached far beyond investors. For example, utility ratepayers were the main victims of Enron's market machinations in California. Recently, the entire world has suffered from the widespread mismanagement of the American financial sector, which led to the collapse of some of the largest investment firms and other banks – in turn threatening not only the American economy, but the global economy. With these scandals, the tide seems to have shifted against corporate governance that only maximizes profits, without regard to the impact on society.

The irony is that the majority of corporate directors of large American corporations are what Lorsch and MacIver call 'broad constructionists' who actually do balance the interests of shareholders in short-terms gains against other factors. Overall, directors rank short-term shareholder gains first (ranked 1st/10) against other factors, but did consider factors such as the company's long-term future (2nd), the CEO's opinion (3rd), legal requirements (4th), customers and suppliers (5th), and responsibilities to the public (6th) and even factored in interests such as competitors in industry (7th), non-management employees (8th), and management (9th). See Table 3-1 in Lorsch, J.W and E.A. MacIver (1989), *Pawns or Potentates: the Reality of America's Corporate Boards*, Cambridge, Massachusetts: Harvard Business School Press, pp. 37–50. Lorsch and MacIver indicate that the largest part of the minority of directors who only consider the interests of shareholders were what they considered 'rationalizers', who believe that what is good for the shareholders is necessarily good for other stakeholders. The remainder are 'traditionalists' who consider it wholly illegitimate to consider any other factor.

Yet, virtually all directors believe that they are required by law to serve only the shareholders' interests. Ibid., at 50–54. Lorsch and MacIver concluded that the failure of corporate directors to reach a common understanding of their purpose makes boards far less powerful in managing the corporation than they are supposed to be. This leaves American corporations in the hands of management – whose interests are frequently at odds with those of shareholders and the broader society. This assessment of the limited power of corporate boards compared with corporate managers is consistent with the Mace's 1971 assessment – which Williamson considers true even in 2008. Williamson, O.E. (2008), 'Corporate Boards of Directors: In Principle and in Practice' *J.L. Econ. & Org.* 24, 247, p. 260, citing Mace, M. (1971), *Directors: Myth and Reality*.

12. Alan Dignam and Michael Galanis argue that changes in global macroeconomic policy such as trade liberalization and deregulation of capital markets have forced corporations irresistibly toward shareholder-oriented 'outside' control of corporate governance. See above, n. 8.

13. Kelly and White, co-founders of the ambitious Corporate 2020 multi-stakeholder initiative to design the corporation of the future, have recently argued that corporate design is the key public policy issue of our time. They articulate six principles of corporate design, many of which inhere in the notion of environmental and social responsibility advanced by sustainable corporation charters:

    1. the purpose of the corporation is to harness private interests to serve the public interest,
    2. corporations shall accrue fair returns for shareholders, but not at the expense of the legitimate interest of other stakeholders,
    3. corporations shall operate sustainably, meeting the needs of the present generation without compromising the ability of future generations to meet their needs,
    4. corporations shall distribute their wealth equitably among those who contribute to wealth creation,
    5. corporations shall be governed in a manner that is participatory, transparent, ethical, and accountable,
    6. corporations shall not infringe on the right of natural persons to govern themselves, nor infringe on other universal human rights.

    The notion of sustainability embodied in their third principle is limited to environmental or ecological sustainability. See Kelly M. and A. White, (2008) 'Corporate Design: The Missing Organizational and Public Policy Issue of Our Time' *New Eng. L. Rev* 42, 761, at pp. 771–773.

14. Though admittedly somewhat thin, the literature produced by progressive corporate law scholars or corporate design scholars has not wholly ignored the role of corporate charters. For example, Charles Cray recently published a working paper to inform the Corporate 2020 Summit entitled 'Revisiting Corporate Charters: Reviving chartering as an instrument for

corporate accountability and public policy' (2007) Corporate 2020 Summit Papers 67. That paper recalled the original history of creating corporations to serve the public interest. Cray suggested three possible approaches: federal chartering of individual companies such as Fannie Mae and Amtrak, uniform state chartering to reinforce the public purpose of every corporation, or federal chartering of corporations in specific industries that require public intervention such as public health, national security, energy, or transportation. However, the approaches suggested by Cray are quite dissimilar to the ideas proffered in this paper. First, Cray and Corporate 2020 adopt a far broader approach that essentially transforms every corporation into a public corporation, organized primarily for public purposes. I am chary of that approach because I fear it would rob corporations of the innovative, entrepreneurial edge that the profit motive provides. Second, Cray suggests federal or uniform state chartering, which to my mind poses an unacceptable threat of corporate flight to foreign jurisdictions.

15. To the best of my knowledge, no other American state has adopted any provision in its corporate law that explicitly allows or requires corporations to consider sustainability or environmental and social responsibility in making business decisions. Judd Sneirson's 'race to the left' by other American states to allow corporations to adopt sustainable corporate charters has not yet begun. Sneirson, J. (2009) 'Race to the Left' *Oregon L. Rev.* 88, 491.
16. Obviously, a sustainable corporation charter and the implementing provisions suggested in this chapter are just the beginning of designing sustainable corporations. The continental European and Japanese models of corporate governance already take another step in redirecting corporate goals and governance from exclusively shareholders to stakeholders.
17. This paper specifically addresses only the classic form of business organization: the corporation. Obviously, any reform of corporate law must consider whether to include parallel provisions in statutes governing partnerships, limited liability companies, limited partnerships, and other forms of business organization.
18. In addition, American corporations must comply with two other sets of laws: federal laws enacted by Congress to regulate interstate commerce and state regulation under the police power.

    While American corporations could be regulated pursuant to Congress' other enumerated powers such as its treaty power, Congress most commonly employs its power to regulate interstate and foreign commerce clause. Laws based on federal commerce clause power include subjects such as labor standards, securities regulation, consumer product safety, and environmental protection. Pursuant to this power, the federal government could, but chooses not to, regulate directly the structure of private corporations that engage in, or as a cumulative matter substantially affect, interstate and foreign commerce.

    American corporations are also regulated by states in which they operate. These laws, however, do not deal with the structure of the corporation, but rather exercise the states' police powers to protect public health, safety, and welfare. States generally seek to avoid regulating, directly or indirectly, corporate structure due to concerns that such regulation would violate notions of comity, constitutional restrictions on adversely affecting foreign and interstate commerce under dormant commerce clause, and state conflict/choice of laws statutes.
19. ORS 60.047(1). For example, the charter must contain the corporation's name, the names and addresses of incorporators and the registered agent, the corporation's office address and its mailing address for notice purposes, and the number of shares the corporation is authorized to issue.
20. ORS 60.047(2)(a)–(c).
21. ORS 60.047(2)(f).
22. ORS 60.047(2)(d).
23. ORS 60.047(2)(e).
24. Testimony of Richard E. Roy, H.B. 2826 Public Hearing, Senate Judiciary Committee, 9 May 2007 [All Oregon legislative hearing materials are accessible through Oregon State archives; written testimony is on file with author].
25. Ibid.
26. Testimony of Jeffrey C. Wolfstone, H.B. 2826 Public Hearing, Senate Judiciary Committee, 9 May 2007.

27. Ibid. Subsequent to Mr. Wolfstone's testimony, Nau, Inc. was dissolved due to financial problems. The moral of the story is not that environmentally and socially responsible companies are doomed to financial disaster, but that any start-up company faces formidable obstacles in establishing financial stability.
28. 'To combine the generosity of the human spirit and the power of technology with business innovation to increase shareholder equity, protect the environment, enhance social justice and provide humanitarian relief worldwide.' Testimony of Jeffrey C. Wolfstone, H.B. 2826 Public Hearing, House Judiciary Committee, 13 March 2007; Testimony of Jeffrey C. Wolfstone, H.B. 2826 Public Hearing, Senate Judiciary Committee, 9 May 2007. Mr. Wolfstone's written testimony in both hearings was essentially identical. [On file with author].
29. Nau's rules of corporate responsibility included:

    - The company will endeavor to conduct all aspects of its business in an environmentally and socially responsible manner, including the promotion of peaceful conflict resolution, the fair and humane management of factory working conditions, the equitable treatment of employees, the implementation of a sustainable process of product creation, waste minimization and recycling, and philanthropy (as described below). The officers and directors of the company are charged with implementing this policy consistent with their fiduciary duty to the shareholders of the company.
    - In exercising their power and discharging their duties, the company's directors and officers are authorized to take into consideration and balance the interests of the environment, human rights, public health or safety, the communities in which the company operates and the dignity of its employees.
    - The company must have in place a program requiring that 5% of the purchase price of goods and services sold be contributed to a charitable organization. To this end, the company has selected several international, regional and local 'partners for change' that will receive donations as designated by customers at the point of purchase.
    - The company will pay its U.S. employees no less than 1.5 times the effective U.S. federal minimum wage and will compensate its non-U.S. based employees in a fair and just manner.
    - Domestic partners (same or opposite sex) will be eligible to receive benefits to the same extent as spouses of company employees.
    - No officer of the company may be paid a cash salary (exclusive of bonus and equity-based compensation) more than 12 times the compensation paid to the lowest paid full-time company employee based in the United States.

30. Above, n. 28.
31. Ibid.
32. Ibid.
33. Minutes of H.B. 2826 Public Hearing, Senate Judiciary Committee, 9 May 2007.
34. ORS 60.047(2) (e).
35. At least two states have toyed with the notion of creating sustainable corporation charters: Minnesota and Hawaii. State legislators in Minnesota have twice introduced a Socially Responsible Corporation bill. Citizens for Corporate Redesign – Minnesota: see http://k2-legal.com/wp-content/uploads/2006/10/SEA-conference-article-final-w-L3Cs.pdf (accessed 17 February 2012). The Hawaii legislature considered a bill similar to the Minnesota bill, but it was amended to create a commission to study alternative corporate charters. Hawaii State Legislature, H.B. 3118 Measure History, http://www.capitol.hawaii.gov/session2006/status/HB3118.asp (accessed 10 February 2012). Even the modest legislation to create a study commission was vetoed in July 2007 by Governor Lingle.
36. ORS 60.074(1).
37. ORS 60.077(2).
38. ORS 60.077(2)(n).
39. ORS 60.077(2)(o).
40. ORS 60.077(2)(p).

41. This claim from academic theorists is based not on law, but on unabashed apologetics for unregulated free markets. For example, a quote frequently attributed to Milton Friedman articulates shareholder primacy as the legal purpose of the corporation: 'the business of business is business.' Friedman stated:

> In a free-enterprise, private-property system, a corporate executive is an employee of the owners of the business. He has direct responsibility to his employers. That responsibility is to conduct the business in accordance with their desires, which generally will be to make as much money as possible while conforming to the basic rules of the society, both those embodied in law and those embodied in ethical custom.

Friedman, M. (1962) *Capitalism and Freedom*, Chicago: University of Chicago Press. For a sampling of other shareholder primacy arguments, see Clark, R. (1991), *Corporate Law*, Boston: Little, Brown, and Company; Fisch, J.E. (2006) 'Robert Clark's Corporate Law: Twenty Years of Change: Measuring Efficiency in Corporate Law: The Role of Shareholder Primacy' *Iowa J. of Corp. L*, 31, 637; Springer, J.D. (1999) 'Corporate Law, Corporate Constituency Statutes: Hollow Hopes and False Fears' 1999 *N.Y.U.L. Rev.* 85; Ehrlich, C. 'Is Business Ethics Necessary?' (2005) *DePaul Bus. & Comm. L.J.*, 4, 55. Another version of the shareholder primacy argument is the 'nexus of contracts' theory, which suggests that corporations merely connect labor, suppliers of equipment, and other factors of production, all of whom receive guaranteed contractual payments for their roles. Corporate shareholders accept the financial risk of doing business and receive all corporate profits. Since shareholders have no contractual guarantee of returns from corporate activities, profits diverted towards CSR 'come directly out of their pockets.' Easterbrook F. and Fischel, D, (1991), *The Economic Structure of Corporate Law*, Cambridge, Massachusetts: Harvard University Press. As Reinhardt, Stavins, and Vietor phrase it: 'from this perspective, CSR is close to theft.' See below.

These theoretical economic views of the corporation, however, have received little support in the case law. Even Reinhardt, Stavins, and Vietor, economists reliant on the legal advice of Robert Clark, concede that the courts have not been willing to second-guess the decisions of directors who refuse to maximize corporate profits:

> The prevailing view among most economists and business scholars is that corporate directors have a fiduciary duty to maximize profits for shareholders. While this view underlies many economic models of firm behavior, its legal basis is actually not very strong. The judicial record, although supportive of a duty to maximize profits for shareholders, also leaves room for the possibility that firms may sacrifice profits in the public interest. The courts' deference towards the judgment of business people – the 'business judgment rule' – prevents many public-minded managerial actions from being legally challenged.

Reinhardt, F.L., R.N. Stavins, and R.H.K. Vietor, *Corporate Social Responsibility Through an Economic Lens*, NBER Working Paper Series, Working Paper 13989 (May 2008), http://www.nber.org/papers/w13989 (accessed 10 February 2012).

42. Testimony of James M. Kennedy, H.B. 2826 Public Hearing, House Judiciary Committee, 13 March 2007, p. 2.
43. States that are home to many Fortune 500 corporations, such as Delaware, Texas, California, and New York, supplement their statutory corporate law with a substantial body of carefully considered corporate law cases. Oregon, however, is home to only a few large corporations and has not developed a substantial body of case law.
44. ORS 60.357(1).
45. ORS 60.357(2).
46. ORS 60.357(3).
47. ORS 60.357(4).
48. ORS 60.357(4). Conflicts of interests are handled separately through allowing the corporation to void conflict of interest transactions unless (1) there was disclosure and authorization, approval or ratification by disinterested directors or the shareholders or (2) the transaction was fair to the corporation. ORS 60.361(1).

49. ORS 60.357(5).
50. The danger, of course, is that this clarification of corporate power will lead to the argument that corporations lacking such a provision lack that power. This is the danger common to any legislative attempt at clarification. The citizens who promoted H.B. 2826 attempted to minimize that danger with their testimony.
51. I remain grateful to Prof. Gordon Clark of the Oxford University Center for the Environment for his kindness in hosting my visit to Monash University during my 1992 Fulbright visit to the University of Sydney. Discussions during his geography seminar in 1992 first brought the strategic sustainability niche to my attention. David Vogel's excellent book summarizes the strategic niche, concluding that there is a market for virtue, but that it is a limited market:

> The main constraint on the market's ability to increase the supply of corporate virtue is the market itself. There is a business case for CSR, but it is much less important or influential than many proponents of civil regulation believe. CSR is best understood as a niche rather than a generic strategy: it makes business sense for some firms in some areas under some circumstances ... There is a place in the market economy for responsible firms. But there is also a large place for their less responsible competitors.

Vogel, D. (2005), *The Market for Virtue: The Potential and Limits of Corporate Social Responsibility*, Washington D.C.: Brookings Institute.
52. Reinhardt, Stavins, and Vieter, above, n. 41.
53. Margolis, Elfenbein, and Walsh conducted a meta-analysis of the results from 167 studies of the relationship between financial performance and socially responsible business practices. They found that 27% of the analyses show a positive relationship, 58% show a non-significant relationship, and 2% show a negative relationship. Margolis, Elfenbein, and Walsh indicate that CSR generally has little effect on profitability, but companies that are profitable are more likely to engage in more CSR activities. Margolis, J.D., H.A. Elfenbein and J.P. Walsh, (2008) 'Do Well by Doing Good? Don't Count on It.' *Harvard Business Review* 86, 19.

Reinhardt, Stavins and Vietor suggest that the lack of any correlation between CSR and profitability is consistent with a market equilibrium in which firms invest in socially responsible projects until the marginal returns decline to the overall market rate of return. As they say, 'In this situation, investing in CSR is not profitable (in the sense that it does not generate economic rents), but neither is it a losing proposition. Instead it means that for most firms, CSR "pays for itself".' Above, n. 42, at 24. Reinhard, Stavins, and Vietor note certain caveats about these conclusions:

> First, when evaluating studies of the relationship between social responsibility and stock returns, it is important to keep in mind that not all companies that are classified as socially responsible actually sacrifice profits. Many operate in industries, such as software development, that by their very nature have little environmental or social impact. Second, many of the measures of CSR used in such studies are not consistent with CSR as we define it in this article. Thus, measured effects on profitability may have more to do with advertising, charitable contributions, or other tangentially relevant factors than with CSR. In summary, evidence on sacrificing profits in the social interest is lacking. The bulk of the available evidence suggests that most firms view socially responsible actions in the same way that they view more traditional business activities, such as advertising and R&D. Instead of altruistically sacrificing profits, they engage in a more limited – but more profitable – set of socially beneficial activities that contribute to their financial goals. Hence, although proponents of sustainable business practices may argue that being environmentally responsible will inevitably lead to higher profits in the long term, the relationship between socially responsible activities and profitability may be best characterized as *some* firms will generate long-term profits from *some* socially responsible activities *some* of the time. (Ibid., at 24–25.)

54. Friend, G. (2009), *The Truth about Green Business*, New Jersey: Financial Times Press. Friend argues though that all firms can benefit from the strategic thinking associated with becoming greener.

55. Corporate Manslaughter and Corporate Homicide Act. 2007, 54 Eliz. 2, c. 19 (Eng.), http://www.opsi.gov.uk/acts/acts1007/pdf/ukpga_20070019_en.pdf (accessed 10 February 2012).
56. According to a Dartmouth study, corporate shareholders may react negatively to any corporate sustainability commitments and react more negatively as the corporate sustainability commitments are more aggressive. That study reported that 46 companies lost almost 1% of their value, about $16 billion, after joining a group of businesses making voluntary commitments to reduce greenhouse gas emissions. Deutsch, C.H. 'Saving the Planet? Not With My Money' N.Y. Times, 26 March 2008, G2. This reaction may be offset by the willingness of respected investment advisers to tout sustainable corporations.
57. Adidas and Nike have suffered adverse publicity due to their questionable labor practices and use of child labor. Wal-Mart had reportedly suffered a 10% decline in customers because of its poor reputation on sustainability issues, before it became a born-again environmentally and socially responsible company. Nestle has been embroiled in controversy from promoting inappropriate use of infant formulas. Exxon/Mobil has endured some modest financial damage from the Exxon Valdez oil spill. Obviously, Bhopal became more than an obscure plant name for Union Carbide's management. A few of these examples are mentioned by Alan Neal, who nonetheless concludes that the volunteerism of corporate social responsibility is a poor substitute for thoughtfully constructed regulatory systems. Neal, A.C. (2008) 'Corporate Social Responsibility: Governance Gain or Laissez-Faire Figleaf?' *Comp. Lab. L. & Pol'y J.*, 29, 459.
58. Above, n. 5.
59. David Weissbrodt noted this difficulty, and the risk that sophisticated corporate lawyers will structure businesses to avoid application of international standards applicable only to transnational corporations, as an explanation why the U.S. Sub-Commission on the Promotion and Protection of Human Rights made the Norms on the Responsibilities of Transnational Corporations and Other Business Enterprises with Regard to Human Rights applicable to all businesses. Above, n. 5, p. 381.
60. In essence, this would be equivalent to the proposals to create an international environmental protection agency and internationalize environmental law. The sustainable corporation charter approach advocated in this chapter is not intended to be a back-door route to accomplishing the goal of those proposals. An international transnational corporation commission would be ill-equipped to engage in the detailed regulatory tasks necessary under such proposals.
61. The non-binding standards against which the corporation's conduct is measured should include those of governments or intergovernmental organizations such as Codex Alimentarius (established by the UN Food and Agricultural Organization and the World Health Organization), those of national standard setting bodies such as the International Organization for Standardization (ISO), and those established by NGOs and industry such as those created by the International Social and Environmental Accreditation and Labeling (ISEAL) Alliance members (Forest Stewardship Council, Fair Trade Labeling Organization, the Marine Stewardship Council, the Marine Aquarium Council, the Rainforest Alliance, and Social Accountability International), the Fair Labour Association, the Sustainable Tourism Stewardship Council, the Program for the Enforcement of Forest Certification, and the Environmentally and Socially Responsible Procurement Working Group. Some of these entities are discussed in Berstein, S. and E. Hannach (2008), Non-State Global Standard Setting and the WTO: Legitimacy and the Need for Regulatory Space, *J. Int'l Econ. L.* 11, 575, which argues that the WTO should consider allowing these non-state market driven governance systems to be considered legitimate international standards that cannot form the basis of a WTO dispute.
62. Braithwaite contemplates having each corporation set its own standards and then measure compliance by its own criteria. Braithwaite, J. (1982), 'Enforced Self-Regulation: A New Strategy for Corporate Crime Control' *Mich. L. Rev.* 80, 1466. This paper proposes keeping the regulatory systems intact, but supplementing them with monitoring and reporting of the corporation's compliance with non-binding standards and its own corporate sustainability strategy.

63. Sigler and Murphy advocate providing incentives for corporations (government contract preferences, tax incentives, reduce penalties on future violations) to engage in compliance audits. Sigler J.A. and J.E. Murphy (1998), *Interactive Corporate Compliance: An Alternative to Regulatory Compulsion*, Westport, Quorum Books.
64. See for instance Duruigbo, E. (2008), 'Corporate Accountability and Liability for International Human Rights Abuses: Recent Changes and Recurring Challenges' *Nw. U. J. Int'l Hum. Rts.*, 6 218; Ruggie, J. (2008), *Report of the Special Representative of the Secretary-General on the issue of human rights and transnational corporations and other business enterprises: Protect Respect and Remedy: a Framework for Business and Human Rights*, delivered to the Human Rights Council, U.N.Doc. A/HRC/8/5 (7 April 2008).
65. http://ozone.unep.org/Ratification_status/montreal_protocol.shtml (accessed 10 February 2012).
66. 42 U.S.C. 7671–7671q.
67. Those interested in direct imposition of international legal duties upon corporations should review. Ratner, S.R. (2001) 'Corporations and Human Rights: A Theory of Legal Responsibility' *Yale L.J.* 111, 443.
68. *Rome Statute of the International Criminal Court.* UN Doc. A/CONF. 183/9 (17 July 1998) (entered into force 1 July 2002). The United States has not accepted the ICC as having jurisdiction over its nationals. Coalition for the ICC, Ratification/Accession and Signature of the Agreement on the Privileges and Immunities of the Court (APIC). http://www.iccnow.org/documents/RatificationsbyUNGroup_14_mar_08_eng.pdf (accessed 10 February 2012).

    UN-sponsored treaties on discrimination, including the International Convention on the Elimination of All Forms of Racial Discrimination and the Convention on the Elimination of All Forms of Discrimination against Women, do create government or state responsibility for the conduct of individuals, groups, organizations or enterprises. Other international treaties and laws, such as the International Covenant on Civil and Political Rights and the Universal Declaration of Human Rights, apply indirectly to businesses. See, Weissbrodt, above, n. 5, at pp. 376–377.
69. U.S.C. 1978. The Pelly Amendment requires the Secretaries of Commerce or the Interior to determine and certify to the President when foreign nationals are conducting activities diminishing the effectiveness of an international fishery conservation program or program for endangered or threatened species. The Act mandates that the Secretaries periodically monitor and promptly investigate activities of other countries that may affect these international programs. The President has the right to impose trade sanctions prohibiting import of wildlife and fisheries products from the violator. However, despite investigations of Norway, Japan, Canada, and Iceland with respect to whaling that violates the International Whaling Convention on Importation/Exportation of Threatened and Endangered Species (CITES), the United States has never issued trade sanctions against these countries.

Index